P9-DVO-040
DODGEM
LOGIC
ADULTS ONLY
£3.5
VOTE CTHU
ON MATHER CANDY

MAGIC WORDS

LANCE PARKIN is a British writer best known as the author of fiction and reference books related to *Doctor Who*. It was in the pages of *Doctor Who Weekly* that he came across Alan Moore's earliest professional writing, and he's followed the comics maestro's career ever since. In 2001 he wrote a pocket guide to Moore's work, which has since been updated and reissued. In addition to contributing pieces to magazines such as *TV Zone*, *SFX* and *Doctor Who Magazine*, and a stint as a television storyliner, he is the co-author of a guide to Philip Pullman's *His Dark Materials* trilogy. He lives in the USA.

MAGIC WORDS

THE EXTRAORDINARY LIFE OF ***ALAN MOORE***

LANCE PARKIN

First published in Great Britain
2013 by Aurum Press Ltd
74-77 White Lion Street
Islington
London N1 9PF
www.aurumpress.co.uk

Chapter title artwork by Caio Oliveira; www.facebook.com/caioscorner

A catalogue record for this book is available from the British Library.

ISBN 978 1 78131 077 9

10 9 8 7 6 5 4 3 2 1
2017 2016 2015 2014 2013

Typeset in Minion by Carrdesignstudio.com
Printed and bound by Clays Ltd, St Ives plc

CONTENTS

INTRODUCTION

> *'My life is peculiar. It's not the one that I was expecting. I'm enjoying it. Terrific. But a bit odd.'*
>
> Alan Moore, *Magus Conference* (2010)

Which one is Alan Moore?

No one ever has to ask the question when Alan Moore is in the room, and it is easy to pick him out in photographs. It is apparently mandatory for anyone writing about Moore to start off by noting that he is a giant of a man (he is in fact 6ft 2in – tall, but hardly grotesquely so), that he has a bushy beard and has taken to wearing chunky, segmented rings and carrying a snake-headed cane. He has been a gift to caricaturists, and works in an industry full of them. His physical appearance has frequently led people to believe he is a fearsome, peculiar person. Moore is fully aware it makes him stand out.

Alan Moore's work is as distinctive as the man himself. His CV includes five-panel newspaper cartoons and a novel that is significantly longer than *War and Peace*; slapstick comedy and the goriest of horror; a five- or-six-page strip about Darth Vader and a three-volume slipcased work of pornography; stories about gaudy corporate-owned characters written under work-for-hire contracts; and a black-and-white self-published, creator-owned anthology magazine opposing a specific piece of Thatcher-era legislation. Moore has worked in collaborative media with over a hundred different artists, each with their own style, but when you're reading stories written by him, even those featuring iconic characters like Superman, the Joker, Jack the Ripper, Han Solo, Dorothy Gale or Jekyll and Hyde, they're clearly all the product of the same creative mind.

The main reason people pick up his comic books is precisely because Moore wrote them. As critic Douglas Wolk notes: 'I still buy anything with his name on it. Even his most minor or slapdash pieces almost always inform the way I understand his major work. And the major work still sends out shockwaves, years after it's been completed. It's not at all correct to say that the past twenty-five years of the history of comics are the history of Alan Moore's career, but it's fair to say that it sometimes seems that way.' You don't *have* to read *Sawdust Memories* (1984), a three-page prose story in the pornographic magazine *Knave*, before you can understand the seminal graphic novel *Watchmen* (1986–7), but there are always connections and commonalities. Moore has a distinctive personal worldview and he is a constant presence in his own stories.

Much of his most prominent work was done for US publishers, has been adapted by Hollywood and is concerned with that distinctly American invention, the superhero. He grew up fascinated by superhero comics and the west coast counterculture, and he's now married to an American underground comix artist. It's forgiveable, then, that there are still people surprised to learn that Alan Moore was born, raised and has lived his entire life in Northampton, a town in the east Midlands of England. Moore has been a consistent champion of the place, once declaring, 'The more I looked at Northampton, the more it seemed that Northampton actually was the centre of the universe and that everything of any importance had originated from this point.'

British readers will understand that this is not a widely held view of a town whose chief exports – besides Moore himself – are Carlsberg lager and Barclaycard bills. His American readers may not. This raises an important distinction. Moore's grim and gritty reinterpretations of superheroes may weigh heavily on British perceptions of him, but they absolutely dominate his reputation in America. Many of his early series imposed 'realism' on hokey characters like Marvelman, Swamp Thing, Batman and the Joker, reimagining their storybook worlds as unsentimental places of mid-life crisis, economic reality and brutal, often sexual, violence. Moore has been happy to play along with this image of him. When he appeared as himself on *The Simpsons* (in the episode 'Husbands and Knives', broadcast in November 2007), we learned that he was the new writer on Bart Simpson's favourite comic, *Radioactive Man*, and had turned him into 'a heroin-addicted jazz critic who's not radioactive'. One of Moore's characters in *Supreme* (1996–2000) was a comic book artist plagued by a British writer intent on telling a 'superdog rape story'. Moore's works for the giant American comics company DC – the major entries being *Swamp Thing* (1984–7), the Superman stories *For the Man Who Has Everything* (1985) and *Whatever Happened to the Man of Tomorrow?* (1986), *Watchmen*, *The Killing Joke* (1988) and *V for Vendetta* (1982–9) – are seen as classics by comics fans and are hugely influential on today's creators, all of them remaining in print and still selling strongly. However, a glance at those dates shows that it represents a mere five-year period in Moore's career, thirty years ago. His work has always been broader than superhero comics for adult fanboys, and while his DC work remains important, clearly it represents a blip in his career, not the bedrock of it.

As we try to learn more about Alan Moore, it should be noted that any attempt to reconstruct his life from his stories would find little to go on. Armed with biographical information, if we delve long enough, we can unearth the odd plum: Quinch's first name is Ernest, the same as Moore's father; Raoul Bojeffries is big and hairy and works in a skinning yard, as Moore did after he was expelled from Northampton School for Boys; the concentration camp in *V for Vendetta* is at Larkhill, which Moore has said was the location of 'one of the most truly horrendous hitchhiking holidays I've ever had', but these are in-jokes, not insights.

To find anything straightforwardly autobiographical in Moore's early work – say the first two decades of his career – it's necessary to venture far from the well-trodden sections of his bibliography. There's *A True Story* (1986), a five-page piece for the fanzine *Myra* which recounts how a schoolfriend died from Hodgkin's lymphoma. *Honk* #2 includes a short essay, 'Brasso with Rosie' (1987), which recounts his family background and very early childhood. And the single-page *Letter from Northampton* (1988), written and drawn by Moore, recounts a trip to America and includes a sly, not-quite-paradoxical, observation on meeting one of his idols, Harvey Pekar, the underground cartoonist who created *American Splendor*, and was the first major comics creator to use the medium for memoir:

Virtually everything Moore wrote before the age of forty was science fiction, superheroes or funny animal satire, and his main concerns involved rethinking genre conventions and storytelling techniques. His most visible work in the eighties was in mainstream adventure comics, and he understood that the editors and readers of *Doctor Who Weekly* or *Green Lantern Corps* weren't looking for anecdotes about his life as a Midlands schoolboy. Moore knew as well as anyone, though, that there was a rich tradition of autobiographical comics, exemplified by Pekar. He was proud to identify himself as coming from a background of underground cartooning. What he never did, though, was create strips with the searing self-analysis and raw confessional that Pekar was famous for.

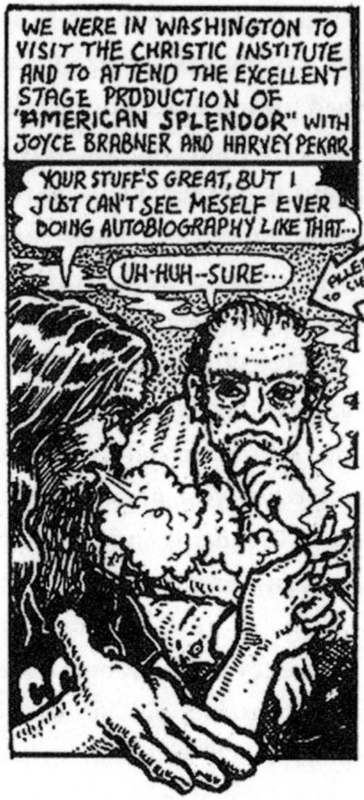

Moore didn't avoid writing about his life only in his fiction. When, from time to time, a comic he was working on would ask for potted autobiographies from its contributors, most other writers and artists would supply fairly straightforward paragraphs. Steve Moore, for example, is a comics writer, Alan Moore's mentor, and his oldest and dearest friend. Here is the biography he supplied for the back pages of *Warrior* #1 (1982):

> Steve Moore is 32, lives in London and has spent most of his working life in the comic-strip industry . . . At present he is the associate editor of *Fortean Times*, the journal of strange phenomena, and has produced a booklet of articles on the Chinese yeti, *Wild Man*.'

And here is *Alan* Moore's:

> A baffling hybrid between Renaissance Man and Piltdown Man . . . great fun to mix with socially until the tranquilisers wear off, Mr Moore believes himself to be possessed by the demon Pazuzu.

Much of Alan Moore's writing from the early nineties onwards has been more personal. Even here, though, it is never a straightforward account of the events of his life. His most overtly autobiographical work to date is the performance piece *The Birth Caul* (1995), which starts with the death of his mother. It soon moves to family, then local, history, before looping back to become a (reversed) account of Moore's childhood, ending with his conception. *The Birth Caul* was created with musicians David J and Tim Perkins, and in places, autobiographical details come from his collaborators – so, for example, each of them contributed a (real) name to the list of three girls the narrator secretly fancied as a boy. *The Birth Caul* mostly avoids the use of 'I' in the narration, preferring 'we', which, as writer Marc Singer puts it, makes the experience more of a 'communal narrative'.

There's a similar technique at work in the last chapter of Moore's novel *Voice of the Fire* (1996); told in the present tense, it describes from Moore's point of view the events of the evening on which he was writing the chapter. Yet it is more of a guided tour of the area he lives in than autobiography per se:

> you'll perhaps notice the extent of my unease regarding personal literary appearances: the words 'I', 'me', 'my' and 'mine' are used nowhere in the final chapter. I think I was originally adopting that device as a way of appearing in my own story without really appearing in it, but as it turned out I quite liked it for the way it left a kind of empty conceptual space at the middle of the narrative for the reader to inhabit and provide their own 'I'. I supposed that really it's just my particular great vanity to try and conceal my great vanity, please don't be taken in by it for an instant.

So if it is not through his work, how do we know anything about Alan Moore's life?

Moore is often portrayed as some kind of recluse. A major BBC interview began by saying he was 'keeping a low profile' and stated he 'dislikes giving interviews'. Nothing could be further from the truth. Soon after he started his professional career, Moore had become a vocal, visible presence in the comics industry. He has given hundreds of interviews over the years, first to fanzines, then to professional magazines, promotional videos, national and local newspapers, radio and television, and latterly to websites. As he said to one interviewer, 'I'm a doddle for interviewing 'cos I'm completely infatuated with the sound of me own voice . . .

you just have to say a few basic words and I'll talk for the next hour or two . . . you prod me if you want me to stop or change to a different subject.' Some interviews with Moore have been long enough to fill a book or whole episode of a radio or TV show. Many concentrate on the development of a particular project – usually his current work – or his creative techniques, career or interest in magic. Very few do more than touch on his biography, but when asked, he will answer, to the point that some early incidents have become familiar anecdotes.

Over the years, then, Alan Moore has spent hundreds of thousands of words going into his background and personal history. He has chosen to tell us his life story, although not – generally – in his art. Moore has suggested in the past that he's avoided autobiographical work simply because he felt his life wasn't very interesting: 'All I do is sit in a room and write – it must be one of the most boring existences in the world.'

Moore's work, like that of any artist, does not exist separately from his experience. He has fictionalised events from his life, and has admitted to becoming more comfortable with doing so as he gets older. When once asked 'How much of your own experience do you encompass in your work?' he answered,

> Eventually you'll use everything. You usually put them in some kind of code unless you're doing a straightforward biography. There's things I did like *A Small Killing* [1991]. The central event in that was a boy burying some bugs in a bottle. I did that when I was eight or nine and it haunted me. In *Big Numbers* [1990] the writer was me, not exactly, but there was enough experience. I borrowed voraciously from my friends' lives, sometimes that can feel a bit dodgy. These people, they're your friends and they'll pour out details of their lives and part of your brain is this cold vampiric thing writing it all down to use later. I can't help it, I'm a writer. I'm getting closer and closer to actually writing about myself. The next thing I do will have a significant autobiographical slant to it. As I get older I'm less worried about revealing myself and looking a prat. It gets to a point where you feel comfortable about being a prat when you do that.

But far more typical of Moore's early work are stories that look for all the world as if they're autobiographical, or which take the form of fictional biography,

but which on closer examination simply don't map onto what we know of their author's life.

Book One of *The Ballad of Halo Jones* (1984), first published in British science fiction comic *2000AD* quite early in Moore's career, is a case in point. It's tempting to see it as a futuristic makeover of Moore's experience of living in an area of Northampton that, for generations, has housed some of the poorest families in the country. The story is set in the fiftieth century on the Hoop, a giant doughnut-shaped structure floating in the Atlantic, built to house the unemployed, or 'Increased Leisure Citizens', as they've been designated. A spoof advert declares:

> If you're one of the jobless of New York State Municipality, then the Hoop is for you! Tethered conveniently just off the Manhattan Peninsula, it provides a floating haven for its many residents – Increased Leisure Citizens who dwell in the picturesque Blister Homes . . . The Hoop: Manhattan Island's Land of Leisure where the wageless pass their time in happy serenity! The Hoop: it runs rings round the Poverty Reduction schemes of other Municipalities.

We quickly see the reality of the situation: the inhabitants of the Hoop are left to fend for themselves in a brutal world where characters panic at the prospect of leaving their homes to buy groceries. The conceit of the story is that the inhabitants take every hardship and bizarre science fiction detail of their lives utterly for granted. When asked what mice are, Halo replies, 'Well, they were like rats only they were littler and couldn't talk.' The inhabitants mask the realities of their existence in euphemistic slang, they distract themselves by watching soap operas set in the twentieth century like *John Cage: Atonal Avenger*. Within the narrative, it takes an historian writing many centuries later to spell out the reality: 'The Hoop was a massive dead end in which to dump America's unemployed. Called a "poverty reduction programme", it didn't reduce poverty . . . it just meant that people no longer had to look at the poor. If you lost your job you were moved to the Hoop, where you lived on a state-provided credit card system called MAM until you found employment. Except that there wasn't any employment.'

The Hooplife spiel is only a little exaggerated from the rhetoric used by the Northampton Development Corporation to lure Londoners to Moore's home town in publications such as *Come to Northampton!* (1972) and *Expanding*

HOOPLIFE

Dataday, day-to-day, I'm ***Swifty Frisko***, love me or leave me! If you're one of the jobless of New York State Municipality, then ***the Hoop*** is for ***you***! Tethered conveniently just off the Manhattan Peninsula, it provides a floating haven for its many residents — ***Increased Leisure Citizens*** who dwell in the picturesque Blister-Homes blossoming from the numerous Lilo-Pads adjoining the Hoop.

As a miracle of quantum-tolerance engineering, ***the Hoop*** stands alone. Gasp in awe as, twice a day, ***the Hoop seals itself off*** and separates its flexible sections in order to prevent the periodic wave-motion from collapsing the entire structure, and washing millions of good and valuable citizens into the Atlantic ocean. ***Remember: Only In America!***

Our friends from ***Proxima Centauri*** know ***the Hoop*** as a truly cosmopolitan society, ready to embrace the Proximan immigrant with open arms — if Proximen ***had*** any arms to embrace with, that is! Nonetheless, these lovable lizards of limited limb, accustomed to the hellish silicone wastes of Proxima, have found a home from home on ***the Hoop***. And let's not forget their more prosperous cousins from ***Alpha Centauri***. The Alphan merchant down on his luck is welcome in our ***"Family Circle"***.

Over 70% of the Hoop's population is female, and even though the Hoop's hyper-efficient police force — volunteers known as ***'Rumblejacks'*** — are usually on hand to cope with emergencies, we prefer to encourage a tough breed of independent women with a flare for self-protection. Of course, if you're independently wealthy, why not try a Ripper? These feisty, ***pseudo-canines***, capable of disembowelling cars, come in five beefy persona-types. On the Hoop, we call it ***"Armed Friendship"***!

The Hoop: Manhattan Island's ***Land of Leisure***, where the wageless pass their time in happy serenity!
The Hoop: It runs rings round the Poverty Reduction schemes of ***other*** Municipalities!
I'm Swifty Frisko, that was a ***'Know Your Neighbourhood'*** information pack.

Northampton: The Next Five Years (1971). As comics scholar Maggie Gray notes, *Halo Jones* was a conscious effort to recreate some of the work of feminist comics:

> key to the second-wave feminist assertion that the 'personal is political', was the practice of consciousness-raising pioneered by radical feminists in New York. Consciousness-raising groups allowed participants to discuss their everyday oppression as a means to critically reconstitute the totality of women's social experience, promote collective solidarity and plan action. This emphasis on subjective experience was reflected in the autobiographical tone of feminist comix, and intimated in *The Ballad of Halo Jones* through first-person narration and Halo's diaries and letters.

The trouble is . . . *Halo Jones* is not autobiographical. Compare Moore's description of himself at Halo's age with his description of Halo:

> [ALAN] I'd always felt I was special and important . . . I didn't realise what a bad situation I was in. I was just convinced that I must get my revenge upon society, no matter what.

> [HALO] She wasn't anyone special, she wasn't that brave or that clever or that strong. She was just somebody who felt cramped by the confines of her life. She was just somebody who had to get out.

Alan Moore was a lanky, long-haired teen from a large family, who bunked off school to ride motorbikes and smoke joints. Halo Jones is rootless, tiny, female, quiet, never shows any inclination to be artistic; she can't wait to get away from the Hoop and never looks back, and as an act of rebellion she cuts off her hair. It's tempting to think Moore carefully crafted Halo Jones to be the anti-Moore.

We see this too in his other work. *Watchmen* takes the form of a succession of different biographical accounts. The back of each issue includes extracts from artefacts like Hollis Mason's autobiography, interviews with Silk Spectre and Ozymandias, and Rorschach's psychological reports. The main narrative is supplemented with captions containing diary entries, first-person narration, recalled memories and other autobiographical forms. *Watchmen* is nothing but biography and autobiography . . . just not that of its author.

*

The Ballad of Halo Jones might not be a thinly veiled version of Alan Moore's own life, but it does contain a thinly veiled expression of his personal politics. Book One, like his earlier series *Skizz* (1983), is concerned with the long-term unemployment that was perhaps the central concern for his teenage readers in the 1980s. Readers and critics have agreed with Moore in identifying a strong political slant as a characteristic of his work. Moore says 'there is an unavoidable political element in life. And if art reflects life or has got any relationship to life, then surely there must be an unavoidable political element in art. I'm not saying that every piece has to be a piece of political polemic, but that all of us have a political standpoint, surely, just as we all have an emotional standpoint, and an intellectual standpoint.' From his earliest work onwards, Moore has seen comics as a place to talk about – suitably dramatised for the stories and audience at hand – issues like child abuse, environmentalism, gay rights or nuclear power. This was, and remains, unusual in mainstream comics, and provokes a fair amount of resistance. These days, the noisiest proponents of the view that comics should avoid politics are not concerned parents, but adult comics fans who don't want anything to interrupt their escapism. The popular comics website Newsarama once listed '10 Easy Ways to Piss Off a Comic Book Reader', and at #7 was:

> COMICS THAT PREACH
> It's the comic books that take an 'issue' and explore it from a character's point of view. Some of the most respected writers in fiction wrap their plots around thinly veiled stands on socio-political views. But in comics, it has to be thickly veiled. In fact, hidden would work better for some . . . As Geoff Johns told Newsarama last year when we asked about the potential for environmental issues in his *Aquaman* run: 'Aquaman cares about that, and it's central to who he is. But you have to be careful not to be preachy.'

Moore is not tacking generic 'save the whales' style issues onto otherwise conventional adventure stories, though. The politics are distinctly, and often idiosyncratically, his own. Another of his early works, *V for Vendetta*, would qualify as 'political' if all it did was take the broad anti-totalitarian line dictated by it being a dystopian tale in the vein of *Nineteen Eighty-Four*, *Fahrenheit 451* and '"Repent Harlequin!" Said the Ticktockman', but Moore steers it into more specific territory. Its concern with the rise of the far right in the UK reflects Moore's own activism in the late seventies and early eighties (he attended Rock Against Racism events and posted flyers for the Anti-Nazi League). Most notably, the lead character V shares Moore's anarchist philosophy – if not his methodology. Moore's expression of his own beliefs in an interview for the book *Mythmakers and Lawbreakers: Anarchist Writers of Fiction* is practically a plot summary of *V for Vendetta*:

> If we were to take out all the leaders tomorrow, and put them up against a wall and shoot them – and it's a lovely thought, so let me just dwell on that a moment before I dismiss it – but if we were to do that, society would probably collapse, because the majority of people have had thousands of years of being conditioned to depend upon leadership from a source outside themselves. That has become a crutch to an awful lot of people, and if you were to simply kick it away, then those people would simply fall over and take society with them. In order for any workable and realistic state of anarchy to be achieved, you will obviously have to educate people – and educate them massively – towards a state where they could actually take responsibility for their own actions.

While this is not a view unique to Moore, neither is it a widespread one. It is not, for example, shared by the co-creator of *V for Vendetta*, the artist David Lloyd: 'That's the irony with V, and people saying it's all about anarchy: they're led from the beginning by V . . . That whole thing is ironic to me. I wish I did believe anarchy was possible. I think people, if they don't have someone, they just get lost. When was the last time there was something like anarchy? What's the earliest form of society? Tribes. Who leads tribes? Somebody. They're not just making pots and spears, someone tells them what to do.'

Moore wants his work to be challenging. At the playful end of the spectrum, that means deconstructing genre clichés and an exploration of some of the absurd impracticalities of being a superhero or living in a science fiction world. At a narrative level, it means using a range of techniques to tell a story. Underlying this, though, Moore has always sought to create work with a deeper meaning, and at least some form of relevance.

For Moore, comics are a way to get *his* ideas across to people: 'What I'm trying to do is to take some possibly unpopular political beliefs and to make them accessible, to give ideas that are quite large and complex to children in a form they can understand. I would much rather put out my stories to children, to people who did not share my political beliefs at all because in that instance I am not preaching to the converted. Given that I've got, say, half a million readers a month, if only ten per cent of those or one per cent of those take notice of what I'm saying, that is still a large number of people.' When working on comics like *2000AD* and *Swamp Thing*, Moore knew that his editors tended to be resistant to explicitly political stories, but he felt that in the carefully moderated world of mass entertainment, the rough-and-ready comics medium was uniquely equipped to sneak in more personal positions: 'There is always the possibility that some of your message is going to be lost, some of it's going to be blunted, but there are strategies, there are ways around these things and if you're smart enough then you can generally find a way to hoodwink your employers into letting you print the most incendiary filth.'

That many comics fans bemoan Moore for bringing 'politics' to his work might indicate the anodyne nature of most comics, even now, when the overwhelming majority of readers are adults. It might expose a naïve understanding of the nature of art among that readership – or just a concern that superhero comics are not the subtle instruments needed for discussing complex real-world issues.

Alan Moore himself has described the real world of Northampton as 'monochrome', echoing the imagery in both *Big Numbers* (1990), a comic set in Northampton which used only tiny splashes of colour, and in a (black-and-white) documentary about his birthplace that he made in 1993, *Don't Let Me Die in Black and White*. His home town is centrally important to him, then, but there is another place he has lived all his life, a polymorphous, radiant domain where people can fly, encounter beings who are beyond human, and find themselves walking in dramatic landscapes of golden skies, giant statues and symbols made concrete – a place he's called 'a bright land without time'.

Moore's imaginative life has consistently been at least as rich and meaningful to him as his 'real' one. His inner life is a land he's been exploring over recent years in increasingly ambitious expeditions, and he now sees art as a way not just to process his imaginative experience, but also to change the mundane world. He calls this 'magic', and his work has become – may always have been – something best understood not as literal autobiography but as extracts of the autobiography *of his imagination*.

1 BEARDLESS YOUTH

'This really sounds Dickensian. I never thought about this before.'

Alan Moore, *The Comics Journal* #138 (1990)

Chapter Five of Alan Moore and Eddie Campbell's graphic novel *From Hell* (1989–98) opens by presenting us with the 'striking juxtaposition' that Adolf Hitler was conceived just as the Jack the Ripper murders began in London. Using the same technique, it's a resonant chronological coincidence that simple arithmetic places Alan Moore's conception around February or March 1953, the very time that Harvey Kurtzman and Wally Wood produced the parody comic strip 'Superduperman' for *Mad* magazine.

Human beings tend not to have the same neat 'secret origins' that superheroes do. Few of us have our lives transformed by a single event that galvanises us and leads us to destiny. That said, the summer's day when a young Alan Moore first read a British reprint of 'Superduperman' was hugely formative, and an idea he had that day would end up defining his early career, transforming the superhero genre and providing a successful template for revitalising a long-running series that spread from comics to television and cinema. If we understand what it was about this eight-page comic strip that engaged Moore, what he understood about its contents and what his response to it represents, we'll be closer to understanding Moore himself.

'Superduperman' originally appeared in *Mad* #4, published by EC Comics in April/May 1953, and was hugely popular. It was one of the first times the magazine had run a sustained spoof of a specific pop culture phenomenon, a format for which *Mad* would become famous. As the name suggests, 'Superduperman' is a parody of the *Superman* comic, and at one level it now looks a little hackneyed. Some of the targets are obvious, such as the spoof of Clark Kent's penchant for changing into costume in a phone booth, while the substitution of the names 'Clark Bent' and 'Lois Pain' for Clark Kent and Lois Lane, or 'Captain Marbles' for Captain Marvel, is not something most adults would find terribly witty. There is far more going on in the strip than that, though. Clark Bent's fawning devotion to Lois and his compulsive desire to sniff her perfume is far from innocent, while echoing the creepiness of the relationship of the 'real' Lois and Clark. By changing the 'camera angle' slightly, the fight between Superduperman and Captain Marbles involves everything a similar sequence in the original comics would, while portraying its 'heroes' as vain, stupid and violent.

Crucially, some of the jokes in 'Superduperman' depend on knowledge of behind-the-scenes drama. Any comics fan back then worth their salt knew that the 'real' Superman and Captain Marvel could never meet, because they were owned by different companies. DC published *Superman*, Fawcett published *Captain Marvel*. The two superheroes had met in court, though, with DC accusing Fawcett of plagiarism. Shortly before 'Superduperman' was released DC had prevailed and *Captain Marvel*, once the best-selling comic on the market, was forced to cease publication. The confrontation between Superduperman and Captain Marbles was, then, as much a commentary on that court battle as on the conventions of the superhero fight scene.

It matters, too, who wrote and drew 'Superduperman'; it's a parody that works because the creators clearly love and understand what they are mocking. The artist, Wally Wood, was one of the stars of the comics industry, and had already worked for three of the biggest names in the business: Timely, Will Eisner's studio and EC. Harvey Kurtzman was another comics legend, the first editor of *Mad*, who'd go on to the *Playboy* strip *Little Annie Fanny* and was the founding father of a style of comedy now familiar from TV series like *Saturday Night Live*, *The Simpsons* and *The Daily Show*. As actor Harry Shearer put it, 'Harvey Kurtzman taught two, maybe three generations of post-war American kids, mainly boys, what to laugh at: politics, popular culture, authority figures.'

At heart, what 'Superduperman' plays on is that anyone reading a superhero comic is exposed to two parallel narratives. The first is the colourful, escapist adventure on the pages of the magazine. The stories in superhero comics are sprawling, interconnected sagas that often seem circular in nature. The same never-ending battles are fought across decades by different individuals who are startlingly similar to those who came before. The same moves are made, the same betrayals occur, old ideas are spliced together to make new ones. The elaborate soap opera cast lists, continuity and traditions that are often baffling and off-putting to outsiders are utterly immersive for the fans. It is always possible to dig down a little deeper, make another connection, spot one more influence, coincidence or unintended consequence. Whole books have been written about the convoluted history of just one comic book character.

By the age of twelve, Alan Moore was already au fait with the tricks used to lure him back month after month:

> my favourite part of the whole comic would usually be the Coming Attractions section at the bottom of the last page. They had all these demented announcements like 'Superman marries Streaky the Supercat! Not a dream! Not a hoax! Not a Red Kryptonite delusion! Not an Imaginary Tale!' After a while I figured out that whichever disclaimer they omitted, that was the punch line to the story. Like in the example above, since they hadn't specifically said 'not a robot!' you knew damn well that on the last page of the story either Superman or Streaky, or both, would open up a plate in their chest to reveal lots of little cog wheels and SP-11 batteries.

As above, so below. Like those who consumed 'Superduperman', even young readers quickly become aware of comics' second narrative, as sprawling and convoluted as anything on the page: the real-life history of the industry and the people working in it. Characters like Superman, Batman, Captain America and Captain Marvel have been around since the thirties and forties. Creative teams have come and gone, bringing different styles of artwork and storytelling choices. Mastery of this second narrative, knowing what was going on behind the scenes, is an essential part of becoming a comics fan. It is not enough to know about *Superman* or *Spider-Man*, a fan must also know about Siegel and Shuster, Lee and

Ditko. Creators like Jack Kirby and Will Eisner are, to a comic fan, as 'legendary' as any superhero.

Alan Moore's description of the shopping trip where he first encountered 'Superduperman' is instructive. As he fished through the racks, he found 'they'd also got a load of the Ballantine *Mad* reprints, which included I think *The Bedside Mad*, and *Inside Mad*, which were reprinting from the *Mad* comics, rather than from the *Mad* magazines. And one of these that I picked up, possibly *Inside Mad*, had got Kurtzman and Wood's *Superduperman*.' At twelve, Moore was already a connoisseur, able to assess a comic's pedigree and make minute distinctions based on only a few clues. With a limited amount of pocket money, he chose his purchases carefully, and the publisher, writer and artist of the comic were at least as important to him as which characters it starred, or whether the cover or story hook were enticing. And Moore was not unique, he was part of an emerging phenomenon, one that publishers had started to cater for: slightly older, more informed comic book fans.

On both sides of the Atlantic, since the birth of the industry in the thirties, virtually all the men and women making comic books had toiled in obscurity and anonymity. Comics were cheap and ephemeral, and anyone older than a small child reading them was assumed to be illiterate. Most writers and artists were happy to sign over all the rights to their work in return for a fairly meagre, but regular, cheque. There were exceptions: Will Eisner, creator of *The Spirit*, signed every strip and aggressively marketed himself and his studio. But more typical was Patricia Highsmith, who before she wrote *Strangers on a Train* and *The Talented Mr Ripley*, had written comics for a number of publishers (including Fawcett), but meticulously avoided referring to the fact, even in private diaries that detailed her affairs and psychiatric problems. Mario Puzo, author of *The Godfather*, and Mickey Spillane also worked anonymously in comics early in their writing careers. People who worked in comics didn't boast about it.

It's fair to say Stan Lee changed that.

Stanley Lieber had done his share of toiling. He had started working at Timely Comics in 1939 as a sixteen-year-old office boy who filled the inkwells for the artists. He wrote his first Captain America story two years later under the pseudonym 'Stan Lee', as he hoped to use his real name for more respectable writing. Twenty years later, he was editor-in-chief for the same company, which had changed its name to Atlas Comics in the early fifties and had just done so again, to Marvel Comics. The company was a small one and rarely innovated, but kept a close eye on trends in the market. It had spent the previous few years producing westerns, romance and comics about astronauts.

In the late fifties and early sixties DC, one of the major comics publishers, found success modernising its superhero line, revamping characters like the Flash, Green Lantern and Hawkman, created for the previous generation of children, by giving them new costumes and more modern stories with a science fiction flavour. In 1961, Lee followed the trend, and set about creating a new superhero team for Marvel. Lee and artist Jack Kirby agreed that DC's heroes were so upright it made them a little boring. Alan Moore concurs: 'The DC comics were always a lot more true blue. Very enjoyable, but they were big, brave uncles and aunties who probably insisted on a high standard of, y'know, mental and physical hygiene.' So Lee and Kirby created a group that was literally a bickering family – the Fantastic Four. Moore's experience was typical of the enthusiasm Marvel generated among its readership. In early 1962, at the age of eight, he had asked his mother to pick up a copy of DC war comic *Blackhawk*: 'I told her it's got a lot of people in it who all wore the same blue uniform. And she went out and came back with, much to my disappointment, *Fantastic Four* #3 . . . but of course I soon became completely infatuated . . . From that point I began to live and breathe comics, live and breathe American culture.'

The Fantastic Four were hugely popular, and were soon joined by Spider-Man, the Hulk, Thor, Iron Man, Daredevil, the X-Men and many more, all of them written by Stan Lee. As Moore put it, the difference between Marvel's superheroes and those of their rivals was simple: they 'went from one-dimensional characters whose only characteristic was they dressed up in costumes and did good, whereas Stan Lee had this huge breakthrough of two-dimensional characters. So, they dress up in costumes and do good, but they've got a bad heart. Or a bad leg. I actually did think for a long while that having a bad leg was an actual character trait.' As he later put it, Marvel's success was down to 'Stan Lee's crowd-pleasing formula of omnipotent losers'.

The stories and art were crucial, of course, but what really marked the company's comics out was that Lee used the covers, captions, letters pages and editorial columns to vigorously and enthusiastically blow his own trumpet. The

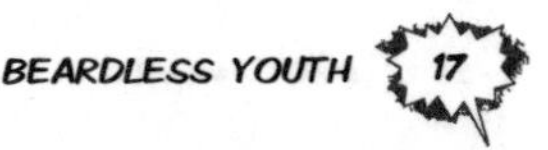

way he did so was so over the top, so hyperbolic, so reminiscent of Robert Preston's performance as a garrulous travelling salesman in the Broadway show *The Music Man*, that it was clearly meant to be impossible to take seriously. So, the cover of the first Marvel Comic read by Alan Moore, *Fantastic Four* #3, declared itself to be

THE GREATEST COMIC MAGAZINE IN THE WORLD!!

And on the cover of *Fantastic Four* #41, readers were promised

POSSIBLY THE MOST DARINGLY DRAMATIC DEVELOPMENT IN THE FIELD OF CONTEMPORARY LITERATURE!'

Marvel were moreover canny enough to make sure that all these stories took place in the 'Marvel Universe'. Spider-Man would swing past the Baxter Building, home of the Fantastic Four, note it had been damaged and speculate on the cause – a caption would helpfully inform readers which issue of *Fantastic Four* to pick up to find out what had happened. The wartime character Captain America was revived and put in charge of the Avengers, a team initially consisting of Iron Man, Thor and the Hulk, who already had their own monthly comics. You *could* just read one Marvel title . . . but why would you when you could read them all?

Lee not only gave the characters nicknames – the Incredible Hulk, the Uncanny X-Men, the Amazing Spider-Man – Marvel Comics were drawn by Jack 'King' Kirby, 'Sturdy' Steve Ditko, Gene 'The Dean' Colan, 'Jaunty' Johnny Romita and the like. Together they were the Marvel Bullpen, and the way Stan Lee told it, no other room on earth buzzed with as much creative energy. Not only did the cover of *Fantastic Four* #10 proclaim

THE WORLD'S GREATEST COMIC MAGAZINE! THE FANTASTIC FOUR. *HOLD YOUR BREATH!! HERE IS . . . 'THE RETURN OF DOCTOR DOOM!'*

but it had a couple of other special guest stars too:

IN THIS EPIC ISSUE SURPRISE FOLLOWS SURPRISE AS YOU ACTUALLY MEET LEE AND KIRBY IN THE STORY!!!

Stan Lee's relentless showmanship demanded and received ferocious brand loyalty from his readers; as Alan Moore has said, 'We were wild-eyed fanatics to rival the loopiest Thuggee cultist or member of the Manson Family. We were True

Believers.' In truth, Marvel was a tiny company and *Fantastic Four* had been a last-ditch gamble. Yet, as novelist Michael Chabon, another Marvel acolyte, put it, 'Lee behaved from the start as if a vast, passionate readership awaited each issue that he and his key collaborators, Kirby and Steve Ditko, churned out. And in a fairly short period of time, this chutzpah – as in all those accounts of magical chutzpah so beloved by solitary boys like me – was rewarded. By pretending to have a vast network of fans, former fan Stanley Lieber found himself in possession of a vast network of fans.'

For UK readers, the comics themselves were artefacts rocketed from a full-colour fantasyland. The Marvel Bullpen intended their version of New York to be ordinary, just the view as they saw it when they looked out of their window, a backdrop to be overlaid with daydreams of the incredible, amazing and fantastic. For Alan Moore, though, a boy living in an English town where the tallest buildings soared to the height of 115 feet, the Manhattan skyline that Spider-Man swung though, or the Lower East Side neighbourhood the Thing came from, or the Hell's Kitchen patrolled by Daredevil were themselves all 'as exotic as Mars. The idea of buildings of that scale, the idea of this modernity that seemed to pervade everything. This was a futuristic science fiction world.'

Merely finding DC and Marvel comics in the UK required a degree of arcane knowledge, as they had no formal distribution. They arrived on freight ships which used tied-up bundles of old magazines as ballast. The bundles were meant to be thrown away, but were sold on to traders by entrepreneurial dockworkers. Seven-year-old Alan Moore had first stumbled across copies of *Flash*, *Detective Comics* and other DC titles on a stall ran by a man called Sid in Northampton's ancient market square, and ever since he'd been back every week.

He certainly understood that there was little chance of finding the best, most recent American comics on the annual family holiday in Norfolk. Every year, Ernest and Sylvia Moore would take their sons Alan and Mike for a week at the North Denes Caravan Camp in Great Yarmouth on the east coast of England. This was around 130 miles from home, the furthest the Moores would typically venture.

In the mid-sixties the bucket-and-spade British holiday was still in its heyday, with practically every family enjoying time at the beach at some point in July or

August. One consequence of this was that seaside towns had a captive audience of millions of bored children. The British comics companies catered for them by printing Summer Specials of their titles, larger comics that often featured reprinted material or activities like colouring pages and stories involving the regular characters on holiday. Unsold stock was also retired to the seaside, ending its life fading on spinner racks and boxes in seafront shops. Moore would trawl through them hoping to uncover some unexpected treasure among the trash. It was on one such family holiday, in 1966, that he found the aforementioned collections of highlights from *Mad*, introducing him to 'Superduperman'. He also came across an old hardback annual featuring the British superhero Young Marvelman, which he was less excited about, but he liked the cover and decided to buy it.

The name Marvelman enables us to make one of those connections that demonstrate how small the world of comics often is. The *Captain Marvel* strip was reprinted in the UK by publisher L. Miller and Co, and one consequence of the lawsuit parodied in 'Superduperman' was that Miller had to find new material once Fawcett ceased publication of *Captain Marvel* in the US. Their solution was to create an almost identical character. Captain Marvel had been a young boy, Billy Batson, who would say the magic word 'Shazam!' and be hit by a bolt of magic lightning that transformed him into an adult who had super strength and could fly. Artist Mick Anglo created a 'new' character, Marvelman, a young boy, Mickey Moran, who would say the magic word 'Kimota!' and be hit by a bolt of atomic lightning ('kimota' is, give or take, 'atomic' spelled backwards) that transformed him into . . . an adult who had super strength and could fly. Where Captain Marvel had a young sidekick called Captain Marvel Jnr, Marvelman had the sidekick Young Marvelman. Their adventures were published for nine years from 1954 to 1963 and amassed a total of 722 issues and 19 hardback annuals.

Even at twelve, Alan Moore knew *Marvelman* to be a rather cheap knock-off, but when he read the stories in the annual, he found them more charming than he had expected. His awareness of the history of the character sparked an idle thought: 'I knew that *Marvelman* hadn't been printed for about two or three years and that Marvelman had vanished . . . It occurred to me then "I wonder what Marvelman's doing at the moment?" three years after his book got cancelled. The image I had in my head was of an older Mickey Moran trying to remember the magic word that would change him back to Marvelman.' Like all good origin stories, the events of that day have been recounted numerous times over the years, and perhaps tidied up a little to make for a better tale. Moore gave the definitive account in an interview in 2010:

> I remember I was reading these two very disparate books back in the caravan, and somehow there was a kind of a cross-fertilisation – well, it wasn't even that much of a cross-fertilisation. I read the 'Superduperman' story, and thought, 'Oh, I'd really like to do a story like that, that was so funny,' and I thought, well, you couldn't do it about Superman, because they've already done it. Could you do a story like that about this British superhero, Marvelman, that I was aware of? And so I just started to think about it – I think at the time I was even planning to submit it to the school magazine, which was the only publishing outlet that was available to me back then. It never got any further than just the idea, but I can remember that I thought it would be kind of funny to have Mickey Moran grown up and become an adult, who'd forgotten his magic word. And, yeah, at the time, that was seen as a satirical, humorous situation, but the idea just stayed in my mind, and over the next twenty or something years, fifteen years, it obviously percolated until it became my version of *Marvelman*.

Throughout his career, Moore has acknowledged 'Superduperman' as being a huge influence on his work, and the links to 'Superduperman' are often pretty concrete. As he implies in that interview, Moore would eventually write his *Marvelman* story (1982–9), and it culminates with, essentially, the battle from 'Superduperman' played straight: the hero does a vast amount of damage to the city he is meant to be protecting and finally defeats his equally powerful opponent only by tricking him; in addition, one of Moore's last pitches to DC Comics was *Twilight* (1986), a series that, had it been made, would have featured an epic battle between Superman and Captain Marvel.

Moore's most substantial debt to 'Superduperman', though, has nothing to do with specific characters or plot points. It relies on his own formulation of how the story fits into the history of comics, and the philosophy it encapsulates: 'The way that Harvey Kurtzman used to make his superhero parodies so funny was to take a superhero and then apply sort of real world logic to a kind of inherently absurd superhero situation . . . It struck me that if you just turn the dial to the same degree in the other direction by applying real life logic to a superhero, you could make something that was very funny, but you could also, with a turn of the screw, make something that was quite startling, sort of dramatic and powerful.' Moore has identified a desire to mimic the density of information in each panel of 'Superduperman' and its cynical take on heroism as the seed of *Watchmen*, but the idea he credits to Kurtzman of applying 'real world logic' is at the core of almost all of his early stories.

The family holiday over, the Moores returned home to their three-bedroom terraced council house at 17 St Andrew's Road, in the Boroughs area of Northampton, opposite a large railway station (then Northampton Castle, later renamed Northampton). Alan lived with his parents Ernest, a labourer at a brewery, and Sylvia, who worked at a printer's, his maternal grandmother, Clara Mallard, and younger brother Mike. The family had lived in the same house for thirty or forty years. Just before Alan was born, it had also accommodated uncle Les, aunt Queenie and their baby Jim (who slept in the wardrobe drawer), as well as another aunt, Hilda, her husband Ted and their children, John and Eileen. Life in such a crowded house had been tense although, as Moore noted at the time, he 'was employed as a foetus and was thus spared the worst effects'.

The Boroughs – now Spring Boroughs – area of Northampton remains one of the most deprived areas of the United Kingdom. The town's main industry had for centuries been boot and shoe manufacturing. The houses were a hundred years old, with outside toilets and no running hot water, although the Moores' house was considered luxurious compared with many in the neighbourhood because the council had installed electric lighting. Ernest Moore earned around £780 a year, when the national average was about £1,330, and once told Alan that £15 a week wasn't enough, and he hoped one day his son might earn £18. This was not abject poverty – the family may have used tin baths filled with water heated in a copper boiler, but that wasn't so uncommon at the time, and they never went hungry. The Moores had a television when Alan was growing up, and every week he was given a little pocket money.

Alan was born in St Edmund's Hospital on 18 November 1953, blind in his left eye. At first he had red hair, a family trait (there were people alive in 1953 who remembered his great-grandfather, Mad Ginger Vernon). He was baptised into the Church of England at the local church, St Peter's, and with both his parents at work, he was raised by his grandmother, 'a working class, Victorian matriarch. She was a deeply religious woman who never said very much but then didn't need to because everybody obeyed her implicitly'. Moore doubts she 'ever travelled more than five or ten miles from the place she was born'. (While his grandmother was devout, Moore did not have a religious upbringing, and has claimed he learned the basics of morality from reading *Superman*.)

In 1967, Jeremy Seabrook wrote *The Unprivileged*, the first book in a long career charting poverty throughout the world. It was an oral history of the working class of Northampton. The portrait he painted was of a community only a few generations away from agricultural peasantry, locked into old rituals of speech, family behaviour, deference to their social superiors and plain superstition: 'The real fear in which their superstitions held them – and at least fifty common phenomena were considered certain forerunners of death – was a grim and joyless feature of their lives . . . Their irrational beliefs were like an hereditary poison, which, if it no longer manifests itself in blains and pustules on the surface of the skin, nonetheless continues its toxic effects insidiously and invisibly.' This is echoed in Moore's description of his grandmother, who had a 'nightmarish array of sinister and unfathomable superstitions . . . she managed through sheer force of will to involve the entire household in her system of Juju and Counter-Juju. Knives crossed upon the dinner table, as an instance, heralded the forthcoming destruction of the house and its immediate neighbourhood by a rogue comet. To avert this peril, the catastrophically crossed cutlery had to be struck forcibly by yet a third knife.' Seabrook concluded that attitudes like this left people insular and ill-equipped to deal with a world that was changing rapidly, that they were 'exposed to an overwhelming sense of loss, seeing the certainties of a lifetime take on a bewildering and terrifying relativity . . . the life of the streets had a devitalising effect and did not allow of any departure from a rigidly fixed pattern of behaviour and relationships.'

The Unprivileged was a study of Seabrook's own upbringing. He was born just a few streets away from the Moores' house, fourteen years before Alan. He recalls:

> As far as working-class Northampton of that time is concerned, it was definitely separated by districts – Far Cotton and Jimmy's End were different from the Boroughs, which were, in any case, in the process of being demolished in the

late fifties, early sixties. The boot and shoe industry was also being eclipsed – it was one of the earliest occupations that were victims of de-industrialisation. The most remarkable thing was the sameness of people's lives – the almost regimented coming and going to work, the predictability of life – the pub, factory, maybe chapel, the pictures, the young people walking up and down Abington Street, the slightly louche places like Becket's Park (clandestinely gay) and around the Criterion and Mitre (prostitution). The arrival of the bus from the American base in the market square on Saturday night was a weekly event.

In the mid-sixties, Seabrook was teaching at the local grammar school, where he was Alan Moore's first-form French teacher the year before he wrote *The Unprivileged*. He doesn't recall Moore specifically, but when he describes the prevailing character of the area, he uses at least some of the same words that have been used to describe Moore over the years: 'The shoe people were generally narrow, suspicious, mean, self-reliant, pig-headed, but generally honourable and as good as their word.'

Moore could not have known as a boy that many of the early comic book writers and artists had grown up in an even more deprived place than fifties Northampton – the Depression-era New York slums. It would be some years before comics fans turned their attention to the history of the 'Golden Age' of the 1940s, and it's perhaps only in the twenty-first century that studies of the period have gone beyond the anecdotal. But Michael Chabon's Pulitzer Prize-winning novel *The Amazing Adventures of Kavalier and Clay* (2000), Gerard Jones' book *Men of Tomorrow: Geeks, Gangsters and the Birth of the Comic Book* (2005) and Michael Schumacher's biography of Will Eisner, *A Dreamer's Life in Comics* (2010) paint a consistent picture of the genesis of the industry and of the superhero genre, revealing a pattern of the young sons of immigrants exploited by companies formed and run using highly dubious business practices . . . often by other young sons of immigrants.

Much later, some of the Golden Age creators would write overtly autobiographical works, like Eisner's *A Contract With God* (1978) and *Life, In Pictures* (2008). Although it was not always so obvious, their superhero work in the 1940s often drew from personal experience as well. Many comics were power fantasies about confronting bullies – from a crook on the corner to Hitler himself. Comics historian Mark Evanier, a friend and former assistant to artist Jack Kirby, has described *Fantastic Four* member The Thing as 'an obvious Kirby self-caricature'. The Thing is a gruff and pugnacious brawler who was a member of the Yancy Street Gang as a kid. Jack Kirby had been a member of the Suffolk Street Gang, and had frequently fought running battles on the streets and rooftops of the Lower East Side in turf wars with the Norfolk Street Gang:

> I had to draw the things I knew. In one fight scene, I recognised my uncle. I'd subconsciously drawn my uncle, and I didn't know it until I took the page home. So I was drawing reality, and if you look through all my drawings, you'll see reality.

Like all artists, the creators of comic books draw on what they know. The life stories of comic book writers and artists are often far darker, stranger and more troubled than those of their creations. There's no contradiction here. Who is going to have the strongest urge to enjoy creating escapist fiction? Someone with a life they want to escape from.

Moore, however, has corrected interviewers seeking to portray his early life as particularly squalid, saying on one occasion 'this is not a tale of extraordinary poverty by any means . . . I had a very happy childhood' and explaining 'I never really thought much about material luxury. That was kind of where I was starting from. My family never had anything. It was never as grim as it sounds because it was normal, in [the] context of what I was used to.' This doesn't mean he waxes lyrical about his background, either. While he remains committed to his roots, and sees much of value – far more than Seabrook does – in the culture found in the terraced streets of Northampton, now and then, there are, Moore concedes, 'things I personally find very sad about the working class. You know, a lot of them are a bunch of racists, a bunch of idiots. They're in these awful social traps that they can't get out of. They blunder through life.'

Moore was reading by the time he was four or five, with his parents – who, unlike many of their neighbours, valued literacy – encouraging him at every turn. They read little themselves (his father occasionally read pulp novels and some anthropology, and Moore suggested once that the second thing he had ever seen his mother read was one of his *Swamp Thing* collections) but Alan quickly became omnivorous. He already had a taste for fantasy stories, and the first book he picked out when he joined the library at the age of five was called *The Magic Island*. He soaked up mythology and folklore.

'I was looked after and cared for and all the other things that a child should be, but in terms of my inner life, or my intellectual life, I was largely left to my own devices. Which suited me just fine. I knew where the library was; I knew where I could find information if I wanted it.' He was an imaginative, precocious child at Spring Lane, the primary school two or three minutes' walk from his home. The school took in boys and girls from the streets around Moore's house, and so he knew every one of his fellow students from his first day there. When he was about ten, he started drawing his own comics in a Woolworths jotter, branding them all as Omega Comics. He charged a penny a read of tales of *The Crimebusters*, *Ray Gun* (featuring a character with a ray gun whose secret identity was Raymond Gunn) and *Jack O'Lantern and the Sprite*. He said at the time it was to raise money for UNICEF, but later admitted it was mainly done in a failed attempt to impress a girl called Janet Bentley. Throughout his early school career he was something of a star pupil.

This was not an idyllic childhood. Moore has talked about how children would attack each other, often in ways that were genuinely dangerous. In one case 'they hanged me from a tree branch by my wrists with string'; in another 'they caved the underground den in on top of me', leaving him 'crawling like a lugworm through the smothering black dirt'. But, on the whole, Moore was happy. Tall for his age, he 'thought I was a miniature god. They made me the head prefect at Spring Lane. I was the brainiest boy in the school and the world was my oyster.'

This idyll was abruptly ended when Moore sat his Eleven Plus.

The intention of the 1944 Butler Education Act had been to level the playing field for all schoolchildren. At the end of their primary education, around the age of eleven, every child sat an examination which measured skills in arithmetic, writing and problem solving. Those who passed – around a quarter of students who sat it – went to prestigious grammar schools for a full academic training; those who failed were consigned to secondary moderns and a more rudimentary preparation for working life. The lion's share of the resources went to the grammar schools, so the secondary moderns, and those who attended them, quickly came to carry the stigma of failure. The theory was that the Eleven Plus was entirely meritocratic, a way to grant a free top-class education to all those who would benefit from it, regardless of background. The system was designed, in large part, to identify and reward intelligent working-class children. In practice, middle-class pupils had many advantages – their parents could, for example, afford to send them to preparatory schools specifically designed to get students through the exam. Some parts of the country had insufficient places for all the pupils who passed; this problem was particularly acute for girls.

The Eleven Plus, then, was crude and in many ways formalised the inequalities it was designed to eradicate, but it worked exactly as it was meant to for Alan Moore. He passed, and was sent to Northampton School for Boys, known locally just as 'the boys' grammar school' (there was a girls' grammar school nearby). It was on the other side of town, and took around 500 pupils from the whole of the local area. It was a shock to the system for Moore: 'Call me naïve, but entering grammar school was the very first time I'd actually realised that middle-class people existed. Prior to that I'd thought that there were just my family and people like them, and the Queen. I had really not been aware that there was a whole stratum of society in between those two positions.' According to Moore there were only 'two or three' other working-class boys at the school and he hardly knew anyone there.

Seabrook suggests that the system had a clear agenda for boys like Moore: 'The grammar school was, for working-class boys, primarily a door to the middle class. Its unacknowledged curriculum was advanced snobbery and social climbing. It separated those who might, at another time, have been leaders of the working class, politicians or trade unionists, so in that sense, while it advantaged the individuals concerned, it could be said to have impoverished the communities. The school was modelled on public school to some degree, but many of the boys resisted the ethos, although perhaps not consciously.' Seabrook had noted in *The Unprivileged*: 'The public boast that "they make proper little gentlemen of 'em at the grammar school" often conceals shame and perplexity when the proper little gentlemen return home, impatient and critical of the way their parents live. They marvel at the remote and inaccessible places in which their children's minds move, and as they leaf timidly through a book left on the kitchen table they wonder who this Go-eth can be and whether it is he who is responsible for their son's alienation.'

There is no indication that Moore's parents felt that way, but Moore himself certainly did. For the first time, he was embarrassed to take his friends home.

He found the school's all-male atmosphere uncomfortable and did not share any particular enthusiasm for sports. The emphasis on authority and rules simply didn't suit his style of learning. 'The school was an odd mixture of strange Dickensian customs and normal, everyday mid-sixties modernism. It was an unusual environment; it was a school I never liked. The Northampton Grammar School was impersonal and cold and incredibly dull and authoritarian.'

A more direct blow to Moore's ego came at the end of the first term, when grades were assigned. He had plummeted from star pupil at primary school to nineteenth in a class of around thirty in the first term at grammar school. He was twenty-seventh in the class by the end of the next term. Some of this was down to his classmates benefitting from the advantages of a better primary education, already having been taught Latin and algebra, subjects Moore had never encountered. Some was a consequence of Moore having been a big fish in a small pond at Spring Lane: 'I thought I was a genuine intellectual light. I hadn't realised that actually, no, I was just about the smartest of a pretty crap bunch!'

Moore gave up academically. 'I decided, pretty typically for me, that if I couldn't win, then I wasn't going to play. I was always one of those sulky children who sort of couldn't stand to lose at Monopoly, Cluedo or anything. So I decided that I really wanted no more of the struggle for academic supremacy.' This was not a case of Moore giving up on learning. Instead he became an autodidact, pursuing his own inner life, and he is clearly proud he ventured off the beaten path in his reading. Most of the books seem to have been fiction – he was particularly fond of Mervyn Peake's *Gormenghast* novels, he went through a Dennis Wheatley phase, a Ray Bradbury phase and an H.P. Lovecraft phase. He would soak up what he read, which was eclectic and idiosyncratic. Even at grammar school, he was reading at a slightly more advanced level than his peers, and occasionally found – for example with *Mad* or, later, Michael Moorcock's *New Worlds* magazine – that he was reading things he was a little too young to fully appreciate.

Less than a handful of his fellow pupils shared his interest in comics, and he failed to impress anyone at the grammar school with his Omega strips, and soon stopped producing them. But Moore continued to read comics. By the late sixties, there was a new batch of Marvel titles like *Silver Surfer*, *Nick Fury: Agent of SHIELD* and *Doctor Strange* for slightly older readers, starring characters who were not quite straightforward superheroes in stories inflected a little towards introspection. The storytelling could now be more stylised and impressionistic, and there were innovations like silent sequences and psychedelic spreads. Moore noted, 'Probably the most remarkable thing that Stan Lee achieved was the way in which he managed to hold on to his audience long after they had grown beyond the age range usually associated with comic book readers of that period. He did this by a constant application of change, modification and development. No comic book was allowed to remain static for long.' These titles did not challenge the sales supremacy of *Archie* or DC's Superman and Batman titles or become the dominant style of mainstream comics, but they found an avid audience among teenage readers who were starting to respond to the medium in a more sophisticated, knowing way. Comics fans were also beginning to talk to each other.

Alan Moore judges that British fandom began to 'catch fire' in 1966, a couple of years later than in America. While their American counterparts tended towards nostalgia, virtually everything was new to British fans, who celebrated the latest American imports alongside material from the forties and fifties that had not previously shown up in the UK, 'so we applauded people like Jim Steranko, Neal Adams; people who were actually pushing the medium forward, trying to make it do things that it hadn't done before. We went berserk when we discovered Eisner, through the Harvey *Spirit* reprints that were done in the mid-sixties. And EC Comics. But it wasn't a nostalgia for Eisner or EC – these were things we were discovering for the first time.'

One of the most prominent of the British comics fans was Steve Moore. He is four years, five months older than Alan, and by the late sixties was working for Odhams, a publisher reprinting Marvel strips for the British market and replicating the Stan Lee formula so slavishly that he was referred to in editorials as 'Sunny' Steve Moore. Along with fellow editor Phil Clarke he also published two issues of what is thought to be the first British comics fanzine, *Ka-Pow*, and organised the earliest British comics conventions. Alan Moore was buying Odhams' *Fantastic*, mainly for its only original strip, *Johnny Future* – written by Alf Wallace and drawn by Luis Bermejo – the adventures of a surviving missing link between modern human and Neanderthal who falls into a nuclear reactor to become a super-evolved being capable of great feats of strength and astral projection. And Alan didn't just subscribe to *Ka-Pow*, he began corresponding with both Steve Moore and Phil Clarke.

Alan Moore and Steve Moore have been friends ever since, and, as we will see, Steve's influence on Alan's life cannot be overestimated. Alan has described him as 'the most influential figure in my life in many ways, this was the guy who taught me how to write comics, got me into magic and is in many ways responsible for completely ruining my existence'. Steve Moore appears unassuming, particularly when standing next to his namesake, but Alan has worked hard to disabuse people of this notion, writing a short story, *Unearthing*, a candid biography that starts at the moment of his friend's conception and encompasses the wide variety of weird encounters he has had. Steve Moore admits to being 'bewildered by all the attention it's getting . . . the whole thing has rather surprised my friends and relatives!', possibly because *Unearthing* includes details of his erotic relationship with the moon goddess Selene.

Alan Moore was a 'supporting member' of the first British comic convention, Comicon, at Birmingham's Midland Hotel in August 1968. He did not attend (he was only fourteen), but helped it financially by buying a fundraising magazine, and his name appeared in the convention booklet alongside those of many people who would go on to work in the British comics industry, either creatively, in editorial or by running comics shops and distributors (see next page).

He was, however, present at the second Comicon, the following year at the Waverley Hotel in London: 'There were sixty or seventy people there and that as far as we knew was the entire number of people who were remotely interested in comics in the British Isles.' The convention was the first time that Alan and Steve Moore met, after a year or so as penpals. Alan also encountered Frank Bellamy, who'd drawn strips like *Dan Dare* and *Fraser of Africa* for the *Eagle* (the veteran artist was a little taken aback to learn that people discussed his work). The main guests were two British artists who had worked for Marvel in the US: Steve Parkhouse – who remembers their meeting: 'I was struck by Alan's demeanour. He was very, very young – but very, very funny. He was undeniably a performer' – and Barry Windsor Smith, who the following year would start an acclaimed run on *Conan the Barbarian* (a comic avidly read by a young Barack Obama). Comicon became an annual event. At this and subsequent conventions, as well as through reading and contributing to fanzines, Alan Moore would come to know (if not always actually meet) many people a little older than him who were starting what would be long careers in the comics industry, and who would end

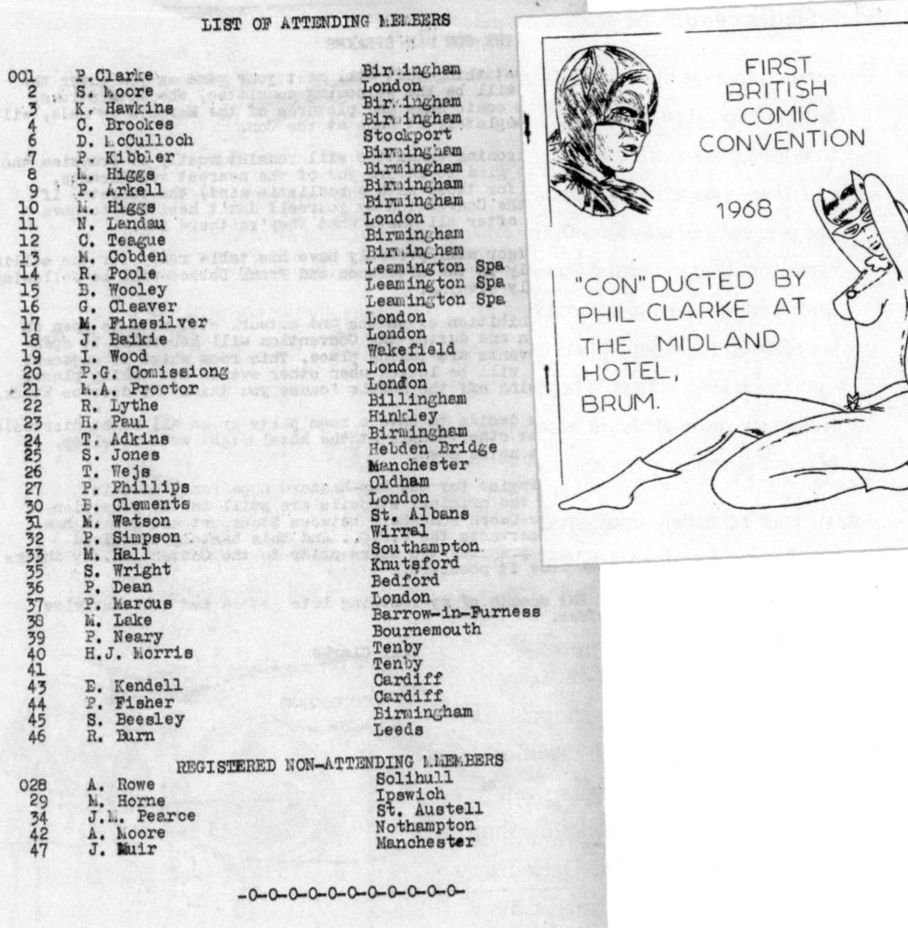

LIST OF ATTENDING MEMBERS

No.	Name	Town
001	P.Clarke	Birmingham
2	S. Moore	London
3	K. Hawkins	Birmingham
4	C. Brookes	Birmingham
6	D. McCulloch	Stockport
7	P. Kibbler	Birmingham
8	L. Higgs	Birmingham
9	P. Arkell	Birmingham
10	M. Higgs	Birmingham
11	N. Landau	London
12	C. Teague	Birmingham
13	M. Cobden	Birmingham
14	R. Poole	Leamington Spa
15	B. Wooley	Leamington Spa
16	G. Cleaver	Leamington Spa
17	M. Finesilver	London
18	J. Baikie	London
19	I. Wood	Wakefield
20	P.G. Comissiong	London
21	M.A. Proctor	London
22	R. Lythe	Billingham
23	H. Paul	Hinkley
24	T. Adkins	Birmingham
25	S. Jones	Hebden Bridge
26	T. Wejs	Manchester
27	P. Phillips	Oldham
30	B. Clements	London
31	M. Watson	St. Albans
32	P. Simpson	Wirral
33	M. Hall	Southampton
35	S. Wright	Knutsford
36	P. Dean	Bedford
37	P. Marcus	London
38	M. Lake	Barrow-in-Furness
39	P. Neary	Bournemouth
40	H.J. Morris	Tenby
41		Tenby
43	E. Kendell	Cardiff
44	P. Fisher	Cardiff
45	S. Beesley	Birmingham
46	R. Burn	Leeds

REGISTERED NON-ATTENDING MEMBERS

No.	Name	Town
028	A. Rowe	Solihull
29	M. Horne	Ipswich
34	J.M. Pearce	St. Austell
42	A. Moore	Nothampton
47	J. Muir	Manchester

-0-0-0-0-0-0-0-0-0-0-0-

up working with him in the eighties – people like Jim Baikie, Dez Skinn, Kevin O'Neill, David Lloyd, Brian Bolland and Dave Gibbons.

Moore's fascination with America, and his avid reading of material like *Mad*, meant he became aware of the counterculture a number of years before it was given that name. He liked what he saw. When asked, 'So would you say the sixties was a really important time for you in terms of your political development?', Moore answered: 'For me it was absolutely formative, if I hadn't have been growing up during that time I certainly wouldn't be the same person that I am today.' Sixties culture, he said,

> seemed to have blossomed from nowhere . . . it was a convergence of several different social trends, there was an awful lot of increase in technology that took place during the war; there was an economic boom after the war; there was a massive generation, the biggest human generation that has ever existed was born in the wake of the war; and all of these things came together in around about the early sixties, so there was this fairly unprecedented explosion of ideas and I think initially the counterculture, as we referred to it then, it was left-leaning but it was it was a very radical take upon even leftist ideas. It tended to reject all kind of authoritarianism and it was much more pleasure based, much more centred upon joy, ecstasy, it was very enlightened in my opinion.

Alan was 'relatively drug-free, fresh-faced and squeaky clean' in 1969 when he first met Steve Moore, but there was a distinctly psychedelic tinge to the comics scene. 'Most of those early English comic fans were hippies, or at least proto-hippies or would-be hippies. They were all hanging out at the only comic and science fiction shop in Britain, which was called Dark They Were and Golden-Eyed, named from a Ray Bradbury short story's title.' Alan's first published work (outside school magazines) was an advert for the shop, an illustration that appeared in the September 1970 issue of the magazine *Cyclops*. He wasn't paid.

Others attending Comicon went on to open comic shops and mail-order businesses. Many published fan magazines, usually fairly eclectic publications that included essays, short stories, illustrations and cartoons about whatever interested them. The print runs of these fanzines very rarely reached three figures: they were almost all made on mimeographs, small machines that used an electric spark to burn type into a wax stencil (hence the alternative name for the device, the electrostenciller). Most schools, churches and offices used them to produce newsletters or flyers. Once they were printed, the editor would collate and hand-staple the result.

Moore contributed to a number of titles. He 'spent a hell of a long time gathering material' for an essay about pulp character The Shadow for *Seminar* (1970). He made a couple of contributions to *Weird Window*: a book review, various illustrations of monsters and the poem 'To the Humfo' appeared in #1 (Summer 1969); #2 (March 1971) had an illustration of a Lovecraftian Deep One by Moore and a prose story, 'Shrine of the Lizard' ('I'd just read Mervyn Peake's excellent *Gormenghast* books at the time, so all the characters have names like Elly Blacklungs and Toziah Firebowels'). An eleven-word letter by Moore appeared in *Orpheus* #1 (March 1971) and he contributed to the horror fanzine *Shadow*.

Soon, though, he wanted to produce his own magazine. 'Myself and a couple of other kids of my age, some from the grammar school that I attended, some from the girls' schools, we decided spontaneously to put together a magazine of bad poetry basically. It was called *Embryo*, it was originally going to be called *Androgyne*, but I found that I couldn't fit that lettering onto the cover so I shortened it. It was very ramshackle.' Its covers were printed on coloured paper, and it sold for 5p, rising to 7p by #5. Moore produced covers, illustrations and poems for *Embryo*. 'I was writing what I thought was poetry. Usually angst breast-beating things about the tragedy of nuclear war, but were actually about the tragedy of me not being able to find a girlfriend.' While it was not a comics fanzine, the last issue featured a four-page comic strip written and drawn by Moore, 'Once There Were Daemons'. Whatever Moore's reservations about the quality of his verse, his work on *Embryo* brought him to the attention of a local poetry group, which he joined.

While Moore had been set back academically, he had never got into much trouble at school; he started smoking, and he would occasionally bunk off to ride a friend's motorbike around the grounds of the local psychiatric hospital. His parents knew he was different, but found this easy to accept:

> I was regarded almost from the outset as unusual, but this was within a family tradition where unusual people were not actually that unusual. There had been previous people in the family line, mostly on my father's side, who were quirky, talented and in certain instances certifiable. Generally my parents seemed to be very impressed that I could draw a picture and string words together, sometimes in rhyme, in a way that they did not feel competent to ... My family accepted me as, in my mum's phrase, 'a funny wonder'. This was an all-embracing phrase that incorporated an awful lot of things. It was something that was wonderful, but funny in the peculiar sense. Such people were not unknown in the bloodline. 'Oh, we get one of these every hundred years or so.' I always had an odd relationship with my family, because turning out to be someone like me did sometimes bring problems with it. It sometimes changes things, luckily with my close family I don't think it did.

The most serious trouble he had got into was when he published a poem in *Embryo* #1, written by his friend Ian Fleming, that used the word 'motherfuckers'. Moore was hauled over the coals by the headmaster, H.J.C. Oliver, and promised to apologise in the next issue. Instead he handed over the editorial to Fleming, allowing a repeat of his offence:

> Also, in passing, a few words about some people's objections to the use of certain streetwords in certain poems. (It's a pity that all the 'NAUGHTY' poems were by the same naughty author.) All, except in one case, ('Motherfuckers', in 'When they see us coming', which was used partly to complete the poem's contrasts, & partly because the word's meaning(s) were used in context with the rest of the poem) were used, not to shock anyone, not to give anyone a cheap thrill, not deliberately, but simply because they were written down as part of the poem, as the poem was formulated, i.e. they were in perfect context.
>
> THE REAL OBSCENITY GOES ON ALL AROUND US, UNDER MANY DIFFERENT NAMES.
>
> (nice rhetoric, man, nice ...)

Embryo was banned, which only increased its notoriety and sales. Despite this, Moore remained in good enough standing with the school that when he

was seventeen and the art department was featured in the local paper, he was the pupil chosen to appear in the photo. Moore had begun growing his hair, but it was shaggy at this stage, rather than shoulder-length. It seems clear that the school and Moore had found ways to cope with him being an artistically minded round peg in a square hole.

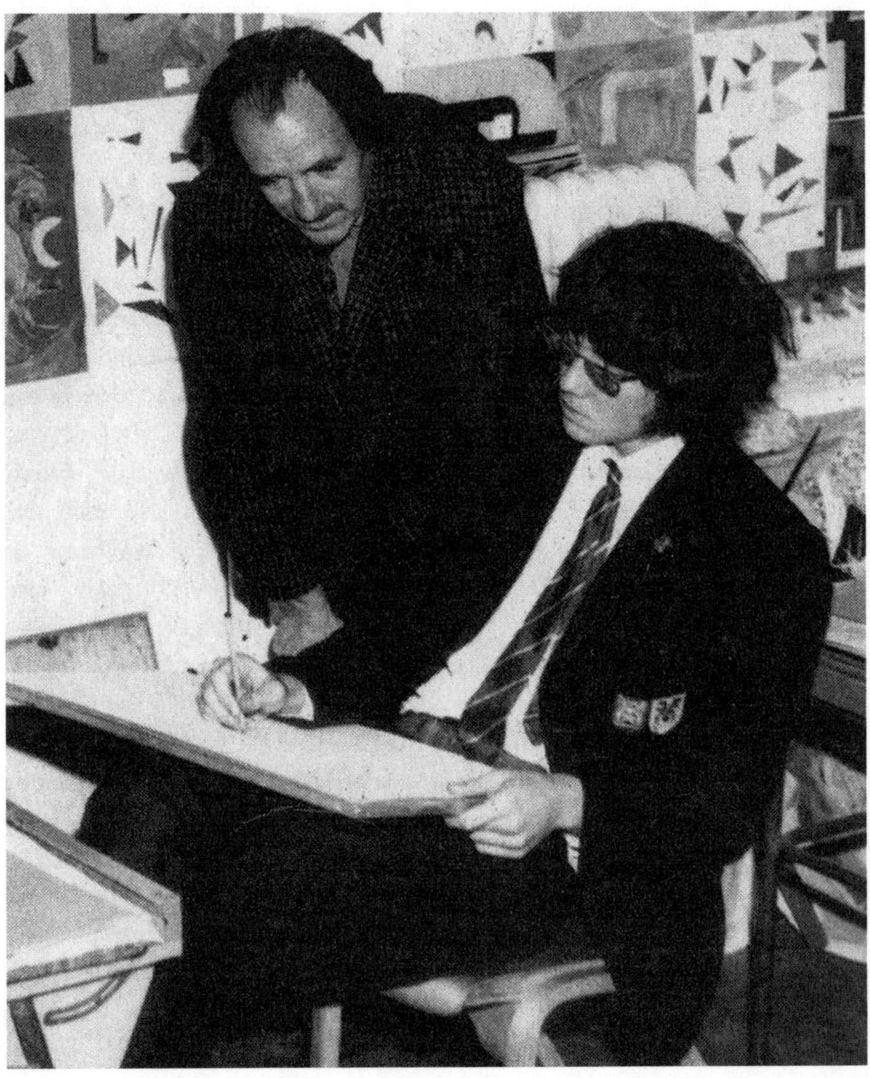

*

It was a second grand egalitarian social engineering project that would devastate Alan Moore and his family, starting in 1965 when Northampton – first settled in the Neolithic – was designated as a New Town.

Britain faced a housing crisis. Millions of Britons still lived in Victorian conditions – their houses were a hundred years old and many were now badly dilapidated. The Second World War had seen the Luftwaffe damage or destroy much of the housing stock, particularly in the cities; after the war, there had been a population boom. The British government set plans in motion to create large towns laid out with cars in mind, and with modern industrial plants, to ease pressure on the largest cities. This construction would be overseen by powerful development corporations. Northampton was part of the 'third wave' of such towns along with Central Lancashire, Milton Keynes, Peterborough, Telford and Warrington. Northampton is about sixty-five miles from central London, so was only about an hour away – in theory at least – by rail or via the brand new M1 motorway. The new arrivals were mainly from London, and tended to be young, aspirational working-class families.

In some cases, like Milton Keynes, the New Towns were essentially entirely new settlements (they were built on the sites of tiny villages). Northampton, however, had an existing population of 100,000 in 1961. That would rise to 130,000 in 1971, with the target of a population of 230,000 by 1981. New Town status brought a great deal of government money, some of which would be used to replace the Victorian slums now considered unfit for human habitation, and on 3 July 1967, Northampton County Borough Council passed the first of a series of resolutions that designated parts of Northampton as 'clearance areas'. The Northampton Development Corporation began operating in 1968, opening new tower blocks in the Eastern District in 1970 and buying up private property with compulsory purchase orders. Most residents, though, were council tenants and simply received a letter saying they were to be relocated. Whole streets were bulldozed.

The Unprivileged ends with a striking image of the abandoned terraced streets; the people had gone, but left what possessions they had behind, including furniture, family photographs and even a bird in its cage. For countless people in

Britain, this was a time of great social mobility and unparalleled opportunity, but according to Seabrook such euphoria did not last long:

> The great clearances of the fifties and sixties were like migrations – people couldn't get out quick enough; you can't blame them, because the conditions into which they were moving were so much better – it is only when all the new things fell apart in their hands that people began to think twice about the meaning of change. There was in the seventies a plan for a ring road in Northampton that would have demolished hundreds of houses which people were proud of, as their 'little palaces' – slum clearance struck at people's contentment with their lot. Redevelopment principally served the building, concrete and steel industries before it served the people who were being moved.

For the Moores, it was a catastrophic disruption. When he was seventeen, Alan Moore's family was relocated to Abington, formerly a prosperous part of Northampton. His eighty-four-year-old grandmother Clara died within six months. The council moved Moore's other grandmother, Minnie, from the house in Green Street where she had lived all her life to an old people's home and she died within three months. Moore has no doubt what caused their deaths: 'Being moved from the place where you got your roots was enough to kill most of those people . . . the place where I'd grown up was more or less completely destroyed. It wasn't that they put anything better there; it was just that they were able to make more money out of it without all those bothersome people.'

Alan Moore was expelled from Northampton School for Boys two weeks after the death of his grandmother Clara. When asked about this in 1990, Moore would only say it was 'for various reasons'; subsequently, one interviewer reported the offence had been 'wearing a green woolly hat to school', a remark Moore doesn't remember making and suspects 'might have been a facetious remark or it may even have been misheard, I'm not sure'. He first revealed the truth in *The Birth Caul* (1995): he was expelled for dealing acid. By the time he spoke to the BBC in 2008, though, it had become an anecdote for Moore the raconteur: 'At the age of 17 I became one of the world's most inept LSD dealers. The problem with being an LSD dealer, if you're sampling your own product, is your view of reality will probably

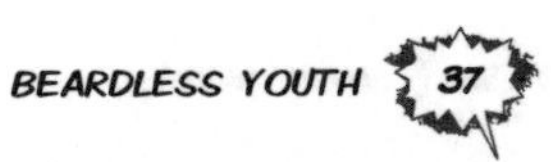

become horribly distorted . . . And you may believe you have supernatural powers and you are completely immune to any form of retaliation and prosecution, which is not the case.' The *Observer* later reported that he had been taken to the headmaster's office and confronted by a detective constable from the local drugs squad. Moore wasn't charged or fined: 'The expulsion was technically groundless. I was searched, but there was absolutely nothing on me and the only thing that they had was the hearsay evidence of a number of my schoolfriends who had named me – we were young then and easily intimidated by the police – and that wasn't conclusive proof. I was expelled from school, but there were no charges brought. I have a clean record.'

Moore's initial reluctance to spell out why he was expelled was out of respect for his parents. It was only after their deaths that he started referring to his drug dealing in interviews. At the time, he had initially told them he'd been framed, but when he later admitted the truth, they were (unsurprisingly) very upset and disappointed. As Moore would say in 1987, 'it must be terribly difficult being my parents'.

Given Moore's countercultural leanings, it would have been odder if he *hadn't* tried LSD. Moore glosses his taking acid at the time as 'purely for ideological reasons, believe it or not', based on reading Timothy Leary's essay *The Politics of Ecstasy*, which argued that people taking LSD were visionaries like the shamans of tradition, tasked with leading others out of the darkness. By this point, Leary was advocating the case that psychedelic experiences unlocked the next stage of human evolution, and so logically the more people who had LSD trips, the more likely it was that society could become more peaceful, harmonious and generous.

Moore had first tried the drug on 12 September 1970, a couple of months before his seventeenth birthday, at a free open-air concert in Hyde Park. It was a wet Saturday afternoon, but the music was pure Californian psychedelic rock. Stoneground opened, followed by Lambert and Nutteycombe, Michael Chapman, General Wastemoreland, and Wavy Gravy. John Sebastian played 'Johnny B Goode'. Even The Animals, originally from Newcastle upon Tyne, had by this time moved to San Francisco – lead singer Eric Burdon celebrated his return to the UK by splitting his trousers during a performance of 'Paint It Black'. Blues-rock band Canned Heat were the headliners. Moore bought some large purple pills from 'some kind of shifty-looking dope dealer straight out of a Gilbert Shelton cartoon' and had his first acid trip to the soundtrack of 'Future Blues', 'Let's Work Together' and 'Refried Hockey Boogie'. In the year between this event and his expulsion, Moore went on more than fifty acid trips – 'LSD was an incredible experience. Not that I'm recommending it for anybody else, but it hammered home to me that reality was not a fixed thing.'

Taking LSD may have given Moore insight into new realms of the imagination, but it was also directly responsible for dumping him out of school in the winter of 1971. He faced the problem that while his consciousness may have expanded, 'I found that my horizons had rapidly contracted. The headmaster who had dealt with my expulsion had, I think, taken me rather personally. He had written to all of the colleges and schools that I might have thought of applying to and told them that they should under no circumstances accept me as a pupil, because this would be a corrupting influence upon the morals of the other students. I believe that he did at one point in the letter refer to me as "sociopathic", which I do think was rather harsh.' Moore has, however, elsewhere described his younger self using exactly that word: 'I did decide to get revenge. I decided that there would be some way in which I could get my own back for this upon everybody that had annoyed me. I was a monster! . . . Very antisocial. Sociopathic.' He concluded that those in authority were out to get him – an idea that's stuck with him throughout his life.

Moore continued to live with his parents on Norman Road in Abington. He soon discovered that having 'the antimatter equivalent of references' meant he would not be going to Northampton Arts School, though he did make one attempt to get a job where his artistic skills would be appreciated:

> I noticed that there was an advert for 'cartoonist wanted', somebody to draw advertising . . . and they asked as a trial 'give us something that would work for a pet shop' and I did this – in retrospect – quite scary dog, and I'd used Letratone on it to show that I was au fait with sophisticated shading techniques. It was rejected of course. What they actually wanted was a smiley picture of a puppy, which I could have done, but I'd thought they wanted to see what a brilliant artist I am. No, they actually wanted to see you could follow a brief intelligently, which I was incapable of doing. So, with that, I gave up. That's when I decided to go down to the labour exchange and take whatever was available.

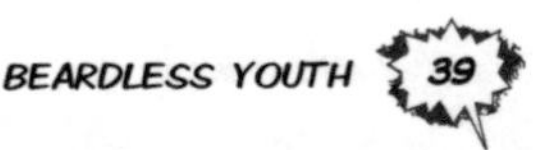

Moore understood what he was in for: his father, grandfather and great-grandfather had all been labourers. The first job he took was in the Co-op skinning yard on Bedford Road. He was paid £6 a week to cut up sheep that had been soaking overnight in vats of water and their own bodily fluids. It was a place 'where men with hands bright blue from caustic dye trade nigger jokes'. He was there for two months before being sacked for smoking cannabis in the tea room. He then worked as a cleaner in the fifty-seven-bedroom Grand Hotel on Gold Street (now the Travelodge Northampton Central), and later he worked in a W.H. Smith's warehouse packing books, magazines and, of course, comics.

When asked about these early jobs, Moore has made the same joke on more than one occasion: 'I tend to think of it as a long downward progression that ends as a comics writer.'

2 Eight Years Later . . .

'When you're at that stage of your career there is a sort of a terror that becomes associated with actually sending your first piece of work in because I think that the reasoning that's going through your head – if you can call it reasoning – is that if I send this in and it gets rejected, I won't even have the dream that I could've been a great writer or artist. Better to never send it in and never have that rejection so I'll always have the dream.'

Alan Moore, *Vworp Vworp* #3 (2013)

The end of Moore's 2011 book *The League of Extraordinary Gentlemen: Century 1969* skips from the aftermath of a sunny, psychedelic pop festival to an epilogue set 'eight years later' in a black-and-white basement punk club. It's a transition that sums up Moore's feelings towards and experience of the seventies, a decade that started at the peak of the countercultural idealism that is close to his heart but ended with wholesale rejection and open hostility towards it. The time jump also matches a relatively uncharted period of Moore's life. Having been expelled from school and consigned to the first in a series of menial jobs, in late 1971, his professional creative career began only with the publication of two illustrations for the *New Musical Express* in October and November 1978, and his first published work in mainstream comics did not appear until the summer of 1980, in *Doctor Who Weekly* and *2000AD*. He's summed up what happened in between by saying, 'My occupation from the time I left school was in a series of thoroughly miserable jobs that I wasn't interested in at all . . . I hadn't got any ambitions other than a vague ambition to make my living by writing or drawing or by something which I enjoyed doing. Since those sorts of jobs weren't on offer I didn't really have any clear idea of how to go about getting one, or even if I was good enough to get one.' His published work in the period adds up to less than two dozen pages of material for local zines and community magazines, none of which were paying jobs.

After Moore was expelled from school, almost all of his friends cut ties with him. He puts this down to their squeamishness over the jobs he was forced to take, but it's clear that the long-haired, sullen eighteen year old who was 'not quite in my right mind, and believed I had supernatural powers' was a very different creature from the shaggy, drug-free sixteen-year-old Moore. Many in his circle of friends took drugs, but those who stayed on at school must have been inclined to see Alan as an example of the terrible fate awaiting them if they didn't hunker down to work on their A-levels.

Moore did however have an oasis of continuity: the Northampton Arts Lab. About a year earlier, he had been a member of a poetry group that teamed up with the Arts Lab to run an event at the Racehorse Inn (it took place on 16 December 1970 and was advertised in *Embryo* #2). Soon after that, the group had merged with the Arts Lab, and from #3 (February 1971) onwards, *Embryo* was billed as a Northampton Arts Lab publication. This would grant Moore a social life and an outlet for his creative energies over the next few years. As he said, 'the Arts Lab was what I was living for to a degree . . . because, all right, I was kind of trapped in terribly miserable circumstances with no obvious way out. In the evenings I could write something that I was pleased with and then a couple of weeks later there'd be a poetry reading – I could go along and read it; maybe do some work with some musicians reading the poems to music . . . And that felt like that was taking me somewhere.'

Arts Labs had sprung up across the country, following the lead of Jim Haynes, co-founder of the hippie magazine *International Times*. Haynes had known John Lennon and Yoko Ono before they knew each other, as well as Germaine Greer and a very young David Bowie. In September 1967, he reopened an old cinema on Drury Lane as a rehearsal room, exhibition space and hangout. The venue had quickly become a hub for London's counterculture, and by 1969 there were more than fifty Arts Labs in towns around England. Each had its own flavour – the Brighton Combination, led by the playwright Noel Greig, for example, produced

work that concentrated on gay liberation themes – but outside the Drury Lane original, the real powerhouse was Birmingham, which put on concerts of classical and rock music, made films and ran an arthouse cinema, as well as publishing numerous magazines and posters. Alumni of the Birmingham Arts Lab would go on to be early players in the punk music scene, as well as key figures in alternative comedy. They also boasted a particularly strong line of comics artists and cartoonists, including the vicious political cartoonist Steve Bell, the less vicious Suzy Varty, British underground comix mainstay Hunt Emerson and the graphic novelists Bryan Talbot and Kevin O'Neill.

In September 1969, fresh from a top-five hit with 'Space Oddity', David Bowie told the magazine *Melody Maker*:

> I run an Arts Lab which is my chief occupation. It's in Beckenham and I think it's the best in the country. There isn't one pseud involved. All the people are real – like labourers or bank clerks. It started out as a folk club. Arts Labs generally have such a bad reputation as pseud places. There's a lot of talent in the green belt and there is a load of tripe in Drury Lane. I think the Arts Lab movement is extremely important and should take over from the youth club concept as a social service . . . We started our Lab a few months ago with poets and artists who just came along. It's got bigger and bigger and now we have our own light show and sculptures, etc. And I never knew there were so many sitar players in Beckenham.

It's a quote that sums up a lot of the appeal and philosophy of the movement. Music journalist Dave Thompson, who has written books about Bowie including *Moonage Daydream* and *Hello Spaceboy: The Rebirth of David Bowie*, says:

> The beauty of the Arts Labs was that they truly were open to all, a precursor in many ways to punk rock – or the equivalent of an open mic night in Los Angeles, except they encompassed all the arts, and not just music. The guiding principle was that all art was valid; the organisers, at least, regarded the 'doing' to be of far greater value than the actual accomplishment. There was no 'quality control' button – if someone claimed to be an artist, a performer, a sculptor, an orator, then that was what they were, and some phenomenal talents emerged from the scene . . .

> A lot of Arts Labs were in pubs (Bowie's was at the Three Tuns), often utilising the same space that was a folk club a few years earlier; a blues club before that; and would become a disco a few years hence. Others used church halls, scout huts, any place where a decent space was available for a once-a-week rental, and a stage of some sort could be erected.

Being part of an Arts Lab was a social activity as much as it was about producing finished work. It encouraged people to be jacks of all trades, rather than concentrating on just painting or poetry or playing an instrument. Or, as Alan Moore put it, the 'ethos of the Arts Lab was that you could do whatever you wanted, that you didn't have to limit yourself to one particular medium, that you could jump about, you could blend media together and come up with new hybrids. This was of course all mixed in with the general soup of sensations that was the 1960s.' There was no formal network of Arts Labs or central leadership. The only things linking them were a newsletter that went to every group and the occasional conference. Some Arts Labs managed to get funding from local government, and applied for grants from the Arts Council, but most were self-funding.

The Northampton Arts Lab was small and particularly ramshackle, consisting at its height of no more than a couple of dozen people, with more men than women. They met every Tuesday evening at 8 p.m. in a hired room at the Becket and Sargeant Youth Centre, and put on poetry readings, light shows and dramatic performances at various other venues. They produced roughly bi-monthly magazines, *Rovel* and *Clit Bits*, which were electrostencilled, hand-stapled, and looked a lot like *Embryo*, the zine Moore put together himself at school. Moore was part of the Northampton Arts Lab for two or three years and – as well as producing three issues of *Embryo* under its aegis – contributed at least one illustration and two-page comic strip to the third issue of *Rovel*. He did learn some of his craft at the Arts Lab: 'That was where I first started writing songs, or song lyrics at least, working with musicians, which gives you a certain sense of the dynamic of words that you don't get from any other field of endeavour. It was where I started writing short sketches and plays, which, again, is very, very useful. It teaches you about the dynamics of setting scenes up, resolutions, stuff like that. All of these things – poetry teaches you something about words and narrative; performing plays: creating different characters, different voices; writing songs . . . although they seem miles away from comics, all of them taught me things that have been incredibly useful since, even though I didn't know it at the time.' He concedes that 'none of the art we were producing was wonderful, and so I can't say that I learned at the feet of any great masters. What it did teach me was a certain attitude to art, an attitude that was not precious, that held that art was something you put together in fifteen minutes before you went on stage and performed it . . . it was messy – no lasting work of art emerged from it. What did emerge from that period was a certain set of aspirations, feelings, an idea of possibilities more than anything.' It was also a forum that stressed performance – Moore couldn't just write a poem, he was encouraged to recite it. He found he had a particular talent: 'If you'd have seen me back then, you might have thought I was good at reading poems, I could engage an audience, I was a decent performer. I'm not saying the poems themselves were any good, but I was increasingly aware of what an audience responded to.'

The Arts Lab also provided a venue for existing artists. Moore was particularly impressed by the Principal Edwards Magic Theatre, a dozen-strong group who lived in a commune in Kettering, just up the road from Northampton. He saw them as 'a model of the sort of thing that I wanted to do', and what they were doing was described by the *Observer* in 1970:

> A group of young people, mostly from Exeter University, are at present touring the country giving what they call mixed-media entertainment under the name of Principal Edwards Magic Theatre. They perform songs, dance, present light shows, intone semi-mystical poetry and enact masques. There are 14 members in all and they have just released an LP of some of their music, called, appropriately, *Soundtrack*.

But perhaps the main benefit Moore got from the Arts Lab was that he acquired a new group of friends, people like Richard Ashby, 'one of my all-time heroes . . . Rich would overcome his own lack of talent in certain areas by thinking up some way to get around the difficulty, and it would usually be simple, ingenious, elegant. He had a mind which I really admired; he had an approach to art which I really admired. That was an influence that stayed with me every bit as much as the influence of people like William Burroughs, Brian Eno or Thomas Pynchon.'

Moore, Ashby and their friends wore their hair long, and they smoked dope on camping trips to Salisbury Plain, Scotland and Amsterdam. Arriving in Holland, on his first trip abroad when he was eighteen or nineteen, Moore was told by a Dutch customs official that his long hair made him look like a girl. So he began growing a beard.

It was through the Arts Lab that Moore met the Northampton-based folk musician Tom Hall, who took him under his wing. The two would remain friends (and occasional artistic collaborators) until Hall's death in 2003. Hall was the first full-time professional artist Moore got to know. He remembers Mick Bunting, a leading member of the Arts Lab, saying once, '"If Tom Hall can't live by his music he can't live." Which was the first time I'd actually heard that spelled out. I remember thinking that was awesome. That that's what I wanted to be: somebody who could be completely themselves, who did not have a master or boss and who subsisted entirely upon the fruits of their own creativity. Tom was a real formative idol.'

But the countercultural movement had already peaked. California and London had moved on, and while the provinces lagged a little behind, the Northampton Arts Lab fizzled out around August or September 1972. As Moore explains, 'The reasons are very similar to those that caused the demise of similar groups everywhere – lack of money, public support at gigs, really good usable premises and equipment, and the general frustration of not getting very far, all of which caused general disillusionment. After around four years the people involved no longer seemed to feel the need for "organised" group activities any more. Many felt they could work better on their own, or with a few friends than in a "big" group; others just seemed fed up.'

Within six months, a successor organisation had formed: the Northampton Arts Group, which was active for around eighteen months from spring 1973. This was a loose association of about twenty people, many of whom had previously been published in *Embryo* or *Rovel*. Moore has said he only had 'some involvement' with the Arts Group, and he appears on one list among those who 'on occasions we're helped by', rather than as a member of the group, but in terms of finished results, it was more fruitful for him than the Arts Lab had been. The group published three electrostencilled zines in 1973 – *Myrmidon*, *Whispers in Bedlam* and *The Northampton Arts Group Magazine #3* – and Moore drew the covers for all of them, as well as contributing pieces like 'The Electric Pilgrim Zone Two' and 'Letter to Lavender' and internal illustrations. He was an 'inevitable' presence at poetry readings, performing 'ever popular' pieces like 'Lester the Geek' and 'Hymn to Mekon'. Neither of those was ever published, but a couple of Moore's Arts Group pieces would go on to have convoluted afterlives.

Moore's cover for the third magazine, which he titled 'Lounge Lizards', stuck with him. He first used it as the basis of his pitch when he entered a talent competition run by the comics company DC Thomson: 'My idea concerned a

freakish terrorist in white-face make-up who traded under the name of the Doll and waged war upon a totalitarian state sometime in the late 1980s. DC Thomson decided a transsexual terrorist wasn't quite what they were looking for . . . Thus faced with rejection, I did what any serious artist would do. I gave up.' Nearly ten years later, however, elements of this idea would provide some inspiration for *V for Vendetta*, and a quarter of a century on, the Doll showed up as the Painted Doll, a major villain in Moore's series *Promethea* (1999–2005).

Moore also wrote a performance piece, 'Old Gangsters Never Die', which would resurface in a number of places in different forms over the years. He has joked that as it was a spoken monologue set to music about gangsters, he therefore invented gangsta rap. He was proud of the piece: 'The language in that, and the rhythms, that was the pinnacle of my style of writing at that time and I'd written it to perform. I realised it had great emotional effect, it had a got a lot of punch, especially with a little bit of music in the background. I also realised it didn't mean anything, other than evoking this rich material about gangsters. It didn't say anything. I started to think the best thing to do would be stuff with the same command of language, but if it means something as well, I might get somewhere.'

As with the Arts Lab, a legacy of the Arts Group was that Moore formed a number of long friendships and industry contacts. These included Jamie Delano, who would follow him into a successful career in British and American comics; Alex Green, who would go on to be the saxophonist for a number of bands, including Army; and Michael Chown, known by the nickname Pickle, with the stage name Mr Liquorice, who Moore would later describe as a 'new wave composer, entrepreneur, and Adolf Hitler lookalike'.

And it was on the way home from an Arts Group poetry reading in late 1973 – they were both taking a shortcut through a graveyard – that Moore met Phyllis Dixon. Another Northampton native, Phyllis was small and slim, a honey blonde. The two soon moved into a small flat in Queens Park Parade together. Within six months they were married, had moved to a bigger flat on Colwyn Road and had acquired a cat called Tonto. By this point, Moore had an office job at Kelly Brothers, a subcontractor for the Gas Board.

The Arts Lab movement had proved short lived, and virtually all of them had vanished by 1975. The only exception was the Birmingham Arts Lab, which

survived until 1982, most likely because it owned its own premises, had always been run with relative professionalism and had secured Arts Council funding. Moore put the end of the movement down to the zeitgeist: 'The tone of the times was changing, that sort of very spontaneous approach to art was something that could only have happened in the late sixties and didn't survive very long into the early seventies. The economic climate was changing, people were changing.' Moore was acutely aware that the sixties were over. The broad utopian vision that global consciousness was expanding and the Age of Aquarius was dawning had been scaled back to a few people living in communes and advocating ecological positions like self-sufficiency. Countercultural and 'underground' art styles became subsumed into the cultural mainstream. The Beckenham Arts Group might have ended, but David Bowie had the consolation prize of seeing Ziggy Stardust go platinum.

Maggie Gray has noted that 'the prevalent narrative of this period . . . asserts an absolute and definitive split between contradictory but previously co-existent sections of the counterculture, usually categorised as its cultural and political wings'. The movement appeared to split into two factions: those who sought radical social change through political activism, and those had come to see the counterculture purely as a mode of art and music. In 1975, Moore found what looked like the perfect vehicle to square that circle. This was the *Alternative Newspaper of Northampton*, which started as a newsletter concerned with grass-roots politics, particularly charting the problems caused by the rapid expansion of the town. Issue #2 boasted of 'Featuring trade unions, household fuel, welfare rights, citizens' advice, arts, community information, education, housing'. Moore's own experiences made him highly sympathetic to *ANoN*'s aims and he took up political cartooning; in the event, though, this effort wasn't entirely successful. He diagnoses the problem as the venue: '*ANoN* was a very tame, very very tame, local alternative newspaper who asked me to do a comic strip for them. I did the rather anodyne *Anon E. Mouse*, which is not one of the high points of my career, but even that was apparently too inflammatory for the sensibilities of the editors and so I withdrew the strip.'

The sum total of *Anon E. Mouse* is five four-panel strips, published in *ANoN* #1–5, December 1974 to May 1975.

The first strip consists of four almost identical panels in which Anon E. Mouse and Manfred Mole are depicted sitting at a bar bemoaning the fact that people only sit around, they never do anything. The second (reproduced here) starts with Anon E. Mouse 'laying it on the line with the Reverend Cottonmouth'. In the third, Anon E. Mouse rejects the idea of being a movie star after seeing a washed-up Mickey Mouse, while the fourth has Anon E. Mouse and Manfred falling out on the day of the revolution over the colour of the flag they'll be flying on the

barricades. The fifth is based around a pun – cartoonist Kenyon the Coyote tells Anon E. Mouse that he's going to try 'biting humour'; 'if you don't humour me, I'll bite your throat out'. And that is it.

There's nothing specific to Northampton or particularly topical, but perhaps most damning – and far harder to pin on editorial policy – Moore does nothing very interesting with the medium. The art is stiff. The 'repeated image' of the first strip exposes just how inconsistent the drawings are. Most panels are straightforward talking heads and all five strips are simple conversations between two characters. There's no visual invention or much in the way of background detail. It's early work, and there's very little of it, but *Anon E. Mouse* is not a good place to look for glimmers of Alan Moore's nascent genius.

Around this time, perhaps at least partially out of frustration with *ANoN*, Moore began planning his own magazine. Having decided on a title, *Dodgem Logic*, he wrote a letter with a list of interview questions to Brian Eno, and received a very thoughtful ten-page set of answers. Moore has remained an aficionado and it's not hard to see why. Eno thinks very hard about a supposedly ephemeral art form like pop music, he's concerned about the purpose of art, about the process of making it, and his work is often collaborative. His influences are science fiction and surreal comedy as much as they are other musicians. In his own words, however, Moore was not 'together enough' to complete an issue of the magazine, and spent a great deal of time doing little more than drawing the cover. Thirty years later, given the chance to interview whoever he liked for an episode of BBC Radio 4's *Chain Reaction*, Moore chose Eno, and took the opportunity to apologise that his earlier attempt never saw print.

In 1976, Moore collaborated on a musical play that must count as his first major completed work: '*Another Suburban Romance* was a surrealist drama, I'm not even sure what it was about, or if it was even about anything. It involved a number of characters that were moving through this series of scenarios that involved meditations upon politics, sex, death and all of the other big issues.' Among Moore's contributions were three songs: 'Judy Switched Off the TV', 'Old Gangsters Never Die' (which, as noted, he had written about three years before) and the finale, 'Another Suburban Romance'. (A surviving copy of the script – which was made on Moore's typewriter – has handwritten annotations by him indicating where musical cues should go.)

While a 29-page script was completed, the piece was never performed in full, and it remains unpublished (although the songs were visualised as comic strips, without reference to the original play, by Avatar in 2003). Alex Green, one of the participants, says it was 'a cross between Beckett and *Peyton Place*, had been written by Alan and Jamie Delano and was then in rehearsal. Glyn Bush and Pickle wrote an incredibly complex score which was exhaustingly perfected and mostly recorded only for the project to founder when a couple of actors dropped out.'

Another Suburban Romance has four scenes, and five characters: Kid, Gangster, Whore, Politico and Death. It was designed to be performed to an elaborate taped backing track, with a number of ambitious lighting effects, and features several long monologues and pieces of beat poetry. Scene One opens in a coffee bar where Kid is lamenting how bored he is when Gangster arrives, and – after he gives a rendition of 'Judy Switched Off the TV' – tells Kid he is looking for the mirror Bela Lugosi was using when he died cutting himself shaving. Gangster then performs 'Old Gangsters Never Die'. Kid decides to track down Whore, who might know where the mirror is.

Scene Two starts with an elaborate mimed routine in which Whore accosts Politico, then Gangster and finally Death. She performs a monologue that starts 'Torn stockings, crumpled silk, lipstick and Benzedrine' then Kid catches up with her. After comparing hard luck stories, they are joined by Gangster and decide to visit Politico. At the opening of Scene Three, Politico is giving a long right-wing diatribe, before Kid enters. Politico is annoyed by Kid and doesn't know anything about Lugosi's mirror, but becomes excited at the thought it might be valuable. Gangster now enters, and reports that he has killed a number of Politico's enemies, as ordered.

Scene Four begins with a long diary entry from Death. The arrival of Kid and Whore interrupts him, and Death goes on to explain the afterlife: you only go to Heaven if you still have your tonsils, and Heaven's located on Pluto. Politico is now looking to cut a deal with Kid to acquire the mirror. Death has the mirror, and shows it to each of them in turn. Whore performs 'Whore's Poem' that starts 'I heard men say she loved a lantern fish'. As they look in the mirror, Kid sees himself in a vast landscape, while Politico sees the Virgin Mary in a mansion. The Gangster arrives, and Kid, Whore and Politico learn that they are to die and depart for the afterlife. Gangster – who reveals himself to be another of the Four

Horsemen of the Apocalypse, Pestilence – now performs 'Another Suburban Romance', after which Death pays Gangster for delivering the other three to him.

We can see here hints of Moore's interests in Americana. There is also a seedy cabaret vibe that recurs in a number of his other works. But *Another Suburban Romance* is an early piece, designed to play to the strengths of specific performers. Moore seems to have written the part of Gangster for himself to perform: we know he wrote the character's songs, as he received sole credit for them in the Avatar adaptation, while Gangster has a similar persona (and gruff American accent) to the narrator of *Brought to Light* (1989), which Moore would later adapt into a performance piece. From the fact that Scene Four is longer than the others, twelve pages out of a total of twenty-nine, and shifts the focus from Gangster to Death, we might speculate that although Moore wrote the majority of the first half of the play, Delano was responsible for the second.

Soon afterwards, Moore and Alex Green started a band, taking a name from a Wallace Stevens poem, The Emperors of Ice Cream. Once they had an album's worth of material – a process that apparently took around a year – they advertised for musicians in the *Northampton Chronicle and Echo* in October 1978. One respondent was David J. Haskins, who met Green but had to decline the opportunity to become a member as he had just joined another band. This was Bauhaus, now usually considered the earliest goth group, whose debut single 'Bela Lugosi's Dead' quickly led to a session on John Peel's Radio One show. Moore did not meet David J until a little later, but theirs would prove to be a lasting creative partnership. The Emperors of Ice Cream, however, neither performed nor recorded. Alex Green has referred to the project as 'the dream band that never got beyond rehearsals'.

In the summer of 1979, another friend of Moore's from the Arts Group days, Mr Liquorice, opened the Deadly Fun Hippodrome, an afternoon venue for local and visiting musicians. David J has said Moore was 'partly behind' the venture, and described it as 'a mad anarchic surrealist cabaret . . . all the eccentric artists in Northampton would crawl out of the woodwork and turn up for this event . . . It was held in an old Edwardian pavilion in the middle of the Northampton race course.' According to Moore, 'over the single summer of its brief duration it built up a loyal audience of, literally, dozens'. One afternoon, there was a gap in the schedule, and Moore formed an impromptu band consisting of himself, David J,

Alex Green (who by now had the stage name Max Akropolis) and Glyn Bush (aka Grant Series, from the Birmingham band De-go-Tees). They called themselves the Sinister Ducks, played for half an hour and 'didn't rehearse or even speak to each other' for another two years afterwards. The spirit of the Arts Lab clearly lived on, with Moore and his mates having fun creating impromptu cabaret-style shows that were evidently more of an elaborate private joke than anything akin to a workable public performance.

Meanwhile, Moore was still following comics. Fifteen years on from the launch of *Fantastic Four*, Marvel had continued to mature with their audience. DC had responded, and American superhero comics were now vehicles for complex running stories with a smattering of social conscience. Future novelists Jonathan Lethem and Michael Chabon – both around ten years younger than Moore – were among those inspired by the Marvel and DC comics of the seventies. In his book of essays *Manhood for Amateurs*, Chabon waxes lyrical about comics of his youth, and particularly Big Barda, a character from DC's *Fourth World* (1970–3). This was Jack Kirby's infectiously bizarre space-age reinterpretation of folklore archetypes that explored cosmic war between good guys called Highfather and Lightray, and evil personified by beings with names like Darkseid and Virman Vundabar. In 2007, Marvel would publish Lethem's take on their equally weird, equally cosmic character from the seventies, *Omega the Unknown* (1976–7).

Moore continued to read American superhero comics – 'by the time I was in my middle twenties, I was still occasionally reading the odd Marvel or DC comic just to see if anything interesting was happening' – but had all but stopped attending comics marts and conventions. He agreed with Steve Moore that fandom was becoming obsessed with the past, when it should be striving to improve the quality of storytelling in new comics, and tellingly he didn't contribute to any fanzines. He did, however, identify the *Fourth World* titles as a highlight: 'We were all really thrilled by them. I remember at the comic convention where I actually saw some early copies of *Jimmy Olsen* work, just how excited everybody was just to see them coming out . . . we were all absolutely devastated when the books seemed to finish without a proper ending.' This interest continued throughout the seventies – Moore has noted, 'I remember reading Frank Miller's first stuff on *Daredevil*, and thinking, "Oh, this was worth buying all those crap comics for; this is something interesting, I can follow this". Miller's run on *Daredevil* began in May 1979, and introduced a noir sensibility to what had been a run-of-the-mill series about an acrobatic superhero.

Two comics in particular spurred Moore on to become a comics creator, not just a reader. The first was *Arcade: The Comics Revue* (1975–6), edited by prominent members of the San Francisco underground scene, Art Spiegelman and Bill Griffith, and designed as a showcase for the best in comics for adults. Moore discovered back issues in the London shop Dark They Were and Golden-Eyed and quickly concluded that the lavish magazine contained 'a collection of comic material that swiftly elevated *Arcade: The Comics Revue* to the Olympian reaches of my Three Favourite Comics Ever In The History Of The Universe. As is usually the way when I encounter something I'm really fond of, my condition escalated rapidly from good natured boyish enthusiasm to an embarrassing display of slobbering hysteria.' Over twenty years later, Moore would explain that he felt '*Arcade* was perhaps the last of the original wave of underground comix, as well as their finest hour . . . As well as showcasing new and radically different artists, *Arcade* also seemed somehow to encourage work from underground artists of long standing that ranked amongst the best they'd ever done.' *Arcade* #4 included *Stalin* by Spain Rodriguez, which Moore 'ranks as one of my favourite single comic strip pieces of all time'. He was spurred on to write an effusive fan letter to the editors and, in late September 1976, received the following reply from Bill Griffith:

> Alan,
>
> Thanks for the entertaining letter. Seeing as it was of such a high intellectual calibre, we'll most likely print it in our next issue . . . You almost found us too late. No 7 is just out and No 8 (out in 6–10 months) will be our last as a magazine. After that we go annual, in paperback form. I'm afraid we're a bit too avant-garde for the Mafia.
>
> Tally ho,
>
> Griffy.

In the event, though, #7 was the last.

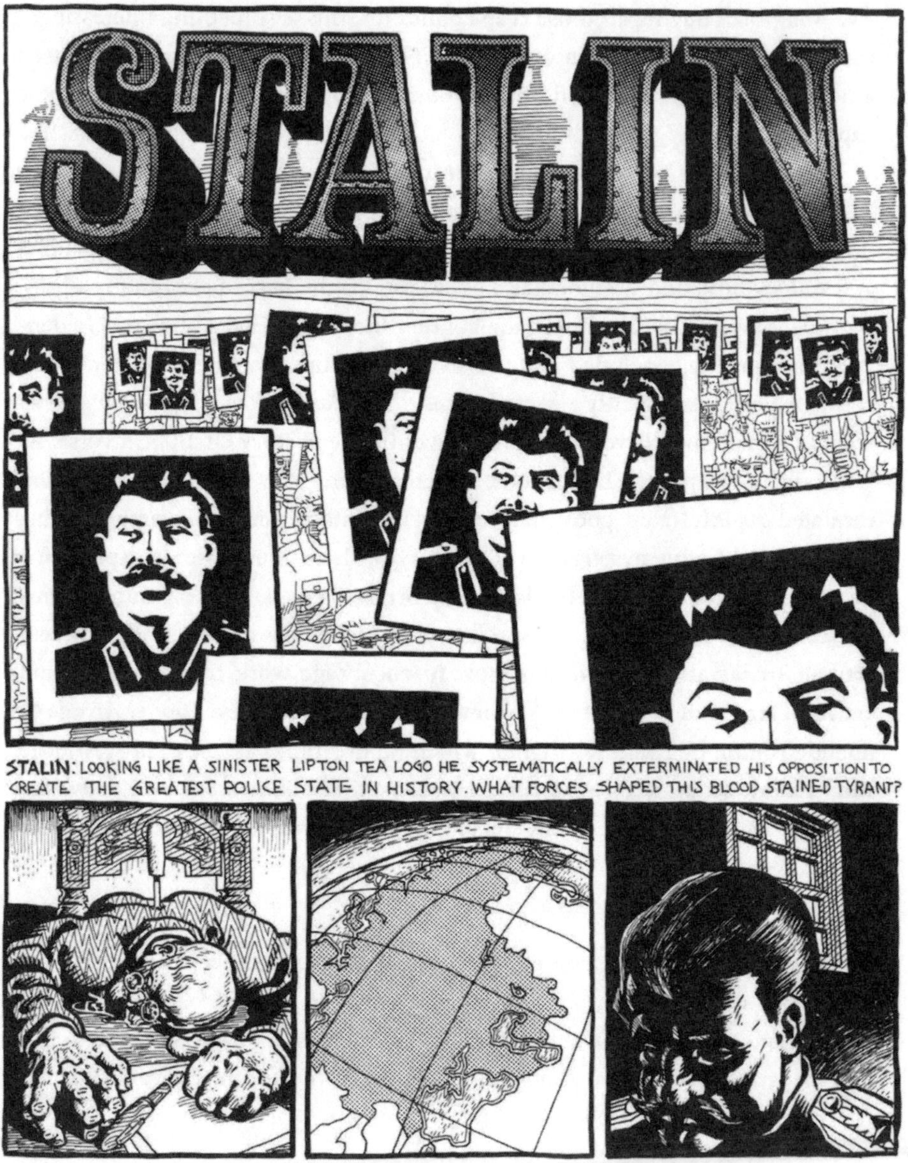

STALIN

STALIN: LOOKING LIKE A SINISTER LIPTON TEA LOGO HE SYSTEMATICALLY EXTERMINATED HIS OPPOSITION TO CREATE THE GREATEST POLICE STATE IN HISTORY. WHAT FORCES SHAPED THIS BLOOD STAINED TYRANT?

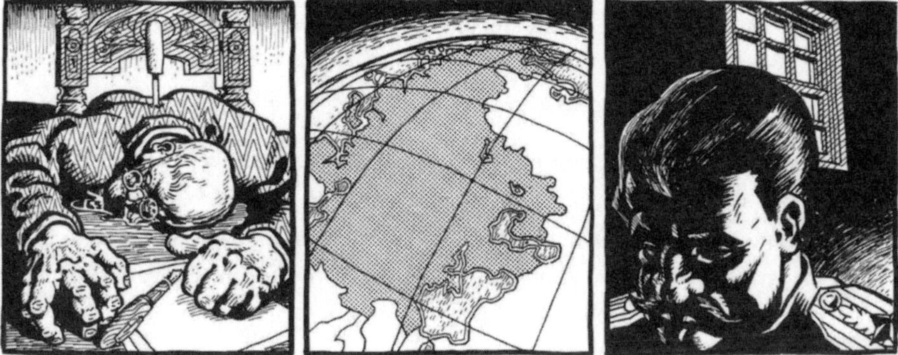

In 1984, Moore wrote 'Too Avant Garde for the Mafia', an essay for the fanzine *Infinity* which surveyed the seven issues of *Arcade* and their contributors. He concluded:

> *Arcade* was an almost perfect culmination of the whole idea of Underground Comix. Granted, there have been worthy individual efforts by the various *Arcade* contributors since then, but somehow without the same flair . . . Balance is what *Arcade* achieved, in a nutshell. It balanced Griffith's metaphysical slapstick against Spiegelman's thirst for self-referential comic material and ground their more explosive experiments with a solid anchor of Robert Crumb's simple and unadorned storytelling. It pushed the medium in all sorts of new directions, the vast majority of which still remain to be properly explored almost ten years later. Anyone seriously interested in seeing what directions comics might go in the future could do a lot worse than checking out just how far they've been in the not too distant past.

On the face of it, the second comic to inspire Moore could not have been more different. *2000AD* was a weekly science fiction comic for boys that launched in February 1977 (and is still running today). It was published by IPC, publishers of children's comics like *Whizzer & Chips* and *Roy of the Rovers*, and the early issues came with free gifts like a 'space spinner' and stickers. It had evolved, though, from *Action*, a comic first published the previous February, then abruptly cancelled after tabloid outrage at the violence of strips like *Look Out for Lefty*, about football hooligans, and *Hellman of Hammer Force*, whose protagonist was a Nazi tank commander. Over the next few years, *2000AD* would thrill its audience with action-packed (i.e. violent) stories featuring characters like Dan Dare, Rogue Trooper, Strontium Dog, Nemesis the Warlock and Slaine – and, towering over all of them, future lawman Judge Dredd.

Picking up an early issue because he liked Brian Bolland's cover (see following page), Moore was pleasantly surprised by the contents. He instinctively understood what *2000AD* was trying to do, and recognised that it was attracting the top British comics talent. More than that, many of the contributors were writers and artists Moore had known for years. 'When I was getting into comics, I'd recognised Dave Gibbons and Brian Bolland's work in *2000AD*, I'd recognised those names and those styles from the underground magazines of ten years before. Ian Gibson, he'd done some stuff in Steve Moore's *Orpheus* fanzine. So a lot of these names, I recognised them from fandom, or from the underground.' But that wasn't what drew him to the comic. As he explained elsewhere: 'You'd got really funny,

KIDS OF EARTH...
WELCOME TO YOUR FUTURE!

2000 A.D.

8p
EARTH MONEY

PROGRAMME 11

DATELINE: 07 MAY 77

IN ORBIT EVERY MONDAY

South Africa 30c. New Zealand 30c. Malaysia $1.00. Australia 30c. Neptune 87g. Pluto 93g. Mercury 17g. Venus 10g. Mars 15g. Asteroid Belt 20g. Saturn 84g.

FOLLOW ME INTO THE SUN... YOU WILL SHARE THE DEATH OF A MARTIAN WARRIOR!

TOP THRILL
DD
DAN DARE

Bollo

cynical writers working on *2000AD* at that time. This was mainly Pat Mills and John Wagner, who had previously spent eleven years working on the British girls' comics. And they had grown cynical and possibly actually evil during this time.' Wagner, continued Moore, had once written a script called *The Blind Ballerina*, in which the title character would find herself in increasingly dire situations:

> At the end of each episode you'd have her evil Uncle saying, 'Yes, come with me. You're going out on to the stage of the Albert Hall where you're going to give your premiere performance' and it's the fast lane of the M1. And she's sort of pirouetting and there's trucks bearing down on her . . . hell, they were funny even in the girls' comics. But when John got a science fiction comic to play with he could really amp up the humour. I saw this stuff and thought these people were intelligent, there's satirical stuff, I could maybe write something that would play to this audience and would also be interesting for me to write.

Moore understood that the creators were sneaking in political and subversive material. Broad satire, to be sure, but *Judge Dredd* routinely took 'tough policing' firmly into the realms of police brutality, if not fascism, and the strip made clear that, in large part, the endemic crime in Mega-City One was a result of social injustice. More to the point, the editors needed to fill pages every week. Finally, there was a venue for the sort of stories Alan Moore wanted to write, and they were hiring new writers.

Alan Moore was twenty-four the year *2000AD* launched. He'd switched employers from Kelly Brothers to Pipeline Constructors Ltd – another office job processing paperwork for a company that supplied and fitted pipes for the Gas Board – while he and Phyllis had moved to a brand new council house in Blackthorn. In the autumn of 1977, Phyllis Moore was pregnant. This represented a decision point for Alan: 'I was married and we had our first child on the way. I always had a vague idea that it would be nice at some point in the future to actually make my living out of doing something that I enjoyed rather than something I despised which was, like, everything other than comics. So, I figured that my wife was pregnant, if I didn't give up the job and make a stab at some kind of artistic career before the baby was born that, I know the limits of my courage, I wouldn't have been up for doing it after I've got these big, imploring eyes staring up at me. So, I quit.'

With the benefit payments Alan and Phyllis Moore received amounting to £42.50 a week, 'the bare minimum they needed to live on', Moore determined that he would measure his success by his ability to earn more through his writing. So he buckled down to the task of becoming a professional comics writer, embarking on a space opera with the projected title *Sun Dodgers* which he thought he could write and draw for *2000AD*, 'an epic that I could've easily filled 300 pages with. A massive story that made *Lord of the Rings* look like a five-minute read'.

> It was all in my head . . . there was a group of superheroes in space, with a science fiction explanation for each of these characters. They were a motley crew in a spaceship, probably going back the kind of strips Wally Wood was doing in *witzend* and *The Misfits* . . . I can remember somebody looked a bit like a futuristic samurai. A humanoid robot thing with a big steel ball for a head, which probably surfaced later as the Hypernaut in *1963*. There was a half-human, half-canine creature who ended up as Wardog in the Special Executive. Thinking back, there was a character whose name was Five, and my vague idea was that he was a mental patient of undefined but unusual abilities who had been kept in a particular room, room five, that might have been an element which fed into *V for Vendetta*.

Moore got very little of this down on paper. 'I think about six months later I'd got one page half pencilled, some inks. I just thought, "Why am I doing this?" I realised it was because I was never going to finish it.'

He sought practical advice from Steve Moore, who by this point was making a living selling comic scripts, and who gently explained that *2000AD* wouldn't just give a new writer a regular series. Writers and artists were expected to start their careers with one-off, self-contained pieces that were typically two to five pages long. Most British comics had slots for stories of this type, not because they allowed editors to test new talent so much as because they allowed for a far more flexible schedule than a roster of regular titles. In *2000AD* these shorter pieces were published in the series *Future Shocks* and *Time Twisters*. Future star writers like Neil Gaiman, Grant Morrison and Pete Milligan would all start at *2000AD* by writing *Future Shocks*; it was how most writers and artists got their break for the magazine. The original idea, and name, for *Future Shocks* is usually credited to Steve Moore himself, and he certainly wrote the first story to appear under that

banner ('King of the World' in #25, 13 August 1977), although such stories had a venerable heritage dating back at least as far as the EC Horror and SF comics of the fifties. Wherever they appeared, the strips tended to be fairly generic tales with a very limited repertoire of twist endings – most concluded with the protagonist dying because he wasn't careful what he wished for, or his greed had led him to walk into a trap, or he didn't realise his world was merely a simulation, or he was rude to someone who was secretly some kind of monster.

Abandoning his space opera, Alan wrote instead a thirty-panel *Judge Dredd* script, 'Something Nasty in Mega-City One!!', complete with design sketches. Steve Moore gave him advice about formatting the script and warned of common mistakes: a writer shouldn't have overlong dialogue; captions aren't needed to convey information shown in that panel's picture; one panel can't (usually) convey a sequence of events or even motion, much of the skill is in deciding which exact moment will appear in every panel. The *Dredd* script was rejected by *2000AD* assistant editor Alan Grant, but he encouraged Moore to submit further ideas.

In an article for *Warrior* published five years later, Steve Moore described his own rise, 'the long way . . . joined Odhams Press as an office boy, way back in 1967 . . . then worked my way up through sub-editor. Started on *Pow!* and *Smash!* . . . ended up at IPC'. The new generation of British comics writers – people like himself, Alan Grant, Steve Parkhouse and Pat Mills – had all started out as junior editors on the staff of comics companies in the late sixties, spending a decade learning their craft and the trade, mainly by reading lots of scripts, networking and seeing the commissioning process from the editor's point of view. Steve Moore noted that 'the other way is how Alan Moore came into the business . . . by bombarding people with scripts from outside'. Moore says: 'I don't think Steve was saying that through gritted teeth, so much as noting he'd never actually seen it done that way before.' He has described his method of breaking into the comics industry as 'a matter of going round the back, poisoning the dogs and going over the fence'.

Moore was not looking to write only for *2000AD*. He cast his net anywhere he found that published comic strips – places like newspapers, underground zines and the music press. And his persistence started to pay off. He was contacted by Dick Foreman, editor of *The Back-Street Bugle*, a fortnightly, Oxford-based alternative paper, who'd been told about Moore by a couple of Arts Lab alumni who'd moved to the town, Ant and Jackie Knight. Moore was offered a full-page strip, and came up with *St Pancras Panda.* This series is usually described as a pastiche of the children's character Paddington Bear, but in fact it is basically a pretext for Moore to be increasingly mean to a sweet little panda. The tone is set in the first part, where our hero is rounded up along with Winnie the Pooh, the *Dandy*'s Biffo the Bear and Dougal from *The Magic Roundabout* and consigned to a furrier's. 'I was still drawing benefits and I still hadn't really got around to submitting anything professionally, but working on the strip I did for *The Back-Street Bugle*, *St Pancras Panda*, I was able to meet deadlines, I was able to find how much time I needed to get the strip looking the way I wanted . . . So that was quite an important magazine, and it was uncovering dirty doings at the local council, it was covering local rock gigs, local alternative activities, very entertaining, very informative.'

Meanwhile, Legendary cartoonist Alan Moore explains to his fans that the absence of a Panda strip in this issue is due to the fact that the lovable little fellow is pissing about with the Quoog space fleet somewhere the other side of Altair 4, and so radio transmissions of his doubtless side-splitting exploits have not yet reached Earth, due to interference caused by someone using a vacuum cleaner in the Tau Ceti sector.

So here instead is a portrait of the fast-growing Moore family:

St Pancras Panda looks sumptuous compared with *Anon E. Mouse*, although Moore put this down to a simple trick, rather than any improvement in his ability to draw: 'I used to cover each picture in tiny stippled dots. For some reason editors love stippling. They buy your work every time. I think, personally, that this is because they feel sorry for you'. He used ten to fifteen small panels per instalment, packing each panel with detail, including Kurtzman-style sight gags. *St Pancras Panda* made its debut in *The Back-Street Bugle* #6. This was published only a few days after the Moores' first daughter, Leah, was born on 4 February 1978, an event Moore would mark with an illustration for the *Bugle*.

Moore's first professional work came in late 1978, when he submitted illustrations to Neil Spencer at the *New Musical*

Express (*NME*). Spencer had been an associate of the Northampton Arts Lab and paid Moore £40 each for pictures of Elvis Costello (published 21 October 1978) and Malcolm McLaren (11 November 1978).

This did not lead to regular work for *NME*; a third illustration depicting Siouxsie and the Banshees was rejected (Moore then submitted it to the *Back-Street Bugle*, and there's a note in #24 saying they hadn't got room to run it). Having the *NME* on his CV, though, Moore was able to get his foot in the door in other parts of the music press.

Dark Star was a British magazine that had started in 1975 by covering west coast music, but had come to embrace British bands like The Teardrop Explodes and Echo and the Bunnymen, and was – a little anachronistically by the end of the seventies – rooted in the underground magazine aesthetic: reporting on Moore's success, *The Back-Street Bugle* described it as 'a magazine for ageing hippies'. Moore was commissioned to write and draw a series called *The Avenging Hunchback*, a broad parody of *Superman* ('our saga begins upon the planet Krapton, a gigantic boil on the bum of the galaxy'), the first episode of which appeared in #19 (March 1979). When the second instalment was lost – the editor's car having been stolen with the original artwork inside – Moore could not face redrawing it and instead was allowed to produce a series of one-off stories. The first was *Kultural Krime Comix* (#20, April 1979) – a strip he also starred in, appearing in 'the vast Alan Moore Studios' alongside a crowd of his creations, such as Anon E. Mouse and St Pancras Panda, lamenting the loss of the second *Avenging Hunchback* chapter. He then teamed up with Steve Moore for *Talcum Powder* (#21) and the more substantial *Three-Eyes McGurk and his Death-Planet Commandos* (#22–25), the latter a four-part strip drawn by Alan, written and inked by Steve. It included the first appearance of the character Axel Pressbutton, a psychotic cyborg who would end up in his *The Stars My Degradation* (1980–3) and Steve Moore's *Laser Eraser and Pressbutton* (1982–6). Moore had designed a bald character with one eye bigger than the other, Lex Loopy, to be the villain of *The Avenging Hunchback*, but instead used the design for Pressbutton.

Again, the work for *Dark Star* was unpaid, but it was in a nationally distributed magazine and so appeared in newsagents around the country. In April 1981, *Three Eyes McGurk and his Death-Planet Commandos* would become his first piece to be published in America, when it was reprinted in Gilbert Shelton's underground anthology, *Rip-Off Comics* #8.

Very shortly after starting work for *Dark Star*, Moore finally secured a regular job that paid. This was *Roscoe Moscow*, a half-page strip for the weekly music magazine *Sounds*.

> Something just happened in my head one day and I did two episodes of a strip called *Roscoe Moscow*, which was a surreal private eye strip that owed more

> than a little to Art Spiegelman's *Ace Hole*. What I owed to it was the idea of a self-referential private eye who talks in the third person, somebody who talks in self-conscious Chandlerese, if you like. I sent in the first two episodes of that and got a telegram back – because we weren't on the telephone at that point – saying that they'd like me to do it as a regular strip . . . *Sounds* was a crummy British rock music weekly; it was quite low-minded in its way, but it did have an interesting array of cartoonists working for them. Savage Pencil had been their mainstay for a long time and he'd been doing half a page a week. Pete Milligan, Brendan McCarthy and Brett Ewins were working upon a punk science fiction nihilist-type rock comic strip for a number of weeks before I applied with *Roscoe Moscow*. Apparently, they'd run out of enthusiasm for their strip or something – I'm not sure of the entire story – but for one reason or another their strip was ending. *Sounds* had a gap for another comic strip and I just happened to send in *Roscoe Moscow* at the right time.

The first instalment appeared in the 31 March 1979 issue of *Sounds*. The paper had a reported circulation of 250,000 copies a week, which if true would mean it was bought by more people than any other publication featuring Moore's work – in either Britain or America – until he wrote for *Image* in the early nineties. The £35 a week Moore got for writing and drawing *Roscoe Moscow* was not quite enough to live on, though, and he adopted a pseudonym to hide his earnings. For the next few years, 'Curt Vile' would prove to be prolific and multi-talented, also writing reviews and interviews, drawing spot illustrations for *Sounds*, contributing to other publications, and even appearing on a single by the Mystery Guests.

And *Roscoe Moscow* saw another leap in quality. While there is a nugget of truth in Moore's assessment that he 'was barely capable of drawing even simple objects in a way by which they might be recognised', he never let that get in the way of an ambition to stretch the medium. In *Roscoe Moscow* he comes up with a number of imaginative panel designs and progressions. The main recurring joke, that the protagonist is delusional, allows Moore to contrast the first-person narration with what the reader can see, and he milks a lot of material from this. There are in-jokes in *Roscoe Moscow* so obscure that Moore could have expected literally only one or two other people to get them. With the benefit of hindsight and a few decades of Moore scholarship, it is fun to spot the cameo by St Pancras

Panda, the blatant plug for the Bauhaus single 'Bela Lugosi's Dead' and a joint credit for a Christmas boardgame given to 'Curt + Phyllis Vile'. In this panel, Moore both reveals his secret identity in a crossword puzzle and namechecks Steve Moore's pseudonym.

Moore gained a certain cachet by having his own weekly comic strip. *The Back-Street Bugle* were clearly proud of him, even though he had to scale back his work for them. *St Pancras Panda* ended in March 1979 (#25), but Moore (or rather Curt Vile) would go on to contribute another dozen or so illustrations. The *Bugle* even marketed the very first piece of Alan Moore-related merchandise: #26 (April 1979) had an advert for a silkscreened poster 'tastefully printed in lurocolor' and sold for 50p. August's #30 also ran a short feature on Moore's *Sounds* work, '*Roscoe Moscow's St Pancras Panda*', announcing that two more instalments of *St Pancras Panda* were planned and that the series might be collected into a comic book.

Early in his career, Alan Moore was happy to identify himself as coming from underground comix roots. In 1982, he would tell artist Bryan Talbot that collaborating with him 'will be the first time I've worked with an artist whose background is as solidly rooted in the underground as my own is'. But even by 1988, he was backtracking a little, framing his *Sounds* work as a way to sneak into the profession 'by entering an area of comic book work that really didn't have an awful lot going for it and wasn't terribly popular'. In 2004 he said he had been 'a kind of sub-underground cartoonist'; in 2010, 'you can look at my early work and see for yourself. I was an average, undergroundish cartoonist who was just making things up from week to week and hoping that the glaring flaws wouldn't be too apparent.' Whatever his feelings about the context in which he was operating, though, Moore has never been keen on the work itself. In 1984, he said he regarded it 'in the same way that anyone who's served their apprenticeship in public would do. For the most part, I see it as a lot of poorly executed drivel'. In the early nineties, he observed: 'There's a lot of repulsive bilge in there; and an awful lot of honest effort in there as well. It's not terribly memorable work, those first strips. It didn't teach me anything about drawing. Well, it taught me that I couldn't draw, which was a useful thing to know before I carried on too far with it . . .' He does admit that 'there were a couple of odd little episodes in there where it was nicely drawn, nicely conceived, there was a nice little gag or a nice little concept', but its value was largely elsewhere: 'it kept me alive for two or three years, and it gave me a hands-on education in comic strips.'

Moore has only ever allowed isolated examples of his underground work to be reprinted (although almost all of it can be found online), saying, 'it will probably remain unpublished. I'm glad, it's nice that it's out there on the 'net. The thing is, I was doing my best at the time . . . I'm really glad that it's out there, so people can see, but I'm glad that . . . I don't even have to look at it!'

Moore was still searching for more mainstream opportunities, and pitched an idea to his local free newspaper, the *Northants Post*. This was *Nutter's Ruin*, a parody of a village soap opera. He drew a half-page strip outlining the cast and their foibles; the characters included Elsie and Eric Nutter, brutal police constable Willard Turk, aristocratic Bradley and Belinda Reighley-Stupid and (in a presumably unconscious lift from *Monty Python*'s 'Mr Hilter' sketch), 'Mr Adolph Hilton, a kindly old Austrian gent who moved to Nutter's Ruin just after the War'.

The paper's editor liked Moore's art but wanted something for children, and suggested 'perhaps a strip about a little cat or something?' So Moore came up with *Maxwell the Magic Cat*, basing the protagonist on his own cat, Tonto. The first strip appeared in the 25 August 1979 edition of the *Northants Post*. The drawing was technically primitive – more like the simple linework of *Anon E. Mouse* than the elaborate stippling of his *Sounds* work – but the jokes were funnier and more elaborate. Moore soon abandoned the idea of telling a running story and came to enjoy the challenge of coming up with a new five-panel gag week after week; because his deadline was only three days before publication, he could make the strip extremely topical. Moore chose to write the strip under the pseudonym Jill De Ray. As he has always taken great delight in recounting, Gilles de Rais was a fifteenth-century demon summoner, child molester and serial killer. Emboldened by having got that past his editor, Moore occasionally steered the strip into dark or overtly political territory, with a healthy regular dose of surrealism.

He enjoyed himself, and *Maxwell the Magic Cat* would continue to run until October 1986 – after the first issues of *Watchmen* had been published and Moore had become the most renowned writer of comics on the planet (a fact his *Northants Post* editors seemed blissfully unaware of). Artist Eddie Campbell's prediction that the next generation of comics historians would reassess *Maxwell* and it 'will be properly recognised as an important work' hasn't yet come to pass, but Campbell best explains the significance the strip holds in Moore's canon: 'Of all Alan's work, *Maxwell* is the most immediate representation of the man's thoughts and idle notions . . . they reach us without being modified by a collaborator or the complicated requirements of the big publishing houses'.

Moore was now earning £35 from *Sounds* and £10 from *Maxwell the Magic Cat*, more than the £42.50 he had been receiving in benefits. Honour satisfied, he signed off the dole and was now officially a full-time professional comics creator.

In May 1980 *Sounds* published a letter from reader Derek Hitchcock accusing *Roscoe Moscow* of being homophobic. Moore replied as Curt Vile, insisting that it was the *character* who was prejudiced, not the writer: 'Curt Vile likes to think of himself as a friend to all the people, irrespective of class, colour, place of worship or whatever the hell they wish to do with their private parts'; in writing this, he wanted 'to make absolutely sure that no impressionable adolescent ran away with the idea that I was outlining my own personal philosophy'. Since, at a number of points later in his career, Moore would worry that his audience were not spotting his 'heavy irony', this exchange may have been one factor that led to him begin to wind down *Roscoe Moscow*, its last chapter appearing in the 28 June 1980 edition. He began a new strip, *The Stars My Degradation*, the first instalment of which was published in July 1980. Dropping all references to the music industry, this was a broad parody of science fiction and superhero stories, the sprawling space opera that *2000AD* would never have let him get away with. Meanwhile, Curt Vile had written glowing reviews of the Mystery Guests and Bauhaus, and Moore struggled with other conflicts of interest: 'Occasionally I'd supplement my income by interviewing people like Hawkwind. Unfortunately if Nik Turner made me a cup of tea while I was interviewing them. I couldn't write anything nasty about them. So I figured journalism wasn't for me.'

Fortunately, there were new opportunities in mainstream comics conducive to the sort of work Moore was keen to write. *Doctor Who Weekly* debuted in late 1979, and was packed with articles about the popular BBC show, both the on-screen adventures of the time-travelling main character and what was going on the behind the scenes. Each issue contained two original comic strips: the first showcased adventures of the Doctor himself, the second was a shorter back-up strip featuring a parade of his old foes, like the Daleks and Cybermen. The latter had until now all been written by Steve Moore, but when from *Doctor Who Weekly* #35 (June 1980) he was promoted to the main strip, he tipped off Alan that they would be looking for a new writer, then passed his friend's trial script, 'Black Legacy', to editor Paul Neary. It was accepted, and was published in the same issue Steve Moore took charge of the main strip. Alan was delighted to realise the artist was the same David Lloyd who, like him, had contributed to the fanzine *Shadow* as a teenager. 'I felt that at the time David Lloyd's strips as an artist were undervalued; he didn't seem to be regarded in the same way that Dave Gibbons or even a relatively young artist like Steve Dillon would be regarded. The perception of David's work back then seemed to be that he was a solid, meat and potato artist who you shouldn't really expect anything spectacular from, but I saw more than that in David's work. I saw a really powerful sense of storytelling and a starkness in his contrasts of black and white.'

Steve Moore had established a formula for the back-up strips. Generally the protagonist would venture somewhere they had been warned not to go, where they meddled with forces they did not understand – this tended to mean unleashing an old *Doctor Who* monster – with a nasty twist at the end when the protagonist thought they were finally safe. Alan had watched *Doctor Who* off and on over the years, but had not been much of a fan since William Hartnell left in 1966 (he had been twelve at the time). With 'Black Legacy', he followed Steve Moore's template perhaps a little too faithfully, but once he had proved himself, he and Lloyd followed it up with the far more unsettling 'Business as Usual', a fast-paced story using the Autons – old monsters made from animated plastic, who infiltrated Earth by taking the form of toys and mannequins. Both stories required a degree of discipline new to Moore, but he enjoyed the challenge: 'Two pages isn't a lot for the reader to be able to remember even by the next week. You've got to kind of establish everything and have each little two-page section come to its own dramatic conclusion. It was trickier than it looked but it was a great way of learning how to write comics . . . the 300-page sci-fi epic was never going to work, whereas what I was now doing was actually starting from something really small.' Each story consisted of eight pages in total, broken into four parts, with an increasingly tense cliffhanger each week, building up to the climax. 'I'm not saying I did a great job of it but it seemed to work, and it is just the best way of learning how to write stories: start off with something that is too small, in your opinion, to tell a good story in and then find a way to tell a good story in that space.'

Alan's last contribution to *Doctor Who* was what he has informally called the *4D War Cycle*, stories set in the early years of the Doctor's people, the Time Lords. This was an ambitious space opera spanning generations, with the Time Lords under attack from the Order of the Black Sun, a mysterious organisation from the future who are retaliating for some offence the Time Lords are yet to commit. The *Doctor Who* TV series had left the origins of the Time Lords a virtually blank slate, and Moore filled it with new characters. The stories are a short, sharp blending of high-concept science fiction and the superhero team book.

> We've got the Order of the Black Sun, who are pretty clearly the Green Lantern Corps but with a different costumier. A gothic costumier. I liked the idea of the Gallifreyans established as a very, very powerful intergalactic force and it's also not just intergalactic, it's throughout the aeons, because they've mastered time travel. So that would make them very, very powerful in any possible universe full of different races. And so I thought you're going to need somebody that is as big and powerful as the Gallifreyans if this is going to be a fair fight. So I started to think of something a bit like the Green Lantern Corps from DC's

Green Lantern comics. At that point there was no chance of me ever working for America, so it just seemed that this might be my only chance to do something that's a bit like those American superheroes that I remember from my boyhood. So I brought in this intergalactic confederacy of different alien races who are all united under this banner of the Black Sun. And yes, I could have carried that on. I forget where I was going to take it. I presume that the battle would get bigger. Perhaps I'd get longer stories to tell it in.'

Moore had planned to write more stories in the *4D War Cycle*, and believes he was next in line to write the main strip. Instead, he quit *Doctor Who Monthly* over a point of principle. One of Steve Moore's strips had introduced *Abslom Daak, Dalek Killer*, a psychotic character 'specifically created as a Pressbutton-style balance to the somewhat lightweight Doctor Who': rather than offer the Daleks a jelly baby, Daak would slice them in half with his chainsword. Having first appeared in *Doctor Who Weekly* #17 (February 1980) and proved popular, Daak returned semi-regularly, and there was talk of a spin-off title. But when Steve Moore learned this was to be written by Alan McKenzie, he stopped working for *Doctor Who Monthly* and, as he says, 'Alan Moore quit writing for the magazine too, in a wonderful gesture of support that was remarkable for someone at that early a stage in their career'. Alan's last story was 'Black Sun Rising' in *Doctor Who Monthly* #57 (December 1981), although neither he nor Steve left Marvel UK altogether, and both picked up similar work in *Empire Strikes Back Monthly*.

Alan Moore had continued to send ideas to *2000AD*'s editor, and 'Alan [Grant] would write letters explaining why they were turned down. Eventually, he wrote a letter saying, "Look, if you just changed this, this and this, I think this one might be acceptable," and on the second or third attempt, I got the form letter back which had lots of robots giving the thumbs up, which means you've been accepted.'

This story, 'Killer in the Cab' (#170, July 1980), was however beaten into print by Moore's second commission, which appeared earlier the same month in the *2000AD Sci-Fi Special 1980*. 'Holiday in Hell' was a five-page story with art by Dave Harwood. The story is almost a textbook iteration of the *Future Shocks* formula. First, the science fiction high concept: Earth of the future is 'a world without war, without crime, without bloodshed', but people book holidays on Mars to let off steam by attacking 'victimatics', perfect robot duplicates of people who 'show terror . . . pain . . . suffering' as they are chopped up or shot. Then we see a 'normal' young couple, George and Gabrielle, enjoy themselves on Mars by brutally attacking victimatics before returning to Earth. Except there's a twist: the real Gabrielle has been replaced by a duplicate who kills George and reveals 'we victimatics need to take a holiday every now and again, too!' and that half the tourists who've returned to Earth are actually killer robots. And so the rampage begins.

With his foot in the door and a little more experience, Moore found it much easier to get commissioned by *2000AD*, and his work – at this stage confined to more *Future Shocks* – was soon appearing in the comic roughly every six weeks. While he continued to write and draw his *Sounds* strip and *Maxwell the Magic Cat*, Moore's contributions to Marvel UK and *2000AD* were solely as a scriptwriter. Not only was he acutely aware that he lacked the technical flair of the regular *2000AD* artists, there was also the practical matter that even half a page for weekly *Sounds* often took him most of the week to draw; he just was not fast enough to produce the page a day he would need if he were to work for *2000AD*. He found he could describe a panel in a script far more effectively than he could ever illustrate it himself.

Moore had a clear ambition for *2000AD*: 'At the time, I really, really wanted a regular strip. I didn't want to do short stories. I wanted to do regular, ongoing series that would bring in regular money. But that wasn't what I was being offered. I was being offered short four or five page stories where everything had to be done in those five pages. And, looking back, it was the best possible education that I could have had in how to construct a story.' Moore came to relish the challenge of developing new twists and ever more elaborate story structures: 'I did realise that in having done a couple of years of a weekly comic strip that I had, almost incidentally, learned how to tell a serialised story . . . I had learned something about the mechanics of telling a story on demand every week that was at least interesting enough to keep the readers entertained and to stop the editor from replacing it with something more commercial.' Moore got into the habit of packing his pages with information and cutting out padding. He got to work with many different artists, and was fascinated to discover the ways different people interpreted his scripts and how it led to a broad range of types of creative partnership, from full and enthusiastic collaboration to an artist wilfully ignoring the script.

It was a key shift, creatively, for Moore, and one that marked him out as a writer who was particularly enthusiastic and thoughtful. Steve Parkhouse, already established by this time as an editor, writer and artist, would go on to collaborate with Moore, most notably on *The Bojeffries Saga* (1983–4); he has identified Moore's great gift as 'the ability to write exactly what the artist wants to draw'.

Moore found he was able to create a few running stories within the one-off format: 'I really wanted to be doing a continuing character. If you were getting regular short story work, one way of doing that was by creating continuing characters or some other form of continuity that linked up your short stories. In *2000AD* I'd done a few stories about a character called Abelard Snazz, "The Double-Decker Dome". He was based upon an optical illusion drawing I'd seen of a man with two sets of eyes which was quite a disturbing thing, visually.' If it went down well, he thought, then he might even get a series out of it: 'If I can come up with a popular character and maybe link up some of these short stories so that they make a bigger narrative to show that I can handle . . . a longer story arc, then maybe that will work out as some future work. I suppose that was the simple mercenary thinking that was behind it.'

Abelard Snazz was introduced in the fourth of Moore's published *2000AD* stories, 'The Final Solution' (#189–90, December 1980, art: Steve Dillon) and the character would eventually feature in eight issues spread over two years. Moore had created his first recurring character for *2000AD*. Snazz was a genius who would 'handle complex problems with even more complicated solutions'. In his first story he solved a planet's crimewave by inventing robot policemen, who promptly established a police state; to solve this new problem, he created robot criminals who were a match for the policemen. To solve the further problem that so many civilians were then caught in the crossfire between ruthless robot police and robot criminals, Snazz's masterstroke was to create a population of robot civilians, and the human population were forced to leave their planet.

Moore was now a visible part of the London comics scene, whose writers, artists and editors would meet up under the aegis of the Society of Strip Illustration (SSI) and compare notes. Shortly after Moore joined, his *Doctor Who* artist David Lloyd became chairman. As Lloyd explains, 'it started in 1977 as something of a glorified lunch club, with a lot of the really great Fleet Street cartoonists and artists.

It recruited some of the guys from *2000AD* and some of the other comics out there, and it was mostly a young organisation at the time . . . we had meetings initially at the Press Club, which was a great, posh place on Shoe Lane just off Fleet Street . . . if people walked in without a tie, they were frowned upon and it was kind of ridiculous to control that, particularly with comic artists. Later on we moved to various pubs, the George at the top of Fleet Street, then we moved to the Sketch Club in Chelsea . . . The Sketch Club is where we were at for the longest time, and it was very good, very vibrant.' There were about forty members, all established comics creators, with two associate members who hadn't been published by that point: Neil Gaiman and Dave McKean. Eddie Campbell, who at the time was based in London and self-publishing autobiographical comics, scathingly depicted the SSI – and Lloyd – as 'an association of professionals . . . Status Quo is the new chairman. They meet upstairs at a pub'. Moore had been welcomed into the group and was much more warmly inclined to it, later describing the SSI as 'at its best a kind of coffee evening, or rather where you could meet up at a bar . . . there were some very nice people there'. These included artists Moore would work with, such as Dave Gibbons, Alan Davis, Mark Farmer, Hunt Emerson, Garry Leach, Dave Harwood, David Lloyd and Mike Collins, as well as most of the editors who commissioned their work. Moore was now firmly in the loop.

Alan Moore had begun his attempt to become a professional comic strip creator around the time his wife Phyllis learned they were expecting their first daughter, Leah, who'd been born in February 1978. When the Moores' younger daughter, Amber, was born three years later, Moore was well on his way. But this is not how it felt at the time, either for Moore, for anyone in the comics industry, or for his readers. He may have begun to earn himself a steady stream of commissions, and was becoming well known in the industry, but he was 'having to work hard to get every little breakthrough to win an inch of ground'. It is only with the benefit of hindsight that we can see this as the beginning of a sure-footed, meteoric rise.

3 REALISTIC WEIRD WARRIOR

'Working for Quality Comics is great! It's cartoon heaven.'

Alan Moore, *Fantasy Express* #5 (1983)

In its May 1981 edition, the editor of the newsletter of the Society of Strip Illustration, David Lloyd, posed a series of questions to 'five of the most respected and reputable strip writers in British comics': Angus Allan, Pat Mills, Steve Moore, Steve Parkhouse and Alan Moore. The other four writers were stalwarts of the British comics scene: Allan, perhaps the least well known today, had been in the business since before Moore was born, and at the time of the interview he was writing virtually all the strips in *Look-In*, a children's magazine that ran comic-strip versions of ITV shows like *The Tomorrow People* and *Worzel Gummidge* – and sold twice as many copies as *2000AD*. Moore was very much a newcomer (this was his earliest published interview), but Lloyd had no hesitation inviting him to the 'round table' discussion (they weren't in the same room – Lloyd had posted the same questions to each writer and collated the responses): 'He became very famous and well known very quickly. He just happened to be brilliant, and accepted as brilliant, and everyone knew he was brilliant when they met him . . . There was no surprise with Alan reaching that position because everyone recognised how brilliant he was.'

Moore was twenty-seven years old, married, the father of two daughters, and the family had just moved across Northampton into a old-fashioned brick council house on Wallace Road. He was now freelancing for *2000AD* and Marvel UK, but was yet to work on a regular series for either of them. It is clear from the interview that he was enjoying his job: 'I find writing comics to be staggeringly easy . . . on an average day, working at a fairly leisurely pace, I can turn out a complete five-page script. On a tough day, I can turn out a couple and still be finished by the early evening . . . I love my work, although having previously been employed in cleaning toilets, this is perhaps less than surprising . . . I think I'm adequately payed [sic]. Actually, just between you and me, I'm grossly overpaid . . . I can turn out a four or five-page script in a single day and get a return of somewhere between sixty and ninety quid for my efforts. On top of this I get to buy ludicrous amounts of comics each month.'

We learn, too, that his *2000AD* editor, Steve McManus, had set him the challenge of telling a story without wordy captions; Moore clearly relished the task, but felt the artist had ruined the final product. The artist in question was Walter Howarth, drawing 'Southern Comfort' for the *2000AD Sci-Fi Special* (July 1980). This early in his career, Moore would have been keen to rack up as many credits as possible, but significantly the strip went out under the pseudonym 'R.E. Wright'. Moore cited the forthcoming 'Bax the Burner' (*2000AD Annual 1982*, published August 1981), as a particular favourite, praising the artist Steve Dillon, and noting: 'I was pleased inasmuch as the story was the only one in which I've hung the plot around a strong emotional content and not had the whole thing come off as being incredibly trite and sentimental.'

Moore was ambitious – 'one day I'd like to have a crack at writing novels, short stories, TV and film scripts, stage plays, kiddie porn and all the rest of that stuff' – but 'at this point I can't see comics as ever becoming anything less than my principal area of concern'. That ambition was not solely personal. His love of comics shines through, and for the first time – but by no means the last – he set down why: 'To me the medium is possibly one of the most exciting and underdeveloped areas in the whole cultural spectrum. There's a lot of virgin ground yet to be broken and a hell of a lot of things that haven't been attempted. If I wasn't infatuated with the medium I wouldn't be working in it.'

This was not what most people working in the British comics industry saw. Twenty or so years later, fellow round-table contributor Steve Parkhouse would say:

> IPC Juveniles were simply regurgitating ideas that were fifty years old. Recycling was the name of the game. Editorial staff were paid next to nothing, installed in draughty old buildings with creaking office furniture and expected to co-exist with the rats, the debris and the general malaise of Farringdon Street and its depressing environs. It was a cottage industry inhabited by middle-aged men in cardigans who smoked pipes. You could see them in the works canteen, spooning down vast quantities of jam roly-poly and custard while discussing the latest developments in model aircraft design.

Pat Mills was perhaps the highest-profile participant in the SSI round table. By any standards he was an energetic and innovative figure, someone who'd fought against the staid, complacent comics industry. Mills had written the acclaimed *Charley's War*, a long-running series in the comic *Battle*, which followed an underage working-class lad into the trenches of the Somme without flinching from depictions of either brutality or the political context. It was he who had launched first the controversial, violent war comic *Action*, as well as *2000AD* and its fellow SF title *Starlord*. For each of these comics, he had created, co-created, developed or written early scripts for virtually all the running characters (including *Judge Dredd*). At the time of the interview, Mills was working on the experimental, satirical, not to mention downright strange *Nemesis the Warlock*, a regular series for *2000AD* with artist Kevin O'Neill. When asked the question 'What ambitions do you have for strips as a whole?', though, Mills' reply was curt and practical: 'Albums, rights – the usual thing. But I don't see it happening. Publishers in this country like things the way they are and I don't see anyone or anything altering their outlook.'

Moore was far more expansive. At the beginning of the eighties, he described the battlefield on which he would be fighting for the next decade, one he reasoned would involve changing the attitudes of publishers, editors, creators, readers and even society as a whole. It practically amounted to a manifesto:

> There's such a lot of things I'd like to see happen to comics over the next few years that it's difficult knowing where to start.
>
> I'd like to see less dependence upon the existing big comic companies. I'd like to see artists and writers working off their own bat to open up space for comic strips in magazines which might not have considered them before.

Secondly, I hope that kids' comics in the eighties will realise what decade they're in and stop turning out stuff with an intellectual and moral level rooted somewhere in the early fifties. Stories concerning the daring escapades of plucky Nobby Eichmann, Killer Commando decimating the buck-toothed Japs with his cheeky cockney humour and his chattering stengun don't have a lot of immediate relevance to kids whose only exposure to war is the horribly grey mess that we've got in Northern Ireland. I'd like to see an erosion of the barrier between 'boys' and 'girls' comics. I'd like to see the sweaty, bull-necked masculine stereotype and the whimpering girly counterpart pushed one inch at a time through a Kenwood Chef.

> I'd like to see, and this is purely whimsy, a return to old-fashioned little studio set ups like Eisner/Iger had in the thirties and forties. This would give the artists and writers a greater autonomy, since they'd be selling stuff to the company as a sort of package deal. It would give them a stronger [sic] the merchandising royalties. And I should imagine that some editors might be quite pleased to save time in commissioning one complete job rather than hassling round trying to commission two or three separate people.

> I'd like to see an adult comic that didn't predominantly feature huge tits, spilled intestines or the sort of brain-damaged, acid-casualty gibbering that *Heavy Metal* is so fond of.

In retrospect, it is striking how Moore's frame of reference is purely the British comics scene. The 'big comic companies' he referred to were the UK's IPC and DC Thomson, not American giants DC and Marvel. Will Eisner was invoked as a legendary creator from before Moore was born, not as the man who had just written and drawn *Contract With God*, the comic that was the first to have been described as a 'graphic novel'. It does not even seem to have occurred to Moore that he might work for the American industry.

But Moore did have one more ambition: 'My greatest personal hope is that someone will revive *Marvelman* and I'll get to write it. KIMOTA!' Of all the things he said in the interview, it was this throwaway line which would change the course of Moore's career, and ultimately the direction of the British and American comics industries.

Alan Moore had just said the magic word.

*

Moore's account of what happened next is that 'Dez Skinn got in touch with me and said by a remarkable coincidence, he had been planning to revive *Marvelman*, and would I be interested in writing it?' In reality, as ever, things were a little more complicated.

Dez Skinn was a key figure of British comics at the time, and certainly the most colourful. Only two years older than Moore, during the course of the seventies he had progressed from writing comics fanzines like *Eureka* and *Derinn Comic Collector* to working at IPC and Warner Publishing (where he devised the successful *House of Hammer*), and launching *Starburst* magazine. Having sold *Starburst* to Marvel UK he had become an editor there, revamping and launching numerous titles like *Conan* and *Hulk Comic* as well as *Doctor Who Weekly*. Along the way he had worked with just about every writer and artist on the British comics scene. Ever ambitious, Skinn had come to understand both that the audience for comics was getting a little older, and that many of the younger generation of creators were frustrated with how hidebound the industry was.

Bernadette (Bernie) Jaye remembers Skinn as 'a blond-haired guy who was on a high, brimming with abundant energy and enthusiasm.' Jaye was a sociology student who had shown up at Marvel UK just to take a look around an art studio, but Skinn hired her on the spot as a freelance colourist before employing her fulltime. Soon to become an editor herself, in which capacity she was eventually to work with Moore, she remembers: 'It was an incredible atmosphere. Working at Marvel was fun in the main. Most of the staff were aged twenty-something. We were often in the office late into the night meeting ridiculous deadlines or in the local pub . . . I hadn't met any "creators" before and I certainly hadn't met people with a passion for a medium that dated back to their childhood. To have viable status in this arena you needed to have a comics collection, an obsession for the historic details and to have contributed to fanzines. I hadn't had any of these experiences, couldn't contribute on any of these levels and as a female I had missed out on all sorts of rites of passage. I never swapped comics in the playground, hunted down comics on my bicycle, made my own comics or had my mother throw some of my comics collection away. What I could do was be supportive of the creators. I had appreciated the freelance work I received from Dez and could offer this opportunity now to others even though it was on a small scale.'

Most Marvel UK titles relied on reprints of American material. Skinn envisioned a comic that would be an anthology of half a dozen all-new strips, ranging across various genres, such as SF, sword-and-sorcery and superheroes. It was to be a showcase for British talent, and a launchpad for new characters. He planned to call it *Warrior*. Skinn has said he would have edited the comic for Marvel, but couldn't get his bosses interested in a showcase for the emerging generation of writers and artists. As Jaye explains, 'I don't think providing work for creators was ever fully supported by the management. They didn't have any history with comics and there was always the feeling it was tolerated rather than enjoyed and promoted. I always felt we were getting by on the blind side.'

So Skinn left Marvel to produce *Warrior* under the aegis of his own company, Quality Communications. In April 1981, just before the SSI roundtable was published, he began putting together the first issue, a process that would end up taking about a year. Pragmatically, he wanted the strips in *Warrior* to be as close as possible to the most popular strips in his old Marvel titles: 'So instead of *Captain Britain*, we had *Marvelman*. Instead of *Night-Raven*, we had *V for Vendetta*. Instead of *Abslom Daak* . . . we had *Axel Pressbutton*. And instead of *Conan* we had *Shandor*.' To that end, Skinn was talking to artists and writers he had worked with at Marvel. Many of the small band of established British comic-book freelancers were keen to work for *Warrior*, and over the next few years they were to do so.

Skinn wanted a superhero as part of the mix, and had already decided that would be *Marvelman* – the old character had fallen into obscurity since his titles were cancelled in 1963, but he was a British superhero and fans Skinn's age would at least remember the name. Skinn originally hoped Steve Moore or Steve Parkhouse would write it, with Dave Gibbons or Brian Bolland drawing. But all four declined the opportunity, although they would all work on other strips for *Warrior*. Gibbons says Marvelman 'appealed, but I was too busy' and this was almost certainly the main reason Bolland declined as well.

For the writers, meanwhile, a factor in their decision to turn down *Marvelman* may have been that *Warrior* was going to allow writers and artists to retain the rights to characters they created. Traditionally, comic book publishers on both sides of the Atlantic had treated creators as hired hands. In 1938, when the American writer/artist team of Jerry Siegel and Joe Shuster sold all rights to the character Superman along with the first strip featuring him, they had been paid just $130.

Forty years on, *Superman* was big business: Warner Communications now owned DC Comics, the publisher of Superman comics, and their movie division had released the blockbusters *Superman: The Movie* (1978) and *Superman II* (1980). Yet the corporation had been shamed into giving Siegel and Shuster pensions and on-screen credits only when it came to light that they were practically destitute.

There were no millions to be made or blockbuster movie adaptations in British comics, and creators enjoyed no glory for their efforts. Slowly, though, things were beginning to change: soon after *2000AD* launched, it had started to put credits on stories, and this revolutionary move had quickly become standard practice. Even so, all the revenue from foreign and domestic reprints, merchandise and other spin-offs remained with the publishers. With *Warrior* giving writers and artists the luxury of retaining the rights to any new creations, it would make far more sense for them to work on their own characters rather than revive someone else's.

Another factor was that superheroes had never caught on in the UK. Since the heyday of *Dan Dare* in the fifties the most popular British adventure comics had consistently been science fiction. The popularity of *2000AD*, the arrival of *Star Wars* and a spike of popularity for *Doctor Who* – both the subject of weekly comics published by Marvel UK – had only cemented that in the late seventies. It was science fiction character Axel Pressbutton who would feature on the cover of *Warrior* #1 – which proclaimed 'He's Back!', although the character's very first appearance had been all of three years before and he was still appearing every week in *Sounds* – and it was Pressbutton who Dez Skinn assumed would be *Warrior*'s signature character. The strip would be written by Steve Moore (using his 'Pedro Henry' pseudonym), and abandoned the 'underground comix' sensibility of Pressbutton's previous appearances. Instead he would star in an action series in a very similar vein to Steve Moore's *Abslom Daak*, using the same artist, Steve Dillon. Except for having a little more violence and bare skin, *Warrior*'s version of *Pressbutton* would not have been out of place in *2000AD*.

Dez Skinn says that when Steve Moore turned down the opportunity to write *Marvelman*, he mentioned he had a friend who 'would kill for the chance'. Alan Moore has suggested that Skinn 'must have seen the thing in the SSI Journal', and would later recall that when David Lloyd was asked by Skinn to create another series, a 'new thirties mystery strip' for *Warrior*, Lloyd 'suggested me as writer'. Taken together, these varying recollections leave the actual sequence of events unclear, but all parties agree that Moore was involved with *Marvelman* before the mystery strip. Skinn says that Lloyd's recommendation came 'perhaps a month later' than Steve Moore's, and 'when David suggested Alan . . . I'd already seen his first *Marvelman* script'; Lloyd states that Moore 'had already said yes to doing the *Marvelman* update'.

Skinn had been keen to work only with people he knew, but was surprised to find he already had Alan Moore's name in his address book. Around eighteen months before, Moore had drawn a couple of pages of single-panel Christmas-themed gags for *Frantic*, a Marvel title Skinn had been editing. And Moore knew all about Dez Skinn. He had subscribed to Skinn's fanzines a decade before, and had 'seen him then, although I probably hadn't necessarily met him' at various comics marts and conventions. He thinks he first met Skinn when he hand-delivered his art to *Frantic*, but Skinn doesn't recall this, and we should probably concede his point that most people who meet Alan Moore remember doing so.

Moore was not an old colleague, or anything like as seasoned as the rest of the creators being lined up for *Warrior*, but if he was as well-known in the industry as David Lloyd said, shouldn't Dez Skinn have heard of him? Skinn did not remember Moore's *Frantic* work, and says at the time he wasn't reading *Doctor Who Weekly* or *2000AD*, where strips by Moore were now appearing. Steve Moore was talking to Skinn about using the Pressbutton character. Wouldn't Skinn have been aware of Alan from the *Sounds* strip Pressbutton appeared in, given that he was its artist? 'You'd expect so, but to me Alan had been very much an "underground" one-off contributor (to *Frantic*). I'd even put such after his name in my mammoth address book so I'd remember who he was (failed though!) . . . Steve Dillon was to draw the strip, so Alan's relevance was purely historical, no more than Mick Anglo and *Marvelman*.'

At Skinn's request, Moore prepared an eight-page pitch document for *Marvelman*, which outlined the main characters and the backstory in some detail. Moore was clearly not in the loop at *Warrior* at this point: at the end of the pitch, he suggested Dave Gibbons or Steve Dillon as suitable artists, unaware Gibbons had already turned down the opportunity, and that there were other plans for Dillon. But the pitch led to a phone conversation, which persuaded Skinn to request a full script for the first instalment, although he made it clear that this was 'on spec' – in other words, Moore wouldn't get paid if Skinn didn't like it.

*

One of the first things Skinn had done when he started putting *Warrior* together was approach David Lloyd asking him to create a '*Night-Raven*-type' series. *Night-Raven* was a prime example of why Skinn had been frustrated at Marvel UK. A Marvel comic from America was, and still is, typically a monthly printed in full colour, with around twenty-two pages of one story featuring one character (Captain America, say) or one team (such as The X-Men). A typical British title was a black-and-white weekly with larger pages and around half a dozen short strips, each featuring a different character. Some comics were padded out with text features – articles about the characters, prose fiction. Marvel UK's comics were mostly straight reprints of American material (often broken up into shorter instalments, and always in black and white), but there would also occasionally be new material by British writers and artists featuring Marvel's American characters like the Hulk. There were even some original characters. British readers were treated, for example, to the all-new adventures of Captain Britain.

Night-Raven was one of these characters. Created in 1979 for Marvel UK's *Hulk Comic* by Skinn and assistant editor Richard Burton, it was written by Steve Parkhouse, drawn by Lloyd, and saw a masked vigilante take on gangsters in the 1930s. It owed a clear debt to venerable characters The Shadow and The Spirit, but had a distinct identity of its own, and while the stories notionally took place in the same 'Marvel Universe' as *Fantastic Four*, *Iron Man* and the rest, the series was set fifty years in the past, so it could plough its own furrow. *Night-Raven* was the favourite strip of many people working for Marvel UK. Despite this, Marvel's American publisher, Stan Lee, insisted on changes after only a few months. He disliked Lloyd's 'blocky' drawing style, and so John Bolton became the new artist. Lloyd was kept busy on other projects, including *Star Wars*, *Doctor Who* and an adaptation of the movie *Time Bandits*. The *Night-Raven* story was moved forward to the present day and the violence was toned down. Skinn saw this as symptomatic of the problems with the industry and, keen for *Warrior* to be a place where writers and artists would not be forced to make such compromises, he invited Lloyd to come up with a new series. Lloyd 'knew it would be a much better piece of work if Alan was on board. I would have been happy to do something, but it would have had nothing like the depth that Alan would add to it.' Many of the foundations of this 'thirties mystery strip', including its artist, had therefore been in place before Alan Moore was involved. Yet it would evolve into one of the series he is best known for: *V for Vendetta*.

Only two years later, when Moore wrote a 'behind the scenes' feature about the origins of *V for Vendetta*, he admitted that when he and Lloyd were asked where they got their ideas from, 'we don't really remember'. Once Skinn set them to work, however, they quickly had numerous telephone conversations and 'voluminous correspondence'; both were clearly on the same wavelength and throwing a lot of ideas around. It was a true collaboration, with the artist working on some of the key story points and the writer putting a lot of thought into the visual style. '"Alan and I were like Laurel and Hardy when we worked on that," Mr Lloyd said. "We clicked"'.

Recalling the 'freakish terrorist in white face make-up who traded under the name of the Doll' he had come up with for a DC Thomson competition about five years before, Moore suggested to Lloyd that the series could be about a character called Vendetta, along the lines of the Doll, rooted in a 'realistic thirties'. This plan was quickly vetoed by Lloyd, who knew from experience that he would not enjoy the level of research and other restrictions this would entail. Lloyd had recently been approached by Serge Boissevain, a French editor who was preparing his own lavish adult comic for the English market, *pssst!* and Lloyd had come up with a single page for a proposed strip called *Falconbridge*. 'The editor was crazy, he was this Frenchman and it was great he wanted to recruit people, but he had this rebellious attitude, and he would say "heroes are dead, so we're not having heroes in my magazine" . . . So Evelina Falconbridge I just imagined would be an urban guerilla fighting these future fascists . . . It was just that one page. I sent it in as a sample, I did it in a kind of French style, used a shading technique on it that was a bit sub-Moebius. It didn't work out.'

Moore and Lloyd agreed that, like *Falconbridge*, the series would be set in the 1990s, in a future totalitarian state. The writer, artist and editor were all keen to have a British setting, rather than an Americanised one. The initial idea 'had robots, uniformed riot police of the kneepads and helmets variety'. Lloyd began coming up with character sketches for a rogue 'future cop' called Vendetta, incorporating the letter V in the costume. Vendetta would conduct a series of 'bizarre murders'

FALCONBRIDGE

in a plotline reminiscent of the Vincent Price movie *The Abominable Dr Phibes*. Lloyd was unhappy they hadn't settled on a motive for their protagonist, and felt that without knowing what made him tick, it was impossible to come up with the right 'look' for him.

The world of the series had been devastated by nuclear war, but there wouldn't be mutants or radioactive deserts. Not only were these clichéd, but the main issue was that *2000AD* mainstay *Judge Dredd* was a future cop living in a corrupt post-apocalyptic city. While Skinn was keen for his characters to mirror existing successes, this would have been a little too close for comfort. But as *V for Vendetta* became less 'futuristic', more austere and Orwellian, it began instead to resemble another early *2000AD* strip, *Invasion!*, about Bill Savage, fearless resistance leader of a near-future Britain invaded by a very thinly disguised Red Army. Most new comics series are built around combinations of old ideas, but Moore and Lloyd knew they needed to find a way to make their series more distinctive.

Getting to this stage had only taken a couple of weeks. A planned holiday at the end of June to the Isle of Wight with Phyllis, Leah and five-month old Amber now became a working break. Moore wrote the first *Marvelman* script and, as he put it in a handwritten comment on his covering letter to Skinn, a 'rough synopsis for *The Ace of Shades*. This is only a first draft. It will hopefully have shaped up into something more complete by the time Dave gets my first script.' Not even Moore liked the new title, which did not survive long. While he was writing up his notes, Skinn and his business partner Graham Marsh – not knowing that Moore and Lloyd had previously tossed around the title *Vendetta* – twisted the Churchillian slogan 'V for Victory' to come up with the title *V for Vendetta*. A memo by Skinn dated 24 June 1981 outlined the plans for *Warrior* and referred to '*V for Vendetta*, written by Alan Moore, drawn by David Lloyd. Set in a future Britain, around 1990. A totalitarian government, Big Brother sort of system. A mystery figure, Vendetta, takes on the system.'

In his 'rough synopsis', Moore had come up with a detailed backstory for the series, directly grounded in contemporary politics. A few months later, he would explain his working method to fellow artist and writer Bryan Talbot: 'A sort of experiment I'm trying is to try and build the story from the characters upwards. This means that before I start on the actual script, I have to know who all the characters are and have a more or less complete life history for each one firmly

established in my head.' He would later tell the fanzine *Hellfire*, 'what I did first was sit down and work out the entire world, all the stuff I'm never going to use in the strip, that you never need to know . . . once I've worked out the politics of the situation, how the government works and all the details like that, I can start thinking about the actual plotlines for individual episodes.'

The results of this cogitation were soon apparent. Moore sent Lloyd a detailed extrapolation of the consequences of a future Labour government unilaterally disarming the UK's nuclear weapons; the Soviet Union was thus emboldened, leading to a nuclear war that left only the UK and China standing. The document got no closer to establishing their main character, though – Lloyd wrote on the sketch of 'Vendetta': 'Just got your notes (28th June) so that makes all this redundant, but my general thoughts and opinions on the character remain unchanged. I'll buzz you at the weekend,' and sent it to Moore. The two of them were acutely aware that they were on to something. Moore had a list of things he wanted the strip to be like – including *Nineteen Eighty-Four*, *The Shadow* and Robin Hood – while Lloyd was coming up with a radical visual style for the series. Each panel would be a regular size, and pictures wouldn't 'bleed' from them. It was a more extreme version of the 'blocky' art that Stan Lee had disliked so much. They were tantalisingly close, but still the strip was failing to crystallise.

Marvelman was proving far more straightforward. Moore submitted the first script to Dez Skinn, along with a cover letter apologising for 'all the errors of typing, grammar and basic literacy that one must expect from a truly great artiste such as myself', as well as for the fact that the story was a page longer than agreed, the ending was a little rushed and 'some of the frames are a little word-heavy'. Skinn read the script on the bus and thought it was 'stunning'. It followed the idea that had occurred to Moore back when he was a teenager: the boy Mike Moran had forgotten the magic word which allowed him to transform into Marvelman. Moran, now middle-aged, ended up in the middle of a heist to steal plutonium from a power station, whereupon he remembered his magic word, transformed into Marvelman and saved the day almost as an afterthought before flying off proclaiming his return.

It was a little under a year before *Warrior* #1 debuted, and when it did, the introduction to *Marvelman* was practically unchanged from Moore's spec script: the main plotlines and most of the details were in place before the artist was assigned. Skinn assigned another relative newcomer, Garry Leach, to draw the story, showing Leach the completed first script to persuade him to come on board. Leach did a lot of work redesigning the costume and thinking through the 'look' of the strip; he modelled Marvelman on Paul Newman and Liz Moran on Audrey Hepburn. Leach has said 'Alan never objected to you pitching an idea in if it was relevant or enhanced the story', and Moore was very happy to adopt some of the suggestions Leach had for improving the visuals – Marvelman acquired a glowing force field that allowed Leach to play with lighting effects, Leach had detailed thoughts on an early fight sequence, and he would call the writer whenever he felt he had other good ideas.

It's fair to say *Marvelman* was less of a collaborative effort than *V for Vendetta*. This isn't to diminish Leach's contribution, but the idea of how to revamp *Marvelman* had been brewing in Moore's mind for fifteen years, and the initial pitch document contained material that would carry the strip for over a year. Leach reorganised a few of the images, but left Moore's captions and dialogue intact. There were only very minor changes: someone exclaims 'Christ!', when it's 'Jesus!' in the script; a caption description of 'cold granite' dawn has become 'cold grey'. Moore asked the artist to establish that the Morans didn't wear anything in bed, and to 'make it really casual and no big deal, so as to avoid that sort of faintly smelly Conan-type voyeurism': Leach has a full-length image of Liz Moran naked, with her back to us. Overall, he does a superb job of bringing a complicated script to life, and squaring the circle of having a flying man in a sparkly leotard appear 'realistic'.

The artist doubled up as art director for *Warrior*, so he worked in the same office as Skinn and they would discuss plot points, but there is no evidence of Moore having the same the lengthy back-and-forth discussions with Leach that he had with David Lloyd and many subsequent collaborators. Leach received a script every month, and when it arrived, 'I'd brew up a coffee, sit back and have a damned good read because they were too dense to skim'.

The decision that the title for the mystery strip would be *V for Vendetta* concentrated Moore and Lloyd's minds, as did the 10 July 1981 deadline all *Warrior*'s writers were set for #1 scripts. The main question became a simple one: what was the motivation for the character's 'vendetta'? Moore now decided that their hero was an escapee from a concentration camp out for revenge. But there remained the issue of what their protagonist looked like. Moore credits Lloyd for finding the solution: 'The big breakthrough was Dave's, much as it sickens me to admit it . . . this was the best idea I'd ever heard in my entire life.' This was that Vendetta should be a 'resurrected Guy Fawkes'. Lloyd included a sketch that's identical to the final V, but with a pointy hat (though he also suggested, 'let's scrub *V for Vendetta*. Call the strip *Good Guy*.') Lloyd's notes also have the prescient comment that 'we shouldn't burn the chap every Nov 5th but celebrate his attempt to blow up Parliament . . . we'd be actually shaping public consciousness in a way in which some Conservative politicians might regard as subversive'.

Moore was enthusiastic: 'There was something so British and so striking about that iconic image, and it played well into the kind of thinking that was already starting to develop on the strip.' This was a reference to both Moore and Lloyd latching on to another Vincent Price movie in a similar vein to *Phibes*: *Theatre of Blood* (1973), which featured Price as a hammy Shakespearean actor who kills off a series of his critics.

In the same letter he suggested the Guy Fawkes look, Lloyd also explained that he wanted to avoid the use of thought balloons and sound effects captions. The idea terrified and excited Moore. Although not unprecedented, it was extremely unusual in mainstream comics and he suspected Lloyd had suggested it 'almost as a joke, I don't think he expected me to go along with it'.

Things moved rapidly from this point. V's mannerisms now took on a more overtly theatrical, Jacobean flavour to match his Guy Fawkes appearance. Moore was able to make this more than a gimmick. In the first chapter, the mentality of the two sides in the battle is efficiently contrasted when a policeman concludes from the odd way V speaks that he 'must be some kinda retard got out of a hospital', failing to recognise that his opponent is quoting from *Macbeth*.

Moore and Lloyd had started out with a series about a vigilante fighting generic totalitarian forces, but the 1997 setting was not very far in the future and Moore had got there by extrapolating current headlines. While most British comics were set in imaginary places like Melchester, Northpool or Bunkerton, *V for Vendetta* was rooted in a Britain with real place names and even some real people. A telling detail is a one-off mention of Queen Zara in the first instalment – Zara Phillips was born in May 1981, only a few months after Amber Moore. As one letter to

Warrior later noted, something catastrophic must have happened to the royal family if Princess Anne's *second* child was now on the throne (Zara was sixth in line when she was born, tenth in the real 1997).

As Moore began drawing up a list of the fascist supporting characters, the various authority figures V was pursuing and the investigators sent after him, it made him look at the situation from their point of view. Whereas the 'hero' of the piece was a masked killer out for personal vengeance, the 'bad guys' were simply ordinary people doing what they believed was best for the country:

> I didn't want to just come into this as a self-confessed anarchist and say 'right, here's this anarchist: he's the good guy; here are all those bad fascists: they're the bad guys'. That's trivial and insulting to the reader. I wanted to present some of the fascists as being ordinary, and in some instances even likeable, human beings. They weren't just Nazi cartoons with monocles and University of Heidelberg duelling scars. They were people who'd made their choices for a reason. Sometimes that reason was cowardice, sometimes that reason was wanting to get on, sometimes it was a genuine belief in those principles.

All this could be read as a simple critique of the usual logic that there had to be goodies and baddies, and everyone was on one side or the other – an idea as prevalent in political discussion as in comic books. However, as Lloyd began interpreting Moore's first few scripts and the finished product started to appear, they both came to realise they were creating something more sophisticated than they had planned.

Much of the credit can be put down to Lloyd. His most recent work, *Golden Amazon* and *Doctor Who*, had included painted wash effects and elaborate grey tones. On *V for Vendetta*, he chose an approach that was a visual joke: 'David Lloyd was using this stark chiaroscuro style where you'd got no bordering outlines on the characters, you've got hard black up against hard white in the artwork. Whereas in the story, in the text, there was nothing but shades of grey in moral terms.' The way characters merge into the shadows, the repeated panel compositions, use of close-ups, the intercutting with flashback scenes . . . all these make the reader work to see what is going on, encourage them to go back and re-read and re-interpret. Some panels almost resemble optical illusions that take a second or two to snap into place. An iconic early example occurs in the second chapter: there's a panel of V standing on a railway bridge, his cloak flapping. Another character glances up and, like the reader, can't quite work out what he's looking at. This panel was later reproduced on house ads, badges and other promotional material.

It is in *V for Vendetta* that we see Moore's first systematic use of what would become a trademark technique, exploiting one of the key strengths of the medium: the artistic effect to be gained by combining a picture and text.

A progression in comic art is evident here. In an unsophisticated early comic, the words would simply support or describe the picture: we might see an image of Superman with red lines coming out of his eyes that connect with a blob in the hand of a gangster and a caption saying 'Superman melts the crook's gun with his incredible heat vision!' The Marvel comics of the sixties concentrated more on the inner life of their characters, revealing them to be troubled. Now we might see a picture of Spider-Man fighting Doctor Octopus, but a thought bubble saying something like 'I hope I won't be late for my date with Mary Jane'.

Comic art was now going beyond that, beginning to explore the far greater poetic effect to be had by using an image and text that seem to contradict each other or to have no obvious connection. It forces the reader to work out what link the creators might be implying. Moore was not the first comics creator to understand that this could add layers of meaning, as well as a degree of ambiguity, but his use of the technique has always been unusually sustained and sophisticated. Moore called it 'ironic counterpoint' in his first *V for Vendetta* script, and there is a good example on the second page of the first chapter.

The text is an announcement of 'the Queen's first public appearance since her sixteenth birthday' where she wore a 'suit of peach silk created specially for the occasion by the Royal Couturier', while the picture is of a very young woman in a bedsit awkwardly putting on a dress. That contrast is obvious, but it's the next page before we learn that this woman, like Queen Zara, is only sixteen years old. (It will be the third chapter before we learn the girl's name is Evey Hammond and find out how her situation became so desperate.) The next panel juxtaposes that

image of Evey in a dress that's too small even for her slight frame with a close-up of V snapping on a glove. We'll learn that both V and Evey are getting dressed to go out onto the London streets at night. Desperation has driven Evey to an ill-thought-through attempt to earn some money prostituting herself, whereas V will orchestrate an elaborate plan to destroy the Houses of Parliament. What Moore has understood is that the act of contrasting the words and images in one panel, then contrasting that panel with the next, creates patterns. The story can say two things, but mean a third, and the narrative can have a highly elaborate, allusive structure.

Without thought balloons giving convenient access to eloquent inner monologues of the characters, the dialogue Moore wrote and the faces Lloyd drew had to become more subtle and expressive. It was not only V who wore a mask – readers of *V for Vendetta* have to imagine what all the characters are thinking, and can never be certain what they really understand about those characters' situations. A fascist government with bold slogans and fancy uniforms and equipment, the population under constant CCTV surveillance, individuals like Evey Hammond dolling themselves up – all of them are 'putting on a brave face'.

There was yet another twist to standard conventions. While comics are full of masked figures, their masks are usually disguises. The readers are in on the secret identity of, say, Batman or Spider-Man. In a similar vein, the early instalments of *V for Vendetta* encourage the idea that we will eventually see the mask come off and learn that V has been one of the other characters all along – that there will be, in Moore's words, 'a satisfactory revelation'. This was a deliberate deception, and Lloyd says 'we never had any intention of doing that'. The people who wrote letters to *Warrior* quickly came to a consensus that V would turn out to be Evey's father, who she had not seen since he was dragged away by the authorities years before – few readers will have noticed that her father resembles Steve Moore, and like him, lived on Shooter's Hill. When the series began in those early issues of *Warrior*, it was essential to keep the man under the mask an entirely mysterious figure, to the point that we can't be entirely sure of V's gender (while V is referred to as 'the man in Room V', some of the inmates were treated with hormones and changed sex).

Instead of pinning down who V is and what he really believes, the story is about piecing those things together. The other characters in the story are trying to, the reader has to. Because the narrative can't look at V directly, we have to see him through the eyes of others. The story was presented in short chapters, and each had to remind the reader of where the story stood – but Moore and Lloyd had banned the use of lengthy captions, so they had to find a less direct way of recapping. By an alchemical combination of design, accident, genre expectation, form and the unintended consequences of storytelling choices, the result is that Moore and Lloyd tell the story as a series of vignettes. We are shown V's world, often the same event or the consequences of that event, from a variety of viewpoints.

There is a main viewpoint character, though, and that's Evey Hammond. She is not mentioned in the *Warrior* article, nor in any of the published notes or sketches, and Lloyd later stated that 'the basic plot, and the characters involved, were all Alan's, apart from Evey'. Lloyd also says, 'she was a late addition to things . . . in *Theatre of Blood*, Vincent Price has a team of people helping him, and this was one of the ideas that Alan was bringing, so there was an idea that V would have an assistant that would help him in his sabotage, like the character Vulnavia in *The Abominable Dr Phibes* . . . that evolved into Evelina Falconbridge becoming Evey. It was a way of introducing Falconbridge, but not as an urban guerilla, just as this girl.' It's worth noting that the *Falconbridge* sample page features Evelina poised to save a woman from being raped by policemen, while the first chapter of *V for Vendetta* sees V saving Evey from the same fate.

Evey is not a major character at the start of the story. She becomes V's accomplice in the murder of the corrupt Bishop of Westminster, but is little seen after that in Book One. V abandons her in the opening chapter of Book Two, then she drops out of the strip for several chapters, and it is only after she returns that she becomes a central character. Evey is immediately appealing and memorable – as well as one of very few women in the story – and it is not hard to infer that Moore was thinking of her when he told Bryan Talbot a few months later he had found 'you can spin entire plotlines out of one supporting character if your character is strong enough'.

V for Vendetta was certainly a story that evolved as it was being told. In 1988, in his introduction to the first American edition, Moore acknowledged that the series changed under them while it was being written: 'There are things that ring oddly in earlier episodes when judged in the light of the strip's later development. I trust you'll bear with us during any initial clumsiness and share our opinion that it was for the best to show the early episodes unrevised, warts and all, rather than go back and eradicate all trace of youthful creative inexperience.' One element that emerged organically was one of the most memorable chapters in the story. It starts in Chapter 11 of Book One, as David Lloyd explains: 'Alan had written a script with V in the Shadow Gallery and said "put him wherever you like", and I put him in a private cinema. The one thing that bothered me at that point about V was that he had no real humanity to him. He was a guy in a mask. So I had him looking at pictures on a screen, and there's this woman and you don't know who she is. It might be a past love or a lost sister, you don't know who they are. And you get this panel where he covers his eyes.'

In Chapter 11 of Book Two (first published in *Warrior* #25, December 1984), we learn that the woman was an actress, Valerie. She is a lesbian, and following the fascist coup, that was enough to have her sent to the concentration camp at Larkhill. She was in the cell next to V and passed him a note explaining her story, and that although she knows she will die, they have not broken her will.

The woman depicted on the screen was in fact an actress Lloyd knew at the time who'd sent him some pictures: 'I wouldn't dream of saying her name – I asked if she minded me using the photos and she was a big fan of V. And so I used those, and that led to the Valerie sequence, which for me is the core of the thing . . .' As he admits, it was 'an accident. And there's a lot of accidents in V. The name is an

accident, the Guy Fawkes thing was an accident . . . It's perfect, but it's an absolute accident.'

Lloyd concludes, 'One of the great things that happens to me is that going to conventions, people come up to me and say the Valerie chapter changed their lives. And that's a great thing, that you've not only created a great entertaining thriller, but it's also meant something.'

What had started out as Dez Skinn simply trying to recreate *Night-Raven* was becoming something quite different. While *V for Vendetta* was grounded in the Britain of the early eighties, Moore and Lloyd started to realise as the story developed that 'the strip was turning out all of these possibilities for things that hadn't been there in the initial conception, but which we could then explore and exploit . . . it could be a love story, it could be a political drama, it could be, to some degree, a metaphysical tale. It could be all these things and still be a kind of pulp adventure, a kind of superhero strip, a kind of science fiction strip. And I think that we were just interested in letting it grow and seeing what it turned into without trying to trap it into any preconceived categories.'

With the first chapters of *Marvelman* and *V for Vendetta* completed, Skinn was very happy with Moore's work. Moore was now more than a voice on the phone, he was visiting the *Warrior* offices and being encouraged to pitch more stories. Skinn explains, 'We'd have regular monthly meetings. In part to up the ante. When artists saw what great work the others were doing I know that made them try harder! It was also to create a feeling of community. We all wanted the same things: more mature products and greater creative rights and freedom. Keeping everybody in the picture helped enable that.'

Moore used the opportunity to build up a list of contacts. Steve Parkhouse recalls: 'When the first few issues were in preparation, I was visiting Dez Skinn's editorial bullpit on a regular basis. On one occasion, I walked into Dez's office to find a very large man with a very large beard looking at some of my artwork.' This was the first time Parkhouse and Moore had met for ten years. Moore said it would be nice to work together on something, which Parkhouse assumed was the usual pleasantry. Shortly afterwards, he was surprised to be presented by Moore with 'a choice of three different scenarios that he had been working on.' We know Parkhouse chose *The Bojeffries Saga*, and that he and Moore started work on the strip shortly after

Warrior launched in early 1982. The three strips Moore developed once *Warrior* was underway signalled major interests that would recur in his later work.

The Bojeffries Saga was the first, and it appeared in *Warrior* #12–13 (1983) and #19–20 (1984). Parkhouse had been the writer and artist on one of the launch series in *Warrior*. Originally this was to be named *Dragonsong*, but it mutated into *The Spiral Path*. Although given carte blanche by Skinn, Parkhouse had found the result – a labyrinthine stream-of-consciousness fantasy story – deeply unenjoyable to create. With *The Bojeffries Saga*, 'Alan made it very easy by delivering scripts of stunning innovation. We both knew exactly what was needed and almost by unspoken agreement we didn't interfere with each other's processes.'

Formally, *The Bojeffries Saga* is a rather straightforward, even old-fashioned strip, with large panels telling a linear story. It even has the dreaded thought balloons. Moore described the series as taking place 'in an unnamed urban mass – possibly Birmingham, possibly Northampton', but he was consciously trying to tie it back to his upbringing. As he said in 1986: 'Me and the artist Steve Parkhouse have been trying to get the feel of the really stupid bits of England we can remember from when we were kids . . . we boiled all this down into a fantasy on the English landscape in which we set these various werewolves and mutants. In a funny way it's a lot more personal than a lot of the strips I've done.' Twenty years on, he stressed the same point: '*Bojeffries* was important in that it was one of the personal things that I've done . . . it looks very surrealistic to Americans, whereas, to me, it's a thing that I've done that I've come closest to actually describing the flavour of an ordinary working-class childhood in Northampton.' In some places *The Bojeffries Saga* is simply Alan Moore's childhood with the names changed and slight exaggeration for comic effect.

Although it's deeply personal, the strip has perennially been overlooked. Partly this is because it's been difficult to find: it took some years for the series to be collected for the American market (as *The Complete Bojeffries Saga*, Tundra Press, 1992, an edition that is harder to track down than the original *Warriors*). That cannot be the only reason for its neglect, though, as *Marvelman* has been even harder to come by and that has only served to inflate its status. Many readers who lapped up *Marvelman* and *V for Vendetta*, particularly in America, have a very hard time 'getting' the strip in the other sense of the word: it seems difficult to categorise generally and as part of Moore's oeuvre in particular.

4 — We went by local transport to the "Sparklesands" caravan camp, where we always stay. Apparently, since last year there's been a full enquiry to find out exactly *why* the sands were sparkling, and now everybody's advised to hire lead wind-breaks and all the deckchairs have had to be encased in concrete until the year six thousand. As usual, me, Dad and "Action Ears" have to sleep on the little built-in vinyl sofa thing, while Ginda gets the fold-down double bed. Uncle Festus is in the wardrobe again, and Uncle Raoul sleeps under the caravan curled round the calor-gas tank.

5 — All the grass around the camp toilets is still dead, and that fat man in the string vest from last year is still washing himself very slowly in one hand-basin. On the way back, disorientated by the many identical caravans, I was almost adopted by a Quaker couple from Hornsby.

6 — On the spinners at the camp at the newsagents I was thrilled to find an eighty-page Giant Jaguarboy Annual, with stories about Radio Ranger (from "My Greatest Comics") and the Violet Mummy (who I've never heard of), but, intriguingly, no Jaguarboy. Unfortunately, as it turned out, I was dreaming the whole episode.

The main reason is simple: *The Bojeffries Saga* is a comedy.

In 1986, Moore described *The Bojeffries Saga* as 'one of the few comedy strips I've done', but from his earliest work onwards, he has written out-and-out comedy whenever he has had the opportunity. At the time he was starting work on *Warrior*, he was writing and drawing weekly instalments of *The Stars My Degradation* and *Maxwell the Magic Cat*. He had written the first *Abelard Snazz* script as a *Future Shock* for *2000AD*, and that would become a short series. All the *Future Shocks* and *Time Twisters*, not just those written by Moore, were meant as light relief. Moore's best-known comedy series, *DR & Quinch*, started as out as a one-off *Time Twister* ('DR & Quinch Have Fun on Earth', *2000AD* #317, May 1983). *The Bojeffries Saga*, then, was part of a continuing and major strand of Moore's work, not some aberration or slight side project.

Neither, though, was it an obvious fit for any British magazine. While it has werewolves and vampires in it, it's not a horror strip. It's not the sort of science fantasy *2000AD* might print. One correspondent to *Warrior* summed up a common reaction in the letters column in #16: 'I liked this story but it was out of place in *Warrior*.' *The Bojeffries Saga* was featured on the cover of its debut issue, with the strapline: 'Makes *Monty Python* Look Like A Comedy . . . a soap opera of the paranormal'. This was more confusing than accurately descriptive, as it's not all that Pythonesque, (although Michael Palin would have made an excellent Trevor Inchmale, the Walter Mittyish rent collector who's the viewpoint character of the first story.) In fact, with a family of supernatural creatures living in a typical home, there is a superficial resemblance to the American TV series *The Addams Family* and *The Munsters* (a comparison Moore and Parkhouse have resisted). But *The Bojeffries Saga* is perhaps most like *The Young Ones*, a TV sitcom about a houseful of unappealing students which debuted on BBC2 in late 1982 and was invariably described as 'anarchic humour'. That show was one of the first flowerings of eighties alternative comedy on television, so it was fitting that the Tundra reprint of the series featured a foreword by alternative comedian (and comics fan) Lenny Henry.

It is more productive to analyse where *The Bojeffries Saga* fits in Moore's development as a writer. The real reason it was in *Warrior* is that Dez Skinn trusted Moore and Parkhouse, and he knew that his readers were keen on Moore. It's fair to say that *The Bojeffries Saga* was the first strip published because the writer is Alan Moore.

Moore would moreover agree with Steve Parkhouse's assessment that 'we never realised its full potential'. Four instalments appeared in *Warrior*, another six would show up in various places over the next ten years. Whereas Moore sees his other *Warrior* strips as done and dusted, he has shown interest in reviving *The Bojeffries Saga*, and for many years Top Shelf, his American publisher of choice, have listed a collected edition with new material as 'forthcoming'. It's an early series, but one that fits quite comfortably with Alan Moore's current work.

Warrior #9 and #10 (January/May 1983) saw the appearance of the second of the three ideas Moore had pitched to Dez Skinn. Moore and Garry Leach's *Warpsmith* was a straight science-fiction strip based on characters Moore had first devised back in his Arts Lab days. One of the Warpsmiths, an alien police force, had appeared on the cover of *Warrior* #4 and in that month's *Marvelman* strip readers learned that the Warpsmiths would become key allies of Marvelman. In their own strip, we learn that the Warpsmiths are a race of teleporters, one whose language doesn't even have a word for 'distance' because they can travel anywhere instantly. The story portrays a number of groups of aliens, all with their own distinctive jargon. It is a high-concept, grown-up science fiction idea, but it's not rooted in the 'realistic Britain' Moore was basing his other *Warrior* strips around, and the strip did not return to the magazine. *Warpsmith* went on to feature in *A1* (1989), an anthology title that Garry Leach would publish (the characters were the cover stars of the first issue) and played an important part in the last book of *Marvelman*. If *Warpsmith* had caught on, no doubt it would have become a soaring science fiction epic with a distinct identity. As it stands, the series is probably best considered a spin-off from *Marvelman*.

Moore ended up taking his third idea, *Nightjar*, to Bryan Talbot, a writer/artist who had been part of the Birmingham Arts Lab and had an extensive background in underground comics, but was now looking for more mainstream work. After drawing a single illustration of Adam Ant for a magazine he found, somewhat to his bemusement, that he had been 'branded as "the Adam Ant artist" and spent most of a year producing pics and logos for various Ant publications'. Comics connoisseurs knew Talbot as the creator of the extraordinary *The Adventures of Luther Arkwright*, a sexy, intricate epic about a war fought across parallel universes. This had begun in 1978 in *Near Myths*, an Edinburgh magazine that also featured some of the earliest work by future comics superstar Grant Morrison. *Near Myths*, though, only ran for five issues. As Moore and Talbot started working together on *Nightjar*, *pssst!*, the magazine that had rejected David Lloyd's *Falconbridge*, had just agreed to reprint and continue *Luther Arkwright* (starting from #2, February 1982) and Moore's initial letter to Talbot congratulated him for that.

The letter seems to have been written just after the launch of *Warrior*. Moore had thought about Talbot's strengths as an artist – his use of white space, his 'sense of Englishness' and familiarity with art beyond the world of comic books – and sensed a kindred spirit, because of a shared background in underground comics. The strip they were to collaborate on was to serve two purposes. First (as we might guess by now), 'I'd like a very believable and realistic 1982 setting'. This would involve a portrayal of magic that was 'more low-key and less pyrotechnic . . . I'd like to suggest a sort of magic reality by the use of coincidences and shit like that'. Moore was interested in featuring working-class magicians. Second, he envisaged 'a vehicle for semi-experimental storytelling devices . . . I should imagine from the episodes of *Arkwright* that I've seen this is pretty dear to your heart as well'. He said he wanted to emulate *Eraserhead*, Nic Roeg and Kubrick.

Moore had a clear advantage over Talbot in his experience of what the readers of *Warrior*, and perhaps more pertinently its editor, would want. He told Talbot that *Warrior* was for 'a 12 to 25-year-old audience', and saw it as important that a series with a female lead should 'educate some of the pre-teen misogynists in our audience about what women are like'. He wanted their protagonist to be unconventionally attractive, though conceded that 'we do have to appeal to people with base sensibilities. Dez for one, 40,000 readers for another.' Indeed, Skinn's pragmatism looms large: Moore advises Talbot that his editor will want a 'broad commercial approach' and an instantly recognisable lead character, and art that can easily be coloured for foreign editions; he suggests they plan for three episodes and then assess 'the Dez/reader reaction'. Moore visited Talbot for a couple of days at home in Lancashire before starting the script and they discussed the concept in more detail.

The results can be seen in the first instalment, which efficiently sets up the premise. Harold Demdyke ('he looks like everybody's dad after Sunday dinner') dies in front of his young daughter, Mirrigan. Years later, her grandmother announces that he was 'Emperor of All the Birds', the most powerful of sorcerers, and that he died at the hands of seven other magicians. Mirrigan is to kill them and take the title for herself. We see the seven antagonists, including the current Emperor of the Birds, the MP Sir Eric Blason ('this guy is about power on a level that drug-addled ninnies like you and I can scarcely conceive', Moore tells Talbot). In the letters column of *Warrior* #8 (December 1982), Skinn was able to announce that 'Bryan Talbot is working on a contemporary sorceress strip from an Alan Moore script'.

But by then the project was clearly on the back burner for writer, artist and editor alike. Skinn admits, 'I was never very keen on *Nightjar* (hated the name) and Bryan was another slow – or busy – artist, so it would never have happened in *Warrior* which *had* to hit deadlines or there'd be no money in the kitty to pay contributors.' By the time *Warrior* folded three years later, Talbot had completed just two and a half pages of the eight scripted and pencilled one other. He simply got a better offer: Pat Mills had approached him to replace Kevin O'Neill as the regular artist on *2000AD*'s *Nemesis the Warlock*. He would follow that with stints on *Slaine* and *Judge Dredd* that would keep him occupied for the next four years (it's worth comparing Talbot's progress on *Nightjar* with the five or six pages a week he was completing for *2000AD*).

Talbot's first work for *2000AD* had been a short strip written by Moore ('Wages of Sin', #257, March 1982), and they would soon work together on 'Old Red Eyes Is Back' (a *Ro-Busters* story for *2000AD Annual 1983*, August 1982), but Talbot hasn't drawn another Moore strip. They did work together on a video project, *Ragnarok* (1983). In the late eighties Talbot completed *The Adventures of Luther Arkwright*, with Moore writing the foreword to the second volume of the collected edition in December 1987 ('he created a seamless whole, a work ambitious in both scope and complexity that still stands unique upon the comics landscape'). Talbot became a semi-regular artist for DC Comics in America, his most high-profile work being on Neil Gaiman's *The Sandman*. From there, he returned to original graphic novels that he both wrote and drew, cementing his reputation as one of the most important and interesting British creators – *The Tale of One Bad Rat* (1995), *Heart of Empire* (1999, the sequel to *Luther Arkwright*), *Alice in Sunderland* (2007), *Grandville* and its sequels (2009–), and *Dotter of Her Father's Eye* (2012). In 2003, William Christensen, editor-in-chief of Avatar Press, contacted Talbot about *Nightjar*, and Talbot was surprised to find he still had the script and pages. Avatar commissioned him to finish the first chapter, then reprinted it along with the script, the initial notes and an essay by Talbot in *Yuggoth Cultures*, a series dedicated to Alan Moore rarities.

Warrior #1 appeared in newsagents in March 1982, and featured the opening instalments of *Marvelman* and *V for Vendetta*, Steve Parkhouse's *Spiral Path*, and four strips written by Steve Moore: *Prester John*, *Father Shandor*, *Laser Eraser & Pressbutton* and *A True Story* (a one-off with art by Dave Gibbons). The last two pages of the magazine were dedicated to short biographies and pictures of the contributors. Alan Moore is represented by a photograph that makes him look particularly demented (see opposite page) and a profile, clearly written by Moore himself, which gave a short recap of his career to date, including the work of his pseudonyms, Curt Vile, Jill de Ray and Translucia Baboon – the latter being an identity adopted by Moore for the early eighties relaunch of The Sinister Ducks.

The second issue contained the same regular strips, with the addition of Paul Neary's *The Madman*. It had a *Marvelman* cover and a text feature on Axel Pressbutton with contributions from Moore as Curt Vile. It also included its first letters column. The letters pages of *Warrior* were a vital part of the reading experience. As he had in his fanzine days, Skinn published correspondents' full addresses, allowing comics fans to get in touch with each other directly. And the creators of the individual strips often replied directly to a specific point raised: in #6 (October 1982) Moore asked one reader who complained about the use of 'Christ' as an expletive why he hadn't complained about all the violence. It is clear that the readers, at least those who wrote letters, were keen on *Pressbutton*, *Marvelman* and *V* in roughly equal measure, and less keen on the other stories. For his part, Skinn 'always thought of *V* as a sleeper hit, like the album track which only grows on you slowly, off the back of more commercial tracks. So I very much saw *Marvelman* and *Axel* as our frontrunners.'

The first three issues of *Warrior* came out on time and to plan but did not sell as well as hoped, with Skinn later noting 'if I'd been an accountant, I'd have . . . cancelled the magazine when I saw the returns on issue one'. While *2000AD* was selling 'a rock solid 120,000 copies a week', sales of *Warrior* fluctuated but it had a reported print run of around 40,000 and, although it failed to make much of a stir across the Atlantic at first, it sold better than expected in America, with US sales accounting for a quarter of the total. Nevertheless, money was tight. Garry Leach said of his position as *Warrior*'s art director: 'That sounds pretty glamorous and high powered, doesn't it? Quality Communications ran from a sleazy little basement beneath a seedy comic shop in New Cross; a rundown low-life area just outside central London. It was festering and alarmingly cheap – which would sum up the entire operation! . . . Dez always had about two thousand reasons why he couldn't pay you that week.' It is a description which makes the 'revolutionary' *Warrior* sound remarkably like the old IPC as described by Steve Parkhouse.

Alan Moore was soon getting plenty of regular work beyond *Warrior*, but Dez Skinn was an editor who encouraged him. Moore was being noticed by *Warrior*'s readers – he was often singled out for praise by letter writers – and he retained ownership of the characters he created (he was granted part-ownership of *Marvelman*). Moore was learning, with *V for Vendetta* particularly, that the comics medium was an alchemic one, where the finished product was more than the sum of the writing and art, and that a running series could progress, adding layers of meaning and resonance.

In late August 1982, around the time *Warrior* #5 was published, Moore wrote to Skinn with suggestions for spin-off series. *Vignettes* would be set in the London of *V for Vendetta* but would tell 'little Eisneresque stories about ordinary people living in a very tough world'. *Untold Tales of the Marvelman Family* would build on the backstory of that series, with Moore suggesting 'we could do a story about Gargunza . . . maybe one describing how he came to build the FATE computer' (FATE was the all-seeing computer from *V for Vendetta*, Gargunza the evil scientist who created *Marvelman*). At this point, Moore saw the two strips as linked, and he and Steve Moore had come up with an elaborate future history that saw 'the Warpsmith takeover of Earth, the Rebellion against the Warpsmiths and their subsequent destruction, the Golden Age of Earth, the Superhero purges, the Exodus of the Marvelmen, the war between FATE and the Rhordru Makers, and so on and so on'. The story continued, in fact, beyond the far future seen in *Pressbutton*.

Only a year or so before, Alan Moore's declaration of intent in the Society of Strip Illustration round table had seemed over-ambitious and a little naïve, but he had already achieved many of those goals. Moore's 'greatest personal hope', writing a revamped *Marvelman*, had proved to be the quickest and easiest part of it.

4 SCRIPT ROBOT ALAN MOORE

> 'Script robot Moore found 2000AD to be an excellent outlet for his ideas. Amongst his work for the Mighty One: many unforgettable Future Shocks, Abelard Snazz – the Double-Decker Dome and the scrotnig series, Skizz.'
>
> 'Meet the Droids', *2000AD Annual* 1983

One of the conceits of *2000AD* is that it is edited by an alien from Betelgeuse, Tharg the Mighty, and that all the actual work is done by an army of malcontent, feckless droids – script robots, art robots, lettering robots. Over the years, occasional biographies or caricatures of individual droids have been published. Script Robot Alan Moore appeared in a poster in #322 (25 June 1983), drawn by Robin Smith (see overleaf).

The image of comics creators as production-line workers under the lash of an alien taskmaster was clearly a joke, but one that contained more than an element of truth. Comics follow a relentless schedule – weekly in the case of *2000AD* – and the creation of most entails a strict division of labour. A writer prepares a script, it is sent to an artist who draws the pages (in American comics, this task is often further split between a penciller, who prepares the layout of the page, drawing in pencil, and an inker, who draws over the pencil art in ink. The inker may have considerable leeway to add details, and is often responsible for adding backgrounds). The word balloons, captions and sound effects are added by a letterer. If it is a colour comic – unlike the vast majority of Moore's British work – a colourist prepares colour guides for the printer. All of this is overseen by an editor, who hires and fires, and who has the

right to alter the script or the art as he or she sees fit. According to Stephen Bissette, an artist who would work with Moore on *Swamp Thing* and *1963*: 'they were assembling comics like we were auto-plant workers. And that's how they saw us. I did the frame assembly, as the penciller. Alan was the car designer. John Totleben put the doors on. Tatjana Wood sprayed the paint on. You name anyone in the process, and we were assembling a car, and that car that had to be out every four weeks was the new issue.'

The arrival of computers in the late eighties allowed better communication and more flexibility at every stage, but the production line has been retained. David Lloyd thinks that this has a negative effect on the value of the final product, that 'the industry depends on the industrial process of creation, which I think is sad. It happened by accident in the old days that jobs had to be split up because they wanted to produce more and more books, so they had finishers, inkers, pencillers and everything was busted up. So in reality you can hardly describe most comics as art because the creative process is fragmented. It's craft, there's excellence in craft, but as artistic expression it falls short.' *Watchmen*'s artist, Dave Gibbons, disagrees: 'Comics is an artform. It's a collaborative artform, usually, although in certain cases the whole writing and drawing is all done by one person. It's an artform along the lines of opera or film, and I don't think there's anything second rate or anything childish about the actual form of comics. It's just that traditionally – and more so in this country than even in the States – they've been used merely to service children.'

In the early eighties, no British comic had the budget to create a large 'bank' of strips, to fund experimental work that would never see the light of day or to cultivate new talent. What editors wanted from writers were striking ideas, but what they *needed* were writers who could produce scripts that fitted the allotted page count and arrived in a workable state, to a deadline. No one was getting

rich, everyone worked for flat page rates and in most instances everything created became the intellectual property of the publisher. There were no bonus payments, royalty payments or windfalls from merchandise or other spin-offs. A writer with one strip in every issue of *2000AD* would earn about the same as a brickie.

Paradoxically, by showing us the 'script robots' and telling us a little about them, the comic gave them a human face. *2000AD* also ran a number of 'making of' features lifting the lid on the production process. Warren Ellis and Garth Ennis, writers who rose to prominence in the nineties, have both credited the same article in the *2000AD Annual 1981* describing the creation of a *Judge Dredd* strip with inspiring them to become comics writers. Young readers tend to have preferences for and loyalties to certain characters, but as they grow older, many become admirers of the work of particular artists and writers. And by putting credits on every strip, *2000AD* had enabled readers to put names to the styles of the artists who worked on *Judge Dredd* or to discover, for example, that *Slaine* and *ABC Warriors* had the same writer (Pat Mills). If a reader of *2000AD* then happened to pick up *Doctor Who Weekly* or chance upon a copy of *Warrior*, they would not see any familiar characters, but they would recognise a lot of the art styles and creators' names. The British comics industry had always been a small world, but now there was a window into it.

The life of a script robot has never been a glamorous one. Moore was a freelancer, never a salaried member of staff, and he worked in the living room of his terraced house in Northampton. He was commissioned by an editor – usually Steve MacManus at *2000AD*, Bernie Jaye at Marvel UK, Dez Skinn for *Warrior*. A writer just starting out would send a full script on spec, but after the first few commissions would progress to pitching ideas to their editor over the phone. Editors would occasionally approach writers with story ideas for them to work up. Moore would go down to London semi-regularly 'and just sort of meet the people at *2000AD*, get together for a drink with them every few months, or you could check up on stuff or talk about your new projects that were in the planning stages'.

When asked about his typical work day, Moore has said 'there isn't one', as he is normally working on a number of projects at different stages of development and each presents its own unique challenges. From the outside, however, his routine seems to have remained basically unchanged throughout his career: long days working from home, punctuated by phone calls from editors, publishers, artists, event organisers, friends and interviewers (and in the evenings, thanks to the time difference, a fresh round of phone calls from America). During the day he makes himself sandwiches, drinks a lot of tea and smokes. In 1985 he claimed: 'I get up at about eight or nine o'clock and lie there on the bed and read comics for two or three hours [laughter]. I'm not one of those hard, fascist people who sits down and says "Now, I will write". [laughter]. I'm incredibly lazy. I lie around until I feel guilty about it. [laughter].' His wife describes a far more disciplined approach, though: 'Alan gets up at eight and works till eight. He has no answering machine, so he can work as few as four hours a day, according to how many phone calls he has to answer. Alan works in silence. He really doesn't watch TV or listen to music much. He doesn't write in other people's presence.'

Moore has echoed that: 'I do need absolute quiet, but I don't get it . . . I don't have music on, or anything else on. I work in absolute silence. All I can hear is the sound of my own thoughts, and then the phone rings, you know?' Earlier in his career, he 'was listening to an awful lot of ambient music on a continuous loop while I was writing those first few John Totleben issues of *Marvelman*. I was listening to *The Plateaux of Mirror* by Brian Eno, which was one of my favorites, and *Lovely Thunder* by Harold Budd.'

When he started writing professionally, Moore used a manual typewriter and three-leafed carbon paper. It was a process that did not allow errors to be erased or TippExed out, so he would overtype any mistakes with rows of Xs. When he was done, he would handwrite any minor corrections or other notes he felt were needed. The copies were often faint and difficult to read, the paper tissue-thin. Moore usually stapled the shorter scripts. The original script and one copy were posted to the editor, who would post the copy (with any amendments) to the artist. Moore kept the second copy. Even now, he does not have an internet connection and sends and receives material by fax.

Taking to heart Brian Eno's view that an artist should not be afraid of examining their own creativity, Moore has described his philosophy and techniques a number of times – in long interviews, in discussions with other writers and most expansively in a four-part essay, *On Writing for Comics*, the first chapter of which was published in the August 1985 issue of *Fantasy Advertiser*. Then, in the mid-eighties, Moore saw writing almost purely in terms of technique, stating, 'all that is required is that one should think about the techniques that one is using, and should understand them and know where they are applicable' (twenty years later he would boil this down to the distinctly Enoesque 'think about your processes'). The implication was that he was unusual among comics writers for doing this.

Much of *On Writing for Comics* is less concerned with Moore's own approach than with criticising the bland, lazy state of the comics industry at all levels; his main target is not editorial or corporate interference so much as his fellow writers' acceptance of received wisdom. Even when writers and artists break away from the big companies, he says, the same patterns repeat themselves: 'With a very few bold exceptions, most of the creator-owned material produced by the independent companies has been almost indistinguishable from the mainstream product that preceded it. It seems to me that this demonstrates that the problem is not primarily one of working conditions or incentive; the problem is creative, and it's on a basic creative level it must be solved.' He skewers the oft-repeated industry maxim that every successful character can be summed up in fifteen words, saying with that approach 'however deep the pool of the character's soul might turn out to be, it's still only fifteen words wide', and goes on to note that 'unwritten laws and conventional wisdoms of this nature really are the banes of the industry.' The plots of comics are 'madly elaborate . . . having no relevance at all to anything other than themselves . . . plot, plot, plot, plot, plot, plot, it sounds like someone wading through mud and it very often reads like it, too'. He despairs of finding 'stories that actually have some sort of meaning in relation to the world about us, stories that reflect the nature and texture of life . . . stories that are useful in some way', and claims that even the most successful writers end up endlessly repeating themselves (as he put it later, the trap for a writer is you find a 'golden rut and plough it until you die').

Moore felt that the weak link was obvious: 'primarily over the last twenty or thirty years it's been an artist-dominated field . . . it is the writing that has let the medium down. And now you are starting to get the emergence of . . . people who do have a different sensibility regarding the writing, people who actually do – can do – stuff that has got as much power or impact as a mainstream novel or film, sometimes more so. That's what's made the difference. I think that is probably what's going to transform the medium more than anything else.'

In a later discussion of his methods, Moore would come up with a striking image when explaining that as he started to write *From Hell*, he read all sorts of books and articles by way of research:

> Obviously, these snippets never found their way into the finished *From Hell*, but they formed a part of my high-altitude mental impression of the Whitechapel events: a kind of fuzzy, low definition map, as seen through cloud where nevertheless certain prominent features of the symbolic landscape could still be seen. Rivers of theory, high points of conjecture and leylines of association. This initial mapping gave me a glimpse of the whole territory in its entirety, if not in detail. I could see what features of the narrative landscape seemed the most significant and promising, even if I couldn't provide a precise soil analysis at that point to say exactly *why* they seemed promising . . . Basically, what I'm saying is that, yes, I did have the broad shape of the whole thing in my head, with many of the details already there, before I started . . . the thing is, if that first high-altitude mapping is perceptive and accurate enough, whatever tiny surface details are unearthed upon closer inspection are bound to fit right into it somewhere.

At each subsequent stage he narrows his focus until he's establishing the minute details within individual panels. While Moore has always filled notebooks with ideas that hit him and pieces of information that he finds interesting, he initially had a 'morbid dread of research' (and little time to undertake it, working on a week-by-week schedule). As his work became longer and more complex, this began to change. By the end of the eighties, when he was writing *Brought to Light*, *From Hell* and *Big Numbers*, Moore became utterly immersed in reading up on his chosen subjects. Ten years after that, writing *The League of Extraordinary Gentlemen*, he had actively come to enjoy it.

As we saw with his initial work on *V for Vendetta*, very early on in the process Moore draws up elaborate background notes about the world the story is set in, the aim being 'to conjure a sense of environmental reality as completely and as unobtrusively as possible'. Writers should hint at the nature of the world of the story by dropping in clues in the forms of fashion, architecture, advertising and brand names. Moore has likened this to going on holiday somewhere new, where you accumulate a working knowledge of what makes a place tick without needing an omnipotent narrator to tell you.

The next stage is to decide on the shape of a story. With many of his comics assignments, the precise number of pages was set by the editor, with little or no flexibility. So, for example, when he began working in the American industry, each issue of *Swamp Thing* had to be precisely twenty-three pages. With *Future Shocks*, the length set by an editor could vary from one page to eight. Once he had a little more control, Moore would often give himself more freedom (individual chapters of *From Hell* range between eight and fifty-eight pages), but he often found it a useful discipline to limit himself (every chapter of *Lost Girls* is eight pages long). Knowing the page count, Moore takes the simple step of writing numbers down the margin of a piece of paper, one line for each page of the final story, to set out the order of events.

A trademark of Moore's work is a concern for structure: 'Back when I was starting out, I was a fetishist for structure, I think. I wanted to know where every last nut and bolt was going before I'd start the story'. This method was extremely calculated. In *On Writing for Comics* he made statements like 'the important thing is that you understand the structure of the work you are creating, whatever that structure might turn out to be' and 'it's quite possible to be inspired toward a story by having thought of some purely abstract technical device or panel progression or something', or 'a plot is the combination of environment and characters with the single element of time added to it'. Moore's description of how a joke works was positively Spock-like: 'the broad mechanisms that actually excite humour as a response and a reaction to certain stimuli.'

Most comics plotting at the time, according to Moore, was hackneyed, a straightforward chronological recounting of events. He outlined three simple strategies to make a story more interesting: starting in the middle; framing the main story in another; telling the story from a specific viewpoint or viewpoints. A great many of Moore's stories, both the shorter and longer pieces, are what he calls 'elliptical': the end of the story echoes the beginning. This takes many forms. At the end of *V for Vendetta*, Evey puts on V's mask and recruits a follower, just as V took her under his wing in the first instalment. *From Hell* has a framing sequence set years after the main events of the story. The first and last panels of *The Killing Joke* are identical pictures of raindrops falling into a puddle. Book One of *Marvelman* ends as it started, with the image of a truck on a motorway and the same caption.

Before the eighties, comics were traditionally ephemeral, designed to be read once and thrown away, or to be swapped with another. Alan Moore, though, was keen to write stories that actively demanded you take a second look. As critic Iain Thomson has said, *Watchmen* 'can only be read by being re-read', since some of the details and connections can't possibly be made out on first reading. In *Watchmen*, re-reading is structured into the narrative itself. The last issue ends with a character poised to pick up Rorschach's diary and read the opening captions of the first issue.

The eighties saw a 180-degree shift in attitude. Since then, comics fans have routinely referred to the comics they own as their 'collection', and have been encouraged to see each comic as a piece of mass-produced fine art. They have agreed strict criteria for the grading of the physical condition of a comic, so that a Fine back issue can cost many times less than a Near Mint because the cover has a slight tear or fold, or the staples are a little loose. In this climate, ever the iconoclast, Moore designed *Promethea* #12 (February 2001) so that the art flows from one page to the next, the whole issue consisting of one long panel; it can only really be appreciated if you prise the staples off and lay out the separated pages (the Deluxe Edition of the *Promethea* graphic novel reprints it as one fold-up page which, when unfurled, is sixteen feet long). The final twist is that the last page flows into the first – so anyone who has laid out the comic to form one panel can then join up the ends to create a loop. Even more ambitious, the final issue of *Promethea* could be read as a comic book and then taken apart and reassembled as a double-sided poster: 'I'd originally had the idea for that 32nd issue of *Promethea* about a year before in the midst of a full-on psychedelic magical ritual . . . the final issue will somehow fold out into this double-sided psychedelic poster but you'll still somehow be able to read it as a comic and this'll be great and people will carry me around in a gold sedan and shower me with confetti wherever I go. And then, of course, I straightened up and realised that I'd got no idea how to do this, so I sat down with Steve Moore, who is often a great help at times like this when I've bragged about something that I'm going to do and then I have to actually sit down and do it.'

Moore's emphasis on formal structure perhaps peaked in 1988, when he drew up a giant grid for all twelve issues of the series *Big Numbers* on a piece of A1 paper (594 x 841mm), outlining the entire sequence of events and the role each of the nearly four dozen characters would play in each issue. He has confessed that 'one of the main reasons I did it was to frighten other writers. Just for the look on Neil Gaiman's face, you know.' He now claims to have a more relaxed approach to planning his work, and says he was 'riding bareback' on the titles he wrote for America's Best Comics (which were published 1999–2005) in order to keep things 'fresh and lively'.

Once he has the structure, Moore works on getting from one scene to the next. 'The movement between one scene and another is one of the most tricky and intriguing elements of the whole writing process . . . The transitions between scenes are the weak points in the spell that you are attempting to cast over [readers]. One way or another, as a writer, you'll have to come up with your own repertoire of tricks and devices.'

It is fair to say that Moore would come to over-employ one trick: overlapping dialogue so that a new scene starts with the last line of dialogue from the previous scene. As Grant Morrison has noted:

> This self-reflected cross-referral of image and text reached fever pitch as *Watchmen* unfolded: a drawing of Dr Manhattan telekinetically looping a tie around his neck for a rare clothed appearance in a TV interview had his estranged lover Laurie Jupiter . . . ask in voiceover 'how did everything get so tangled up?', while a scene in which she crushed a mugger's balls in her grip was cross-cut with another character's words to Doctor Manhattan: 'Am I starting to make you feel uncomfortable?' . . . this relentless self-awareness gave *Watchmen* a dense and tangible clarity.

Those examples, though, are meant to be deliberately jarring. Elsewhere, Moore employed the technique to more subtle ends, switching scenes with an echo of a panel composition, or even just the use of the same colour, providing a smoother segue.

And once we get to the layout of individual pages, Moore's advice is straightforward: 'The simplest and most mechanical way to understand comic book pacing is to work out how long a reader will spend looking at a panel.' The creators of a comic can control that reading speed by altering the levels of information in each panel – the more detailed the art or the more dialogue it contains, generally, the longer it takes to read. Many comic creators fail to recognise, for example, that a fast-moving fight scene will be slowed down if the antagonists are making lengthy speeches to each other. The example of *Watchmen* (along with Frank Miller's *Dark Knight Returns*) would prove highly influential on the superhero genre, and nowhere was this more obvious than the influence the series had on the way fight scenes were portrayed. Very soon after *Watchmen* was published, superhero comics had all but abandoned the lengthy monologues and parades of thought balloons that had previously cluttered fight scenes. It was a quick fix, one that creators and editors could easily implement.

Once he has an idea of the structure and transitions, Moore draws extremely rough thumbnail images of each page, entirely for his benefit and generally indecipherable by anyone else. These allow him to see the layout of panels on the page and the pacing of his story: 'I can then transform these incomprehensible scribbles into quite lavish and detailed panel descriptions.' This was never an entirely cold, cerebral process. Moore has talked about acting out the parts, adopting, for example, the hunched pose and snarling voice of the Demon. 'I think to write emotionally with any real conviction, you have to work yourself into a self-induced state of near-hysteria, emotionally speaking. It's a bit like method acting, and it takes a lot out of you.' He then writes out the script, first as a draft in longhand using 'biro and scraps of paper' (for prose pieces, he generally goes straight to his keyboard). When those notes are done, he types them up. He very rarely redrafts his work:

> you have to understand that anything you've ever read of mine was probably a first draft. I don't do rewrites because . . . god that's boring! It's generally been such a grind writing the thing in the first place that the idea of rewriting it is a nightmare. Also, if I was a novelist and I get to chapter eight and suddenly realise that there was something that I wanted to introduce back in chapter one, I could do that, but if you're a comic writer, then by the time you're up to chapter eight, chapter one had already been published for about three months. The deadlines are really fast and furious, you haven't really got time to do multiple rewrites on a story, and it's not possible to go back and amend or fine tune earlier chapters.

This is a habit Moore has retained, even when he has had the time to redraft. With his first novel, *Voice from the Fire*, 'the first eleven chapters were pretty much exactly as they were when I first wrote them, other than a word here or there that got changed'. Moore stresses that this first draft is 'a very deliberate and deliberated over first draft'.

One of the legends about Alan Moore is that his scripts are immensely long. And, like many legends, it has a basis in truth.

The form a comics script may take varies tremendously, but can be boiled down to a handful of basic styles. The most common way of writing comics in the US in the early eighties was 'Marvel Method', the house style at Marvel Comics (it was also used at other companies, although never became popular at arch-rivals DC). The writer gave a very basic plot summary, usually no more than a paragraph per page of finished comic book, so that the script for a comic of around twenty pages might be three pages long. The artist would then decide on the layout of every page and the composition of individual panels. Once the artwork was completed, the writer would come up with dialogue and captions to fit the pictures. Many artists, in particular, favour working this way. Mike Wieringo, who drew for both Marvel and DC in the nineties, said: 'I prefer using the Marvel method because it gives me more input as opposed to DC's full script method, where you're sort of just a hired hand asked to draw the writer's vision and not able to put any of your own in it.' That said, on longer or more acclaimed runs, artists have often come to criticise it, because they feel the writer gets disproportionate credit for work where the artist has made so many of the major storytelling decisions. The Marvel Method has fallen out of favour, but still has its champions. As Howard Mackie, another Marvel stalwart, wrote: 'Just to drive the point into the ground . . . all of the favorite comic books done by Marvel in the 60's, 70's, 80's or 90's . . . all the comics that fans and pros reference . . . were done using the Marvel Method of plot followed by script. There had to have been SOMETHING to it.'

The approach favoured at DC Comics and most British comics publishers – and by Alan Moore) – is 'Full Script', where the writer describes the page layout and the composition of each individual panel, and the script spells out the dialogue, captions, thought bubbles and sound effects. The decline of the Marvel Method was in no small part due to Moore's success and the spotlight he placed on the quality of writing in comics, alongside the fact that other Britons like Neil Gaiman, Grant Morrison and Warren Ellis, who went on to work in America, directly emulated his style of scripting. Moore was always dismissive of the Marvel approach: 'If the artist has just got a plot that says "Daredevil talks to so-and-so on this page and at the end, so-and-so will come in", then from that the artist won't know what expression to put on the mouth. So if he draws a chap grinning and then Chris Claremont comes along and gives a huge balloon to it saying "my wife and family have just died . . ."'

Claremont was the writer of the best-selling comic on the market, *The Uncanny X-Men*, and in May 1985 he and Moore were interviewed together in London by the fanzine *Speakeasy*. The readers of *Comics Buyer's Guide* had just voted Moore second in the Best Comic Writer category – and Claremont had won. Moore was evidently a little put out by this. He had criticised Claremont's writing a number of times in the past. Three years before, as Curt Vile, he had told *Warrior* he parodied *The X-Men* in *The Stars My Degradation* because 'Chris Claremont's got a whole string of Eagle Awards and I haven't got any. There's no justice in that. I must admit, though, I'm not over-enamoured with his writing, and I thought there were enough absurdities in it to get a bit of mileage for some sort of cheap shots and low-minded 'umour.'

MOORE: This comes down to one of the big differences between me and Chris, beyond any stylistic differences. It's purely in the way we work, in that Chris writes plots and then writes the dialogue, and I write a full script.

CLAREMONT: Just because I'm a lazy sod!

MOORE: The only difference is that I wouldn't like to do it your way you know because of the amount of control. I write very, very full scripts.

. . .

CLAREMONT: The conscious decision I made was to sacrifice a measure of that control for the advantage of the artist's contributory creativity. I find when I am working with someone like Frank (Miller) or Walt Simonson or (John) Byrne or Paul Smith or John Bolton, to name just a few, that there is a barrier: their suggestions, their thoughts of pacing. They know better how to visually construct a scene than I do.

MOORE: My attitude is the same as Chris's. I value serendipity, and I value the artist's input a lot and with every script I have written, I write a full script and then say 'throw it out'.

The skill of the Full Script approach is in choosing the best moment to depict, and in relating each panel to those around it. It is a format a lot like scripts for television or cinema. As Moore noted, 'comics are spoken of in terms of the cinema, and indeed most of the working vocabulary that I use every day in panel directions to whichever artist I happen to be working with is derived entirely from the cinema. I talk in terms of close-ups, long shots, zooms, and pans'. Something about this nagged at him, though. 'If you see comics only in terms of cinema, then all it can be is a kind of cinema that doesn't move.'

Ultimately both the Marvel Method and Full Script are meant to produce compelling stories, and whichever approach is used comics will always be collaborations between a writer and an artist. There's no right or wrong way to format a script. A team can employ the Marvel Method to create experimental, intricate work or derive a linear, plodding comic from a full script. The reason British comics prefer full scripts and Marvel Comics developed their own method was nothing to do with concern for the quality of the finished result, and everything to do with the circumstances of production.

Marvel's 'Bullpen' was actually a studio in Manhattan where the writers and artists worked together and comics were assembled. When the company launched its range of superhero comics in the 1960s, publisher Stan Lee oversaw them all. They were drawn by established artists like Jack Kirby and Steve Ditko, who had a genius for strong graphic design and dynamic images. Their version of the method was quite casual: Lee would occasionally not even write down the plot summary, instead simply spelling out its events in a brief conversation or phone call, while for his part, Kirby has admitted he would draw individual pages of fight scenes and shuffle them around or retain them for the next issue. As Marvel expanded, bringing in more writers and artists, the method became more formal, with an editor checking the plot summary and adding notes before passing it on to the artist, but the basic principle remained that the artist had a huge amount of involvement in how the story was told. The method perfectly suited an arrangement where the artist could call the writer over from the other side of the room to ask if the picture he was working on was what the writer had in mind. By the early eighties many artists were working from home or their own studios, but the Bullpen still existed as a large, central room at Marvel's offices where final amendments were made to pages.

Creating British comics was always a far more compartmentalised, one-way process than it is even at American companies like DC. The writer's job was finished once he sent in his script, the editor having assigned an artist to draw it. And like the writers, the artists were freelancers working from home. They were expected to follow the script, although they had licence to make changes if it would give the pages more impact. The final stage, the lettering – when the speech bubbles were added – was usually done at the publisher, with editors routinely cutting out or adding captions to fit the art if they felt the storytelling needed improvement. At this stage, artwork could be altered by someone on staff. (Images involving smoking and drinking were often redrawn, as were pictures deemed too gory or sexy.) Writers and artists wouldn't always see the finished pages, or know what had been changed, until they were published. In the interests of diplomacy, if major changes had been made, a writer might be informed, but could do little about it except ask for the strip to go out under a pseudonym.

By the time of his later *Future Shocks*, Moore would often know who his artist was going to be, and could write to their strengths. Knowing he would be working with, say, Dave Gibbons, an artist who specialised in panels that were crammed with detail, he came up with 'Chronocops' (*2000AD* #310, April 1983), an intricate time-travel story where the same events recurred with slight variations, as indicated by some clever sight gags.

For longer projects, although editors wanted to remain party to any discussions, Moore and his regular artist would have long telephone calls and exchange bundles of notes and sketches. They could take the opportunity of comics marts and conventions (usually in London) to meet over drinks, and would occasionally even visit each other at home. The reality, though, was that once a series was underway, maintaining a weekly schedule took up a lot of time, particularly for the artist. There were few people, particularly those early in their career, who worked in comics full time. Alan Davis, for example, saw drawing *Captain Britain* as 'a bit of extra cash and a lot of fun' and had a day job working in a warehouse. Jamie Delano was a taxi driver, Eddie Campbell a metal fabricator. It left little free time in their schedules. If an artist fell behind, he would be replaced, not always temporarily – though this only happened to Moore once, when Garry Leach stepped down as the artist on *Marvelman*.

As a rule of thumb, then, the only opportunity a British comics writer had to communicate with their artist was through the script itself, and so anything the writer wanted to get across needed to be in his script. It is fair to say that Alan Moore has taken this to an extreme. While most comics scripts are no-nonsense descriptions of what the writer would like to see in each panel, Moore's are often far more discursive, explaining the exact effect he is trying to achieve, framing things in terms of longer-term planning, listing his influences and making jokes. The most obvious attribute of his scripts is that they are extremely long. For example, here is the first panel of *The Killing Joke*, published in 1988 with art by Brian Bolland:

And here is Alan Moore's script for that panel:

PAGE 1, PANEL 1:

WELL, I'VE CHECKED THE LANDING GEAR, FASTENED MY SEATBELT, SWALLOWED MY CIGAR IN A SINGLE GULP AND GROUND MY SCOTCH AND SODA OUT IN THE ASHTRAY PROVIDED, SO I SUPPOSE WE'RE ALL SET FOR TAKE OFF. BEFORE WE GO SCREECHING OFF INTO THOSE ANGRY CREATIVE SKIES FROM WHICH WE MAY BOTH WELL RETURN AS BLACKENED CINDERS, I SUPPOSE A FEW PRELIMINARY

NOTES ARE IN ORDER, SO SIT BACK WHILE I RUN THROUGH THEM WITH ACCOMPANYING HAND MOVEMENTS FROM OUR CHARMING STEWARDESS IN THE CENTRE AISLE.

FIRSTLY, SINCE I'M NOT ENTIRELY SURE HOW THESE GRAPHIC NOVELS ARE SET OUT, MIGHT I SUGGEST THAT IF THERE ARE END-PAPERS OF ANY KIND THEY MIGHT BE DESIGNED SO AS TO FLOW INTO AND OUT OF THE FIRST AND LAST PANELS OF THE STORY. SINCE BOTH THE FIRST AND LAST PANELS CONTAIN A SIMPLE CLOSE-UP IMAGE OF THE SURFACE OF A PUDDLE RIPPLED BY RAIN, THEN MAYBE A SIMPLE ENLARGEMENT OF A BLACK-AND-WHITE RIPPLE EFFECT TO THE POINT WHERE IT BECOMES HUGE AND ABSTRACT WOULD BE IN ORDER? AS WITH ALL MY VISUAL SUGGESTIONS, BOTH HERE AND IN THE PANEL DESCRIPTIONS BELOW, PLEASE DON'T FEEL BOUND BY THEM IN ANYWAY. THEY'RE ONLY MEANT AS WORKABLE SUGGESTIONS, SO IF YOU CAN SEE A BETTER SET OF PICTURES THAN I CAN (WHICH I'D SAY IS QUITE LIKELY, ALL THINGS CONSIDERED) THEN PLEASE FEEL FREE TO THROW OUT WHAT I'VE COME UP WITH AND SUBSTITUTE WHATEVER YOU FEEL LIKE. I WANT YOU TO FEEL AS COMFORTABLE AND UNRESTRICTED AS POSSIBLE DURING THE SEVERAL MONTHS OF YOUR BITTERLY BRIEF MORTAL LIFESPAN THAT YOU'LL SPEND WORKING ON THIS JOB, SO JUST LAY BACK AND MELLOW OUT. TAKE YOUR SHOES AND SOCKS OFF. FIDDLE AROUND INBETWEEN YOUR TOES. NOBODY CARES. ANOTHER GENERAL NOTE WOULD REGARD STYLE AND PRESENTATION. I'VE ALREADY GONE INTO THIS IN THE SYNOPSIS, SO I WON'T DWELL ON IT TOO MUCH HERE, EXCEPT TO UNDERLINE A COUPLE OF THE MORE IMPORTANT POINTS, ONE SUCH POINT WOULD BE OUR TREATMENT OF THE BATMAN AND HIS MYTHOS, INCLUDING THE BATMOBILE, THE BATCAVE AND WHATEVER OTHER ELEMENTS MIGHT FIND THEMSELVES INCLUDED IN THE STORY BEFORE ITS END. AS I SEE IT, THIS STORY ISN'T SET IN ANY SPECIFIC TIME PERIOD. WE DIDN'T SHOW ANY CALENDARS, OR ANY NEWSPAPERS WITH HEADLINES CLOSE ENOUGH TO READ THE DATE. THE ARCHITECTURE AND THE SETTINGS IN GENERAL THAT WE SEE ARE EITHER OBVIOUSLY OLD AND DATED, AS IN THE CARNIVAL SEQUENCES, OR HAVE AN AMBIGUOUS SORT OF LOOK TO THEM THAT'S BOTH FUTURISTIC AND ANTIQUE AT THE SAME TIME, AS WITH THE FLEISCHER-SUPERMAN/LANG'S METROPOLIS LOOK THAT I SEE OUR

VERSION OF GOTHAM CITY AS HAVING, AT LEAST ON IT'S UPPER LEVELS. THE LOWER AND SEEDIER LEVELS OF GOTHAM ARE MORE INCLINED TOWARDS A TERRITORY SOMEWHERE BETWEEN DAVID LYNCH AND THE CABINET OF DR CALIGARI, ALL PATCHES OF RUST AND MOULD AND HISSING STEAM AND DAMP, GLISTENING ALLEYWAYS. I IMAGINE THIS STRIP AS HAVING AN OPPRESSIVELY DARK FILM NOIR FEEL TO IT, WITH A LOT OF UNPLEASANTLY TANGIBLE TEXTURES, SUCH AS YOU HABITUALLY RENDER SO DELIGHTFULLY, TO GIVE THE WHOLE THING A REALLY INTENSE FEELING OF PALPABLE UNEASE AND CRAZINESS. SINCE I KNOW THAT YOU LIKE USING LARGE AREAS OF BLACK ANYWAY, THEN MIGHT I SUGGEST THAT WE USE THE DARK AND SHADOWY NATURE OF OUR BACKDROPS AND THE BLACKNESS OF THE BATMAN'S COSTUME TO GIVE US AS MANY INTERESTING PRIMARILY BLACK COMPOSITIONS AS WE CAN GET AWAY WITH? THE FACT THAT THE JOKER IS SUCH A BLEACHED AND BLOODLESS WHITE PLAYS OFF INTERESTINGLY AGAINST THIS, I RECKON, SO PLEASE FEEL FREE TO GO COMPLETELY LOOPY WITH THE QUINK ON THIS ONE. AS FAR AS THE CHARACTERS THEMSELVES GO, I'LL DESCRIBE THEM IN DETAIL WHEN THEY MAKE THEIR APPEARANCES, BUT MY ONLY GENERAL NOTE WOULD BE THAT LIKE THE LANDSCAPE AND THE VARIOUS PROPS, THEY HAVE A SORT OF TIMELESS AND MYTHIC QUALITY TO THEM WHICH DOESN'T FIX THEM FIRMLY IN ANY ONE AGE RANGE OR TIME PERIOD. THE JOKER LOOKS EITHER OLD OR BADLY DEPRAVED, BUT THEN HE'S ALWAYS LOOKED THAT WAY. THE BATMAN IS BIG AND GRIM AND OLDER THAN WE ARE, BECAUSE AS I REMEMBER THE BATMAN HE'S ALWAYS BEEN BIGGER AND OLDER THAN I AM AND I'LL FIGHT ANY MAN THAT SAYS DIFFERENT. GIVEN THIS TIMELESS AND MYTHIC QUALITY, IT ALSO STRIKES ME THAT THERE ARE CERTAIN ELEMENTS OF THIS STORY THAT HAVE STRONG OPERATIC ELEMENTS. BOTH THE BATMAN AND THE JOKER HAVE A POWERFUL OPERATIC QUALITY TO THEIR APPEARANCE IN THAT THE JOKER IS AN EXTREME VERSION OF THE HARLEQUIN FIGURE WITH THE BATMAN'S CAPE AND MASK LOOKING LIKE SOMETHING STRAIGHT OUT OF DIE FLEDERMAUS. I DUNNO WHY I MENTION THIS EXCEPT TO UNDERLINE THE SORT OF GRAND EMOTIONAL INTENSITY I WANT THIS BOOK TO HAVE WITH BOTH THE BATMAN AND THE JOKER BECOMING POWERFUL AND PRECISE SYMBOLIC FIGURES IN A NIGHTMARISH AND ALMOST ABSTRACT LANDSCAPE. ANYWAY, BEFORE I WANDER OFF INTO A COMPLETELY IMPENETRABLE AESTHETIC FOG I SUPPOSE

WE OUGHT TO ROLL OUR SLEEVES UP AND GET STRAIGHT DOWN TO BUSINESS WITHOUT FURTHER ADO.

THIS FIRST PAGE AND A COUPLE OF THE SUBSEQUENT ONES HAVE NINE PANELS APIECE, ALBEIT WITH VERY LITTLE OR NO DIALOGUE TO CLUTTER THEM UP. I WANT THE SILENCE AND THE METRONOME-LIKE VISUAL BEAT THAT THE PANELS WILL HAVE TO CREATE A SENSE OF TENSION AND INTRIGUE AND SUSPENSE WITH WHICH TO DRAG THE READER INTO THE STORY, WHILE STILL LEAVING US ENOUGH ROOM TO SET UP ALL THE NARRATIVE AND ATMOSPHERIC ELEMENTS THAT WE WANT TO ESTABLISH. IN THIS FIRST PANEL, WE HAVE A TIGHT CLOSE-UP OF THE SURFACE OF A PUDDLE. (SEE? AND THERE WAS YOU ALL WORRIED THAT I WOULDN'T GIVE YOU ANYTHING FASCINATING TO DRAW.) WE ARE SO CLOSE TO THE PUDDLE AS TO SEE IT ONLY AS AN ALMOST ABSTRACT IMAGE OF WIDENING RIPPLES SPREADING ACROSS A SHADOWY AND BLACK LIQUID SURFACE. IT IS NIGHT TIME, AND THE RIPPLES THAT WE SEE IN THE FOREGROUND ARE CAUSED BY LARGE DROPLETS OF RAIN THAT FALL THROUGH THE FOREGROUND IN DIAGONAL SLASHES. MAYBE WE CAN SEE ONE DROPLET AT ITS PRECISE MOMENT OF IMPACT WITH THE PUDDLE, SO CLOSE ARE WE TO IT. ALTHOUGH I DON'T SUPPOSE THAT THIS INFORMATION WILL MAKE MUCH DIFFERENCE TO THIS CURRENT PANEL, FOR YOUR FUTURE REFERENCE IT IS MID-NOVEMBER AND BITTERLY COLD. HERE, ALL WE SEE IS THE RAIN SPLASHING INTO THE PUDDLE AND THE SILVERY WHITE RIPPLES SPREADING OUT ACROSS THE DARKNESS.

No Dialogue.

Moore believes his record is a ten-page description of a two-page spread in *Promethea* . . . and that was one of the few times he was forced into a rewrite. The pages depicted characters having a circular conversation while walking along a Möbius strip, but a miscommunication meant artist J.H. Williams placed the twist the wrong way round, so the original dialogue did not fit the art. Rather than have the artist redraw the pages, Moore rewrote the dialogue.

Each issue of *Watchmen* had twenty-eight pages of comic strip (except the final issue, which had thirty-two). According to Dave Gibbons, the *Watchmen* scripts were:

#1: 91 pages

#2: 90 pages

#3: 100 pages

#4: 84 pages

#5: 106 pages

#6: 91 pages

#7: 111 pages

#8: 110 pages

#9: 53 pages

#10: 65 pages

#11: 78 pages

#12: 53 pages

As this indicates, Moore's scripts for succeeding instalments tend to be shorter and more functional. Eddie Campbell has suggested that, on the flipside of that, 'Alan's speed of production tends to trail off towards the end of a project so that the artist is receiving the pages one at a time'. This has led to suspicion, and in a couple of cases open accusation, on the part of some artists that Moore does not share, to the same degree, their long-term commitment to a series. Though, it seems fair to acknowledge that even if Moore begins each project with a ferocious burst of activity and creativity that later cools off, that is probably to be expected once a series is underway and the tone and design work are settled.

With only a few exceptions, Moore's basic method, from the artist's vantage point, has looked the same throughout his career: he identifies for himself the strengths and tastes of an artist (what he thinks they will enjoy drawing), brainstorms with them a few times (often in letters, faxes and long telephone calls), phones to agree a rough outline for an issue, then goes off and types up a full script which ends up far, far longer than the artist had been expecting.

It is a running joke among many of the artists who have worked with Moore that the first question they'll be asked at a signing or convention is 'What's Alan Moore like to work with?' – as Eddie Campbell notes, 'I know what they really want to hear is one of those anecdotes that make him appear windswept and interesting and just a little eccentric.' But the length of Moore's scripts is another perennial question those artists find themselves fielding. And many have admitted feeling overwhelmed at first. Dave Gibbons quickly mastered a technique to cope: 'What I tend to do is read the script very carefully . . . and then what I like to do is to mark the script up with highlighters, so that I can separate the wheat from the chaff, so that I can have the stuff that's really essential to the job of drawing the story separated from the asides and things, and to separate the lettering out as well, so that slowly from an impenetrable mass of grey typescript we get some sort of order and some sort of graphic sense to the whole thing.'

A few artists have not been able to clear the first hurdle of understanding the demands of the script. In 1994, Moore wrote the first issue of a series originally called *Swordstone*, later renamed *War Child*, for Rob Liefeld at Image. Set in a near-future America after the government had collapsed and been replaced by criminal organisations, it featured a fascist biker gang, the Weimar Knights, fighting the Magical Mafia. But the series never materialised, at least in part because Liefeld could not find an artist able to draw what Moore had written: 'A couple of the artists I gave it to handed it back. The first ten pages is some of the most difficult, visually, it's hard to crack . . . There's someone standing atop a building, looking in through the window at a certain angle, while the person is sitting doing their hair looking at themselves in the mirror . . . and the panel descriptions, you go, how do I shoot this? I could shoot it with a camera, but like all the storyboards? It's just very difficult.' Most, though, say that Moore's style, rather than being impenetrable, prescriptive, bullying or limiting, makes for a far more interesting job than a purely functional script does. Stephen Bissette says:

> They were like long, narrative letters to the cartoonist. And they were playful in a lot of ways, too. We did a two-part zombie story that was set in the antebellum South and Alan's script for the first page of the first issue, it was a page where you're underground and you're looking at a body in a coffin. And in every panel description, Alan had a beetle family. He had a description to me of the beetle family, that these two beetles are on the body, and they're arguing. Now this is nothing I was supposed to draw, it was just like a joke. And at the sixth panel, he said 'I've decided to kill the beetles. They don't have any character potential, and there's no future for them in this comic series.' So Alan's scripts were fun to read! But they were also these elaborate blueprints of

not just what was happening on each page and panel, but where it was going to go. Like 'This object is here because on page 22, it's going to come back in. So be sure to emphasise it.' And it was unusual at that time to have scripts not just of that length and that detail, but scripts that carefully thought out.

John Totleben, who worked with Moore on *Swamp Thing* and *Miracleman*, agrees: 'He was really clear. Alan is the kind of writer who pretty much nails everything down. There's really no guessing in terms of what has to be done in a panel from an artist's standpoint. He has a pretty good visual sense of how to move the story along with images and what will fit and what won't work. That's something that some writers tend to lose sight of'.

Moore calls the process 'collaboration', and it clearly involves two creative people bringing their talents to a project, but it is not always the two-way exchange of ideas that word implies. David Lloyd felt his work on *V for Vendetta* in the *Warrior* days was truly collaborative, but that changed when Moore came to finish the series for DC, mainly because of Moore's workload:

it was to do with the fact that the last three issues were written in one chunk. One of the best things about it when we were doing it for *Warrior* is that we were doing it step by step and, in fact, when we started we didn't have any idea how it was going to end. We didn't know how it was going to develop and in fact it developed very organically through suggestions and chats we were having. Alan would write a synopsis of the first book, we'd talk about that, I'd say what I liked and didn't like and what we could maybe change and this that and the other. I would get scripts month by month. I'd make suggestions and sometimes we'd argue about those but mostly not. Most of the things I changed were frame breakdowns, pacing things.

The point is it grew organically. There was a course change in the middle of *V for Vendetta*. An accidental change of course. Those things couldn't happen with the work for DC ... There were no real chats, no discussion about any of it. I remember him calling me after I got it and asking what did I think. It was great, of course it was, very good. But I felt sad it was a done deal, there was none of that chat. There was none of that organic ... it was very like being in a band and jamming, and incredibly enjoyable. And the great thing about *Warrior* is that it was six to eight pages a month. Alan would not write the script for the next episode until he'd seen the last one, and he would be inspired by things that happened.

Eddie Campbell was the artist on *From Hell* for ten years and ended up self-publishing the collected edition, but doesn't seem to see it as a true collaboration:

> it's Alan's book, I'm just illustrating it. It comes in as always horrifying, I try to take the horror out of it, try to play this real deadpan … it kind of works, actually. They just produced a book of Alan's scripts, in a ninety dollar hardback, I did some spot illustrations for it, but it's really interesting to read because Alan's one of the most interesting writers in comics. In an Alan Moore script he *describes* it, his prose is unbelievable. Any other writer of comics says 'in this panel it is raining'. But Alan says 'the rain beats out in staccato morse code the rhythms of a dreary Russian novel'. It's raining. I make it rain. But Alan's scripts do that all the time, they're just so dense with poetic metaphor, they're a great read, and none of it ever gets on to the page. It's just for my benefit, to help me visualise the picture.

Rather than 'jamming', a better musical analogy might be that the artist is a musician interpreting the work of a songwriter. Aware that his own drawing skills are limited – certainly compared with the professional artists he's worked with – Moore has often stressed that an 'artist will almost certainly have visual sensibilities fifty times more sound and reliable than your own'. His philosophy about his scripts is that 'I give the artists the freedom to change them, because my ideas might not always be the most inspired. But my ideas will work as a basic place to start from, or to fall back upon. If they can't think of anything better, my way of doing it will work.' He had formed this opinion early enough to say in 1981, 'It doesn't really bother me unduly that such and such an artist might have decided to do a number of frames differently to the way I've specified in the script. As far as I'm concerned the only important consideration is whether the artist enjoyed the script and had fun translating it into pictures. If this is the case then nine times out of ten you'll get a good story roll off the conveyor belt.'

Campbell was one artist who was not afraid to bring his own spin to the material. In one sequence for *From Hell* (for Chapter Five, page 26), for example, Moore's script had the direction 'NOW WE REVERSE ANGLES SO THAT IN THE

FOREGROUND WE CAN SEE POLLY, SITTING IN PROFILE TO US'. It used the grammar of cinema, not of comic strips. Campbell drew the scene differently: 'My idea was to take "cutting" away and replace it with a keen observation of body language. In order to see subtle interactions between two bodies, the leanings toward, the leanings away, the slight turnings, superior straightenings, lookings down, lookings away, while not necessarily leaning the same way, lookings inwards, subtle changes in the emotional temperature, but instinctively dealing with it and not categorising it like this, etc, etc . . . then the two bodies need to be seen in each and all of the pictures.' In the book *From Hell Companion* (2013) Campbell outlines examples of how he interpreted the scripts and notes Moore's objections to the changes, which the writer seems to have limited to sarcastic asides in subsequent strips.

Across the comics industry, writer/artist partnerships have broken down, sometimes very acrimoniously and spectacularly, over the directions of stories, who first came up with a particular idea, the quality of the work or perceived disparity in the commitment to a project. This tends to come with great success – Stan Lee fell out with Jack Kirby in the sixties, Chris Claremont with John Byrne when they worked together on *The Uncanny X-Men* in the eighties.

Moore gets a lot of attention, and so a lot of credit. It's all too easy to give primacy to the writer, to fall into the shorthand of describing 'Alan Moore comics', 'Moore's work', his co-creator as 'Alan Moore's artist', or to see the artists as interchangeable components. Articles about Moore frequently don't acknowledge the artists' existence, for instance: 'He jolted the comics world with *Watchmen* and a dramatic updating of Batman in *The Killing Joke*. Three of his works – *From Hell*, *The League of Extraordinary Gentlemen* and *V for Vendetta* – have been made into films, and he has disavowed them all. On *Vendetta*, he went so far as to take his name off the credits.'

Even praise for the artists can be phrased in a way that underplays their contribution, merely crediting them with following Moore's instructions particularly adeptly. It would be natural enough if his artists resented this, but most genuinely don't seem to. This may be because even by the mid-eighties, artists knew what they were getting into when they agreed to work with Moore. It may be because artists recognise that working with Moore spurs them on to produce some of their best work. Perhaps it is because Moore himself takes pains to counterbalance a focus on him, saying as early as 1984: 'It annoys me when people talk about "Alan Moore's *V for Vendetta*" or "Alan Moore's *Marvelman*" and I'm not going to enjoy hearing about "Alan Moore's *Swamp Thing*". I can't claim to be an individual artist in my own right. The end result, the strip you see on the page, is the meeting between me and the artist. That's where the creation is.' Moore is commonly effusive about the art. So, early on in his career, he singled out John Stokes' work on the *Doctor Who* strip 'Stardeath' (*Doctor Who Monthly* #47, December 1980) for praise: 'Everything I asked for was in there, no matter how ridiculous or time-consuming, and as an additional bonus lots of little details had been squeezed into the backgrounds which contributed greatly to the old-fashioned space opera atmosphere that I'd been aiming for.' At other times, he has been happy to give the artist credit for salvaging something from his own lacklustre writing, saying for example, '*The Killing Joke* is another thing that I'm rather embarrassed by. I mean it's a wonderful piece of work by Brian Bolland, but for my part, I don't think the story's anything spectacular.' It can't be stressed often enough how many of the major decisions that make projects like *V for Vendetta*, *Swamp Thing*, *Watchmen* and *From Hell* so successful come from the artist.

Perhaps this is why, even though Alan Moore has a reputation for being difficult to work with, his 'creative differences' tend to be with the management at his publishers or with rival writers. Moore has written for well over a hundred artists and – as far as we know – very few of those relationships have broken down while a project is running. That's not to say that he's *never* had a dispute with a co-creator. An entire chapter of *V for Vendetta* went unpublished because David Lloyd felt it wasn't up to standard. Stephen Bissette did not want superheroes in *Swamp Thing*. But those disputes always seem to have been relatively amicable. Moore *has* fallen out with a number of his artists – including Bissette – but it's always been over business issues, and long after the project has concluded.

In a career so far spanning around thirty-five years, Moore has publicly blamed his artist for problems with a project precisely three times. The first, as he noted in his 1981 Society of Strip Illustration interview, was Walter Howarth's work on the *Future Shock* story 'Southern Comfort'. The second was Bill Sienkiewicz on *Big Numbers* (1990), a major work set in a town closely resembling Northampton (and self-published by Moore), which ground to a halt after just two issues. Sienkiewicz and Moore had previously worked together on *Brought to Light*

(1988), an extremely dense and visually complex project. Moore had contributed the introduction to the *Bill Sienkiewicz Sketchbook*, saying 'What I have come to appreciate more fully is the breadth of his talent . . . Bill has worried at the work in question until he finds that part of it that seems most central in the light of his individual vision.' The artist had a great deal of trouble, though, with Moore's scripts for *Big Numbers*. Moore's side of the story is: 'I still don't know what the problem was but he couldn't do the work. Now why that should be I don't know. The two issues he did were beautiful – they're amongst the best work he's ever done. Bill liked the idea of *Big Numbers* and respected the cutting-edge aspect of its publication . . . the problem seemed to be having to draw all these miserable terraced streets and Northampton people just drove him mad, or at least it was boring for him.'

Sienkiewicz has explained that he was relying on photo reference, and was finding it hard to wrangle his cast: '*Big Numbers* started to become a money pit. Too much time and effort was involved in getting the reference, leaving very little time to create the artwork. Time. The ultimate tool. The ultimate foe. But with *Big Numbers* one of the demands – prerequisites – I'd placed upon myself was to work almost exclusively from the model as possible. I was going for as great a degree of illustrative photographic verisimilitude as I could muster. Dammit, I was going to adhere to the accurate reference no matter what. It was, in retrospect, a vain attempt to control everything – everything – completely, as things swirled and collided in mid-air all around. This was my Stanley Kubrick period. Of course, the more I tried to control everything, the more real life kicked my ass.' The final straw came when his model for Christine, the main character, got married to a soldier and relocated to Germany. In this case Moore remained generous in his praise for the quality of Sienkiewicz's work; his problem was solely with the quantity.

Moore spoke about the third time an artist disappointed him when interviewer Alex Fitch noted that 'the only occasion I can think of where the art was fairly lacklustre was some of Rob Liefeld's drawings for *Judgment Day*' (a 1997 series that was a gigantic crossover between series in Liefeld's Awesome Studios stable). Moore answered, with a very long chuckle:

> Rob Liefeld. There's a name to conjure with. I can remember when I was working for Awesome Comics – and I suppose really that the name of the

comic company should have given me a couple of tips going in the door really as to what I was in for – I can remember that Rob Liefeld asked me through an intermediary what I actually thought of his artwork . . . I was trying to be as honest as possible, and I said 'Well, there's obviously something about it that appeals to the readers, but for me it looks lazy and there are never any backgrounds, all of the characters look the same, it looks like there's been no involvement between the artist and the script that he's working from at all. There are no backgrounds in any panels, there's just a series of characters posing or gritting their teeth and looking resolute.' And I think his response to that was '(sigh) Well, who cares about windows?'. Which I suppose pretty much defines his approach to comic book storytelling.

Perhaps it is significant that Liefeld was Moore's publisher as well as his artist, and that, as Moore was self-publishing *Big Numbers*, in that instance Moore was Sienkiewicz's publisher. This was not purely a writer and an artist disagreeing on creative choices, there was another relationship in play.

This isn't to say that being the artist on a project written by Moore is free of tension. The root cause for most disputes between comic book writers and artists is that it is almost always far easier, and faster, to write a page than it is to draw one. Naturally, different people work at different rates, but as a rule of thumb most artists working in American comics can just about maintain a monthly schedule of delivering one complete comic a month – around twenty-three pages, so one completed page every weekday. For example, on *Swamp Thing*, Stephen Bissette has said 'John [Totleben] and I took five weeks to do an issue', whereas Moore 'did eight pages a day, handwritten and then typed'. It means that writers can work on three, four or five books a month (and often do, if they can find someone who'll commission them), but artists work very strictly on one title at a time. Alan Moore's career presents a textbook example of this: the America's Best Comics line published by Wildstorm from 1999 to 2005 included four regular titles (and various specials, miniseries and spin-offs), initially all scripted by Moore, but each book had its own art team. In the meantime, Moore was also able to finish off *Lost Girls* and work on other projects.

Melinda Gebbie, artist on *Lost Girls*, acknowledged the problem: 'He had to work quite hard at any one time on seven or even eight other projects, while he was working on *Lost Girls* as well, so he had a very, very rigorous schedule, and I needed time to work on *Lost Girls* . . . Being an artist was quite frustrating because, I mean, he was able to do so much work during that period, many different things, and I was only able to do that book.' Bissette raises a more long-term issue: 'Alan could do *Swamp Thing* in a week to a week and a half, and he still had two and a half to three weeks to do other stuff. Like *Watchmen*. And as we watched Alan's career skyrocket, you know, we were still the lowly *Swamp Thing* cartoonists. So that was a schism.'

The vagaries of publishing mean that working with Alan Moore might not be the biggest payday of an artist's career, but they tend to find it is the work that endures the longest and which they are asked about most often. The majority of artists who have worked with Moore are already successful in the comics field, and have racked up other high-profile work. Many are, or go on to be, writer/artists. The list of artists who have done substantial work with Moore but who are better known for something else – a highly contentious call to make, complicated by the fact that some comics haven't travelled well across the Atlantic – might be said to include Bryan Talbot, Rob Liefeld, Todd McFarlane and Brian Bolland, but surprisingly few others. Some artists are clearly a little resentful that their own work or projects with other writers have been overshadowed, that they are known mainly as one of Alan Moore's artists. Very few, even those who have fallen out with the man, seem to blame Moore himself for that.

When Avatar Comics reprinted the *On Writing for Comics* essay in 2003 (as *Alan Moore's Writing for Comics*), Moore wrote a new afterword in which, having re-read his old essay, he describes his younger self as a 'far less complex individual, someone a few years into his career attempting to describe the processes of his craft as honestly and lucidly as he was capable of doing at the time'. He warns established authors they are 'in danger of becoming a joke' if they repeat their stylistic tricks too often and suggests 'make things hard for yourself'.

Certainly Moore's methods worked and he swiftly built his reputation. Having started 1982 as the writer of a handful of one-off strips, he ended 1983 as the award-winning writer of five regular series, with a steady stream of work from three British publishers.

In 1982 and 1983, Moore wrote a string of short prose stories, numerous non-fiction articles – including pieces on haunted houses and CB radio for the

Scooby Doo and *BJ and the Bear* annuals – and a script for a video science fiction project, *Ragnarok*. March 1983 saw the last of his strips for *Sounds*: *The Stars My Degradation*, which had been winding down, and he had thought about producing a new strip centred on Mycroft the Crow from *Roscoe Moscow*, but in the event he was getting so much writing work that he simply didn't have time to continue drawing a half-page strip every week (for the last year, Steve Moore had been writing the series). Happily, though, Moore did find the time to continue writing and drawing *Maxwell the Magic Cat* for the *Northants Post*, even managing to negotiate a pay rise . . . from £10 to £12.50 a week.

He was also involved in various musical projects with Northampton bands, the outcome being a number of commercial releases. He wrote songs for the Mystery Guests – Mr Liquorice, Alex Green and Buster Skinner: 'The Merry Shark You Are' and 'Wurlitzer Junction' (1980). He composed and recorded a poem used by Bauhaus in the sleeve notes to *Masks*, on the cover of the album *This Is For When . . . Live* and as a taped spoken introduction to live performances of 'Double Dare' (it appears on the live album *Press the Eject and Give Me the Tape*). And the Sinister Ducks reformed – their line-up was Moore, David J and Alex Green – for three live performances, and to record 'March of the Sinister Ducks' and a version of 'Old Gangsters Never Die' (1983). Moore even wrote a song for *V for Vendetta*, 'This Vicious Cabaret', which David J set to music and released, with other compositions inspired by the comic, as the *V for Vendetta* EP (1984).

His most high-profile work, though, was in comics, where he wrote in excess of six hundred pages of material over two years. He was inarguably prolific, but it is worth noting that the weekly schedule of British comics kept a lot of writers very busy. Steve Moore, Steve Parkhouse, Angus Allan, Alan Grant, Pat Mills and John Wagner certainly all wrote more in the same period. Alan Moore was not at all unusual in being a freelance writer working on many projects for 'rival' publishers. If anything, it was unusual that virtually everything he was writing fell within such a narrow waveband of science fantasy aimed at teenage boys (with a high proportion of it quirky and comical in nature). Most comics writers were happy to take work where they could find it in titles aimed at very young children, girls, or about football, horror or war.

One way in which Alan Moore was exceptional was that he became one of the stalwarts of the British comics industry remarkably quickly. There were other people in comics who enjoyed a rapid rise, but these tended to be artists: Steve Dillon, the artist on *Pressbutton* in *Warrior* and *Abslom Daak* for *Doctor Who Weekly*, had been sixteen when Dez Skinn first commissioned him for *Hulk Weekly* in 1979; Alan Davis, Moore's co-creator on three series in this period, made his professional debut after Moore, in 1981. Even for artists, though, this was unusual. Kevin O'Neill, David Lloyd, Dave Gibbons and Brian Bolland all served lengthy apprenticeships on obscure publications before getting regular work.

Because he produced so much material for so many publishers in such a short period, it is hard to give specific examples of a neat chain of cause and effect where Moore was given a job because of a particular previous piece of published work. We know the publication dates, and we know that typically it would be four or five months between a script being accepted and its publication, but that doesn't always represent when Moore first had an idea or pitched it to an editor, when he was commissioned or when the script was handed in. One-off strips in particular could be put on file and used to fill gaps in the regular schedule. British comics publishing in the early eighties, as now, was a small, interdependent world. The editors of one British comic typically would not only have read the other comics Moore was writing for, they would usually have a pretty good idea of their rivals' plans, and what everyone was busy with. Moore was just as likely to get work based on advance word of what he was working on as from an editor reading a published comic and getting in touch. We can say for certain that Moore got the chance to write for *Captain Britain* on the strength of his *Marvelman* work, but beyond that, Moore has confessed he is unclear himself of the exact order he wrote this material, and that as far as he's concerned, 'It all started to happen at the same time . . . once *2000AD* and Marvel knew I was being given series work by somebody else, they became more inclined to give me series work as well.'

Many of the people who read *2000AD* in the early years are hugely nostalgic about it now, but they remember *Judge Dredd* and his supporting cast, *Strontium Dog*, *Rogue Trooper*, *Slaine*, perhaps *Flesh*, *Nemesis the Warlock* and *Ro-Busters* . . . not the *Future Shocks*. Moore's work from this period is often very entertaining, and some of the short pieces like 'Chronocops', 'The Reversible Man' and 'Sunburn' are excellent, but much of what he wrote was not leaps and bounds ahead of other material and rarely so distinctive as to be unmistakably his work – indeed, there is some dispute about whether a number of *Future Shocks* written under a pseudonym are by him. Likewise, a number of *Doctor Who* stories credited to 'Moore' are by Steve Moore, but appear in some reference books as the work of Alan Moore. Even working across so many titles, if Alan Moore had quit comics at the end of 1982, it is doubtful that anyone would really have noticed.

We can look down the list of credits of pretty much any issue of *2000AD* from the early eighties and it now looks like a Band Aid-style assembly of comics superstars. It was a time when many talented creators, many of whom have now been the biggest names in comics for a generation, were emerging. How did Alan Moore manage to move to the forefront of this strong field?

Moore was fortunate not only that he had arrived on the scene just as writers and artists were starting to receive creator credits but that the market in the early eighties supported three publishers producing the boys' science fiction adventure magazines he wanted to write: Quality (*Warrior*), IPC (*2000AD* and *Eagle*), and Marvel UK (a number of titles, including *The Daredevils* and *The Mighty World of Marvel*). The most obvious advantage was that there were plenty of pages that needed filling. Working for three publishers, though, also meant Moore's career was not dependent on the patronage of one editor, or the survival of one magazine.

All this was equally true for everyone else. But Moore's analysis in *On Writing for Comics* was fair: the world of British comics was a staid one, in which even the new generation had accepted a lot of received wisdom. A good example was *Marvelman*. The smart money had made its judgement: British audiences didn't like superheroes because they were inevitably very silly; Marvelman was a horribly derivative, hokey example of the breed; science fiction stories with dashes of black comedy were the way to go. At one level, the received wisdom was proved right – for all the talk of Freedom's Road, you would never make your living writing for *Warrior*. Nevertheless, Moore arrived fired up with an entirely original, extremely clear vision for the character and, with his first chapter of his first regular series, created a template for superhero storytelling that would prove to be the most important contribution to the genre since Lee and Kirby's first issue of *Fantastic Four*.

But in the British comics industry of the early eighties, success for a writer still depended in no small measure on being a good script robot: someone who could deliver thoughtful, imaginative work to a deadline and who never seemed to have too much work on his plate. And Moore was an exceptional script robot. He wrote stories that fitted perfectly with the publications he was writing for, and when talking to his editors he was enthusiastic and constructive. Dez Skinn remembers, 'Alan was never off the phone! He'd call up at all hours, often saying "Got you out of your pit, have I?" if I sounded blurry after a late night. He'd mail a script in and then phone me to tell me the entire story. He was very enthusiastic and yes, very flexible – hence the Big Ben appearance in *Marvelman* as a springboard for a character I'd been dragging around with me for years. He even suggested to his *Sounds* editor that I'd be the perfect person to put together an intended comic they wanted to launch.' Bernie Jaye agrees: 'Alan Moore used to pop into Marvel when he was in London for conventions or meetings, as did many other writers and artists. We exchanged a few home visits. He was a consummate professional. He was conscientious, answered lots of mail from fans. Nothing was too much trouble. He was especially brilliant on panels, articulate, thoughtful, humorous and entertaining. He worked well with Alan Davis and their pages were always in on time. You couldn't have asked for a better contributor.'

One thing that Moore, unlike his peers, seems to have noticed was that while *2000AD*, *Warrior* and *The Daredevils* were very similar, they were not interchangeable. Each offered distinct opportunities and allowed him to demonstrate different talents. Moore is fond of Brian Eno's remark that only a few hundred people ever listened to the Velvet Underground, but they all formed bands, and that's the perfect description of *Warrior*'s place in the history of British comics. Writing for *Warrior* had given Moore his first opportunity to write regular strips, while learning the benefits of collaborating closely with an artist on longer project – *V for Vendetta* in particular.

Writing for *Warrior* would not, however, confer the other obvious advantage of having regular work – a regular income. The publication was already paying less than its competitors – Moore received just £10 a page for his *Warrior* work. As Dez Skinn says, 'The rates increased after the first year, but I based them on being two-thirds of *2000AD*'s rate. Cheaper because I wasn't IPC! And I was only buying first publication rights. Profits would come from syndication and merchandising, both of which we achieved. The badges alone earned the creators a *lot* of money'. Artists were paid £40 a page at *Warrior*, proportionately less than at IPC and Marvel. What's more, *Warrior* was on a monthly schedule, whereas *2000AD* was weekly – a regular strip in *2000AD* meant more pages to write and draw, but the combination of extra work and higher rates meant that you could expect to earn ten times as much working there. Writers and artists still had reasons to work for *Warrior*, but many were highly sceptical of Skinn's promise of future profits (he'd said in one memo to contributors that *Warrior* would be 'not only fun to produce, but lucrative to us all'). As David Lloyd observed, 'If you spoke to anyone involved with *Warrior* who thought it would make them rich, I'd love to know who they are. Dez might have thought he was going to be rich at some point. I can't imagine anyone else thinking that. We were pleased to be working on something that we owned and had freedom to do.'

And while Moore and Lloyd maintained a monthly schedule on *V for Vendetta*, all the other strips soon saw some sort of disruption. Within the first year, Garry Leach left *Marvelman*; *The Madman* ended abruptly; Steve Parkhouse ended *The Spiral Path* (halfway through the run, he brought John Ridgway onto the strip to assist with the art), and Steve Dillon's contributions to the *Pressbutton* strip began to dry up. *Warrior* #4 was planned as a Summer Special but was quickly retasked, a clue that regular material was already running late.

Skinn believes 'creator ownership was both the blessing and the curse of *Warrior*. Initially it was a blessing. People tried harder because they owned it! If you're making something for somebody else, whether a wardrobe, a suit or a comic strip, you look first at how much they're paying and time yourself accordingly. But if you're doing it for yourself, you know that the better it is the more you'll benefit long term. I was the editor/publisher. But, as I soon realised, for the first time I had no way of exercising my role. Usually if an artist disappeared, you'd find a replacement. If a writer lost his way, you'd either help him get back on track or once again replace him. But we had creative anarchy going on. We were banned by [the newsagent] W.H. Smith for being too "naughty" for a mere comic. One artist disappeared for over six months halfway through a serial. One writer totally frustrated an artist by a cop-out plot twist (as the artist perceived it).' Skinn nonetheless took on a bullish tone in editorials and letters columns. Teething troubles were to be expected, they were learning from their mistakes. Besides, Alan Moore was still there, eagerly filling any gaps that emerged with scripts for *Young Marvelman*, *Warpsmith* and *The Bojeffries Saga*.

With a steady flow of commissions from Marvel UK and *2000AD*, and with more to prove than his more established contemporaries, Moore could afford

to keep working at *Warrior*. It brought him renown, or at least the UK comics industry equivalent; in 1982 he won two Eagle Awards for *V for Vendetta* (Best Comics Writer, Best Story), as well as helping *Warrior* to Best UK Title. In 1983, he won Favourite Writer, Favourite Comic Character (Marvelman), Favourite Villain (Kid Marvelman) and Favourite Single or Continued Story (*Marvelman*), while *Warrior* won Favourite New Comic and Favourite Comic Cover. Moore was later fairly dismissive of the awards, saying, 'they're voted for by a couple of hundred comic fans . . . it's no indication of quality, but I won them for two or three years running which didn't mean anything really'. He was clearly proud of winning the awards at the time, though. He'd had the ambition to win them, they certainly did no harm to his career and he saw the positive reaction to his work as confirming his instinct that he was on the right track.

A regular strip or two in *2000AD* was the grand prize for a British comics writer in the early eighties. The anthology comic was the epicentre of the British comics scene, the place to find virtually all the top creators and characters.

2000AD had been smart enough to grow up with its audience. It had launched in 1977 as a science fiction adventure comic for ten or eleven year olds who loved *Doctor Who* and *Star Wars*, and the magazine was brash and surprisingly grim. Five years on, its readers were now teenagers facing their own dark future of mass unemployment and Thatcherism. Strips in *2000AD* became a parade of stories where ordinary people and friendly robots were ground into the dirt by mean bosses, fascist policemen or crazed tyrants, or just swept away by a brutal universe. It is possible to pick out specific instances of topical satire – *Nemesis the Warlock*'s parody of the royal wedding of Charles and Diana, for example – but the most subversive thing about *2000AD* was that virtually every strip rammed home that the world isn't fair, life is cheap and people are mean.

Once again, Alan Moore made himself very useful to his editor. He may not have had a 'regular series', but his *Future Shocks* and *Time Twisters* appeared in nearly half the issues of *2000AD* in 1982 and 1983. When he pitched a *Judge Dredd* spin-off, *Badlander*, it was not accepted, but instead he was rewarded with his first regular series.

The movie *E.T.* was being hyped at the time ahead of its June 1982 release in the States. But it would not be released in the UK until December, and Moore was given the job – without having seen the film – of coming up with a similar story about a cute alien being marooned on Earth and befriending a child. The result, *Skizz* (1983), was an interesting strip for *2000AD* because it was actually set in Thatcher's Britain, rather than some SF analogue of it. Its main influence is, perhaps a little too clearly in places, Alan Bleasdale's *The Boys from the Blackstuff*, a BBC television drama about a group of unemployed working-class men that had been running in late 1982 as Moore wrote *Skizz*. The main human cast of *Skizz* are young people about to leave school and enter a world where there are no jobs. Moore makes it a story about human dignity as much as cute aliens, but it didn't matter. While he and artist Jim Baikie were developing their strip, *E.T.* became a huge cultural phenomenon and commercial success: it remained in the top two at the US box office for over six months, and was also hugely popular in the UK. When *Skizz* arrived in March 1983, it was completely overshadowed by what had become one of the most beloved and commercially successful movies of all time.

Moore hated the strip, describing it in an interview in November that year as 'the horrible *E.T.* rip-off that I did for *2000AD*, you've got this cuddly little alien that everybody likes who's having a really bad time on Earth 'cos everyone's beating on him 'cos he's little (that's the plot so you needn't read it)'. Twenty years on, he was able to see a brighter side: 'It was great working with Jim Baikie, who is a wonderful artist. It was interesting to have an ongoing strip in *2000AD* where I could explore character development and maybe press a few unusual buttons for *2000AD*. But it kind of really whetted my appetite for doing something better.'

His opportunity wasn't long in coming. Alan Davis had suggested Moore take over as the writer on Marvel UK's *Captain Britain* when Dave Thorpe, the writer Davis had been working with, quit after a series of disputes with the management. *Captain Britain* had begun in 1976, the particularly literal-minded result of a plan to create a 'British Captain America'. As Bernie Jaye explains: 'The managing director was concerned about the political content of *Captain Britain* and read the riot act. This was a bit of a crisis to say the least and I do remember there were hours of phone discussions. Dave, quite understandably, wasn't willing to compromise and I couldn't risk the whole project being sabotaged. We needed a different take on the story. Paul Neary, who I trusted, vouched for Alan Moore, and Alan Davis independently also vouched for Alan Moore. It was thought he could take the story in a more acceptable superhero direction.'

Under Thorpe, *Captain Britain* stories had been odd mélanges of science fiction and folklore, and Moore admitted he picked up the assignment 'halfway through a storyline that I'd not inaugurated nor completely understood'. But his run on *Captain Britain* was to continue almost uninterrupted for two years, even if the strip itself moved across three Marvel UK publications: *Marvel Superheroes* (July–August 1982), *The Daredevils* (January–November 1983) and *The Mighty World of Marvel* (December 1983–June 1984).

Dez Skinn was unhappy that Moore and Davis were the creative team on both *Marvelman* and *Captain Britain*, the only two British superhero strips running at the time. Bernie Jaye at Marvel was far more relaxed: 'I trusted Alan Moore and Alan Davis not to compromise their own work.' And in the event, the strips were very different. While there were a few nods towards realism – for example, Captain Britain struggles to work out a method of carrying around the helmet of his superhero costume when he is in his civilian identity – *Captain Britain* was a story about parallel universes and Arthurian magic. Moore was now writing stories set in the Marvel Universe he'd explored so avidly as a boy, where, as he said, 'these sort of things are willingly accepted, whereas in the *Marvelman* continuity they would look stupid and completely out of place'. He brought back the Special Executive from his *4D War* stories in *Doctor Who Monthly*, and contrived to have Captain Britain fight inside London's Forbidden Planet comic shop, but the strip is perhaps best remembered for a relentless cyborg, the Fury, who presented Captain Britain and his allies with a lethal and durable antagonist.

In retrospect, however, Moore's most important work for Marvel UK was the cheap filler material he came up with. Marvel UK was a shoestring operation, and while they published a few original strips like *Captain Britain*, most of the pages of their magazines were black-and-white reprints of American titles. Bernie Jaye recalls 'I was always relieved when he said yes. I was happy that he was able to sustain such a prolific output. I don't think he ever turned down any request.' There are issues of *The Daredevils* – the anthology comic in which Marvel UK reprinted Frank Miller's much-acclaimed recent *Daredevil* strips – where Moore seems determined to appear on every page. He wrote short stories, but he also wrote volumes of non-fiction: articles about the history and social context of comics, their relationship with pop music, their problems with the depiction of women. By 1983 specialist comic shops had started to appear in most British cities, places like Forbidden Planet in London, Odyssey 7 in Manchester and the Sheffield Space Centre. There you could find full-colour imported American comics – the true aficionado did not need to pick up reprints. The text articles, though, were clearly designed with the hardcore fan in mind. Bernie Jaye says: '*Daredevils* was a conscious attempt to include the fans. I think I had been to a few comic conventions by then, I loved being around artists and writers, they were obviously the lifeblood of the medium and I was keen to do my bit to provide creative opportunities. It was a breath of fresh air in the midst of all the reprints. I enjoyed the interaction and engagement.'

In this spirit, Moore instigated and wrote a fanzine review column for *The Daredevils*. Fans were now more savvy about the creators of their favourite comics, and the advent of cheap photocopying had given them a way to publish their thoughts: soon, Moore reported that he had been inundated with fanzines to review. While this was hardly a great seat of power, it allowed him to reach out to the network of British comics fans and positioned him as an authority and arbiter of taste. Moore clearly enjoyed reading the fanzines he was reviewing, and he attended the comic marts at which the creators of fanzines hawked their wares. It is doubtful he was enacting some Machiavellian scheme to win the hearts and minds of the people who voted in the Eagle Awards – more likely his hidden agenda in volunteering to write the review column was simply to get some freebies – but Moore was so physically distinctive that it was difficult not to notice and remember him. He proved loquacious and entertaining on panels and in interviews, wrote letters to fanzines, mingled with their editors, happily contributed ideas and articles. He quickly came to realise he was becoming well known: 'I used to go down to the comic marts that they'd have at Westminster Hall. And we'd all gather in the Westminster Arms just down the road. This would be comic fans, comic professionals, there was no differentiation. And you'd have a couple of people saying, "I saw that story you did in *2000AD*, I thought that was really good." And you'd say thanks and you'd perhaps buy each other a drink and then stand and chat. I noticed after a few of these that I was getting four or five people coming up and saying that they liked my work. Then I was noticing that I was getting about twenty people. Now this is tiny. But I started to think, "Hmmm.

If this trajectory continues the way it's going, it's going to be a lot more people, isn't it? And so I might end up being famous.'

Alan Moore's success was not down to being tall and having a bushy beard, of course. Ultimately, there is a simple explanation: he was very good at writing comics. If you only read one of the magazines Moore was writing for in 1982–3, you would start to spot his name cropping up over and over again. If you read more than one, you'd see the same man in a variety of different roles: writing dark, adult stories in one place, silly throwaway gag strips in another, fanzine reviews and articles about feminism in another. Moore managed – and this is what distinguished him from all his peers – to consolidate a diverse portfolio into one solid body of work with a distinctive voice. While writers like Steve Moore and John Wagner were happy to stay relatively anonymous, even pseudonymous (Steve Moore's most acclaimed series was probably *Laser Eraser & Pressbutton*, which was only ever credited to 'Pedro Henry'; Wagner used half a dozen pseudonyms, the most prolific being 'T.B. Grover' and 'John Howard'), Alan Moore instead ended up creating the character 'Alan Moore', someone with an instantly recognisable appearance who was enthusiastic, affable, if a bit loud and weird, and always willing to share his opinion.

Was this all part of a three-front strategy with a clear endgame? While Moore is not a ruthless man or a cunning businessman, he clearly does not like coming second. He has always understood himself to be a better writer than most of his contemporaries. In an interview barely four years into his professional career, he was quite comfortable saying: 'I know quite a bit about writing comics. It's a problem I've been applying my admittedly limited intelligence to for the past five years, and it'd be pretty remarkable if I didn't. Without wanting to sound egotistical, I reckon there are maybe a dozen people in the Western world who know as much or more than I do about writing comics. This says more about the paucity of the medium that it does about my personal talents, but the point still stands.'

Moore understood the paradox: he needed to be a script robot, but one who stood out from the crowd. One of the articles in *The Daredevils* that brought him particular attention was 'Stan Lee: Blinded by the Hype, An Affectionate Character Assassination' (#3–4, March/April 1983). While it wasn't hard to find

Marvel employees who had some choice things to say about their publisher and company figurehead, the pages of Marvel's comics themselves had always treated Lee with reverence. Moore was happy to call Lee a 'flawed genius' and characterise his recent editorials as 'geriatric gibberings' (Lee had just turned sixty). The main problem he diagnosed was that what had once been bold had been repeated and diluted so many times it was now simply formulaic, and more depressingly it had become the only game in town:

> All the other companies of the mid-sixties . . . Charlton, ACG, Tower and so on . . . opted not to follow Marvel's lead and subsequently went bust, leaving the comic field populated solely by pale ghosts of Lee's former glories. Even the independent publishers that have recently sprung up seem largely unable to do anything more radical than tinker feebly with Lee's basic formulas. *Captain Victory* is little more than *The Eternals* playing at the wrong speed and Ditko's *Missing Man* would not have looked out of place as a sub-plot in *Doctor Strange*. Oddly enough, it is imitating the superficial stylistics of Mr Lee's 'Marvel Renaissance', most of these imitators seem unable to recognise the single most important quality that he brought to the comic medium.
>
> Stan Lee, in his heyday, did something wildly and radically different. And as far as I'm concerned, his vacant throne will remain empty until we come up with someone who has the guts and imagination to do the same.
>
> Any offers?

Moore identified what he saw as the problem, though it's unclear whether he had a candidate in mind. Unlikely as it seems in retrospect, is he making a case for *Warrior*'s iconoclastic approach to the subjects comics could tackle and the rights creators enjoyed there? Probably not: Moore seems to be talking solely about American superhero comics. There is, though, the possibility he was proposing *himself* as the solution.

Moore has claimed he did not see working in British comics as a stepping stone to the more lucrative, full-colour shores of the United States. He said, twenty years later, 'I wasn't thinking about America at all. I was thinking, "this is great, I'm doing what I've always wanted to do. I'm doing a regular series for British comics. In fact, I'm doing four regular series for British comics".' This was clearly true in 1981 when he was interviewed just before starting on *Warrior*. But things had changed by the time he wrote 'Blinded by the Hype'. That article appeared in March 1983. In January that year, he had told *Fantasy Express*, 'On the American front, there are loads of characters I'd like to write . . . *Superman*, *Martian Manhunter*, *Challengers of the Unknown* and so on. But the two main features I'd really like to deal with are *Tales of the Bizarro World* and *Herbie*.'

This wasn't a pipe dream. American publishers had begun to look at British writers. In 1983, Brendan McCarthy and Pete Milligan (working with artist Brett Ewins) became the first British-based writers to be commissioned by an American comics company, when they contributed stories to Pacific Comics' *Vanguard Illustrated* anthology series. British writers were meeting American editors at conventions and pitching projects. Moore himself had written to DC, volunteering to take over as writer of the struggling series *Thriller*. And a number of artists *were* finding work across the Atlantic. One of the first was Brian Bolland, a stalwart of *Judge Dredd* in *2000AD*. In late August 1979, Bolland was at Seacon, a convention held in Brighton. Len Wein, an editor at DC, was in attendance, actively looking to recruit artists from *2000AD*. Bolland was commissioned to draw a few covers for DC Comics, and persisted in his attempts to gain more substantial commissions: 'I had been appearing at DC every summer for four consecutive years. The first time I went, Paul Levitz – not knowing who the hell I was – gave me the standard tour of the premises and away. The next year, one or two people knew me through liking *Judge Dredd*, and the third year I was taken out, wined and dined and I met all sorts of people.' Wein commissioned Bolland to draw an ambitious and prestigious miniseries, *Camelot 3000*. The story, by American writer Mike W. Barr, would not have been out of place in *Warrior* – King Arthur returns at England's time of greatest need: the year 3000AD, with the solar system under attack from Morgana Le Fey.

One of Bolland's friends was the artist Dave Gibbons. Their careers had developed in close parallel. Both had been part of the early British comics fandom, then worked on underground comix; they had worked together on *Power Man*, a superhero comic sold in Nigeria. Gibbons had become even more of a presence in *2000AD* than Bolland, with strips like *Dan Dare*, *Harlem Heroes*, *Ro-Busters* and *Rogue Trooper* appearing virtually every week in the comic's first two years. By 1983, Gibbons was perhaps best known for his work on Marvel UK's *Doctor Who Weekly*. He had been hired for the job in 1979 by Dez Skinn and worked there from the title's launch in 1979 until 1982, drawing the main strip for sixty-five of the first sixty-nine issues. DC originally thought Gibbons would be ideal for their *Star Trek* comic, although Gibbons 'only heard later this was DC's plan . . . I would certainly have turned it down, who wants to draw half a dozen likenesses every time you show the bridge of the Enterprise?' He was set to work instead on *Flash* and *Green Lantern* back-up strips, quickly impressing his editors enough to become lead artist on *Green Lantern*.

The name of the game at DC was to revamp existing characters, not to create new ones. After long discussions with Gibbons, Moore typed up pitch documents for at least two such series. *Martian Manhunter* was set in the McCarthyite fifties and got as far as Gibbons making sketches, while *Challengers of the Unknown* would be a way of telling 'an essential and definitive DC Story'. Set in the present day and making extensive use of flashbacks, it would be an exploration of how Superman's arrival on Earth represented a huge divergence from our history. In particular, it would make 'the Soviet Union feel very insecure. This might have some interesting long-term political repercussions'. (The idea of an all-powerful American superhero impacting the course of the Cold War was to be a central plot point in Moore and Gibbons' series *Watchmen*.) In the event, before either series was formally pitched to DC, Gibbons was told the characters had already been promised to other creators.

More fortuitously, in early 1983, DC editor Len Wein was searching for a new artist for horror title *Swamp Thing*, and invited Gibbons to submit sample pages. Neither Wein nor Gibbons liked the results, and agreed Gibbons' clean linework did not suit the swamp creature. But Wein was a *2000AD* reader, and was familiar with Moore's work. He later called Gibbons asking for Moore's phone number.

So, it wasn't completely out of the blue when, on an evening in May 1983, as Alan Moore sat down to dinner with Phyllis, Leah and Amber, he received a phone call from Len Wein at DC Comics in New York, asking him if he would like to work for them . . .

5 HEADS UP AMERICA . . . HERE I COME!

> 'There's nowhere to go in this country . . . no space. Not like in America, that's what it's really like to be on the road. THE road is in America.'
>
> Kid, *Another Suburban Romance*

Swamp Thing inhabits a murky backwater of the DC universe, on his own far from the soaring towers of Superman's Metropolis or Batman's Gotham City. This was also the status of the comic book *The Saga of the Swamp Thing* in DC's 1983 line-up. The character had been created in 1971 by Len Wein and Bernie Wrightson for a one-off appearance in *House of Secrets* #92 (1971), which had led to a short-lived *Swamp Thing* comic (twenty-four issues from 1972 to 1976). The movie rights were optioned in 1979 and the resultant movie, directed by Wes Craven, was released in March 1982, whereupon DC revived the comic to cash in. Alan Moore was contacted a little over a year later, and as he later summarised, 'I was given this book called *Swamp Thing* which was really the pits of the industry. At the time it was just on the verge of cancellation, selling 17,000 copies and you can't do comics beneath that level.'

Swamp Thing's protagonist was Alec Holland, a scientist who had been caught in an explosion and stumbled out of his laboratory engulfed in flame, then fallen into the neighbouring swamp and sunk into the murky waters, where his flesh transformed into vegetation. *Swamp Thing* stories concerned Holland's attempts to restore his body to human form while protecting people from other monsters and supernatural creatures. Moore knew, 'It was a dopey premise. The whole thing that the book hinged upon was there was this tragic individual who is basically like Hamlet covered in snot. He just walks around feeling sorry for himself. That's understandable, I mean I would too, but everybody knows that his quest to regain his lost humanity, that's never going to happen. Because as soon as he does that, the book finishes.'

The Saga of the Swamp Thing was one of a very few non-superhero books published by DC, the only remaining horror comic in its line-up (the venerable *House of Mystery* had been cancelled after 321 issues in October 1983). There had been horror comics since at least the fifties, when EC Comics set the standard for short tales with a nasty twist. A moral panic about the role of comics in inspiring juvenile delinquency had led to the introduction of the Comics Code Authority (CCA) in 1954. This saw the comics industry self-regulating by agreeing to abide by a draconian set of guidelines. Even after the Code was revised in 1971 to relax many of the restrictions it still decreed, among many other things:

> 1. No comic magazine should use the word 'horror' or 'terror' in the title . . .
>
> 2. All scenes of horror, excessive bloodshed, gory or gruesome crimes, depravity, lust, sadism, masochism shall not be permitted.
> 3. All lurid, unsavoury, gruesome illustration shall be eliminated.
>
> . . .
>
> 5. Scenes dealing with, or instruments associated with walking dead or torture shall not be used. Vampires, ghouls and werewolves shall be permitted to be used when handled in the classic tradition such as Frankenstein, Dracula and other high-calibre literary works written by Edgar Allen Poe, Saki (H.H. Munro), Conan Doyle and other respected authors whose works are read in schools throughout the world.

Although the code would be revised again in 1989, these were the standards a horror comic published in 1984 still had to follow. The production of horror comics continued, but under the aegis of the CCA the genre had been neutered and only ever traded in the same sort of tame trick-or-treat imagery as *Scooby Doo*.

It so happened that Alan Moore would have been perfectly suited to write EC-style stories. Thanks to his long interest in comics, he was very familiar with the original material. When Steve Moore came up with the *Future Shocks* format for *2000AD*, it had owed a clear debt to those old EC stories, and Alan had mastered the form. There's no indication, though, that Len Wein even knew about that part of Alan Moore's CV. What interested him was Moore's skilful revamping and reinvention of characters like Marvelman and Captain Britain. Wein sent Moore a set of recent *Swamp Thing* issues, and Moore drew up a fifteen-page document explaining what he thought the problems with the character were and how they might be addressed.

Moore decided that the key was to make it work as a 'horror comic' fit for the early eighties. There is no evidence he was an avid fan of the horror genre at the time, although he had read Dennis Wheatley and H.P. Lovecraft as a teenager. Steve Moore was however an aficionado, and a contributor to the Dez Skinn-edited *House of Hammer*, which had been running (under a number of variant titles and two publishers) since 1976. That magazine featured comic strips by artists like John Bolton and Brian Bolland, which might have piqued Alan's interest. He would have been aware that in the late seventies a new style of horror novel had emerged, exemplified by the work of writers like Stephen King, Clive Barker and Ramsey Campbell. Nor was the trend just a literary movement; in interviews, Moore contrasted the tame 'horror comics' of the time with movies like *Alien*, *Poltergeist* and John Carpenter's *The Thing* – 'I'm very conscious that we're competing for kids' money with video, with films, and with Stephen King books – not with *Tomb of Dracula* or *Werewolf by Night*.' As with his *Warrior* work, the key was to ground the story in reality. It was a lesson learned from King, whose books had all the shocks and twists the genre demanded, located in a defamiliarised small-town America:

> We're going to try and actually focus upon the reality of American horror and see if we've got some good material there to turn horror comics out of . . . I tend to think that the horror that existed in the forties with the Universal films, it's played out, it's a different audience now. I mean what frightens people these days is not the idea of a werewolf jumping out at them, it's the idea of a nuclear war or any of the sort of things that we have coursing through our society at the moment. I think that to really frighten people, you have to somehow ground the horror in their own experience, things that they're frightened of.

Moore felt it was important to return Swamp Thing to his swamp, and took pains to emphasise the setting, although he never visited Louisiana and his method of establishing a sense of location was to buy maps and guidebooks. Someone sent him a copy of a phone directory from the state so that the names in the stories sounded local.

His artists were to be Stephen Bissette and John Totleben, two friends who had joined the book shortly before Moore, with #16 (August 1983). Swamp Thing had long been Totleben's 'all-time favourite comic book character', but neither artist was keen on the direction the previous writer, Marty Pasko, had taken (Pasko later reported that he had been annoyed to receive story suggestions from them). The artists were fans of *Warrior*, and delighted to learn Moore would be their new writer. He sent them a four-page letter outlining his plans and inviting their contributions. Straight away, it was clear that writer and artists were on the same wavelength. Unlike Moore, Bissette was an avid horror fan and keen to make the book genuinely scary. They all agreed that the protagonist had to change his appearance. Swamp Thing had been depicted merely as a large, hunched man with green skin and some roots that looked like the veins of bulging muscles. He was redesigned to emphasise, particularly in close up, that he was a mass of moss, mud and living plants, with leaves, twigs, buds, roots, shoots and even flowers protruding from him. Bissette and Totleben found that Moore would eagerly adopt their ideas for individual visual sequences or character designs, while he had a strong sense of the 'whole network', the direction of the running stories.

Moore faced the same problem he had dealt with when taking over *Captain Britain*: he had been handed an existing series – not just one with a 'dopey premise', but with nineteen previous issues of accumulated story and supporting cast that he was simply not interested in. He solved it the same way: with a swift cull of the characters he didn't think were working . . . and, as with *Captain Britain*, that included the protagonist. Alan Moore's first issue of *The Saga of the Swamp Thing* ends with Swamp Thing shot through the head and killed.

Moore's vision for the series really kicks in with #21, *The Anatomy Lesson* (February 1984). An autopsy is performed on Swamp Thing, during which the very idea that a human can be 'turned into a plant' is mocked as scientifically illiterate. Swamp Thing's 'brain' and 'lungs' and so on are functionally useless vegetable structures that only physically resemble human organs. The pathologist deduces that this wasn't Alec Holland's body, that the man had died in the swamp, his memories somehow being imprinted on the plant life there. While it may seem like an obscure or minor change, the entire premise of the series to that point had been that Holland was on a quest to convert himself back to flesh and blood. Now it transpired that Swamp Thing had never *been* Alec Holland. If – it's a big if – Swamp Thing really is 'Hamlet covered in snot', then the equivalent would be for Act Two to end with Old Hamlet showing up alive and well and wondering why his son is moping around so much. The doctor's second conclusion is a punchline delivered with perfect timing: 'You can't kill a vegetable by shooting it in the head'. Swamp Thing revives, learns its true nature and, in an inhuman rage, kills the man who captured it. As Warren Ellis, then an eager regular reader of *Warrior*, soon to be an acclaimed British writer of American comics, would put it:

> This story was the first hand grenade thrown by what you might call the British sensibility in American comics. In using the surgeon's monologue as narration, it avoids all the purple prose that otherwise characterises much of the early British work in American comics (including some of Alan's own). *Miracleman* predates it, but this was the first time a wide audience in modern comics had been shown a character they knew well, and told that everything they knew was wrong. Now, it's a cliché. Then, it was explosive.
>
> Structurally, it's untouchable. Perfectly paced, a complete short story, powered by hate and Moore's sudden grasp of the possibility in the 24-page form. As a British writer, he'd been restricted to the 6 to 8-page form before now. It was like seeing a clever piccolo player suddenly get access to an orchestra.

Horror fans would gradually learn about Moore's work on *Swamp Thing*, and he would manage the virtually unheard-of task of persuading older readers who were fresh to comics to buy a monthly ongoing series. Early on, though, Moore understood he needed to entice existing comics fans. He made a calculated attempt to locate the series in the wider DC Universe. An early story showed the Justice League of America – the team that includes all DC's big names like Batman, Wonder Woman and Green Arrow – watching helplessly as the plant life of the Earth rebels, then demonstrating how Swamp Thing can fight that threat in a way that Superman and Green Lantern can't. His stories were set in the same fictional space as all the DC superhero comics, but would be covering different territory. That point made, Moore would bring in as guest stars a large number of existing DC 'supernatural' characters, like the Demon, the Spectre, Dr Fate, Zatara and the Phantom Stranger. Some were well-known and were appearing in other comics at the time, like the magician Zatanna, a member of the Justice League; others, such as the minor demons Abnegazar, Rath and Ghast, were obscure to all but the most obsessive fan. Moore set about integrating the disparate characters, created over six decades by many different writers and artists, into a broadly consistent narrative framework.

Editors at DC were astonished by what Moore, Bissette and Totleben had managed to make out of such unpromising material. An editorial that ran across all DC comics in late 1984, 'Spotlight on . . . Swamp Thing', declared that 'if any book could be called a sleeper or, in this case, a buried treasure, it's *The Saga of the Swamp Thing*'. Bissette talked about the nature of the support DC were giving them: 'Being more positive about the work. Letting Alan, John and me have this exchange of energy and letting it pretty much go. We're free to work with each other and work these things out, and we're pretty much trusted with what we're doing. Plus, they're putting the PR machine behind us now. We're going to be doing some ads. They're doing a new *DC Sampler* this year, that free comic with just double page ads for all their characters, and they gave us the centre spread which is a pretty choice position. So they're really starting to showcase *Swamp Thing*.' Another piece of evidence that the title was starting to make waves was that Bissette made those comments in *The Comics Journal* #93 (September 1984), the 'Swamp Thing Issue!' with a painted cover by himself and Totleben, and long interviews with the team. By the end of 1984, the efforts of the new team had led to a sales increase of about 50 per cent.

Len Wein met Moore when he visited England in early 1984. Wein was soon to move on, though, and Moore gained a new editor, Karen Berger, from #25 (June 1984). If anything, this proved to be an even more fruitful partnership. To Moore's eternal delight, Berger defended his corner when *Swamp Thing* #29 (October 1984) fell foul of the CCA. As he explained when interviewed in 1986 by a young journalist called Neil Gaiman:

> For anyone who doesn't know what the Comics Code is, back in the Fifties, when America was in the throes of all kinds of witch hunts, a man called Frederick [sic] Wertham produced a book called *The Seduction of the Innocents* [sic]. He said that disturbed kids he had treated had all read comics at some time or another – he could probably have drawn the same conclusions about *milk*. He printed panels from comics out of context: one, for example, showed a tight close-up of Batman's armpit, so it's just a triangle of darkness – Wertham managed to imply that this was a secret picture of a vulva the artist had put in to titillate his younger readers. Reading Batman must have been an endlessly enriching erotic experience for Wertham . . . I mean, if you can get that much out of an *armpit*! Well . . . As a result of the book, the comic's publishers imposed a code of practice on themselves.

Moore's generation of fans grew up regarding Frederic Wertham as the comics industry's equivalent of Joe McCarthy and the Comics Code Authority as akin to the Hollywood Blacklist. *Seduction of the Innocent* had roughly the same connotations as *Mein Kampf*. This is not an exaggeration: comics historian Mark Evanier has described Wertham as 'the Josef Mengele of funnybooks'; comics publisher Cat Yronwode claimed 'probably the single individual most responsible for causing comic books to be so reviled in America is our good friend and nemesis Dr Fredric Wertham . . . We hate him, despise him . . . he and he alone virtually brought about the collapse of the comic book industry during the 1950s.' The normally level-headed comics scholar Scott McCloud depicts Wertham as an almost demonic, bookburning figure (see right).

The spectre of a return to those dark days hung over the industry for decades, along with the nagging fear that any attempt to produce a comic an adult might be interested in would somehow fall foul of authority.

There are huge problems with this version of events, particularly with the depiction of Wertham, a non-practising Jew who had fled Nazi Germany and who was ahead of his time in raising issues like media depictions of the female body and racial stereotyping. An article he wrote criticising segregation in American schools was cited in *Brown v Board of Education*, the 1954 landmark case that found the practice unconstitutional. He was no foam-mouthed anti-comics zealot: his last book, *The World of Fanzines* (1973) praised the imagination and expertise of fandom, seeing the creativity and active engagement of the participants as a model for young people.

That said, there's clearly some truth in the 'standard account' of the *Seduction of the Innocent* affair. The whole subject of censorship is complex and eternally sensitive, but we can generalise that freedom of speech is a good thing and that the urge to ban books is a bad thing. There *was* a moral panic in the mid-fifties around comic books and juvenile delinquency, and at its heart was an absurd confusion of correlation and causation: most teenage hoodlums had indeed read comics as children, but only because at the time 90 per cent of all children did. Articles by Wertham reached huge general audiences in *Reader's Digest*, *Collier's* and *Ladies' Home Journal*. There were two Senate Sub-committee hearings run by Democratic Senator Estes Kefauver, an ambitious politician looking to pick opportunistic fights on 'values' issues. The Comics Code was established as a result and it did become all but impossible to sell crime or horror comics.

There were those in the comics industry who asserted that the Comics Code Authority stifled the industry's creativity and it was therefore the prime reason the medium remained in a state of arrested adolescence. This reeks a little of scapegoating though. The CCA was not a vast government agency: in the early eighties it consisted of a man called J. Dudley Waldner and his wife. With hundreds of comics published every month, they could not carefully scrutinise every word and line. As Dick Giordano, vice-president of DC Comics, explained in 1987: 'The two of them read the same things differently, because there are no real standards. It's basically how they feel on that given day. So, for example, and this is what caused us to take *Swamp Thing* from the Code, one part of a two-part story that had bodies in it and flies flying around in it was approved, the second part of the two-part story which had the same elements in it was disapproved, simply because it had been read by two different people.'

What tipped them off was this double spread at the end of *The Saga of Swamp Thing* #29:

Once alerted, they went back and read the issue more carefully. The zombies in question were moving because their insides were masses of insects, which is pretty unpleasant. The real problem, though, was that the story involves the female lead, Abby Cable, learning that her husband Matt has been possessed by the spirit of the series' arch-villain, Arcane. A casual glance at the comic would lead the reader to think that Abby was traumatised by that simple fact. A more careful reading would reveal that Arcane is Abby's uncle, that Abby and Matt have recently slept together, and so the story is about a woman suffering a sexually abusive, incestuous relationship.

DC – initially in the form of Berger, then her boss Giordano – stood by the story, and took the almost unprecedented step of publishing it without Code approval. *Swamp Thing* #29 appeared in comic shops and on news-stands alongside the other DC titles. When asked how he felt about that, Moore savoured his victory, answering, 'Well, given the insufferable size of my ego, what do you think I think of it? It's something that gives me immense pleasure and an overwhelming feeling of smugness every time it crosses my mind.'

From #31, the decision was made to publish *The Saga of the Swamp Thing* without Code approval. Moore, Bissette and Totleben didn't look back. The series became a venue for crawling body horror and disturbing images, yoked to a political consciousness that, while mostly shared by Bissette and Totleben, was distinctly Alan Moore's worldview. *Swamp Thing* became a champion of environmentalism, but that is a description that sells the content short. Moore and his artists did not adopt a simplistic approach to the material: it was difficult, personal work. As Douglas Rushkoff put it,

> *Swamp Thing* was an ideal conduit for Moore's memes . . . Swamp Thing is totally dependent on the condition of his environment, but maybe, as the comic implies, so are the rest of us who are just as dependent on the plant kingdom for food, air and a balanced biosphere. The psychedelic agenda is presented in equally bold strokes. Many psychedelic users believe that the drugs function by giving human beings access to 'plant consciousness' . . . in Alan Moore's hands *Swamp Thing* became a media virus to promote this pro-psychedelic, pro-plant kingdom agenda.

Swamp Thing #34 featured 'The Rite of Spring', the consummation of Swamp Thing's relationship with Abby. She ingests a tuber she plucks from his body, and goes on an LSD trip where they form a perfect, orgasmic union. In the *American Gothic* sequence (beginning with #37, June 1985), Swamp Thing began touring America, fighting supernatural creatures who symbolised the rot Moore saw affecting the country: racism, misogyny, gun violence, corporate pollution, the nuclear industry.

Not everything in the garden was rosy, however. Stephen Bissette would later confess: 'I hated the intrusion of superheroes into the pages of *Swamp Thing* (and said so, apparently with enough vigor for Len to tell me it was *his* idea, a white

lie told to me so I wouldn't direct my ire at Alan, who was the real catalyst for the coming of the Justice League into *Swamp Thing* with #24), and even having bucked and shucked the Comics Code with *SOTST* #29, we were still working under mainstream comics restrictions. That forced us to be inventive with our subversion, but the necessary (to my mind, essential) evolution of horror comics required something more radical and unfettered.'

As ever, one of the more prosaic restrictions of a monthly comic was the necessity to work to a rigid timetable. Moore could write a comics script quickly, but now he was being called on to do so quite frequently. *Swamp Thing* #19 was already complete and heading to the printers when he was commissioned for #20. Various other production bottlenecks meant that, for example, the script for #29 had to be written in three days, that the 'inventory' issue he wrote to be used as a fill-in for use in an emergency was used immediately (#32), and that Moore had to come up with a way to dress up a reprint of the first *Swamp Thing* story with a new framing sequence (#33).

The biggest problem was that *Swamp Thing* was subject to what senior DC figure Paul Levitz once called 'the worst contract DC has ever made'. In the early eighties, the company led the way in improving the deal for creators. Previously – and at Marvel, this was still the case for many years afterwards – the publisher could turn, say, a cover illustration into a poster or T-shirt without any further payment to the artist. That had changed under DC's new president, Jenette Kahn (appointed in 1981), and now creators received a cut of the revenue from any exploitation of characters they created or artwork they had drawn. One exception, though, was *Swamp Thing*. The 1979 movie option included the right to use any or all of the characters and situations created for the series, as well as the merchandising rights. The main practical effect was that DC could not market posters or T-shirts based on Bissette and Totleben's art, or any of the toys or badges that other DC characters enjoyed, let alone pass on a share to the creators.

Even so, working for DC was lucrative for Moore. Only four years before, he had considered himself a success for being paid £45 a week for his writing. Now his earnings from *Swamp Thing* alone were equivalent to the average UK salary: DC paid $50 a page, so Moore was earning $1,150 an issue. Due to fluctuating currency rates in 1984, this would convert to anywhere between £810 and £890 a month. Perhaps the most salient exchange rate is that Moore got paid more for his first issue of *Swamp Thing* than for all the work he had done on *Marvelman* in the three years to that point.

Moore had come to DC's attention because of his British work, but his two best-regarded series for *2000AD* started *after* his *Swamp Thing* debut.

The first was *DR & Quinch.* The characters had been created by Moore and Alan Davis for a *Time Twister* that appeared when Moore had been about halfway through writing *Skizz* (#317, May 1983). That was intended as a one-off, but the reaction to it was so positive that the characters were given their own series, which proved wildly popular when it debuted in January 1984. *DR & Quinch* was – by Moore's own admission – a rip-off of *OC & Stiggs* from *National Lampoon.* Two teenage delinquents, aliens with a flying hotrod, create havoc wherever they go – whether they're chasing a girl, being drafted into the army or attempting to make a Hollywood movie. Davis was pleased, saying, 'I'm very proud and fond of them; they're easy to draw, they look funny no matter what they are doing, and it was fun to see what they could do and how far I could push them.'

Moore was less keen: '*DR & Quinch* are probably the comic strip that I shall ask to have eradicated and destroyed upon my deathbed. What DR & Quinch are is a continuation of the Great British comic tradition of making heroes out of juvenile delinquents. If you imagine Dennis the Menace with a thermonuclear capacity, you're probably pretty close to the idea of *DR & Quinch.* Maybe it's a sign of the times, I don't know, but certainly in this country they are probably the most popular creations I've come up with.' He later clarified his position: 'It makes violence funny, which I don't think is right. I have to question the point where I'm actually talking about thermonuclear weapons as a source of humour . . .' He admitted, however, 'There were a lot of good things about *DR & Quinch.* I think Alan Davis and I both put a lot of nice work into it and some of it is amusing. But it has no lasting or redeeming social value as far as I am concerned.'

Moore was a lot happier with another new creation for *2000AD. The Ballad of Halo Jones* was a story about an ordinary young woman in a vast science fiction landscape. The artist was Ian Gibson, who had brought his fluid, cartoony style to numerous strips for *2000AD*, most notably *Judge Dredd* and *Robo-Hunter.* He was keen to work with Moore and was introduced to him by *2000AD* editor Steve MacManus at a party. Gibson suggested they could work on a story with a female

lead, and they quickly agreed she should be 'a totally unexceptional character, somebody who could just be the girl next door', a celebration of the triumphs and tragedies of everyday life. Moore's preferred technique was to meticulously build up his worlds through little details, and he found a kindred spirit in Gibson, who Moore credits with 'providing as many of the main concepts and small touches as myself'. It was Gibson who provided the basic idea for the story of Book One: 'I told Alan that the best way to get to know a place is to go shopping in it. And it seemed like an ideal "girl" story – without being too chauvinist, I hope. I remember saying to Alan "Imagine what it is like if going shopping is like a military expedition, requiring planning ahead of time. If there is a hostage situation in Sainsbury's and a fire bombing of Tescos etc." He turned my suggestion into a very fine tale!'

Moore had finally achieved his ambition of creating a running space opera for *2000AD*. Now, *Halo Jones* is regularly cited as a high point of the magazine's long history. Then, it was a different story. Every week the magazine polled its readers on their favourite strips, and *Halo Jones* was notably unpopular during its first run (#376–385, July–September 1984). Moore accounted for this as follows:

> Naturally, given its nature, the strip wasn't really for everyone. Some found our decision to dump the reader straight in at the deep end with a totally alien society and let them figure it out for themselves to be merely confusing and irritating. Then, of course, there were those readers who complained that very little happened in the strip. Personally, I think what they actually meant was that very little *violence* happened in the strip, but it *was* their 24p a week and they had every right to be bored if they damn well want to be. In short, for numerous reasons, not everybody liked *Halo Jones* Book One. But we did. And the people at *2000AD* did.

Meanwhile, another project that had been among Moore's earliest writing ambitions was coming off the rails. *Warrior* #21 (August 1984) saw the last appearance of *Marvelman*. Artist Alan Davis has offered the most succinct reason why: 'By the time I had given up on *Marvelman* it was really a bit of a snake pit of egos.' Five years later, Moore would pass both the writing duties and his stake in the character on to Neil Gaiman with the words 'this may well be a poisoned chalice'. *Marvelman* became the focus of a great deal of ill will, much – but by no means all – of the animosity being between Moore and editor Dez Skinn. As

Moore explained: 'I was not on the best of terms with Dez Skinn by the end of the *Warrior* experience. I didn't trust the man, and my opinion – for what that is worth – is that there was knowing deceit involved in the *Marvelman* decision.'

The dispute over Marvelman would have subsequent implications for Moore's work for *Warrior*, Marvel UK and *2000AD*. Earlier in his career, he had stopped working for *Doctor Who Monthly* in solidarity with Steve Moore, and there's some evidence of friction over editorial changes to work for *ANoN* and *Sounds*. The dispute with Skinn, though, was the first of several truly spectacular fallings-out Moore would have with his publishers, disputes which have tended to conform to a pattern.

Moore's understanding of the dynamic between himself as a writer and his editor/publisher has always been that he (and his artists) should be trusted with total creative freedom and that his publisher's job is to deal with the commercial side of things: marketing, rights issues, legal matters, merchandising and so on. In 1983, Moore had said: 'The major benefit of working for *Warrior* is that we're all allowed to do more or less what the hell we like. Dez knows we're all competent professionals and tends to trust in our judgement on aesthetic matters. From the response we've had I don't think we've let him down so far. If anything I think *Warrior* has benefited immensely from the diversity and outlandishness of much of its content. It sets us apart and makes us different. It enables us to make artistic progressions of a sort that the major companies are too nervous to even contemplate.'

Generally speaking, Moore's editors are initially very impressed by his enthusiasm and the level of thought that has gone into his scripts, and tend to leave him alone. Inevitably, though, at some point, an editor will suggest some change to a script that Moore disagrees with. When asked about *Warrior* in 1986, Moore told interviewer Neil Gaiman that the promised 'creative freedom was only gotten after a lot of arguments with the editor' and Skinn had said, even in happier times, in the pages of *Warrior* itself: 'Alan and I have such arguments you wouldn't believe. He cares about his characters with a passion that's quite unbelievable. It can make an editor's life hell! . . . But the alternative, of not caring, merely hacking the scripts for unknown artists, and never looking at the end product is far more frightening to me.'

There had been a number of specific disputes. In *On Writing for Comics*, Moore related: 'I have had at least one editor within the field tell me that there was no point in risking the alienation of even one reader, the solution being to soften the dialogue of the sentence in question until it had no teeth left with which to maul even the most sensitive member of the audience . . . there is such a thing as being offensively inoffensive.' The editor in question was Skinn. Comics journalist Pádraig Ó Méalóid asked them both about the incident. Skinn's side of the story is: 'For Alan, I think things got tarnished when I suggested we edit out such words as "chocolate" (about [black character] Evelyn Cream), "virgin" (in the context of a twelve-year-old boy) and "period" (about Liz missing hers) – all from the same *Marvelman* script (#7, I've just checked specifics). We'd lost W.H. Smith only a few weeks earlier because somebody's mum had complained about the "adult nature" of the *Zirk* strip in #3 . . . I couldn't afford a trade backlash against us.'

Moore elaborated on the consequences:

> *Warrior* was aimed at a fairly intelligent readership, we hadn't had any complaints, and I tended to think that this was a hangover from Dez Skinn's days at Marvel, and he mentioned lots of things – 'Why offend even one reader?' – to which I responded, 'Because the alternative is to gear your entire product to the most squeamish and prudish member of the audience'. I said that I'm not happy going along with that. Eventually, the argument got down to, well, if I'd just change one of them, and it didn't matter which one it was. At which point I said, so, basically, they're all alright to go in, but you want me to change one of them? And Dez Skinn had said, yes, and that it was a matter of him not losing face, at which point I said, no, that's an even more ridiculous reason . . . Probably the breaking point came in a meeting in the New Cross offices. We were arguing over some other issue, at which point I had reminded Dez [about this]. At which point he said, 'That never happened, Alan.' This was calling me a liar about something we both knew was true in front of, I suppose, Garry Leach and Steve Moore. At this point I was halfway across the office, and Steve Moore and Garry Leach were saying, 'Leave him, Alan, he's not worth it,' and at that point I ceased my work for *Warrior*.'

Note that the original dispute was over the script for *Warrior* #7, which would have been a couple of months before its publication in November 1982. Yet Moore's last *Marvelman* appeared in #21 (August 1984) and the last *V for Vendetta* was written for #27 (unpublished at the time, it was scheduled for publication in March 1985), so the fisticuffs took place at least two years after the initial incident.

A year after that, Moore would contrast Skinn's squeamishness over the word 'period' with Karen Berger's willingness to run a *Swamp Thing* story 'entirely about menstruation without the slightest qualm'.

The corollary of Moore's position is that if an editor starts interfering with his storytelling, Moore feels authorised to start finding fault with their business skills. Moore was not the only person disillusioned with the way *Warrior* was being run by the time it had entered its third year of publication. As was normal, after a peak at launch, sales of the magazine had levelled out and eventually started to drop. The prospect of sharing profits had evaporated, with *Warrior* racking up losses of around £20,000. When many of the creators started prioritising better-paid work elsewhere, it triggered a vicious circle that cut the frequency of *Warrior*'s publication to bimonthly, and so halved its already fairly meagre income. Many of the later strips were little better than filler material, with reprints and new strips written by Skinn himself, while he continued to pay flat page rates to all his creators. Alan Davis has indicated that there was frustration among some of the *Warrior* writers and artists: 'There was a situation where the most successful strip was carrying the book and the other strips weren't earning their way . . . it started to be an issue that various creators thought they deserved more because their work was receiving more attention than other people's work. And so it just got pretty nasty.' Davis had his own reason to be upset:

> When I was first asked to pencil *Marvelman* I never regarded myself as Garry's long-term replacement – I was only asked to pencil two issues for Garry to ink. I believed I was simply doing some donkey work to help Garry make up time on deadlines . . . When it was finally made clear that Garry was going to quit *Marvelman*, to work on *Warpsmith*, I said I would only agree to continue drawing *Marvelman* if I was given an equal percentage of the trademark and character copyright Dez, Garry and Alan claimed to own. Each gave me a percentage that made me an equal quarter partner. Remember, *Warrior* was paying £40 per pencilled and inked page as opposed to £80–£95 from Marvel UK or *2000AD*, so working for *Warrior* was a gamble to secure an equitable, or enhanced, payscale through royalties.

The issue of who owns what rights to *Marvelman* has been highly contentious for a long time. We can say with confidence that at this point Moore and Leach

understood that they had equal shares and that either Dez Skinn or Quality Communications also had a share (there are differing accounts of the size of Quality's share). To recognise his contribution, Davis was cut into the deal, ending up with the same share as Moore and Leach, with Quality Communications also retaining a share.

Moore had clearly lost his enthusiasm for *Warrior*. He was no longer pitching new series, writing one-off strips or contributing articles. He stuck with *V for Vendetta* simply because he had always seen that story as being finite, and as it was two-thirds complete, he felt an obligation to his readers and artist David Lloyd to finish. Lloyd in contrast was more than happy to keep working: 'Other artists had to go off and do other things to make more money. I was very happy to keep doing it because Dez was still paying me money. And I was doing other work . . . I don't know if Alan felt as much loyalty to it as I did, though he probably did. He was doing other things, but it was very important to me. That was fantastic, a great character, I had sympathy for the character. Nothing was more important to us . . . it was ours. And we could do what we liked with it . . . We could talk about things we couldn't talk about anywhere else, because we had that control. I'm not saying I'd have kept doing it if I hadn't been paid . . . but we would have still done it.'

Nor did Alan Davis have any complaints about Skinn at this point. 'Various people had warned me off about working with Dez, because he had a bit of a reputation at the time. Again I don't know how he warranted that because Dez never ever did anything to me.' Everyone knew that *Warrior*, never awash with cash, was in trouble, and tensions were clearly fraying. Davis felt 'there was no heroic melodrama or valiant struggle for creators' rights, just practical business decisions muddied by ego and legacy building. Dez had invested heavily in *Warrior* and was struggling to keep it alive.'

The last, great hope for a lifeline was the prospect of *Warrior* material being licensed to the lucrative American market. Skinn had been actively pursuing this since early 1983, and initially 'everybody was cool to let me go with my gut instinct, it had got us this far, so it made more sense than a dozen or more writers and artists all pitching individually. Outside of the expense for them to all fly to the States, not many of them were really that used to negotiating US contracts or pitching and bartering!' At the 1984 San Diego Comic Convention, over the weekend of 28 June to 1 July 1984, he talked to representatives of the 'Big Two' US publishers, Marvel and DC, and was invited to pitch to both companies in New York. The flagship strip of *Warrior*, *Marvelman*, was in the paradoxical position of being precisely what the American comic publishers were looking for – a critically acclaimed, adult superhero book, by a writer who was a rising star – but which was also unpublishable by either DC or Marvel because its name contained the word 'marvel'. Skinn says Jim Shooter, editor-in-chief at Marvel, 'definitely didn't want *Marvelman*, for a quite logical reason. Despite the name, which would make it sound like a figurehead for the company, what we were doing with the character didn't really represent where Marvel overall was heading. Dick [Giordano] laughed at the thought of publishing *Marvelman*. They'd had a bad enough time with Captain Marvel! Of course this wasn't much of a surprise. We realised that *Marvelman* would be a major stumbling block for anybody.'

The obvious solution would be simply to change Marvelman's name. There were two options. The first was what DC had done with Captain Marvel for many years: comics starring Captain Marvel were named *Shazam!*, after his magic word. The comic in which Marvelman appeared could simply be named *Kimota!*, after *his* magic word. Alternatively the name of the character could change: as Marvelman has an MM insignia on his costume, the name would have to begin with an M (while speech balloons could easily be edited, correcting art would be far more complicated, and trademarks would also be affected).

Moore had in fact jokingly referred to changing the name to 'Miracleman' as far back as the original pitch to *Warrior*. He and Davis had shown (and quickly killed off) Miracleman, a character who looked just like Marvelman, in a *Captain Britain* episode featuring superheroes from a parallel universe. In early 1984, however, Moore told *Comics Interview* 'I'm not prepared to change the name', and had already told Skinn and Davis the same thing. Skinn was furious: 'With *Marvelman*, we'd all poured our souls into making it work. For Garry Leach, Alan Davis and me, this was where we'd get some financial return for our efforts. We really didn't care what America wanted to call it. So long as they'd print it and pay us that rare beastie in comics called a royalty. But Alan felt it would somehow destroy the property if the name was changed. That he couldn't continue writing it as anything other than Marvelman. Great, he'd already made it to big payer DC, on *Swamp Thing*. Everybody else was still waiting for the call and could use the money. I seem to remember it took almost a year to get him to see sense.'

It's a characteristic aspect of the pattern of his disputes with publishers that once Alan Moore starts losing patience with them, he adopts a point of principle that seems, to the other side, at best eccentric or self-defeating. This principle is usually straightforward and the logic behind it coherent, but it can come out of the blue. While there's invariably a noble philosophical cause at stake, it is also clearly a tactic which has the effect of forcing the publisher into bending over backwards to keep him happy.

Skinn had many other *Warrior* properties to offer. Giordano and DC's publisher Jenette Kahn were keen on *Zirk* and *Pressbutton*; across town, Archie Goodwin at Marvel's 'adult' line Epic also reportedly wanted to publish *Pressbutton*. Skinn, though, had a sticking point of his own: he wanted a publisher to commit to reprinting every strip from *Warrior*. He envisaged a range of titles, ideally co-branded with Quality Communications, and had prepared dummy issues using photocopies of *Warrior* pages and reusing painted cover art: 'I wouldn't *let* them cherry-pick! DC loved *Zirk* and *Pressbutton* I remember . . . But we'd had a very democratic way with *Warrior*, everybody was an equal, so I felt it unfair to dump any strip in favour of getting a deal with some of the others. I was going the movies-on-TV route, where to get *Jaws* you'd have to agree to take a few of Universal's other maybe less sellable movies as part of a bundle. We hadn't known who'd be our *Judge Dredd*/*Tank Girl* when we started, but the magazine wouldn't have worked without everybody pulling together so I certainly wasn't about to dump anybody now we could see who the front-runners were. Instead, I put the shorter-run strips or the less flavour-of-the-month ones into US anthologies, with titles like *Challenger* and *Weird Heroes*. Only *Marvelman* and *Pressbutton* had their own titles.' This was not something either Marvel or DC were interested in. Skinn returned to the UK empty-handed, and began preparing pitches to smaller American publishers.

Marvelman now ground to a halt. Moore told Skinn he would not be writing any more *Marvelman* scripts for the time being. This was no problem in itself – he had already delivered scripts for several future issues – but now Alan Davis joined in, withholding his artwork because he hadn't been paid for his last batch. Skinn was prompted to explore at least one other avenue: a young Scottish writer named Grant Morrison had submitted a spec *Kid Marvelman* script, and Skinn sounded him out about becoming the regular *Marvelman* writer. Many years later, Morrison would recall:

> I didn't want to do it without Moore's permission, and I wrote to him and said, 'They've asked me to do this, but obviously I really respect your work, and I wouldn't want to mess anything up, but I don't want anyone else to do it, and mess it up.' And he sent me back this really weird letter, and I remember the opening of it, it said, 'I don't want this to sound like the softly hissed tones of a mafia hitman, but back off.' And the letter was all, but you can't do this, you know, we're much more popular than you, and if you do this, your career will be over, and it was really quite threatening . . .

For Moore, this is a version of events that 'as far as I know has no bearing upon reality at all'. He remembers Morrison's script and that 'Dez had rather sprung it on me out of the blue, and it didn't fit in with the rather elaborate storyline that I was creating . . . I can only imagine that Dez Skinn told Grant Morrison what I'd said. As far as I remember, and this would be quite a serious aberration if I'd forgotten something like this, but I am almost 100 per cent certain that I never wrote any kind of letter to Grant Morrison, let alone a threatening one. Of course, if you were able to produce this, I would be willing to think again.' In a 2001 interview, Skinn implied he had been the one to pass the news to Morrison – 'Alan's reply was, "Nobody else writes *Marvelman*." And I said to Grant, "I'm sorry, he's jealously hanging on to this one"' – but he says now 'I do remember the situation. I never saw or asked to see the letter Grant got, though . . . I enthusiastically sent Grant's wonderful little cameo story up to Alan Moore, ill-aware of his growing possessive paranoia (for want of better terminology). But I quickly became aware of (and surprised by) how jealously he was guarding his position.'

Whatever the rancour in the air, Skinn clearly bore Alan Davis no ill will, assigning him a three-part *Pressbutton* story. For his part, Davis made it clear he wanted nothing more to do with *Marvelman*, and returned his stake to Garry Leach.

Alan Moore wasn't only losing patience with Dez Skinn and *Warrior* in the summer of 1984, he had also severed ties with Marvel UK. Two reasons were stated: first that the company's accounts department had become slow to send out cheques; second that his favourite editor, Bernie Jaye, had left the company. He also decided to end *DR & Quinch*, 'a Frankenstein monster that got out of hand. I was going to do a one-shot story . . . It went on beyond the point where I would rather have finished it off.' The net effect was that he had abruptly stopped working with Alan Davis on all three strips they'd been collaborating on at the start of the year. Their last regular *DR & Quinch* appeared in #367, in May 1984; their last instalment of *Captain Britain* appeared in June; their last *Marvelman* was published in August. For the moment at least, however, they remained friends. Davis continued to draw *Captain Britain* and *DR & Quinch*, with Moore's recommended successor, Jamie Delano, his old pal from the Arts Group days, writing the scripts for both.

While Moore claimed he had left *Warrior* and Marvel UK on principle, Davis notes that he 'clearly quit both *Captain Britain* and *Marvelman* at virtually the same time but claims external, unconnected reasons for both. Isn't it simpler to accept that with *Swamp Thing* and new offers from DC – which were far better paid – the volume of work increased to a point where choices had to be made? I know I, amongst many other creators, was hoping for a call from DC.' Moore continued to work in British comics – not just on *Maxwell the Magic Cat*, but for *2000AD* and a variety of smaller publications – but whatever was motivating his choices, his American breakthrough had clearly changed things. Barely a year before, he had been happy to let Dez Skinn try pitching to US publishers; now he was in direct contact with senior management at DC. They were keen for him to take on more projects with them, and offered lavish production values and generous deadlines. It wasn't just the promise of jam tomorrow: DC were publishing *Swamp Thing* every month without fail. He was now a star name at DC Comics, with Dave Gibbons only half joking when he referred to him as DC's 'golden boy'.

Moore's second project for DC was a short *Green Lantern Corps* story, drawn by Gibbons (*Green Lantern* #188, May 1985), but characteristically, he had plenty of plans for the future. He worked with Kevin O'Neill on developing *Bizarro World* and *The Spectre*, and at least considered reviving the Demon (who had made a couple of appearances in *Swamp Thing*). By December 1983, he had pitched a Lois Lane series and expressed interest in the Metal Men. He and Gibbons also talked about revamping science fiction series *Tommy Tomorrow*, although they seemed motivated solely by their amusement that the lead character wore shorts. Meanwhile Moore wrote one-off strips for *Green Lantern*, *The Omega Men*, *Green Arrow* and *Vigilante*. And DC signed up Moore and Brian Bolland to produce a *Batman/Judge Dredd* crossover series: as Bolland explained in October 1984, 'the whole premise would have been that Judge Dredd is an organ of the law whereas

Batman represents justice, and the story revolved around the conflict between these two, and the misunderstandings that would arise from the two completely different ways of looking at how society is run.' The project fell through, Bolland claimed, when IPC could not be convinced 'that Batman was a viable character'. By the beginning of 1985, Moore and Bolland had moved on to start work on a story that pitted Batman against the Joker.

Moore's *Swamp Thing* editor, Karen Berger, was delighted with his work and encouraged him to take risks, backing him up when he did so. Or, as Moore rather pointedly put it, speaking at a 1985 convention: 'Karen's great. She's really nice . . . She reads the stories, and she supports us. I think one of the problems we have in Britain is that editors feel they've got to edit. It's like policemen who don't get promoted until they've made a certain number of arrests . . . They want to deliberately change something just so that they can say, "Yeah, I edited this"'.

While DC were not able to publish *Marvelman*, they were interested in other stories from Moore that applied real-world logic to superheroes. The DC Universe was a playground full of interesting characters, but permanent change was not possible – a writer couldn't blow up New York or have a nuclear war, or even age the characters. So Moore began drawing up plans for a superhero story set in its own self-contained world. Originally, he used the Archie Comics superheroes the Mighty Crusaders, but when he was told that DC had bought the characters previously owned by defunct publishers Charlton, he decided they would be ideal for his story, and started referring to it as *The Charlton Project*. The heyday of the Charlton heroes had been a period in the late sixties when characters like the Peacemaker, the Question and Blue Beetle had appeared in a coordinated line of superhero titles created by writers and artists like Steve Ditko, Jim Aparo, Denny O'Neill and Dick Giordano. Part of the appeal for Moore was precisely that the characters were so generic. He drew up a proposal for a six-part limited series, *Who Killed The Peacemaker?*, a story in which the Question investigates the murder of one of his colleagues, only to uncover a conspiracy to destroy New York with a faked alien attack.

Dick Giordano received the unsolicited proposal in early 1984. His first instinct had been to encourage Moore to take the characters further into 'adult' territory, but he balked when he saw just how far Moore wanted to go. Dave Gibbons had successfully lobbied to become the artist on the project at a comics convention in Chicago (and, while there, also persuaded long-time Superman editor Julius

Schwartz to commission a *Superman* Annual from himself and Moore). A few years later, Gibbons produced a mock-up cover of *Comics Cavalcade Weekly*, featuring the Charlton superheroes as a prototype for a weekly anthology comic:

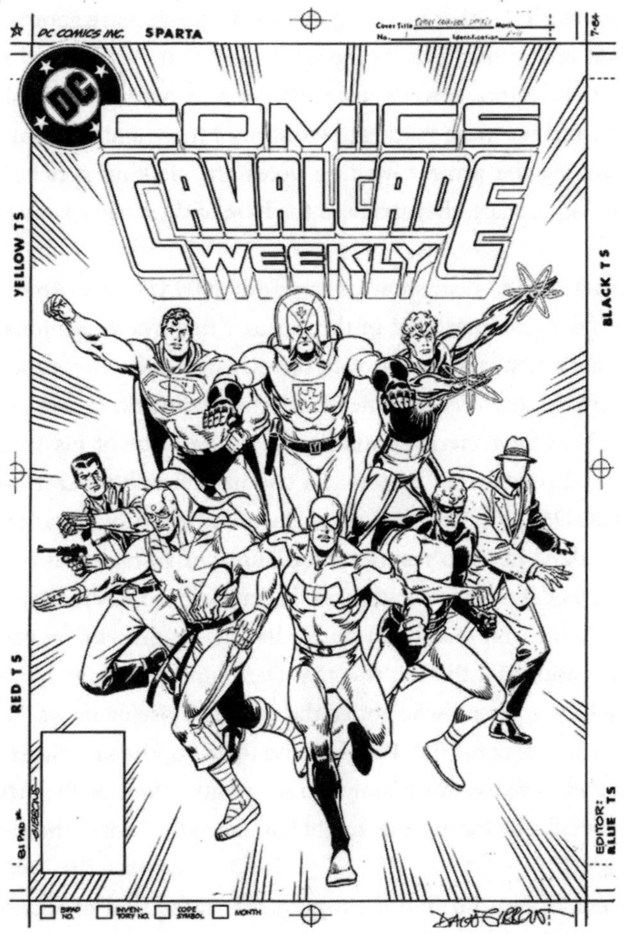

This had been what DC had in mind for the Charlton characters – an integration into the DC Universe's superhero community (note the presence of Superman). Giordano telephoned Moore and persuaded him, after some initial reluctance, that he should rework the story with original characters. The Charlton characters were given to other creators, and over the next few years books like *Blue Beetle*,

The Question and *Captain Atom* showed up. Moore and Gibbons were surprised how much creative freedom using new characters gave them, but the biggest consequence was that they were offered a contract that classified their series as 'creator-owned', meaning they would own the rights and would be given a share of the merchandising and other licensing deals. This progressive approach appealed to Moore, as it represented exactly the same ideal that *Warrior* had aspired to: a free hand for the creators, a savvy business operation getting the finished product out to readers, and everyone sharing the rewards. Moore and Gibbons spent many months discussing the project, writing notes and making sketches. After one Westminster Comic Mart, they finalised the look of their new characters.

Warrior had acted as a talent showcase – as did *2000AD* – but American editors proved to be far more interested in the creators than their creations, and could bypass the middleman, getting in touch directly with the writers and artists who interested them. Moore was only the most prominent British comics writer who was now working for American publishers. In the wake of his success, DC in particular would send senior editors to London to headhunt creators. Tellingly, in *Warrior* #26 Dez Skinn characterised this mass recruitment as an 'American attack on UK talent'. Just two years after the launch of *Warrior*, it was Alan Moore, another fan-turned-pro, one who'd barely had a professional credit in mainstream comics when Skinn commissioned him, who was reaping the rewards. Moore's take on the situation is 'I think it was that Dez Skinn . . . wanted to be Stan Lee. He wanted to be the person who got all the credit, whose name was on the whole package – Dez Sez, back in *Hulk Weekly* – and that's how he saw himself . . . I think that the fact that *Warrior* was mainly attracting attention for the artists and the writers, and specifically for me, that might have been the root of the problem – I'm only guessing.'

Nevertheless, Skinn did find a US publisher interested in republishing the whole Quality Communications range: Pacific Comics. 'It was the whole lot or nothing,' he says. 'I didn't want any of the gang left out. So Pacific became the only game in town. Obviously until I had a deal in place there was nothing to tell the creators.' Pacific were a small company, but they published Jack Kirby's new series *Captain Victory* and – to great critical acclaim – Dave Stevens' *The Rocketeer*, and were known for their high production values and commitment to creators' rights. Skinn helped prepare mock-ups of issues. Proceeding as though it was a done deal, in the late summer of 1984 Pacific sent an order form to shops advertising eight comics that they planned to release in September. One of these was *Challenger*:

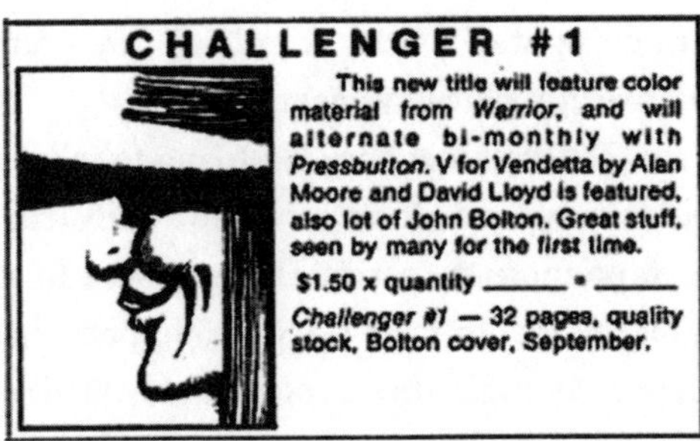

This was clearly premature. Moore and Lloyd knew Skinn had been negotiating with Pacific, but both were very hazy on the details, and nothing had been signed. Lloyd admits, 'There was no clear agreement or we'd have run it . . . It was a very foggy area for me . . . Dez did all that. He was effectively agenting it.' It also proved academic – at the end of August 1984, employees at Pacific were told that the company was winding down, and the following month they declared bankruptcy.

Shortly after that, Moore went to the United States for the first time – at DC's expense – to attend the Creation Convention. A limousine whisked him from JFK airport to DC's Fifth Avenue offices. He was greeted by Paul Levitz, then the vice-president of the company, with words that confused Moore: '"So, Alan Moore. You are my greatest mistake". Sort of ambiguous to say the least. I just figured it was a kind of neurotic, American business thing that I didn't quite understand.' Moore met Karen Berger, John Totleben and Steve Bissette on the first day, and a number of other esteemed comic book creators (including Marv Wolfman, Walt and Louise Simonson – Walt showed Moore his new gadget, a 'word processor' – Rick Veitch, Howard Chaykin, Len Wein, Frank Miller and Lynne Varley) over the remainder of his visit. He participated in a *Swamp Thing* panel at the convention, then met Julius Schwartz, the legendary editor of the *Superman* books he had loved as a child, now seventy and still very much in charge of the character. Moore 'knew his name before Elvis Presley's . . . being a megalo-star of some stature myself, I obviously feel awed by very few people, and Julius Schwartz happens to be one of them . . . we hit it off immediately'. They discussed the *Superman* Annual Moore would be writing, and when Moore flicked through Schwartz's scrapbook of souvenirs and mementoes he was astonished to catch sight of a letter from H.P. Lovecraft, and to learn that Schwartz had been Lovecraft's literary agent.

Moore, Bissette and Totleben met Dick Giordano to talk about their plans for further issues of *Swamp Thing*, and Moore recorded a fairly lengthy video interview DC planned to use to promote the series. He then went to stay with Bissette in Vermont, stopping on the way to meet Gary Groth, publisher of Fantagraphics, and editor of *The Comics Journal*. After a couple of idyllic days in the tranquillity of Vermont, he returned to New York, where he visited Marvel ('I don't seem to have an awful lot to say to Marvel and they don't seem to have much to say to me') before returning to Northampton, via Heathrow.

It was around this time that Moore indicated to Dez Skinn that he wanted to take *V for Vendetta* to DC. Skinn considered what DC were offering 'a far poorer deal', but he also had a different objection: 'I know I was baffled and shocked because it was a sudden move away from our all-for-one/one-for-all approach, but I can't put a time frame on it. *V* had definitely been in the dummy US titles which Garry Leach and I had put together so it was a late-on change he suddenly dropped on us . . . Alan Moore really was starting to be his own worst enemy. Instead of going along with the rest of us and selling a single publishing right on *V for Vendetta* to Pacific (ultimately Eclipse) he went with a lower page rate and sold the whole caboodle, rights and all, to DC. Outside of them being his new best buddy at the time (Marvel UK, *2000AD* and my own little show having served their purpose as his springboard to America) I never could understand what made him do something so insane.'

It would be almost a year before Moore and David Lloyd finalised their *V for Vendetta* contract with DC. The reasons Moore signed are self-evident: he trusted DC, they would pay him the highest page rates in the industry plus a royalty, they were keenly interested in publishing anything he had to offer and making all the right noises about creators' rights. In 1984, Moore's back catalogue divided neatly into four categories: 1) his work for Marvel UK and *2000AD*, which he didn't control the rights to; 2) his work for *Sounds*, *Maxwell the Magic Cat* and *The Bojeffries Saga*, which were all unsuited to the mainstream US market; 3) *Marvelman* (and the related *Warpsmith*), which DC couldn't publish; and . . . 4) *V for Vendetta*.

Within a month of Pacific collapsing, *Warrior* received another blow. On 21 September 1984, Marvel's lawyers sent Skinn a letter objecting to the use of the name 'Marvelman'. This had been triggered by Quality republishing a number of old Mick Anglo *Marvelman* strips in a one-off comic called the *Marvelman Special*. It was the first time the name had appeared in the title of a magazine, although in his reply, Skinn noted that Marvel UK had known all about *Marvelman* appearing in *Warrior* for years and not objected. Four more letters were exchanged, with Marvel seeking a clearer assurance that Marvelman would not reappear. The threat of legal action proved useful to Skinn, as it acted as a smokescreen for the behind-the-scenes problems with the strip. He published the correspondence in *Warrior* #25 and #26, gaining sympathy from fans.

It also, briefly, saw Moore on the same side as Skinn. Temperamentally distrustful of lawyers, Moore saw the legal action as something akin to an assault on the natural order: 'Despite the fact that "Marvelman" has been a copyrighted character in England since 1954, it was feared that a certain major American comic company (not DC) might take exception to a comic entitled *Marvelman* being published upon its own turf. Despite the fact that the company concerned hadn't adopted their name until the very late sixties, it was decided that corporate clout and legal muscle would be more likely to decide the issue than such comparative trivialities as the concepts of right and wrong.' In the same issues he published the exchange of letters with Marvel's lawyers, Skinn was able to trumpet the American reprints of *Warrior* material, starting with *Axel Pressbutton* #1 (cover dated November 1984). The small US comics company Eclipse had swiftly bought Pacific's intellectual property in a bankruptcy sale, and this included the reprint rights to some, but not all, material from *Warrior*. The deal included *Pressbutton*, *Marvelman* and *Warpsmith*, but – for reasons about which now not even Moore, Lloyd or Skinn are entirely clear – excluded *V for Vendetta* and *The Bojeffries Saga*.

It came too late to save *Warrior*, though. Issue 26 (February 1985) was the last to be published. It saw the first contribution by writer Grant Morrison, an instalment of *The Liberators*, a new series created by Skinn. Another chapter of that, and of *V for Vendetta*, were complete but would remain unpublished for some time. That summer, Skinn told *Amazing Heroes* magazine *Warrior* would return, but from now on he would insist that he owned any new characters.

Meanwhile, Eclipse Comics pressed on with their plans for *Marvelman*. Co-founder Cat Yronwode loved the series: 'It's a great story. Great art. I thought it was one of the most adult – and I don't mean pornographic – stories I had seen in comics. I loved where Alan Moore was going with the story from what I'd read in *Warrior*. And I knew that if he had kept it up, it would be a masterpiece.' For the time being, though, Moore had little involvement with Eclipse. Even with each American comic reprinting four *Marvelman* chapters from *Warrior*, it would be #7 (provisionally scheduled for March 1986, eventually published in April) before any new material would be required from him.

Eclipse had aggressive plans for *Marvelman*; they made moves to secure the rights to the character, trademarks and the continuation of the story beyond the *Warrior* material, signing contracts with Quality Communications for Skinn's company to supply them with completed pages equivalent to twelve issues of both *Marvelman* and *Pressbutton* – in both cases, the first six issues would be *Warrior* reprints, the next six issues all-new material. Most of the comics sold exclusively in comic shops – the 'direct market' – were premium products for avid collectors, with a higher cover price than the regular comics sold at news-stands. Eclipse would sell *Marvelman* only to the direct market, but at the same price point as a news-stand comic, 75¢. It was a conscious attempt to muscle in on DC and Marvel's territory.

As *The Comics Journal* reported in February 1985, the name 'Marvelman' remained a sticking point whichever side of the Atlantic it appeared, and Eclipse weren't quite sure how to proceed. Moore therefore wrote to Archie Goodwin, a senior editor at Marvel, issuing an ultimatum. Although he had already vowed not to work for Marvel UK again, he still had some leverage, as Alan Davis explains: 'At the time Alan Moore and I were producing *Marvelman* and *Captain Britain*, UK-originated comics were not being taken seriously. There were no contracts between Marvel UK and its freelancers, and the *Warrior* contracts only ever covered the broad concepts of the series, *not* specific pages. Because we were being paid so little by both Marvel UK and Quality/*Warrior*, we were able to sell our work as "first English language edition only." That is, we sold the company the right to print the work *once*. After that, they would have to renegotiate for further publication.'

Moore wrote Marvel a further letter in which he stated that he was denying Marvel – both Marvel UK and the American parent company – the rights to reprint any of his work, and to avoid doubt (not everything he had written had been credited to him in the comics) sent them a list of the work. It would be some months before Alan Davis, whose *Captain Britain* strips formed the bulk of that list, learned Moore had done this, while industry legend suggests that the result was only uncovered years later when someone was clearing out Jim Shooter's desk. As Moore recounts: 'Archie Goodwin had said, "Alan Moore's not going to be working for Marvel in any way, or letting us reprint *Captain Britain* unless we ease up on the *Marvelman* deal," and he'd said, "I suggest that you go along with him." But Jim Shooter, who was another one of these comic book industry führers, whose will is not to be meddled with, he'd petulantly screwed this letter from Archie Goodwin up and thrown it in the bottom of a drawer somewhere.' Moore now allowed Eclipse to rename the character 'Miracleman'. Eclipse's statement to *The Comics Journal*, reported in July 1985, that the name change was 'suggested by Moore' gives no hint of his mood when he did so. The first issue of *Miracleman* sold 100,000 copies, making it easily the best-selling Eclipse comic in the company's history.

With apparently no behind-the-scenes drama whatsoever, Eclipse continued to publish Steve Moore's *Axel Pressbutton*, relaunching the series as *Laser Eraser & Pressbutton* when they started printing new strips instead of *Warrior* reprints. As planned, twelve issues (and a *3D Special*) were published, from November 1984 to July 1986. Other one-off strips from Quality occasionally appeared as back-up strips in other titles, but there was nothing like the range-within-a-range Skinn had envisioned when he was talking to Pacific.

All the while, Moore continued to keep himself busy. He had scaled back his work in British comics, but had not abandoned it altogether, saying 'I do still want to be involved in the British comics scene, so I don't feel like a deserter'. After vowing not to work for Marvel UK, however, and with no interest in continuing *DR & Quinch*, his only major British work at the time was *Halo Jones*. The lukewarm reaction to Book One meant there had been no guarantee of a Book Two, but it appeared a few months later (#405–415, February–April 1985). This was in part because *2000AD* wanted to keep Moore working for them, and 'both Ian and I were excited about the strip and, to their credit, the editors of *2000AD* know that the best chance of getting first-rate work out of creative people is to give them something they're excited about.'

Book Two sees Halo away from the hermetic world of the Hoop, working as a hostess on a luxury spaceliner. It has more action, less futuristic slang, Halo shows a lot more skin and the story finds a much larger role for her robot dog, Toby, who'd proved very popular. Moore worried at the time that this had been at the cost of fleshing out the world he and Gibson had created, and said that while he was writing it that it was 'more of a compromise than I'd have liked . . . having to make concessions to the younger audience tends to blunt the edge of the strip for me', but in his Introduction to the first collected edition he admitted that 'looking over the current volume as one complete work, I think we just about managed to pull it off'. Book Two certainly proved extremely popular, and Moore was careful to lay down in it some hints for Book Three, which *2000AD* were keen to run as soon as he had time to write it (it would appear in #451–466, January–April 1986).

His other British work tended to be obscure, and was clearly done because it entailed short pieces for friends or projects that intrigued him. Moore was far more prolific in America. He continued to write *Swamp Thing*, and June 1985 saw the publication of his longest single work to that point, the story *For the Man Who Has Everything* in *Superman* Annual #11. He also did a variety of one-off pieces for other companies – including his only work for Marvel US: three pages as part of the famine relief comic *Heroes for Hope* and a strip for glossy *Epic Illustrated*.

In the summer of 1985, Moore was approached by Malcolm McLaren, former manager of the Sex Pistols and now working for CBS Theatrical Productions, the feature film arm of the TV network. McLaren had recently discovered Moore's work (naming a 1985 album *Swamp Thing*). They spent an afternoon together, and were joined by McLaren's girlfriend, the model Lauren Hutton. When the impresario told Moore he had ideas for a number of movies and needed a writer, the concept that caught Moore's eye was *Fashion Beast*, a retelling of the Beauty and the Beast myth channelled through a fictionalised version of the life of Christian Dior. The idea's originator had been the writer Johnny Gems (who would go on to work with Tim Burton, notably on *Mars Attacks!*), while Kit Carson, screenwriter of the 1983 remake of *Breathless* and of *Paris, Texas*, had written a treatment the previous Christmas. Memno Meyjes, who'd adapted *The Color Purple*, had also developed a treatment. Moore completed a draft of the screenplay and was paid £30,000 for it, but CBS Theatrical Productions was closed in late November 1985, and *Fashion Beast* went into 'turnaround' – essentially it was shelved. Moore, however, clearly considered *Fashion Beast* to be an ongoing project for some time after this – he mentioned the movie in a March 1986 interview with the *NME* and it was listed as one of his forthcoming works in the collected edition of *Halo Jones*, published in July of the same year, while McLaren continued to shop it around, with Moore's script attached. (Although never filmed, it was adapted for comics by Avatar in 2012–13.)

Moore made his second trip to America a year after his first, this time taking Phyllis. In early August 1985 he was a guest at San Diego Comic-Con, which was attended by about 6,000 fans. Here he met Cat Yronwode, his *Miracleman* editor, in person for the only time. He, Bissette and Totleben and *Swamp Thing* were showered with Kirby Awards, the American industry's top accolade: Best Single Issue (Annual #2), Best Continuing Series, Best Writer, Best Art Team and Best Cover (#34). While Moore basked in such accolades, he was far more impressed that he was able to meet the man the awards were named after: Jack Kirby, artist of the issue of *Fantastic Four* (and so many other comics besides) that had changed Moore's life. Moore shared a panel with Kirby and Frank Miller – he was embarrassed to hear Kirby praising him and Miller for what they had done for comics – but did not get much time with his idol, saying, 'all I remember was that aura he had around him. This sort of walnut coloured little guy.'

Moore also held court in a solo panel; a transcript that appeared in *The Comics Journal* #106 was accompanied by the assertion that based on sales 'Alan Moore may not be the most "popular" writer in comics right now, but he certainly is the most respected'. It was the first time the American convention scene had been treated to what had become a regular occurrence in Britain – a wild, bearded, surprisingly jovial figure getting an audience to eat out of his hand. Moore threw questions open to the audience and was able to talk about a huge slate of work. He had just finished *Batman Annual* #11 and his last *DR & Quinch* story, and was continuing to work on *Swamp Thing* and *Halo Jones* (which he was planning to write many more books of). He would like to do a Congo Bill story 'because he's a really stupid character'. He was due to start on 'the graphic novel' (he used the term) *The Killing Joke*. He was just about to sign contracts on the DC version of *V for Vendetta*, and had written the first chapters of Book III. 'I'm going to be doing a *Superman* graphic novel, and Julie [Schwartz] wants me to do some occasional stories during his tenure on the book.' He had also resurrected the title of his unpublished seventies fanzine, *Dodgem Logic*, as the title of an anthology comic for Fantagraphics, a black-and-white magazine that would feature one 48-page story per issue, drawn by a different artist. (Moore had said elsewhere of the project, 'If I do this right I hope I'll be able to bridge a little of the gap between what can be achieved with comics and what can be achieved with serious literature.') He would never again work for Marvel (following their legal action against the name Marvelman). And he also took the opportunity to announce 'I've ceased all contact with Dez Skinn.'

Around this time, Alan Davis was talking to Jamie Delano, now the writer of their *Captain Britain* series: 'He told me about Alan being snubbed by Jim Shooter and, in retaliation, denying Marvel permission to reprint *Captain Britain* – nothing to do with the Marvelman name. I confronted Alan, told him to withdraw his objection to the *Captain Britain* reprints or I would deny Eclipse my *Marvelman* rights. Which I eventually did! Eclipse, Dez and Alan all ignored my protests/refusals.'

To add insult to injury, *Captain Britain* was an ongoing series – Moore's writing stint fell between runs by Dave Thorpe and Delano. By blocking the reprints of the middle of the story, Moore hurt the chances of *any* of Davis' *Captain Britain* run being collected. Davis was annoyed that Moore had taken this course of action in, as he put it, a 'fit of anger', but the real issue was that 'Alan hadn't bothered telling me . . . I found out, sort of like, five months after he had actually said that and just because someone assumed I already knew'. Reacting to Marvel's intransigence over the use of the Marvelman name and the departure of Bernie Jay, Moore says: 'I just thought that me and Alan Davis were pretty much on the same page with everything, although that may have been a misunderstanding upon my part and I perhaps didn't do enough to make sure that was the case.' But the relationship

between the two men became strained – Moore believes Davis purposefully avoided him at a convention they attended around the time.

Davis had just had his break in the US industry. He became the artist on *Batman and the Outsiders* from #22 (June 1985; it sold about 140,000 copies a month compared with *Swamp Thing*'s 95,000), and would be promoted to the main Batman title, *Detective Comics*, the following year. Moore was able to block reprints of *Captain Britain* because he had only granted first English language edition rights, and, despite the artist having returned his stake in the character, the same applied to Davis' artwork on *Marvelman*: Davis could make a very simple tit-for-tat response. On 16 July 1985, Dez Skinn wrote to Moore to inform him that Davis was refusing permission to reprint *Marvelman* Book Two, or to let Eclipse use his designs for characters like Evelyn Cream, Sir Dennis Archer and Marveldog. He also informed Moore that Garry Leach was happy for his work to be reprinted, but had not agreed to his designs being used in any new material (Leach's designs, critically, included the series logos, the Marvelman insignia, Marvelman's costume, and the main characters Mike Moran, Liz Moran and Johnny Bates). Skinn told Moore he 'would appreciate being informed of your intentions'.

What happened next is hotly contested, and ended Moore and Davis' friendship. Davis later said, with some regret, 'Alan and I had a great working partnership and what I thought was a solid friendship for more than three years. We were both there at the end. We *both* know the truth. If his version differs from mine it becomes a matter of who you choose to believe.'

Moore does not seem to have addressed the *Captain Britain* issue, and did not contact Davis. Instead he concentrated on resolving the issue of Davis withdrawing his consent to use the *Marvelman* material. Cat Yronwode asserts that Davis 'sold . . . his one-third share of *Miracleman*, to Eclipse', and Moore says he 'was told that Alan Davis had sold out his rights'. Davis' position is a flat denial: 'I did not give or sell anything to Eclipse. I have only ever sold a single right, to one English language publication, of any of the *Marvelman* pages I drew, for their first appearance in *Warrior*.' Moore told Yronwode he would not contribute any new *Miracleman* material until he had written proof that Davis had given permission. Rumours about the dispute were inevitably to end up in the comics press: Cat Yronwode took a hard line with Davis, telling *Speakeasy* magazine in late 1985, 'Dez Skinn signed a contract with Eclipse allowing us to reprint material from *Warrior*, and we intend to reprint that material. If Alan Davis granted Dez Skinn the power to make that contract, and has since changed his mind, that is unfortunate for Alan but he is legally bound to that contract. If Dez Skinn represented himself to Eclipse as having the power to represent Alan Davis when in fact he did not, that is a matter for Alan Davis to settle with Dez Skinn. In any event Eclipse will be reprinting the material.'

Of course, Moore was now far from happy about the idea of working with Skinn, and took active steps to ensure he would not have to. In October 1985, Skinn was in America. There mainly to liaise with Eclipse about *Miracleman*, he had met with DC and understood he had been offered an editorial job there. An article on Skinn's blog explains:

> Dick Giordano was an old friend from the days of Neal Adams' Continuity Studios, and told me he welcomed me taking on the job – especially as he'd spent the last few years using *Warrior* and my address book as a takeaway menu for getting hold of new DC contributors! A match seemingly made in heaven. Except it wasn't to be. Immediately prior to the meeting, Jenette [Kahn – DC President] had excitedly called one of my old *Warrior* team and announced that he'd be able to work with me again soon as I'd also be joining DC's ranks. His response is said to have been 'If Skinn works for DC, I quit!'. I also discovered later that Dick had kindly mentioned, almost prophetically, he thought I'd be a safer long-term bet. But unbeknownst to me at the time, Jenette could obviously see the immediate revenue her star Brit writer was bringing in and so our somewhat brief and terse meeting went nowhere. A month or two later Mike Gold got the job.

It's not hard to work out who the 'star Brit writer' was, but Moore says 'it was a little more nuanced than that. I had Jenette Kahn in the middle of a dinner say that she was very excited because they'd got this British professional who was going to be working for DC and it was Dez Skinn, and what did I think of that? And I said to her that she really ought to ask somebody else because personally I really didn't like Dez Skinn but that might not be a fair appraisal. I said that I didn't want to work under Dez Skinn, not that I'd quit DC.' Skinn elaborates: 'What happened? Jenette went with the short-term option so I wasn't able to take all the gang over to US comics in the same way I'd taken them into Marvel UK a few years earlier.

Of course they pretty well all made it later under their own steam, they were a talented bunch. But it was more diffused, diluted without their little old catalyst to whip up a storm for them.'

As 1985 drew to a close, Skinn and Eclipse needed new material for *Miracleman* #7, due to be published in March 1986, but Moore still hadn't supplied his scripts. He says

> I wanted to be absolutely sure that the artist at that time, Alan Davis, was happy about his work being reprinted. And I told them that I could not commence writing any new work until they had got that affirmation. They finally left it until the last minute, and then asked me why I hadn't got the new *Marvelman* work in, at which point I reiterated my request for some proof that Alan Davis was okay about the whole thing. They said that they were getting this proof – and that they really needed me to start work – that this proof existed, that it was on its way, and they would be showing it to me as soon as possible. I started work because I believed that they were telling the truth. I later found out this was not the case.

Davis has a scathing response to that: 'When I first read the above, I felt really sad that Alan's work had been so badly impaired by deep concern over the legality of Eclipse publishing *my* art. He was so distraught in fact, that he must have forgotten he had my address and telephone number, or if he was too nervous to call, could have contacted me via a mutual acquaintance, like Jamie Delano, rather than suffer such creatively debilitating doubts. But I suppose Alan's recollection, for what it's worth, proves my case. The reason Eclipse could not furnish the proof Alan required to commence work is because it didn't exist . . . I had withheld my permission to have my work reprinted.' Moore says, 'By the time I was enmired with Eclipse I wasn't in contact with Alan Davis, and I was totally at the mercy of what I was being told . . . genuinely the reason I was stickling over delivering new work to Eclipse was because, while I didn't much like Alan Davis at that point, and I thought he was a bit of a grumpy person who I hadn't got any interest in talking to again, I didn't want him to be cheated. I didn't want anyone to be cheated. I perhaps should have done more. In retrospect I should have demanded.'

Dez Skinn's suggestion that someone besides Moore could write the continuation

material was given short shrift by Eclipse. It was now obvious, if it hadn't always been so, that the publisher was interested in Alan Moore writing a dark superhero series for them, not in forming a strategic partnership with Dez Skinn to reprint Quality Communications' back catalogue. By February 1986, Skinn, Garry Leach and Davis hadn't been paid for the *Miracleman* reprints, even though the series had started monthly publication in August 1985. Eclipse now offered to buy both Skinn's and Leach's one-third shares in *Marvelman* for $8,000. Both were happy to wash their hands of it. Everyone involved now believed Eclipse and Alan Moore owned a two-thirds and one-third share in the character respectively. Moore and Eclipse signed a new contract, formalising this and laying out terms for Moore to continue writing the series for another ten issues, with Eclipse given world publication rights.

Alan Davis' career as an artist of US comics has continued for thirty years and encompasses *Detective Comics* and the *Justice League* for DC, and long stints on many Marvel titles including *The Avengers*, *X-Men*, *Fantastic Four*, *Captain America* and *Wolverine* – as well as an adaptation of the first *Spider-Man* movie and a continuation of Captain Britain's story in *Excalibur*. But he was left feeling battered by his dispute with Moore: 'My memories of the creative process have been tainted by the petty politics, inflated egos, and, ultimately, the fact my *Marvelman* work was published against my wishes by Eclipse Comics. The fact that I was never paid is secondary to the fact people I trusted behaved so shabbily.'

Skinn soon set up Quality Periodicals Inc, a company that would repackage British material (mainly from *2000AD*) for the US market. He told *The Comics Journal* he planned to relaunch *Warrior* under the new imprint, and *The Comic Buyer's Guide* that he would eventually be releasing the original titles *Intruders*, *Liberators*, *Projectors* and *Warworld*, but while Quality continued to reprint *2000AD* strips for the next four years (including a twelve-issue run of *Halo Jones*), no new material ever appeared. According to Skinn: 'Bryan Talbot said to me a few years later, during an industry party that both Alan Moore and I were attending, "This industry isn't big enough for a feud. Why don't you two make up?" I thought that seemed reasonable so I went to the bar, tapped him on the shoulder and said, "Alan, why don't we just make up?" He replied (rather wittily), "Dez, why don't you just fuck off!"'

Moore evidently regrets the fallout from the dispute, though. He was not alone in finding Cat Yronwode a little abrasive at times, and lamented that 'there had been lost friendships in the course of *Miracleman*. There had been a lot of things that kind of soured the project.' He would finish Book Two of *Miracleman* with #10 (December 1986). Book Three's publication history was far more erratic, but Moore completed his story – and his contractually stipulated ten issues – with #16 in December 1989. He wrote other pieces for Eclipse, and is proud of his work as part of the *Real War Stories* project (1987), a venture which put combat veterans and comic book creators together to depict the realities of modern warfare and its psychological aftermath. In 1989 Eclipse stepped into the breach and published Moore's *Brought to Light* after a number of other publishers got cold feet.

By the time he resumed writing *Miracleman*, though, most of Moore's creative energy was going into a project with a working title *Who Killed the Peacemaker?*, his and Dave Gibbons' creator-owned superhero book for DC. There had been a vast amount of preliminary work: it had taken almost a year between the initial discussions and Gibbons receiving his first script from Moore on 27 March 1985. Gibbons was rather surprised to find that script ran to ninety-one pages, but completed the art by late June. The first issue would however not be published until May of the following year; Moore explained at San Diego that they wanted to complete six issues before it was launched, to ensure the series maintained a monthly schedule.

And along the way the comic had changed its name to *Watchmen*.

THAT ISN'T FUNNY. HA HA HA HA HA!

'Yeah, I know I have done some quite horrible comics, and certainly some with very adult themes, but that's not all I've done.'

Alan Moore speaking at N.I.C.E. (2012)

Much has been written about *Watchmen*, including the definitive account of the development of the series, the book *Watching the Watchmen* (Titan Books, 2008), by its artist and co-creator, Dave Gibbons. For good and ill, *Watchmen* came to define the changes in the comic market in the mid- to late eighties. It propelled Alan Moore from star to demi-god within the comics field and attracted unprecedented attention outside it. It was showered with honours, including many that no other comic has received before or since. It attracted extensive attention from academia, where it's since been the subject of conferences and has generated books with titles like *Watchmen and Philosophy*, and *Watchmen as Literature*. It was reviewed and continues to be discussed in the mainstream media. It has been a consistent bestseller since publication. *Watchmen* is, simply, as the trailer for the 2009 movie version puts it, 'The Most Celebrated Graphic Novel of All Time'.

Thanks in large part to *Watchmen*, the word 'serious' appears a lot when Alan Moore is discussed. Moore, we're told, creates stories where superheroes are 'taken seriously', and forces even those sceptical of comics to take the medium 'seriously'. He is a 'serious writer' who deals with 'serious issues'. Comics fans, ever sensitive to charges that the superhero genre is childish, are eager to stress how 'adult' and 'sophisticated' *Watchmen* is. Academics' textbooks on Moore invariably start with an introduction explaining that yes, *Watchmen* and *From Hell* are comic books, but despite this they are worthy of 'serious study'.

The result of taking Moore's work so seriously is that even when he writes a comic called *The Killing Joke* that ends with the Joker, a man dressed as a clown, telling a joke in a funfair before collapsing in fits of laughter . . . his most avid fans and his most highly trained critics fail to allow for anything but high seriousness. Likewise, *Watchmen* starts and ends with a bright yellow smiling face. Dave Gibbons explained the bad guy's plan in these terms: 'in the end, what Veidt did was a joke, a hoax, a bloodsplattered joke, which is what the smiley badge is'. By treating *Watchmen* as a work of great solemnity, this scholarly attention, the subsequent imitators, and the movie version have almost universally missed the point:

Alan Moore was joking.

The publishing industry is keen to pigeonhole works into genres. Moore has sharply critiqued this tendency, initially during an interview in *Mustard* magazine, and his words have been turned into an inspirational greetings card by one American company – 'My experience of life is that it's not divided up into genres; it's a horrifying, romantic, tragic, comical, science fiction cowboy detective novel' – although that version omits the punchline: 'You know, with a bit of pornography if you're lucky.' Yet academics, publishers, critics and comics fans all like sharp categories, and under their taxonomy, *Watchmen* is a superhero story that treats the genre seriously. It is an exercise in articulating comics history, a deconstruction of existing superhero story conventions, a warning against applying 'comic book' views of good and evil to the real world, as well as a masterclass in the use of, and subversion of, techniques of comics storytelling.

That's plenty for people to get their teeth into, but still it sells the story short. *Watchmen* is also a science fiction story. It's a detective story, a conspiracy thriller, a political satire, a historical family saga. It has elements of romance stories and war stories. It contains a comic-within-a-comic, a pirate adventure. It is packed with all manner of jokes: sight gags, running jokes, ironies, satire, parody, pastiches, characters telling each other jokes or making witty remarks, both intentional and obvious only to the reader. The book is soaked in verbal and visual puns. It is also unarguably, very dark in places.

It's worth noting that *Watchmen* is not *literally* a dark book. In the movie version, the colour palette is muted – blacks, greys, dark greens, browns and blues, and even people who are very familiar with the comic probably think the movie is faithful to the source material. But the pages of the comic, even when they depict scenes set at night, are made up of vivid greens, reds, blues, oranges and yellows. It's more reminiscent of the garish *Batman* TV series (1966–8) than Christopher Nolan's more recent *Batman* movies. Often, there is a narrative reason for such gaudiness – for example, Moloch's apartment is intermittently lit by the neon sign from the nightclub next door – but just as often the colours used make no pretence at naturalism. As *Watching the Watchmen* makes clear, colourist John Higgins worked hard, and closely with Gibbons, on the colour scheme for the book. It's fair to say the printing techniques that comics used in the mid-eighties were limited: however, when Higgins took advantage of advances in technology to redo the colouring for the 2005 *Absolute Watchmen* edition, he retained the overall palette, even if he made many small alterations. Compare that with the 2008 re-release of *The Killing Joke*, where artist Brian Bolland dramatically reworked the colouring, making it far more subdued than the original release. The candy colours in *Watchmen* are an artistic choice.

The creators themselves nevertheless called *Watchmen* 'grim'. Before it was released, Dave Gibbons described it as 'gritty, grim, rugged and realistic, the title all you superhero fans have been waiting for'. Moore has described the series as a 'dark take on superheroes', and in 2002 he bemoaned the way many other superhero stories aped it: 'Get over *Watchmen*, get over the 1980s. It doesn't have to be depressing miserable grimness from now until the end of time. It was only a bloody comic. It wasn't a jail sentence.' Moore almost instantly regretted *Watchmen*'s effect on the superhero genre. But when he surveyed mainstream comics in 1992, five years after *Watchmen* was published, he made an important distinction between *his* grim and gritty series and those that had followed: 'Now everywhere I turn there're these psychotic vigilantes dealing out death mercilessly! You know? With none of the irony that I hoped I brought to my characters. And I felt a bit depressed in that it seemed I had unknowingly ushered in a new dark age of comic books . . . there is now this sort of nihilism in comics. Which is all right if you're a smart, cynical adult: you can chuckle at the violent behaviour. But if you're a nine or ten year old, I wonder what sort of values that opens up?' *Watchmen* was intended for an adult audience – one that would recognise 'irony' and 'chuckle at the violent behaviour'.

The whole of *Watchmen* is soaked in a brand of black comedy that's distinctly recognisable from Moore's more overtly humorous work . . . if you've seen that other work. Moore had written plenty of funny comics before *Watchmen*, but it's understandable why 90 per cent of its audience would be unaware of that. His work for the American market ran seamlessly from the horror series *Swamp Thing* to *Watchmen*, *The Killing Joke*, then on to the completion of both *V for Vendetta* and *Marvelman*. Most of his fans had not seen the counterbalance, the strips for *Sounds*, *Maxwell the Magic Cat* and *The Bojeffries Saga*. Some of his work from *2000AD* – including his *Future Shocks* and his best-known comedy series, *DR & Quinch* – was reprinted for the American market but it appeared in a scattershot way, and Moore's name never appeared on a cover. In the eighties, he wrote plenty of short strips for smaller American comics companies, and these were often humorous – but they were seen by a fraction of the 100,000 readers buying *Swamp Thing*, *Miracleman* or *Watchmen*, and were easy to dismiss as a serious artist letting off steam.

The book *Alan Moore: Comics as Performance, Fiction as Scalpel* strays from the beaten track of *Watchmen*, *V for Vendetta* and *From Hell*, and has an admirably extensive analysis of what it calls 'Moore's lesser-known output, such as *Halo Jones*, *Skizz*, and *Big Numbers*'. But it barely touches his comedy writing. It only namechecks *Maxwell the Magic Cat*, and doesn't find room to even mention *The Stars My Degradation*, *DR & Quinch* or *The Bojeffries Saga*. When the book explores Moore's America's Best Comics line, it dismisses the five comedy series in *Tomorrow Stories*: 'The mannerist quality of many of these episodes gives the impression that Moore considered them a sort of formal exercise to be dutifully performed while he concentrated his efforts on fewer important elements in works such as *The League of Extraordinary Gentlemen* and *Promethea*. The latter are part of ABC too, but despite sharing their frequently playful atmosphere with the other serialisations, they are the sites for Moore seriously to explore themes like identity and magic.' The supposition that Moore churned out *Jack B Quick*, *First American* or *Cobweb* due to some sense of obligation is not supported by what he says in interviews: 'They're so intense, and doing *Jack B Quick*, to follow that example, was really difficult because to write *Jack B Quick* you have to sort of get your mind into this completely irrational state. You have to take scientific ideas to absurd lengths. You have to be able to think in a certain way to do those stories. I couldn't do them all the time, and I certainly can't see myself being able to do ones that are more than six to eight pages long.' The strips that Moore drew as well as wrote, mostly early in his career, were almost without exception comedies. The very early underground work, which merged into the work for *Sounds*, is made up of savage parodies. When Moore introduced the 'Ex-Men' into *The Stars My Degradation*, he – or rather Curt Vile – explained, 'I suppose what I was trying to do in my own pathetic and puny way was to sting people into re-evaluating the X-Men rather than just coasting along out of loyalty to the creative team or the characters . . . In fact I suppose you could say that my entire limited concept of satire revolves around kicking a man when he's down. I don't have to be nice. I'm handsome.'

Moore's early stories do tend to have very bleak endings. *St Pancras Panda* ends with a fictionalised version of Moore shooting himself in the head, as does his one-off strip *Kultural Krime Komix*. *The Stars My Degradation* ends with the accidental obliteration of the universe. Roscoe Moscow goes insane, *Three Eyes McGurk* and *Ten Little Liggers* end with the detonation of nuclear warheads. When Moore wrote for the younger *2000AD* audience, his contributions were mostly twist-ending stories of the EC Comics or Roald Dahl variety – concisely portraying a world of just desserts, where the protagonist always found himself condemned to some terrible, and usually terminal, fate. Moore has accounted for his return to end-of-the-world themes by saying 'it's the equivalent of the sick but understandable jokes that kind of spring up like a rash when there's any public disaster'. Around the time he was writing *Watchmen*, Moore added that he was worried his audience wasn't getting the joke: 'I started to question the ethics of doing humour based upon nuclear weapons because I wasn't sure that my audience was understanding it with the heavy irony that was intended and, in fact, sometimes I wasn't even sure that I was understanding it with the heavy irony that it really needed.'

Maxwell the Magic Cat appeared innocuous enough, and the *Northants Post* was a provincial local newspaper, not exactly an underground zine in the Crumb tradition. Yet although Maxwell was a little cat, he was also cruel and arrogant, happy to chomp up talking mice and birds.

There may moreover be a more nationalistic cultural difference in play. British comics tend to be black comedies with anti-heroes as their main characters. A male British comics reader has traditionally been weaned on the *Beano*, moved on to adventure comics like *Battle* or *2000AD*, and then perhaps on to underground comix and fanzines. British comics all share a taste for mayhem and violence, usually gleefully directed against authority figures, suitably tailored for their audience. The most enduring current 'serious' British character, *2000AD*'s Judge Dredd, is a broad satire on heavy-handed policing. Co-creator of the character Alan Grant was shocked when American convention-goers kept telling him they wished the real police were more like Judge Dredd. The British creators of comics were far more suspicious of 'supermen' using violence to lay down their version of justice, prone to see fascist overtones rather than a heroic ideal. As a former editor of *2000AD* put it, 'American comics tend to be much more bright and optimistic. Naïve, even. The British sense of humour is much darker, more ironic. Morally ambiguous. American readers don't seem to be big on moral ambiguity, they seem to prefer things to be simple and clear-cut. They don't seem to realise that *Dredd* isn't always meant to be taken seriously. Sometimes it's serious, sure, but sometimes it's out-and-out parody. Sometimes Dredd's the hero, sometimes the villain, sometimes he's barely a supporting character.'

The study *Knowing Audiences: Judge Dredd* takes the 1995 guidelines for merchandising of the (British) comic and the (American) movie version of *Judge Dredd* and concludes 'they have almost nothing in common'. The movie guidelines describe *Judge Dredd* as 'a futuristic action thriller about how the toughest, most upright and respected of all the Judges saves Mega-City One from destruction'. Those for the comic are 'written in a self-reflexive half-mocking style . . . the implication is that *Dredd* merchandising should carry some of the comic's mocking attitude', and includes a line that's equally applicable to Rorschach, the mentally disturbed vigilante in *Watchmen*: 'Though he is capable of a very black sense of humour, we can never be sure if he thinks his remarks are funny.'

Alan Moore had parodied comics set in a grim and gritty New York before he ever wrote one. In *The Daredevils* #2, Moore offered the four-page strip *Grit*! (art: Mike Collins, February 1983). This depicts the hero Dourdevil in a bombastic world not so far from Miller's, one of casual violence and people with rather inconsistent or sketchy motives. As one character notes:

By the time Moore was writing *Watchmen*, he and Miller had met and become friends. Miller's *The Dark Knight Returns* was published the same year as *Watchmen* (*Dark Knight* ran February–June 1986, *Watchmen* started in May). It had a similar theme, with a middle-aged Batman coming out of retirement into a far more brutal world than was usually depicted in comics. Soon after *Watchmen*, Moore's own 'dark' take on Batman, *The Killing Joke*, was released. Articles about 'serious comics' invariably roped Miller and Moore together, linking *Watchmen* and *The Dark Knight Returns*.

There are parallels between the two. Moore would write the introduction to the collected *The Dark Knight Returns*, Miller would contribute to Moore's anthology *AARGH!*, and Dave Gibbons' next major project after *Watchmen* was as artist on *Give Me Liberty*, scripted by Miller. Like Moore, in the nineties Miller would write and draw creator-owned comics for an adult audience, such as *Sin City* and *300*. Unlike Moore, though, he happily returned to DC in the early 2000s to produce a sequel to *The Dark Knight Returns* (*The Dark Knight Strikes Again*) and work on other Batman projects (*All Star Batman and Robin the Boy Wonder*, and *Holy Terror* – the last, a Batman v Muslim terrorist book, was dropped by DC and ended up as a non-Batman title at Legendary Comics). And perhaps the major difference is that Miller has embraced the movie versions of his comics, co-directing, producing and even making cameo appearances in them. It's also fair to say that his work, while ambitious, has a far narrower range than Moore's, and tends to be violent, masculine and hard-boiled.

While Miller cites Spillane and Chandler as influences, when Moore and Gibbons began putting together *Watchmen*, they were guided in large part by comedic treatments of the superhero genre. Once again, Moore returned to 'Superduperman': 'We were thinking that probably the best superhero stuff was the *Mad* parodies of it – that superheroes never looked better than when Wally Wood was parodying them. So we decided to sort of take some of those elements from the *Mad* parodies – you know, we were having massive amounts of background detail but it wasn't sight gags: it was sight dramatics, if you like.'

What Moore called 'sight dramatics' fill the pages of *Watchmen*. There are countless examples. One of the more whimsical consequences of a world with real-life superheroes, one close to Moore's heart, is that there would be no demand for superhero comics. Instead, the market in the world of *Watchmen* is dominated by pirate adventures. We see excerpts from *The Tales of the Black Freighter*, and one of the text features lovingly explains the parallel history of this comics industry. Eagle-eyed readers can also see a pirate-themed comics shop, Treasure Island, in the background of the New York street scenes.

The most iconic image of the *Watchmen* series is that with which it begins: a smiley face with a splash of blood on it, in the position where five to midnight would be on a clock face. The original badge (and blood) belonged to the murdered superhero, the Comedian, but it is wiped clean in the first issue and tossed into the Comedian's grave in the second. The image continues to echo throughout the story, everywhere from photographs to pareidolia. What in the fictional world is 'coincidence' or 'accident' is, of course, very carefully placed there by Moore and Gibbons.

The title has a number of meanings and resonances throughout the book. One of the many clocks and watches and countdowns that appear in the story is the Doomsday Clock – 'like most things in *Watchmen*, it was a kind of pun that had got two or three different meanings' – and it appears on the back cover of every issue, ticking closer to the apocalypse – or at least the end of the series. 'Watchmen' is also a reference to a quote from Juvenal, one that's daubed as graffiti across New York, 'Who Watches the Watchmen?' – if you have guards, you need to have some way to keep those guards in line, all the more so if they have superpowers and secret identities.

One thing 'Watchmen' is not is the name of a team within the story – our heroes never all worked together, let alone called themselves 'the Watchmen' (during the Comedian's lifetime, as far as we know, they were all in the same room only once). However, their predecessors were the Minutemen – a moniker that alludes variously to a mobile militia in the War of Independence, a number of right-wing volunteer groups, including a militant anti-Communist group in the sixties, and (after *Watchmen* was published) a vocal group of civilians who patrol the border with Mexico. No doubt Moore was also aware of punk band the Minutemen, and it goes without saying that in a book about the threat of nuclear war, the name is a conscious reference to the ICBMs that had been in service since the sixties (Moore possibly even knew that one of his favourite authors, Thomas Pynchon, worked as a technical writer on the Minuteman project) . . . and so on.

Every name in the comic is a telling, multiple pun – Sally Jupiter's retirement home is Nepenthe Gardens, a reference from Greek myth, via Poe, via a limerick by Aleister Crowley. There's a nightclub called the Rumrunner, a restaurant called the Gunga Diner. And character names like Rorschach, Dr Manhattan and Ozymandias are a little more allusive than standard superhero names like Ant Man and Power Girl. One essay on *Watchmen* dedicates three pages to the significance of the seven-name list of Adrian Veidt's favourite musicians.

Another comedy was also an influence on *Watchmen*: Robert Mayer's 1977 novel *Super-Folks*. On his website, Mayer notes:

> The novel was supposed to be funny. Reviewers said it was. It was a spoof on all those heroes. But something unexpected was happening out in the universe – well, in America and Great Britain. Adolescent boys were growing up who

> wanted to write comic books. They read *Super-Folks* – and they thought, aha, look at all the nasty things you can do with superheroes. They plunged the men in tights into twilight, made a lot of money doing it, and the entire genre was changed forever . . . Among the spawn, many critics say, were much of Alan Moore's work, including the 'classic' *Watchmen*. To my knowledge Mr Moore has never publicly acknowledged a debt to *Super-Folks*.

In fact Moore had done so: '*Super-Folks* was a big influence on *Marvelman*. By the time I did the last Superman stories [in 1986, at the time he was also writing *Watchmen*] I'd forgotten the Mayer book, although I may have had it subconsciously in my mind.' However, readers who track down *Super-Folks* expecting a 'serious' treatment of superheroes, a bleak novel that Moore has shamelessly ripped off, discover it's more like a prose version of 'Superduperman' or National Lampoon's *Bored of the Rings*, an exuberant romp full of seventies pop culture references. There are similarities – both *Super-Folks* and *Watchmen* feature beaten-down, middle-aged former superheroes and a conspiracy theory – but it's nothing like *Watchmen* in terms of tone, technique or intended audience. Nevertheless, *Super-Folks* became something of a collector's item following *Watchmen*'s success and, in one of life's little ironies, when the book was reprinted in 2003, Dave Gibbons drew the cover.

Mayer does, however, point the way to a criticism that's consistently been levelled at *Watchmen*: that, as Carter Scholz's review of the graphic novel put it, 'the superhero genre was never made to take the strain he [Moore] puts on it . . . he has taken an untenable concept absolutely as far as it can go'. Critics who raise objections to *Watchmen*'s 'serious tone' seem to think Moore was oblivious to the idea that superheroes are inherently childish and open to ridicule. This, though, is a misapprehension. When Moore embarked upon the project he did so in the belief that a relatively expensive, direct-sales-only comic had no appeal except for existing comics fans, and deliberately played to that fanbase. But in the introduction to the original hardback edition of *Watchmen*, he noted that, once the series started receiving wider attention, what 'started life as merely a more cynical and baroque take upon the Justice League of America and their ilk suddenly found itself standing in the public marketplace of mainstream fiction, dressed in only a cloak and a pair of brightly coloured tights'.

But by 1986, as we've seen, comics readers were getting older, and with that came demands for more sophisticated storytelling. Those readers now expected to see stories that tackled social themes, had soap opera-style character development and displayed a keen awareness of comics history and tradition. Readers accepted the 'brightly coloured tights' as genre convention, just as fans of detective stories accept the murderer blurting out a confession as soon as he's identified. But *Watchmen* acquired a second audience: a more mainstream one of adults familiar with superheroes mainly from television and movies, and who had last read a comic in childhood. Much to the despair (or disdain) of comics aficionados, such people's view of superheroes was still dominated by the colourful Adam West *Batman* TV series and Lynda Carter's *Wonder Woman* (1976–9), which had been in much the same vein. Try as they might, even the Christopher Reeve *Superman* movies couldn't avoid camp – indeed *Superman III* (1983) and *Superman IV* (1987) all but surrendered to it. It was therefore ironic that – thanks to *Watchmen, The Dark Knight Returns*, *The Killing Joke* and the 1989 *Batman* movie directed by Tim Burton, which took cues from Moore and Frank Miller's work – the public perception of what made a good Batman story would soon swing hard the other way. Ten years after *Watchmen*, Joel Schumacher's Batman movies would be rejected by audiences as being too camp and not gritty enough.

The superhero conventions *Watchmen* (and *The Dark Knight Returns*) aimed at were therefore those of the *Batman* TV series, not anything from comics produced in the early eighties. The story opens with a superhero climbing up a skyscraper on a grappling line, like Batman and Robin, while the Batman-like Nite Owl's costume parodies Adam West's TV costume merely by copying it. The heyday of the superheroes in *Watchmen*, moreover, had been in the swinging sixties. It's also significant which notes *Watchmen* doesn't play – the lack of '*Ka-pow!*', '*Splat!*'-type sound effects and 'Meanwhile, in stately Wayne Manor' style captions.

And *Watchmen* addresses the most familiar absurdity of the genre head on. The Comedian and Silk Spectre wear fairly standard superhero outfits. Nite Owl does indeed wear his underpants on the outside, while Dr Manhattan fights the Vietnam War in *only* his underpants – he later disposes even of those, preferring to be naked. In some later attempts to tell more grown-up superhero stories (including the movie version of *Watchmen*), 'brightly coloured tights' give way to more practical solutions like leather and moulded body armour; others, like the television series *Smallville* and *Heroes*, would give their superheroes ordinary clothes. Yet, rather than thinking Superman would become plausible if only he wore a jacket, Moore and Gibbons turned the 'real world logic' on its head and asked who would pull on a cape and tights: 'It wouldn't always be a terribly healthy person. Some people would be doing it purely for the sexual excitement of dressing up, others for the excitement of beating somebody up. Some are doing it for political reasons, many are doing it for altruistic motives, but there would certainly be a percentage who would have rather odd psychological afflictions in their make-up . . . There's just something about anybody who would dress up in a mask and costume that's not quite normal.'

Any adult – every vaguely thoughtful small child – understands that you don't fight crime by putting on a leotard, and this inevitably short-circuits any attempt to treat superheroes 'realistically'. Moore and Gibbons understood this. The *New York Times* may have hailed the series for its 'staggeringly complex psychological profiles' but this is not a claim that survives contact with the book. As Grant Morrison noted, it deals in stock action-narrative types:

> Dazzled by its technical excellence, *Watchmen*'s readership was willing to overlook a cast of surprisingly conventional Hollywood stereotypes: the inhibited guy who had to get his mojo back; the boffin losing touch with his humanity; the overbearing showbiz mom who drove her daughter to excel while hiding from her the secret of her dubious parentage; the prison psychiatrist so drawn into the dark inner life of his patient that his own life cracked under the weight. The *Watchmen* characters were drawn from a repertoire of central casting cyphers.

The characters are a series of different punchlines to the same joke. Nite Owl, the equivalent of Batman, is flabby and impotent; the analogues of Captain America and Superman killed civilians in Vietnam; Silk Spectre, the generic superheroine, has gone from being jailbait to being on the government payroll as an escort; Ozymandias has used his great genius to market action figures of himself. These are not keen psychological insights. *Watchmen* is not an attempt to rehabilitate the concept of the superhero, it's an effort to test it to destruction. However dirty the city where the superheroes live, however much graffiti it has, however much you psychoanalyse superheroes, however many 'real world' problems you saddle them with, the answer to 'how can you depict superheroes realistically?' that *Watchmen* inevitably comes to, from many different perspectives and directions, is 'you can't'. As Moore would later say of *The Killing Joke*, 'Batman and the Joker are not real characters and they do not resemble anyone you'd ever meet.'

The humour nevertheless runs more deeply than just the observation that superheroes are silly, or a narrative suffused with a mass of incidental details, visual and literary puns. The bigger picture is also underpinned by black comedy and vicious ironies. One way to understand this is to examine the 'joke' Dreiberg tells to Laurie Jupiter at the end of the first issue. The former Nite Owl and Silk Spectre are reminiscing about Captain Carnage, a minor villain they had both encountered who gained sexual pleasure from being beaten up (there are hints that Dreiberg became Nite Owl at least partly for similar reasons). Captain Carnage's career came to an abrupt end when 'he pulled it on Rorschach and Rorschach dropped him down an elevator shaft'. Laurie and Dreiberg start laughing:

LAURIE: Oh God, I'm sorry, that isn't funny. Ha ha ha ha ha!

DREIBERG: Ha ha ha! No, I guess it's not.

Is it funny? Yes, from certain perspectives; no, from others. As an event it would be a tragedy, as an anecdote it's amusing.

Or take another example: in Chapter VI of *Watchmen*, Rorschach kills two dogs with a meat cleaver, then throws their corpses at a paedophile, Grice, who had murdered a young victim and fed her to those dogs. The vigilante then handcuffs the killer, douses him in kerosene and sets fire to him, sticking around to watch him die. From what possible perspective is *that* funny?

That scene is one of those in which the differences between the comic and the movie adaptation are instructive. The *Watchmen* movie is consistently more violent than the comic, and never more so than in this sequence: on the silver screen we see Rorschach split Grice's head in half with a meat cleaver, then keep hacking – nine times, in total. The comic implies violence, but cuts away before we see any and the vivid colouring adds to the lurid unreality. Moore has said of his relationship to comedy, 'I don't think I'm one of those crying-on-the-inside clowns so much as sort of sniggering on the inside tragedian. My favourite comedies are ones that have an edge of tragedy. My favourite tragedies are the ones where you almost find yourself laughing. It's too awful, and you're taken to that edge.' Or, to paraphrase Oscar Wilde: to have one bright red dead bloodstained dog thrown at you is a misfortune, but to have *two* thrown at you borders on absurdity.

Traditionally, darker narratives have used comic relief that takes the form of an interlude between serious scenes. Moore rarely does that, instead tipping throwaway puns, ironies or absurdities into the darkest material in the story, making it even more unsettling. There's more than a touch of the Grand Guignol to much of his work, a theatrical exuberance that leads to fully fledged musical numbers in stories like *The Killing Joke* and *The League of Extraordinary Gentlemen: Century 1910*. A good demonstration of this is 'This Vicious Cabaret', which kicks off *V for Vendetta* Book Two, first published in *Warrior* #12 (August 1983). Formally, it's a summary of the story so far, presented as a song, sung by V who sits at a piano, inviting us to the show. The musical notes are printed below the panels (the song was recorded at the time by David J from Bauhaus and released as a single). It ends with a flourish, and a nasty twist:

There's thrills and chills and girls galore
There's sing-songs and surprises.
There's something here for everyone,
Reserve your seat today!
There's mischiefs and malarkies
But no queers, or yids, or darkies.
Within this bastards' carnival,
This vicious cabaret!

The effect is almost one of lifting the audience a tiny way before a final plunge. Again, there's the 'ironic counterpoint' between the pictures of a man singing a jolly song and the nasty words. As with *Watchmen* (and *The Killing Joke*), whatever is happening, whatever horrors the words are telling us about, we're confronted with the image of a fixed grin.

Critics who've accused *Watchmen* of an adolescent preoccupation with nihilism and violence focus on Rorschach and assume Moore is endorsing Rorschach's view of the world, setting him up as a hero to be emulated, or even using him simply as a mouthpiece for his own ideas. With that reading, Moore's view is that Grice's fate represents a just punishment for a cruel man.

Thinking Rorschach is the main character is an understandable mistake. The story opens with Rorschach's narration, while the first issue follows his lonely investigation of the Comedian's murder. And it's through Rorschach we first meet the other superheroes, as he goes to each of them in turn and warns them to be on their guard. Rorschach sets the scene and the tone. But Moore has said, 'I don't think there is a centre of the book. I mean, part of what *Watchmen* is about is that all of the characters have got very, very distinctive views of the world, but they're all completely different.' Subsequent issues are told from the points of view of other characters with contrasting perspectives; as Moore has also said, 'I don't think Dr Manhattan is dark; I don't think that Nite Owl is dark.' Even reading the first chapter of *Watchmen*, before we've seen chapters told from other viewpoints, it ought to be clear Rorschach is not 'right', or representative of the norm. It quickly becomes clear he is, as Moore put it at the time, 'a psychotic vigilante, driven by strange fascistic notions, who's not particularly fussy about whom he kills'. It might be possible to imagine that *Watchmen*'s opening line, presented as an entry in Rorschach's journal – 'Dog carcass in alley this morning, tire tread on burst stomach. This city is afraid of me. I have seen its true face' – is Alan Moore presenting his own view of New York, through Rorschach. An avid fan might recall Moore's write-up of his visit to the real New York City, and – if that fan felt Moore was invariably 'serious' – conclude that he had a particular vision of the place: 'making sure I don't get eaten by subway cannibals or end up sleeping on the grating . . . the [hotel] room is big enough to induce agoraphobia . . . there is a little plate informing me I should keep the door double-locked at all times and always look through the peephole before answering it, in case it's a bag lady with a meat cleaver and a shopping bag full of index fingers . . . I pass the night without hearing a single murder . . . manage to walk all the way to the DC offices without getting shot or sexually assaulted'. Although that fan should also have spotted there are clear echoes of *Grit!*, Moore's spoof of grim and gritty comics (see right).

It might equally be possible to read a subsequent line, also from Rorschach's Journal and the first page of *Watchmen*, at face value: 'They could have followed in the footsteps of good men like my father, or President Truman. Decent men who believed in a day's work for a day's pay.' A few pages later, when a policeman describes Rorschach as 'crazier than a snake's armpit and wanted on two counts Murder One', we might distrust this authority figure and imagine that a corrupt regime has framed our hero for crimes he didn't commit. (As it happens, Rorschach *is* eventually framed for a murder he didn't commit, even though he admits to the two mentioned here.) For similar reasons, we might distrust Laurie's summary of him, 'I just don't like Rorschach. He's sick. Sick inside his mind. I don't like the way he smells or that horrible monotone voice or anything. The sooner the police put him away, the better.' But by the end of the issue, when Rorschach asks himself 'Why are so few of us left active, healthy and without personality disorders?', there's unmistakably a gulf between what we readers can see and how Rorschach is interpreting it.

A key exchange in the first issue is this:

RORSCHACH: Maybe someone's picking off costumed heroes.

DREIBERG: Um. Don't you think that's maybe a little paranoid?

RORSCHACH: That's what they're saying about me now? That I'm paranoid?

Rorschach's last line is, of course, a straightforwardly set up and paid-off joke, but not one that the character himself is in on. Elsewhere, tellingly, Rorschach has trouble recognising irony or when someone is trying to be funny. His belief that he is the only sane man in a crazy world is, of course, what every crazed loner thinks. By the end of the first issue, at the very latest, every reader should understand Rorschach is over-the-top, 'too awful' – at that edge Moore identified between tragedy and comedy.

There's a broader point being made. Moore based Rorschach's writing style on the notes left by the serial killer 'Son of Sam', whose second note, from May 1977, is practically a description of the first page of *Watchmen*:

> Hello from the gutters of N.Y.C. which are filled with dog manure, vomit, stale wine, urine and blood. Hello from the sewers of N.Y.C. which swallow up these delicacies when they are washed away by the sweeper trucks. Hello from the

cracks in the sidewalks of N.Y.C. and from the ants that dwell in these cracks and feed in the dried blood of the dead that has settled into the cracks.

Towards the end of *Watchmen*, when the editor of the newspaper *New Frontiersman* hears the first line of Rorschach's journal, he declares, 'Jesus, who's it from? Son of Sam? Sling it on the crank file.' The joke is that the real-world equivalent of the only superhero in *Watchmen* who hasn't compromised his principles is a notorious serial killer.

There are further ambiguities about Rorschach's character. His insistence that, like his mask, the world is sharply divided between black and white is clearly a symptom of mental illness. But the idea that the world – or at least its superhuman population – can be neatly divided up between 'superheroes' and 'supervillains', 'good' and 'evil', underpins the whole of the genre. In those terms Ozymandias' plan, as he says himself, is reminiscent of a Republic Serial villain, whereas Rorschach, in overcoming all obstacles to investigate and confront Ozymandias in his base, is the hero.

At heart, Ozymandias' plan to destroy New York to shock Russia and America into co-operating is an entry-level moral dilemma: 'Is killing X number of people justified if it saves more than X number of people?' The familiarity of the question does not mean there's one morally absolute answer. It is also, of course, a dilemma familiar from the history of atomic weapons. In Chapter VI, we learn that a young Walter Kovacs (who would become Rorschach) had written, 'I like President Truman, the way dad would of wanted me to. He dropped the atom bomb on Japan and saved millions of lives because if he hadn't of, then there would of been a lot more war than there was and more people would of been killed. I think it was a good thing to drop the atom bomb on Japan.' Yet Rorschach is the only one of the heroes who defies Ozymandias. He sees *this* mass killing as unjustified. Is this because of some form of patriotism? Millions of Americans die, America comes to co-operate with Soviet Russia – does Rorschach truly believe 'better dead than Red'? Or, as has been speculated, is it a gender issue? Does Rorschach think Truman and war are masculine, whereas Ozymandias is liberal and effeminate? Moore gives us plenty of material to work with, including a whole chapter dedicated to an in-story psychiatric analysis of the character, but leaves us to interpret what we're told.

This holds true throughout *Watchmen*. The character who stands for 'the American Way' is the Comedian – a man we see attempting rape, shooting a pregnant woman, and who almost certainly assassinated JFK. Dr Manhattan is the only character with 'superpowers', and is compared with both Superman and God in the story . . . but while they are by definition moral paragons, Dr Manhattan is utterly amoral, capable of saying 'a live body and a dead body contain the same number of particles. Structurally, there's no discernible difference. Life and death are unquantifiable abstracts. Why should I be concerned?' When he walks among the ruins of New York in the last chapter, his deterministic, materialistic view of the universe means he's unable to make a meaningful distinction between the corpses and the rubble. Moore's point is that none of these people are 'right' or 'wrong', it all depends on your perspective; not even the creators of *Watchmen* can make such rulings.

So can Alan Moore's own opinion be disentangled from the narrative?

There's a deep irony evident in *Watchmen*, one that we see in Moore's other work, and so we might identify this as approaching a cohesive Alan Moore worldview. The critic John Loyd identifies the sequence where Rorschach kills Grice as containing one of the keys to such a worldview, which he terms the 'Big Joke'. As Rorschach recounts the story to his psychiatrist, he concludes that the human condition is that we are 'Born from oblivion; bear children hell-bound as ourselves; go into oblivion. There is nothing else. Existence is random. Has no pattern save what we imagine after staring at it for too long. No meaning save what we choose to impose. This rudderless world is not shaped by vague, metaphysical forces.' The 'Big Joke' is that although various characters insist that the world is 'rudderless', in fact it isn't. *Watchmen* the comic is the opposite of 'rudderless'; it was almost certainly the most carefully designed comic ever created, with extraordinary attention to detail. In the first script, Moore takes fifty-six lines to describe the opening panel, the close-up of a smiley badge lying in a gutter. Throughout, Gibbons finds room to add even more intricacies than appear in the scripts. And as the series progressed, the writer and artist became ever more confident and the end result grew ever more complex. Issue 5 is structured as an elaborate palindrome, with an almost perfectly symmetrical sequence of events. So does this mean Dr Manhattan is right? He has the ability to remember the future as well as the past, so he sees nothing but pattern. But this isn't liberating, it means he is constrained within a clockwork mechanism of cause and effect, condemned to see every one of the connections that bind the world, to be locked into a fixed course of action, to merely be the only puppet with the ability to 'see the strings'. Dr Manhattan and Rorschach can't both be right – at least not comfortably – but, ultimately, it doesn't matter: either way is equally bleak and nihilistic.

Watchmen presents a world where the driving force of destiny is a dark irony. It is, as more than one character observes, all one big joke.

COMEDIAN: Listen . . . once you figure out what a joke everything is, being the Comedian's the only thing that makes sense.

DR MANHATTAN: The charred villages, the boys with necklaces of human ears . . . these are part of the joke.

COMEDIAN: Hey . . . I never said it was a good joke! I'm just playing along with the gag . . .

There are similar sentiments at work in *The Killing Joke*:

JOKER: It's all a joke! Everything anybody ever valued or struggled for . . . it's all a monstrous, demented gag! So why can't you see the funny side? Why aren't you laughing?

BATMAN: Because I've heard it before . . . and it wasn't funny the first time.

And it's there even in a light-hearted example Moore gives in a 1986 essay about the craft of comics writing, when he illustrates character by having a stamp-collecting policeman describe his formative moment as follows: 'I was just standing there, looking at my stamp album and the priceless collection that it had taken me years to build, when all of a sudden I realised that since I had foolishly pasted all of them directly into the album using an industrial-strength adhesive, they were completely worthless. I understood then that the universe was just a cruel joke upon mankind, and that life was pointless. I became completely cynical about human existence and saw the essential stupidity of all effort and human striving. At this point I decided to join the police force.'

*

It's possible to see this consistent, extremely pessimistic worldview across a lot of Moore's work from the eighties. The world is a fragile place, on the brink of economic, social and environmental collapse. The 'man on the street' is wilfully oblivious to politics, but it doesn't matter because the apocalypse is imminent and it's only a question of *how* society is going to collapse under the weight of intractable social problems. The proximate cause is the right wing – Norsefire in *V for Vendetta*, Nixon and his cabal in *Watchmen* – using the logic of the Vietnam War: that it's necessary to bomb the village to save it. The liberal left might mean well, but do more harm than good. In *V for Vendetta*, CND get their way, the UK disarms unilaterally and a nuclear war promptly starts. In *Watchmen*, the 'liberal' Ozymandias kills millions. *V for Vendetta*, *Watchmen* and *Marvelman* all end with the collapse of the old order. In the end, everything we've strived for is pointless, and it's all going to be swept away.

So is this also Moore's view of *our* world (or, more precisely, was it his view around the time he was writing *Watchmen*)? This is how he saw things in 1988:

> The big chill is coming down for sure. All that bad science fiction and all those paranoid hippy prophecies about the way the country was going . . . as it turns out they were true! Outside my door the other day was one of those 'Dark Riders of Mordor' policemen, those with the visor and the cloak, the horse wears a visor too. One of these horses was shouldering a couple of kids up against the garage door. Just football fans on the way down to the match. We ran outside to get a photo of it and one of those vans with the rotating video cameras came by. The police stated in the paper: 'We are looking forward to this match so we can try out our new crowd control methods.' It was obvious looking at it that it wasn't designed just to handle football fans. You don't put that much money into stopping trouble erupting at games between Northampton and Sunderland! Sure enough, two weeks later at the Clause 28 rally the police had them out again. They turned up and arrested girls for kissing and for holding placards, saying they were offensive weapons.

The eighties saw Margaret Thatcher's Conservative Party win successive landslide General Election victories, doing so on a platform of an economic policy based on closing down or selling off great sections of manufacturing industry, taking power from local councils and centralising it in Westminster, breaking the trade unions, selling off council housing and opposing at every turn the 'permissive sixties'. Every feature of the British political landscape of the eighties appalled Moore, although – erudite and opinionated as he was – he was reticent about what could be done: 'Please understand that I'm not yet so drug-addled or enthused by my own intellect as to suggest that we're going to reach a solution, or anything like a solution. All I want to do is present the questions as I see them in as interesting a light as possible.'

More recently, Moore's view has remained similar, but has mellowed: 'The apocalyptic bleakness of comics over the past 15 years sometimes seems odd to me, because it's like that was a bad mood that I was in 15 years ago. It was the 1980s, we'd got this insane right-wing Boadicea running the country, and I was in a bad mood, politically and socially and in most other ways. So that tended to reflect in my work . . . I wouldn't say that my new stuff is all bunny rabbits and blue-skies optimism, but it's probably got a lot more of a positive spin on it than the work I was doing back in the eighties. This is a different century.' When he describes the world, he does so in terms that Ozymandias might have in *Watchmen*: 'We're an inventive bunch and when things sort of get as dire as they are at the moment, it comes down to a basic thing whether we will come out of it with some way round this or we won't . . . impending death hanging over us does tend to focus the mind wonderfully, so it might be that some of these problems incite their own solutions. That's what I'm hoping.' And while he still can't see the broader solution for civilisation, there's a recognition of some resolution at the human scale:

> For all of us, life is a matter of trying to come to terms with the universe and I think that in its most benign sense, apocalypse is the moment of revelation, where we realise that all of our attempts to make sense of the universe are hopelessly off the mark and in the ruins of our theories we kind of get a glimpse, we have what drunks call a 'moment of lucidity' of the things that are really important . . . revelations can come in sorts of ways in everybody's life.

So is *Watchmen* a comedy? Well, its jokes tend towards the dark, the cruel and even the sick, but there are plenty of jokes in there. Comedies have happy endings, and *Watchmen* . . . might. The world is not destroyed, and it no longer seems inevitable that it will be. Dreiberg and Laurie, the most 'ordinary' characters in the story, have put aside the emotional baggage from their past and started thinking about their future together. Is *Watchmen* cheerful and life-affirming, then? No, not for the most part, but neither is it written in a monotone, endlessly dark and dreary. While it is 'by the writer of *V for Vendetta* and *The Killing Joke*', to fully understand *Watchmen*, it's important to understand that it's just as much 'by the writer of *DR & Quinch* and "March of the Sinister Ducks"'.

7 WATCHMEN II

'I'm a comic book messiah for the 1990s, and having risen from my humble terraced street origins, and having survived my tenure as one of the dole queue millions, I've now become a successful small businessman of no mean repute, and I believe that this is the face of success in Mrs Thatcher's Britain.'

Alan Moore, *Monsters, Maniacs and Moore*

With the dust settling from *Watchmen*, 1987 saw perhaps the pivotal point in Alan Moore's creative life, as both he and the comics industry tried to figure out what would come next.

Moore and Gibbons' work on *Watchmen* finally came to an end around May 1987, over three years after they first conceived the project. They knew the series was a huge critical and sales hit before they had started on the final issues. In the event, though, finishing the book had become something of a scramble, with Moore sending individual pages of scripts over to Gibbons by taxi as he completed them and the schedule slipping by a couple of months so that the last issue had to be resolicited (that is, the original orders placed by comic book stores were cancelled and they had to order the issue again). *Watchmen* #12, the final number, was published on 11 July 1987. The series would be collected into a 'graphic novel' in December, and quickly become a bestseller.

In the UK, style magazines and Sunday supplements were now running articles heralding the advent of comics for grown-ups. One of the first was by Neil Gaiman, in the 27 July 1986 edition of the *Today* newspaper, and it serves as a template for practically every subsequent mainstream article. It informed readers that comics were not just for kids any more; that the quintessentially American superhero was now being written and drawn by British talent with an outsider's perspective on US society; and that comics like *Watchmen* included political commentary. It noted that Alan Moore was one of a new breed of British comics creators whose work could be found in *2000AD*, referenced Frank Miller's *Dark Knight* and mentioned the Forbidden Planet comic shop in central London. A longer piece by Don Watson in the *Observer* in November 1986, 'Shazam! The Hero Breaks Down', followed almost exactly the same pattern, noting, 'Alan Moore's fearsome appearance (over six feet tall, shoulder-length hair and beard) belies a character of gentleness and restless intelligence. Despite the fact that the title that made his name, *Swamp Thing* monthly, is set in the rotting opulence of the American South, he himself still resides in his native Northampton.'

The hype was carefully nurtured by publisher Titan. Not only did Titan Books publish collected editions of both British and American material, its distribution arm supplied comics to shops, and its London comic shop, Forbidden Planet, was the largest in the UK. Titan had hired a PR man, Igor Goldkind, to find ways to market comics to a wider audience. He popularised the name 'graphic novel', admitting 'I stole the term outright from Will Eisner', but it was a strategy that persuaded bookshops to stock comics.

The PR effort was augmented by the publication as collections of three superb comics that had previously appeared in serial form: *The Dark Knight Returns*, *Watchmen* and *Maus* – 'the Big Three', as they became known. Alongside their regular references to *Dark Knight*, the British press would often mention *Maus*, Art Spiegelman's account of the Holocaust told using cartoon mice, but they would always concentrate on *Watchmen* and Alan Moore. Moore's striking figure and *Watchmen*'s smiley badge illustrated almost every article. By 1988, the badge was cropping up in all sorts of places: as set dressing in a Lenny Henry sitcom, on a *Doctor Who* companion's bomber jacket, ubiquitously as the emblem of electronic dance group Bomb the Bass. Moore and his work were name-checked by all sorts of bands. The Chameleons sang 'Swamp Thing', Transvision Vamp were 'Hanging Out with Halo Jones'. In 1989 Pop Will Eat Itself released 'Can U Dig It?', a list of songs, movies, TV and comics they liked, which name-checked *V for Vendetta* and had the repeated refrain 'Alan Moore knows the score'.

Moore was now skirting the boundary between being a cult figure and a celebrity. His parents were pleased for him. 'As I started to realise some of my idle teenage ambitions, I don't think they quite believed it at first, at least to start with. They thought it was going to end in disappointment and it would prove to be impossible . . . my father was very impressed when he saw me on television for the first time. He never read my work . . . but he understood that if you appeared on television and people were saying nice things about you, you were doing well.' Moore was everywhere: he appeared on Radio 4's arts show *Kaleidoscope* and in the very first issue of *Q* (October 1986). Having talked about *Swamp Thing* during one appearance on children's Saturday morning show *Get Fresh*, he then sat on a panel with Cliff Richard, Shakin' Stevens, Alvin Stardust and a dog from *EastEnders* to judge that week's pop singles. He was interviewed on an arts programme by Muriel Gray and by Paula Yates on the 14 November 1986 edition of late night music show *The Tube*. 'At that point I was the most successful comic writer that had ever been. I felt weird because with the best will in the world you can get cut off from people if you become a success; all of a sudden your time is taken up doing TV things, doing interviews – not like this one, but interviews with some magazine in Holland, another in Germany, another in France; you're filming documentaries about your life . . .'

That last point was a reference to *Monsters, Maniacs and Moore* (1987), a half-hour TV documentary made by Central Television as part of their long-running *England Their England* series, and which took the form of Moore interviewing himself. He makes the case for comics in the programme by stating that their low price means they are 'within reach of anybody'. There's a long discussion of the environmental themes of *Swamp Thing* and his work for *2000AD*. He shows us around Northampton, explains the political intent of his comics, reads 'A Cautionary Fable' (from *2000AD* #240) to his daughters Amber and Leah, and provides a detailed exegesis of 'The March of the Sinister Ducks'. Asking himself if he has a messiah complex, he notes 'would I have a haircut like this if I didn't?'

One aspect of Moore's life that wasn't picked up by the press was that around this time Debbie Delano, a mutual friend for many years, had moved in with Alan and Phyllis to their house on Birchfield Road. Moore says they tried a 'sort of an experimental relationship, I suppose you'd call it. It was something we were very serious about, and it endured for two to three years, which was a mark of that seriousness.'

As with much of Moore's personal life, it's a mistake to confuse his choice not to throw the relationship into the limelight by writing about it with secrecy or evasion. The three were open with friends and family about their relationship. Moore drew Phyllis and Debbie in a piece for *Heartbreak Hotel* (see next page).

Public exposure brought with it a degree of anxiety for Moore, who in 1986 admitted, 'I like the undeserved adulation, but in some ways I'd almost rather write anonymously.' He understood the game he had to play, though. Much to the amusement of some of his peers, Moore bought a shiny white suit cut fashionably – for the summer of 1986 – short at the sleeves and made himself available to anyone who wanted to talk to him. As Igor Goldkind noted, Moore 'was adopted as a kind of spokesman for adult comics – a task he fulfilled with great patience, as virtually every interested journalist buttonholed him for his views. He was soon dubbed

"Britain's First Comics Megastar", and for once the media analysis rang true.'

Moore tirelessly heralded the coming of the adult comic. He knew, though, that his main role in the revolution would be to write some of the 'graphic novels' everyone was hearing so much about. His fans were interested in a follow-up to *Watchmen*. After the success of *The Dark Knight Returns*, Frank Miller had been commissioned to write *Batman: Year One*, a 'grittier' origin story, and it was a huge hit. From the time *Watchmen* started publication, Moore and Gibbons had said they weren't interested in a continuation of their story, but they were open to the idea of exploring other aspects of that world. Moore commented: 'We might do a series called *Minutemen*, detailing the superheroes of the 1940s. We've also thought of maybe doing a series called *Tales of the Black Freighter*, which would be this pirate comic-book series that we've mentioned running in that alternate world. But, no, there will not be another series of *Watchmen*.' Gibbons confirmed this: 'Obviously, Alan and I could make ourselves a fortune on *Watchmen 2* next year. I just can't think of any reason to do it other than the obvious monetary ones. *Minutemen* appeals because it's a different era and a different story.'

They both stuck to this line in interview after interview, although Moore occasionally alluded to an important caveat (my emphasis): 'The only possible spin-off we're thinking of is – maybe in four or five years time, *ownership position permitting* – we might do a *Minutemen* book. There would be no sequel.'

As *Watchmen* reached its conclusion, Moore's fans were not short of further reading. Though he vetoed a couple of reprint projects – he didn't think his *Sounds* work was of high enough quality, and continued to block reprints of his Marvel UK material – almost all of his early British work was repackaged and reprinted for both the US and UK markets. The best of his *Future Shocks* and *Time Twisters* were branded by name in the collections *Alan Moore's Shocking Futures* and *Alan Moore's Twisted Times*; Moore wrote introductions for them (possibly because although he wasn't due payment from the reprints themselves, the writer of the Introduction was on a 1 per cent royalty), and contributed a page to a strip in *2000AD* #500 – his last work for the title. A four-volume set of all the *Maxwell the Magic Cat* strips was published, a fact that embarrassed Moore so much he donated his fee to Greenpeace. Eclipse were publishing *Miracleman,* and by this point it was all new material. Moore was a frequent contributor to small press comics in Britain and America, providing a vast range of pieces encompassing everything from a dramatised account of real soldiers' experience of war to an illustration of Godzilla. DC were due to publish *V for Vendetta*, with Moore and David Lloyd completing the story that had been abruptly halted by the cancellation of *Warrior*. The long-gestating Batman/Joker graphic novel, *The Killing Joke*, would soon be released, and Moore was interested in writing a *Mr Monster/Swamp Thing* crossover.

Astute readers could spot, though, that all was not well between Alan Moore and DC. There were no longer any shorter pieces or guest writing from Moore in DC comics. Previously prolific, he had finished work on his last issue of *Swamp Thing* around the same time he completed the script for the twelfth and final issue of *Watchmen*. The script for *The Killing Joke* had been written in 1985. Two-thirds of *V for Vendetta* was to consist of reprints from *Warrior*. Even if it wasn't going to be a sequel to *Watchmen*, where was Moore's new major project, and why weren't DC publishing it?

The answer was that there had been a major falling out between Alan Moore and DC Comics. Early in 1987, Moore had declared publicly that he would never work for the company again.

*

Moore had begun writing *Watchmen* on extremely good terms with DC. *Watchmen* #1 was published in May 1986, but a full year earlier, as the first issues were being assembled, those at DC understood it was something special and had proudly shown it off to people visiting the offices, including the author Michael Crichton. Artistically, Moore and Gibbons were given a virtually free hand and DC's resources allowed innovations with such matters as the format of the comic and the graphic design. The writer and artist trusted each other, DC trusted them. They were not working within the constraints of an existing 'line', and this removed whole layers of corporate oversight and editorial concern. Gibbons has said that while the series was being developed, there was no time pressure on them. *Watchmen*'s editor was kept busy, though. Barbara Randall, who assumed the role midway through the series, says 'There was a hell of a lot to do: music rights, production issues (you wouldn't believe how many hours it took to create a "paper clip" in those days before personal computers, scanners, and Photoshop!), long calls with Alan walking through the content of the back matter, mostly just congratulatory calls to Dave because his work was excellent.'

Moore continued to be given other plum jobs at DC, who were undertaking a relaunch of their entire range to make it more appealing to modern readers. In 1986, Julius Schwartz commissioned him to write *Whatever Happened to the Man of Tomorrow?*, a send-off for the 'original' Superman before the character was given a major revamp; there are rumours Moore had to turn down the offer to become one of the writers for the revamped version because he was too busy with *Watchmen*. He wrote a number of one-off strips, and while writing *Watchmen*, he'd continued to pitch ideas to DC. Moore and Gibbons discussed the idea of working together on a lighthearted version of Captain Marvel after *Watchmen*, as an antidote to all the darkness. One of Moore's last pitches to DC would be *Twilight* (also referred to as *Twilight of the Superheroes*), a vast series set in the future of the DC Universe, with the same end-of-days feeling as *The Dark Knight Returns*, but applied to the entire pantheon of superheroes. It had big roles for characters Moore had created, such as John Constantine and Sodom Yat, but also for Superman, Batman, Wonder Woman and so on. The pitch document is undated but internal evidence suggests it was written in late 1986. Moore thinks,

'*Twilight* was the *Watchmen II* sort of proposal . . . It was just this big crossover . . . I guess that they were very pleased by the success of *Watchmen* and . . . I think we could have done more or less whatever we wanted.' By the beginning of 1987, though, Moore was 'starting to realise DC weren't necessarily my friends.'

DC's business model was based around long-running ongoing monthly comics featuring superheroes created decades before – Superman, Batman and Robin, Wonder Woman, the Flash, Green Lantern, the Teen Titans and many more. By 1987, the oldest titles, *Action Comics* and *Detective Comics* (featuring Superman and Batman respectively), were both heading towards their 600th issue. There had been legal disputes over the creation and ownership of many of these characters, but DC treated them all, from the household names to the most obscure one-off supporting character, as corporate property, licensing merchandise as well as producing their own.

Watchmen was unusual in being a creator-led limited series that used original characters, but these were not entirely uncharted waters for DC. Mike W. Barr and Brian Bolland had co-created *Camelot 3000* (1982), Frank Miller had created *Ronin* (1983). By the time Moore started working for DC, creators were beginning to enjoy a few more rights. Contracts changed so that writers and artists received payments if their characters were reused. *Swamp Thing* #37 had seen the debut of John Constantine, a working-class magician who proved instantly popular and was eventually given his own monthly title, *Hellblazer*, which inspired a 2005 feature film starring Keanu Reeves. If Constantine had been introduced just a year earlier, they would have received nothing; now, with every appearance, the creators split a small payment. Writers and artists also became eligible for at least some form of royalty payment for strong sales and reprints. Artists were paid royalties if their work was sold as a poster. Original art was returned to the artists, who could sell it on directly to fans, or in batches to comic shops.

Watchmen was commissioned in the knowledge that there was now a distinct demographic of older comic fans, keen for less childish stories and willing to pay a premium for them, and that the best way to produce such comics was to let creators have more creative freedom and a financial stake in the success of the project. Moore's *Swamp Thing* contract had been a simple work-for-hire arrangement that came into force when he cashed his cheque; the *Watchmen* contract was a far more substantial, complicated legal document.

Watchmen told a complex and intertwined story where small events that initially seem unconnected converge towards a surprise apocalyptic finale that sees a demigod withdrawing from the mortal realm. As above, so below. Moore and Gibbons' series became the flashpoint for behind-the-scenes disputes that had been brewing within the industry for a number of years. Although no one seems to have put it in these terms at the time, *Watchmen* can be seen as the moment when comics stopped being magazines (ephemeral, editor-driven, deadline orientated, ongoing) and became novels (enduring, authored, carefully composed, complete). It was a change that caught out publisher and creators alike – and one that provoked a fierce rearguard action from the former. It's entirely fitting that the dispute culminated in an argument about what happened when a comic was *literally* turned into a novel.

The first crack in the relationship between DC and Alan Moore appeared soon after *Watchmen* went on sale, in the summer of 1986, and it was one that all parties involved considered to be trivial. The *Watchmen* deal gave Moore and Gibbons a cut of merchandising revenue, but there was one loophole: DC were allowed to distribute 'promotional' items without paying the creators. It was a standard clause, understood to cover small things commonly given away in comic book stores or at conventions: buttons (badges, as they would be called in the UK) or flyers that folded out to become posters. For *Watchmen* replicas of the smiley button depicted in issue #1 were given away in great quantities, but some comic shops began charging for them, believing DC had set a recommended price of $1. Even when money was charged for the buttons, however, the DC marketing department classified them as 'self-liquidating promotional items', rather than merchandise. Moore and Gibbons received no money.

'Self-liquidating promotion' is a common marketing term, typically used to describe an offer where a consumer collects, say, proof-of-purchase tokens and sends them in for a 'free gift'. In reality, the consumer has paid for their 'free' gift, because the cost has been added to the price of the items they've had to purchase to get the tokens. So the promotion pays for itself (hence 'self liquidating'). When a comic shop 'gives away' a button to a customer buying a comic, there's no argument that it's exactly the same process. The disagreement came when DC's marketing department asserted that as they were the same item, the buttons were still 'promotional material' even if customers bought them. Moore and Gibbons disagreed with this interpretation, and as Gibbons diplomatically put it, 'discussion and eventual resolution ensued'; he 'spoke and wrote extensively to DC's executive vice-president, Paul Levitz, who, whilst not conceding the legal point, agreed to pay a sum equivalent to an 8 per cent royalty on the buttons'.

The dispute nevertheless created ill will between Moore and DC, and demonstrated to the writer that however accommodating they were, ultimately DC held all the power. 'It was these little bits of meanness. Well, really, to make one happy would have cost a few thousand dollars. And they would have kept my goodwill and that they haven't kept my goodwill I'm sure has lost them more than a few thousand dollars over the years.' Moore's estimate of how much he was owed seems about right. Eight per cent of retail price would be 8¢ per badge, split between Moore and Gibbons. In other words, Moore was due about $1,000 per 25,000 badges sold.

Before this, Moore had publicly expressed his happiness with the *Watchmen* deal. At a convention appearance in September 1986, he and Gibbons responded to the question 'Do you actually own *Watchmen*?' as follows:

MOORE: My understanding is that when *Watchmen* is finished and DC have not used the characters for a year, they're ours.

GIBBONS: They pay us a substantial amount of money . . .

MOORE: . . . to retain the rights. So basically they're not ours, but if DC is working with the characters in our interest then they might as well be. On the other hand, if the characters have outlived their natural lifespan and DC doesn't want to do anything with them, then after a year we've got them and we can do what we want with them, which I'm perfectly happy with.

Rights reversion clauses are absolutely standard across book publishing. The deal is that if a book is kept in print, its publisher retains the rights, and if the book goes out of print then, after a period defined in the contract, the rights revert to the author. What 'the rights' include varies from contract to contract, and the *Watchmen* contract has never been made public, but statements by a number of parties to it indicate that they understand the *Watchmen* contract to

say that DC have the rights to the property lock, stock and barrel – giving them the absolute legal right to publish the book, exploit the characters, publish a sequel, sell merchandise, license foreign language editions, and negotiate movie and television deals. It was only as *Watchmen* neared completion that Moore came to understand that 'if DC kept it in print forever, then they would have the rights to it forever.'

It's easy to gloss this as a howler on Moore's part, or as the familiar story of an artist signing a Faustian contract without reading the small print. Alan Moore is a man very knowledgeable about the comics industry and had been fully aware that in the past publishers had exploited creators. Did he not read the contract? Gibbons remembers 'calling Alan when I first received the contract to discuss it. He told me he'd already signed it. I got a few changes made, mainly relating to equalising the starting point of royalties to writer and artist, before I signed.' Moore rarely contradicts himself, but over the years he has portrayed the *Watchmen* contract as both a hard-fought victory for creators' rights . . . and as a document he never bothered to read. He has even said both things in one interview answer:

> That was the understanding upon which we did *Watchmen* – that they understood that we wanted to actually own the work that we'd done, and that they were a 'new DC Comics' who were going to be more responsive to creators. And, they'd got this new contract worked out which meant that when the work went out of print, then the rights to it would revert to us – which sounded like a really good deal. I'd got no reason not to trust these people. They'd all been very, very friendly. They seemed to be delighted with the amount of extra comics they were selling. Even on that level, I thought, 'Well, they can see that I'm getting them an awful lot of good publicity, and I'm bringing them a great deal of money. So, if they are even competent business people, they surely won't be going out of their way to screw us in any way.' Now, I've since seen the *Watchmen* contract, which obviously we didn't read very closely at the time. It was the first contract that I'd ever seen – and I believe that it was a relatively rare event for a contract to actually exist in the comics business.

It should be stressed that this is no replay of the creators of Superman selling the rights for all time in return for $130, or of the countless cases where the creator of a lucrative character lives in poverty while the publisher makes millions.

Many would think Moore is in an enviable position. When the 'graphic novel' of *Watchmen* came out at the end of 1987, it quickly sold more copies than any individual issue (although contemporary press reports that it sold 'millions' within a year or so of release were exaggerated). The mainstream media attention generated by the original comic piqued the curiosity of readers who'd never dream of setting foot in a comic shop, or of laboriously collecting back issues. *Watchmen* was sold in ordinary bookshops, and it has kept selling year in, year out. The standard paperback is now in its thirty-third printing, and four other editions have been published in the US market alone. Thanks to the movie adaptation, *Watchmen* was the best-selling graphic novel of 2009, but even in 2007, before that peak in interest, it sold over 100,000 copies. In 2012, DC's senior vice-president of sales, Bob Wayne, stated *Watchmen* had sold 'over two million copies' to the mainstream book trade.

Moore's contract granted a 4 per cent royalty for *Watchmen*. By 1991, he was able to say '*Watchmen* has made me hundreds of thousands of pounds', and he has since stated that he has earned 'millions' from it and turned down millions more. Before *Watchmen* #4 was published, the movie rights had been optioned and Moore and Gibbons received money for that. Movie producer Don Murphy has claimed Moore was paid $350,000 for the movie rights, although Gibbons says 'we got a fraction of that between us'. Although that first attempt to film *Watchmen* collapsed – as did a couple of others – in 2009, when a *Watchmen* movie was finally completed, Moore was due some money from the movie and more from its merchandising, even though he passed his share of the latter to Gibbons. Moreover, he enjoyed a windfall from increased sales of the graphic novel thanks to interest in the film (his contract does not, however, entitle him to money from the *Before Watchmen* follow-up series that ran a couple of years later). The same deal applies to *V for Vendetta*, his other creator-owned DC work.

Moore's dispute with DC is not about money, then, at least it is not that he feels DC are withholding cash the contract says he is owed.

Neither is it a legal dispute. Over the years many, many comic book creators have taken their publishers to court. Most of the cases involve the same basic problem: material that has proved to be lucrative for far longer than originally envisaged and has been adapted for media and markets that barely existed when the original deal was struck. It is a situation complicated by the, at best, vague

wording of industry contracts, inconsistent or non-existent copyright notices, and the problem that many familiar elements of long-running characters were added over the years by a range of different creators. Just as Superman is the archetype for the superhero, he's come to be the archetype for the legal dispute over superhero creator rights. Joe Siegel and Jerry Shuster created the *Superman* strip published in *Action Comics* #1, the first appearance of the character, but that first issue didn't feature the familiar Superman symbol, the *Daily Planet*, Kryptonite, Smallville, the Fortress of Solitude, Lex Luthor, Jimmy Olsen, Superboy or Supergirl. In his first appearance, Superman couldn't fly, didn't have X-ray or heat vision. Which of these elements would the owners of 'the rights to Superman' own?

The legal dispute over Superman was underway before Moore started working in American comics, and has continued, literally, for generations. Moore knew this before he started working for DC. Legal issues make Alan Moore very uncomfortable, though, and it's tempting to see this as a class issue, or one stemming from his countercultural sensibilities: an instinctive distrust of the system. On the other hand, it may simply be that he understands that one tactic the media corporations use is to draw out proceedings to fight a war of attrition, and that if he initiated legal action he could spend the rest of his life, not to mention all his money, in court.

As long as there have been comic books, there have been men who have balanced a creative flair with business savvy, men like Will Eisner and Stan Lee. And in the eighties a new generation of entrepreneurs emerged: people like Dave Sim, Todd McFarlane, Neil Gaiman and Frank Miller cut deals, got rival publishers to enter bidding wars for their services, kept a keen eye on rights issues, the merchandising and spin-offs, and weren't afraid to lawyer up. A veteran comic book creator, who wishes to remain nameless, told me that he realised at some point his career goal had become to earn enough money freelancing for one major US comics publisher to be able eventually to afford to sue them for what he was really owed.

This is not Alan Moore. It is clear that, as Stephen Bissette has noted, 'Alan hates doing business.' That is not to say he is naïve or conflicted about the idea that a comic book publisher wants to make money. In pitch documents he would talk about merchandising potential and explain how his plan would increase sales of his and other books, but there was always the implication that it was up to someone else to implement all that. He writes the comic, he's delighted to do interviews and knows how to generate a headline, but the actual marketing and legal negotiations, the settling of disputes and rights clearances are not his job; that is what the other 92 per cent of the revenue is meant to be paying for.

Moore wants to create art, and to leave the commerce and legal stuff to people he trusts. In 2010, after DC approached him hoping to negotiate over a *Watchmen* follow-up project, he said (my emphasis): 'And so I would imagine that given our understanding of the industry standards during that time . . . there may be . . . I mean, *it's occurred to me that I could possibly get a lawyer to look into this*. There may be some problem with the contract, or some potential problem that may require my actual signature saying it's okay to go ahead with these prequels and sequels. It might be that they can't just do this.' There have been disputes over the *Watchmen* contract for twenty-five years, with millions of dollars at stake. Was Moore really saying that he had never so much as had a quick chat with a lawyer in all that time?

That interview caused a stir online, and commentators (both comics fans and professionals) accused him of naïvety, irony or flat-out dishonesty. But, no, it would be 2011 before Moore took legal advice: 'More recently,' it was reported, 'Moore says some lawyers involved with another of his projects offered to review the *Watchmen* contract he'd signed nearly three decades earlier. "It was a nostalgic moment seeing it after all these years," he says. "There was a clause that essentially said that, if in the future, there were any documents or contracts that I refused to sign, DC was entitled to appoint an attorney to sign them instead".' Whether or not DC are able to override the withholding of his consent in the way Moore describes, his falling out with the publisher in early 1987 was not because of a dispute over interpretation of the small print in a contract. Regardless of the legal position, it is clear that at the time he thought DC were following the wording of the agreement he had signed.

Given that he has received millions of dollars, that DC have fulfilled the terms of the contract to the letter, and that his work has been enjoyed by countless more people than he could ever have dreamed of, in what sense has Moore been 'swindled'? The obvious answer is that he wasn't swindled, that he's being irrational and stubborn, and has no grounds for complaint. In 2012, Len Wein, editor of the first issues of *Watchmen* and a writer of *Before Watchmen*, said. 'I think Alan has developed over the years a mindset that's really his own mindset, that bears no real resemblance to the truth . . . and somehow decided at one point that he was betrayed by DC.'

The issue is that Moore believes he and Dave Gibbons ought to have certain rights over *Watchmen*. He believes that control of *Watchmen* should have reverted to them a long time ago, and that for DC to retain the rights is not in the spirit of what was agreed. Given that DC clearly control those rights legally, he asks that they at least respect him. His position is that DC have consistently made decisions that are at odds with his clearly stated wishes, to the extent that he has, at times, interpreted their actions as being motivated by something approaching malice. (The publisher would, of course, reject this.)

Creatively, he also bemoans the continued exploitation of his work as a dearth of imagination:

> It's tragic. The comics that I read as a kid that inspired me were full of ideas. They didn't need some upstart from England to come over there and tell them how to do comics. They'd got plenty of ideas of their own. But these days, I increasingly get a sense of the comics industry going through my trashcan like raccoons in the dead of the night. That's a good image, isn't it? They weren't even particularly *good* ideas. For Christ's sake, get some of your own ideas! It's not that difficult.

It is fair to say that Moore has added other grievances to his list over the years, and that time has obscured, elided or added some details. To take one example, he now remembers 'starting to feel a little put out and used in the fact that I had revamped the entire occult line'. It is entirely true that DC would build on the success of his run on *Swamp Thing* and launch a number of other horror-fantasy comics in a similar vein, often using the same characters. This hadn't happened in early 1987 when Moore split with DC, though. It didn't come to fruition for a couple of years and, early on, had his blessing. Moore's successor on *Swamp Thing*, Rick Veitch, had worked as an artist on the title and was a friend. Moore encouraged one of his oldest friends, Jamie Delano, to pitch for the John Constantine comic, *Hellblazer*, and the first issue appeared only in January 1988. Another friend, Neil Gaiman, created *The Sandman*, which did not debut until a year after *Hellblazer*, in January 1989. The Vertigo line, launched in 1993, incorporated those and other 'DC occult' titles, but the line-up also included many other comics like *Enigma* and *Sebastian O* that were entirely independent of Moore's work.

Over the years, *Watchmen* has continued to sell and Alan Moore has grown increasingly more resentful of DC. It is crucial to understand, though, that his objection to the collected version of *Watchmen* was not an example of clouded hindsight, or something that only began to brew after the book became a success. It's easy enough to prove this: Moore had fallen out with DC before *Watchmen* was finished, let alone before the graphic novel version had been released. Moore was talking publicly about his split with DC by February 1987; the collected edition didn't come out until December of that year. When Moore first raised the issue it was a dispute about DC's *plans* to issue a collected edition and keep it in print as long as there was a demand for it.

DC's position is perhaps best summed up by Len Wein: 'It's not our fault the book continues to sell.' When Moore signed the contract for *Watchmen* in 1984, there was no 'graphic novel' section in every bookshop, the business models of the comics publishers did not depend on trade paperbacks of every monthly title. At the time, as Moore knew probably as well as anyone, there was simply no market in the US for collections of recent comics. But the market was changing, and these changes were endlessly discussed at the time by those in the industry and by the fan press. Many creators had seen how innovative approaches might be rewarded.

The most visible of these changes was the advent of the 'graphic novel' itself. Will Eisner, a pioneer of the medium since the 1940s, came up with the term in 1978 when pitching his book *A Contract with God* to Oscar Dystel at Bantam. Dystel wasn't interested, but Eisner went on to publish it regardless, and would write other personal, often directly autobiographical works. That same year, Don McGregor and Paul Gulacy, popular with comics fans thanks to their freelance work at Marvel, made their 'comic novel' *Sabre* solely available through comic shops, and its success would lead to the establishment of Eclipse Comics (eventual publishers of Moore's *Miracleman* and *Brought to Light*).

The first graphic novels were usually fairly slim albums, self-published by the artists, advertised in comics fanzines and hawked at conventions. But by the early eighties, Marvel and DC had got in on the act with original graphic novels that often used existing characters, like the X-Men book *God Loves, Man Kills* or Jack Kirby's *Fourth World* book *The Hunger Dogs*. But these were all new stories. Even series like *Camelot 3000* and Frank Miller's *Ronin*, the comics closest in form to *Watchmen*, were never intended to be collected in one book. If you wanted to read them, you bought the back issues. Comic shops dedicated most of their floorspace to the section where their customers could catch up on comics they had missed. Fans might have to pay a premium for 'hot' comics they'd been foolish enough to ignore on original publication, but that was all part of the game. *Ronin* was published in 1983, but the collected version was not released until 1987, thanks to intense interest in Miller's work after *The Dark Knight Returns*. It would be fifteen years before *Camelot 3000* was collected. There were digest-sized reprints and 'graphic albums' – usually oversized replicas of the first appearances of popular characters, or a repackaging of movie adaptations – but there weren't any books which collected recent comics.

Alan Moore would reasonably have expected the twelve issues of *Watchmen* to be published and for that to be that; when he signed the contract, there was not a single precedent to suggest otherwise. He, Gibbons and DC all fully expected that within a few years all rights would revert to the creators. Even as the early issues of *Watchmen* went on sale, however, the game was changing. One catalyst was Dave Sim, creator and self-publisher of *Cerebus the Aardvark* (1977–2004), a series which had transformed from a pastiche of *Conan* and *Howard the Duck* comics into a literate, complex discussion of religion and politics. Sim had been publishing slim collections of old material for a number of years, but found that keeping supply matched to demand was a challenge, and his printing bills were expensive. In 1985, DC began negotiating to publish graphic novels of the *Cerebus* back catalogue, and offered Sim $100,000 and a 10 per cent share in the royalties and merchandise. This looked like an extraordinarily good deal for Sim, but he was unhappy at having to sign over so much control of his intellectual property. He came up with the alternative of self-publishing thick 'phone book' paperbacks collecting twenty-five issues at a time, which would be far easier to keep in print. Sim published a 512-page volume, *High Society*, in June 1986, and by cutting out every possible middleman he had earned himself $150,000 within weeks. He would become a champion of self-publishing, putting his money where his mouth was by supporting dozens of ventures.

The corporate publishers, though, could learn the lesson of *Cerebus*: there *was* a market for collections of recent comics, and DC would soon reap the rewards. The collected *Dark Knight Returns* was published in October 1986 with an introduction written by Moore. As *Watchmen* neared completion, the idea that – as a limited edition for hardcore fans – it would have a similar afterlife in book form excited its writer. When it became clear that there was a market for a paperback collection of *Watchmen*, which would give the book an unusually long lifespan, Moore assumed that he and Gibbons could renegotiate terms with their friends at DC to reflect the new situation. (It has been suggested that they had already had informal conversations in that vein with people at DC, although the details of any such discussions remain unclear.) For his part, Moore evidently *felt* there was a gentlemen's agreement in place that the rights would revert to the creators in any event after no more than three years. All seemed to be well.

And at some level, Len Wein is wrong. DC did not accidentally fall into a situation where people were buying the *Watchmen* graphic novel. The marketing department had seen the positive publicity around the release of the individual issues of *Watchmen*; they had seen the success of the collected *Dark Knight Returns*. In their wildest dreams, no one at DC would have expected *Watchmen* still to be a bestseller twenty-five years down the line, but a movie version had been optioned in the autumn of 1986, and so a *Watchmen* book could reasonably be expected to have a shelf life of several years. They were planning the release of the graphic novel edition for over a year before it happened, setting up a special arrangement with Warner Books to distribute it. The trade paperback would stay in print, Moore and Gibbons would not be getting the rights back, and that was all in accordance with the contract. To Moore, it 'seemed to us as if we were being punished for having done a particularly good comic book'.

This was not, for Moore, anything to do with legal or financial pedantry. At heart, the tragedy of Moore's realisation that DC 'were not necessarily his friends' is that he had genuinely believed they *were*.

Up until the dispute over the *Watchmen* buttons, Moore had enjoyed a cordial relationship with people at the company. They had quickly developed a mutually beneficial deal where he was given great creative freedom, and where in return he produced comic books that won awards and made a lot of money. He had found people at DC open to his imaginative suggestions, and had been lucky enough to start working for the company right on the cusp of a number of changes that benefited the talent producing comics. Unlike the UK comics industry, DC had the resources to do his work justice. They had flown him to New York and San

Diego, handed him copies of rare comics and given him a chance to meet his idols like Jack Kirby and Julius Schwartz, as well as his peers like Frank Miller and Walt Simonson. He had got to work with Curt Swan, artist of the Superman stories he had loved so much as a child. Senior staff at DC smiled at him, shook his hand, told him they loved his work, fought his corner. In early 1986, Moore clearly thought that he had landed in a place that delivered everything *Warrior* had merely promised: 'This is the sort of thing that makes America a very attractive proposition . . . being trusted enough as a professional and an artist to be granted almost total license. If the financial situation was reversed and there was more money available over here, I'd still be working predominantly in America purely on the grounds of the creative opportunities they have to offer.'

Once the disagreements over the buttons and the graphic novel had changed the tone of discussion with DC the issue of a sequel to *Watchmen* inevitably became the elephant in the room. It was clear that such a sequel would be hugely lucrative. Research by comics journalist Rich Johnston indicates that it was decided at an editorial retreat in late 1986 that Andy Helfer would be approached to write *The Comedian in Vietnam*. Barbara Randall, *Watchmen* editor, alerted Moore and Gibbons, who made it clear they were not happy, and the plans were dropped. Interviewed the following summer, Dave Gibbons revealed that DC had also floated the idea of prequels, including *Rorschach's Journal* written by Michael Fleisher and *The Comedian's War Diary*, set in Vietnam, but he was not impressed. Neither was Moore, who said: 'I actually felt that the work we did on *Watchmen* was somehow special. I have got a great deal of respect for that work. I do not want to see it prostituted. This has always been my position. I don't want to see it prostituted and made into a run of cheap books that are nothing like the original *Watchmen* which, anyway, wouldn't work if it was dismantled. Those characters only work as an ensemble. A comic book about Dr Manhattan would be really obtuse and boring. A comic book about Rorschach would be really miserable.'

Johnston quotes Mike Gold, a senior editor at DC at the time, as saying: 'there most certainly was a lot of conversation around the joint about sequels. Many people – certainly Barbara, but others as well – thought that a follow-up was aesthetically contradictory. Of course, that's why we were editors and not in the marketing department. And many people – including all of those in the former group – knew Alan would rebel against the idea. Any of us who had ever worked with him, including me, knew that with complete certainty. After he reacted adversely and loudly to some marketing/promotion stunt, you'd have to be on the Bizarro World to think he wouldn't scream to the heavens had DC done anything *Watchmen*-like without him, and certainly he was not going to play along.' While investigating the early brainstorming session for the *Watchmen* spin-offs, Johnston found that 'another, very well placed DC source who wishes to remain nameless confirms much of Barbara's account, but differs in the motivation for those on the retreat, the spinoffs being positioned as a response to the fight that Alan Moore had had with Bruce Bristow over *Watchmen* merchandise being labelled "promotional" and thereby not paying out royalties.'

There is a common thread here: Moore had fought with the marketing department over merchandising royalties; it was marketing that came up with the idea of a collected *Watchmen* that would remain in print; it was now the marketing department that was the driving force behind *Watchmen* sequels. Now it is possible, perhaps even likely, that management at DC were caught out when Moore pushed to get money from the sale of buttons. They may have been surprised when he asked for the contract to be amended if *Watchmen* was going to remain in print. However, they definitely knew that he would object to the idea of *Watchmen* prequels. Moore was already in 'a bad mood' with DC by the end of 1986, 'which never helps', but it's clear that this was not some form of unilateral antagonism on his part. There were those at DC already working on contingency plans if there was a future dispute with him. That dispute did not take long to materialise.

At the Mid-Ohio Comic Con, held over the Thanksgiving Weekend at the end of November 1986, Frank Miller got wind that DC was about to impose a new ratings system that would divide their books into Universal, Mature and Adult categories, with detailed guidelines as to what could and couldn't appear in each category. Miller spread the word to the other freelancers at the convention, and also telephoned Moore. Moore then called Rich Veitch, who remembers, 'when Alan heard about it, he hit the ceiling . . . HARD! I still remember the phone call I got from him and boy, was he pissed! REALLY pissed!! He took the whole thing as a personal affront.'

With so many comics creators coming from a countercultural background, it is no surprise that they were suspicious of even the abstract concept of censorship, but they had a specific historical reason for being especially sensitive. This felt like a beginning of a return to the fifties, *Seduction of the Innocent*, Senate hearings and the creation of the Comics Code Authority. For the ever self-mythologising comics world, the darkest of days appeared to be returning.

There had been those, including Moore himself, who had understood that in Reagan's America, the forces of social conservatism and 'family values' would, sooner or later, turn their baleful eye on the comics industry. Yet, when it came, the pressure was so light it was barely detectable. A Christian cable show (no one could say quite which one) had declared modern comics like *X-Men* to be 'pornographic'. Around the same time, one comic shop owner, Buddy Saunders of Lone Star Comics, had written a letter to his distributor, Diamond, saying he was worried that none of the solicitation information he was given when he ordered stock for his store told him whether a book was suitable for children or not (he singled out Moore's *Miracleman* #9, an issue with graphic images of childbirth, as one of particular concern).

Diamond were the largest comics distributor in the US. Their founder and CEO, Steve Geppi, wrote to DC and Marvel echoing Saunders' concern: 'We are not censors. We no more want someone deciding for us than you do. We cannot, however, stand by and watch the marketplace become a dumping ground for every sort of graphic fantasy that someone wants to live out. We have an industry to protect; we have leases to abide by; we have a community image to maintain.' Within weeks of that statement, DC announced their ratings system.

The freelancers quickly reached the consensus that this was unacceptable. Moore and Miller took a particularly hard line on the whole concept of censorship; Moore said, 'My feelings on censorship are that it is wrong, full stop. It is a thing which I utterly oppose. I believe there is nothing in this world that is unsayable. It is not information which is dangerous; it is the lack of information which is dangerous.' Interviewed by Gary Groth for *The Comics Journal*, a magazine that was giving comprehensive coverage of the controversy, Moore spelled out the absolutist line he took on the issue, saying he would not even take steps to block children from accessing hardcore pornography. 'I would think that in reality there would be a certain sort of common sense element creeping in. I would try to handle it in as non-authoritarian a fashion as possible.'

There was a political dimension to this reaction. Both Moore and Miller were writing comics that explicitly satirised right-wing extremism, and neither was

happy with the idea of caving in to the religious right. Miller said, 'these are evil, evil people and I believe that as a force in our country they should be fought tooth and claw wherever they appear.' But the speed with which DC gave in became in an issue in itself, shocking Moore in particular: 'I will never accept that one can oppose a social evil by cowering guiltily and hoping to avoid its notice. I believe a ratings system, or indeed any kind of censorship, to be akin to shooting oneself in the foot in the fond hope that this will make people feel too sorry for you to shoot you in the head . . . If any person or publisher seeks to negotiate a surrender or truce with the book burners, they are at liberty to do so, but not on my behalf. Not without telling me first.'

There were worries about the practicalities, about what it would mean for their existing projects. Moore was happy to accept that some comics were for children, but felt many characters fell within a grey area – Batman was one such. He had the immediate concern that his Joker v Batman story *The Killing Joke*, in progress at the time, would be altered without his consent or labelled in such a way as to harm its sales. There was a difference, he felt, between taking on a project knowing the rules and finding that the rules had changed halfway through.

A couple of years earlier, Moore had said: 'I have nothing against a rating code that would provide a description of the contents . . . "For Mature Readers" or "Full of Tits and Innards" or something like that. In fact I can see that an idea like that would have a lot of practical appeal in the current rating debate going on in the States. But that's description, and not censorship.' Which would seem to be all DC were proposing. The crucial distinction, Moore felt, was that rather than reading a completed work and labelling it appropriately, DC were planning to alter the nature of the work to make it conform to a rating category. Fittingly, a key question was who would watch the watchmen – who would decide what comics went into which category, who would decide what was acceptable? And there was a related sticking point: none of the creators (nor, it turned out, many of the editors) had been consulted. DC staff had drawn up the guidelines and presented them as a fait accompli. After months of petty disputes with DC management, Moore now simply didn't accept the company's ability to make those judgement calls on his work.

There was an obvious tension in the current situation, where the general public assumed superhero comics were for very small children but publishers

had started targeting comics at people of college age. The previous year, DC had run a campaign with the tagline 'DC Comics Aren't Just For Kids Any More'. As a number of people (including Moore) pointed out, though, book publishers marketed some novels to adults and others to children and people did not need warning labels to tell them apart. It would be hard to look at the cover of *Care Bears,* then the cover of *Watchmen* and conclude they were intended for the same audience. For one thing, to see *Watchmen* you had to be in a specialist comic shop.

Clearly, though, the content of some comics was becoming more 'adult'. On the whole, comics shop owners are very knowledgeable about the products they sell and very careful (and in many US states legally obliged) not to sell unsuitable material to children. With comic shop owners like Buddy Saunders having to order comics after reading no more than a short paragraph on an order form and deciding how many they were likely to sell, and most comics being supplied on a non-returnable basis, if a shop wasn't legally permitted to sell a comic, it was stuck with those copies. Saunders conceded that there were some titles, like *Swamp Thing*, that he knew were not suitable for his youngest customers, but argued that it was impossible to make that call with new titles, or when DC relaunched characters like *Blackhawk* and *Green Arrow* and made their adventures violent and sexually explicit.

Moore and Miller now circulated a petition that signalled their alarm, taking out a full-page advert in *The Comic Buyer's Guide* in February 1987. When the writer/editor Marv Wolfman was among twenty-four DC freelancers to sign it, the company removed him from editorial duties for speaking against the ratings system. Senior management at DC were clearly caught out, and began arranging a series of meetings and phone calls aimed at placating creators.

But, for Moore, things had already come to a head. Late in 1986, he and Dave Gibbons had met DC president and publisher Jenette Kahn in London to discuss plans for a *Watchmen* movie over lunch with producer Joel Silver.

> This was right at the end of our relationship, when things were looking very, very dodgy, and this was a meeting with Joel Silver and Jenette Kahn. As I remember it, we were in some hotel lobby. We met Jenette Kahn first. Joel Silver would be joining us. And in the time we were waiting for him to arrive, Jenette Kahn said that they were talking about doing prequels to *Watchmen* including

> Andy Helfer writing one, I think, somebody else was doing the Comedian in Vietnam. And then she said 'but of course we wouldn't do this if you were still working for us'. And I just went silent while I processed that. I think Dave Gibbons said, 'Well, I've been assured that you won't be doing that anyway,' and she seemed to accept that. But I was thinking, 'you just threatened me, I know what that was, I don't know if you can do it or not, but you just threatened me and this is not how I want to conduct business relationships'... we left as soon as the meeting was concluded, and, yeah, that was one of things that made me sever contact with DC shortly thereafter. That was on the negative scale that was starting to add up.

Telling Moore they could go ahead with sequels without him was a change in position, but it is by no means evident that Kahn intended it as a threat. Even so, that was Moore's interpretation: 'I really, really, really don't respond well to being threatened. I couldn't tolerate anyone threatening me on the street; I couldn't tolerate anyone threatening me in any other situation in my life. I can't tolerate anyone threatening me about my art and my career and stuff that's as important to me as that. That was the emotional breaking point.'

To his mind, it was a replay of Marvel's threats to *Warrior* over the Marvelman name – a big American company acting like a bully and showing more concern for what was legal than for what was fair. It was all the more hurtful, given that DC had seemingly been so supportive and had apparently been making progress with creators' rights. Up until now, Moore had won his battles – notably when DC ran *Swamp Thing* #29 despite its failure to be approved by the Comics Code Authority. They had supported Moore then, and losing the CCA label had done nothing to dent the rise in sales – his last issue of *Swamp Thing*, #64 (September 1987), sold six times as many copies as his first.

But there is little doubt, when Dick Giordano told *The Comics Journal* that labelling comics 'wasn't a moral issue for me and there was no way I could respond to people who were becoming so emotional about what seemed to me a very simple marketing device', that he was talking about Alan Moore. Clearly Moore's personality is a factor here. We might recall Jeremy Seabrook's description of the working class of Northampton: 'narrow, suspicious, mean, self-reliant, pig-headed, but generally honourable and as good as their word', along with Moore's own admissions that if he can't win he doesn't want to play and that 'reconsidering things is not really generally one of my strong points'. The breakdown with Dez Skinn followed the same pattern: Moore works with someone if he trusts them, and if he loses that trust, he does not want to negotiate, he wants to get out as soon as possible.

This of course would be to place the blame for everything that happened solely on some personality defect of Moore's. If that were true, the implication would be that the multimedia giant TimeWarner, used to dealing with pop divas and movie stars, had been caught out by the stroppiness of a single successful creative person. Without assigning 'blame', it seems more likely that DC management knew how Moore would react to the ratings system, but went ahead anyway.

One problem was that Moore and DC dealt over the telephone rather than face to face. The other big-name freelancers such as Miller, Chaykin and Wolfman, along with the vast majority of the comics community at the time, were based in or around Manhattan and saw each other regularly, during office hours and afterwards. Like the British comics industry, the world of American comics was a small one that tended to sort things out over drinks, and the creators and editors based in New York were able to come to an understanding. At the San Diego Comic Con, held over the weekend of 6–9 August 1987, Chaykin said: 'I got bored with the ratings system argument soon after it started as a result of my inability to take it personally.' At the same event, Miller joined Dick Giordano on a panel and declared 'the issue resolved'.

On the other hand, Moore was receiving his information via phone calls, hearing rumours, Chinese whispers and wild stories from comics journalists eager for quotes. As he admitted, 'I'm relying upon second-hand information for this.' Left to stew, Moore joined up whatever information he had. He may well have inferred more Christian fundamentalist involvement than there had actually been – Buddy Saunders, who wrote the original letter raising his concerns, has said he's 'not particularly religious', and neither is Steve Geppi.

Giordano's *Comics Journal* interview repeats something that may hint at the true source of the problem (my emphasis): 'We thought the labelling was an appropriate *marketing device*. We really did think of it as mostly that . . . it seems to me that that was a simple *marketing device*, and I really was quite surprised by the emotionalism that came from it . . .' There is a great deal of evidence that the received wisdom at DC is that *Watchmen* is a good comic, but that it was DC's marketing prowess that enabled its success and cemented its reputation.

Moore has expressed disgust that some at the company credited the success of *Watchmen* and *Dark Knight* to the format the comics were printed in, rather than their contents:

> if it wasn't for the enthusiasm that decades' worth of writers and artists have invested into, say, Batman, then what's so great about Batman? . . . some guy who dresses up as a bat to fight crime. And well, it's not Tolstoy, is it? . . . I remember that the buzz in the DC marketing department was that what had made *Dark Knight* #1 a success was the format. Not Frank's art, not the storytelling, not Lynn's colouring, nothing like that – the approach to superheroes. What had made it a success was the only thing the marketing department had contributed to, which was what size it was and what kind of cover stock it had. So it would be inconceivable that they would say 'hey, you think that *Dark Knight* thing – do you think it sold because of the quality of the material?' They could not even consider that concept; it had to be something that they had done.

From an accountant's eye view, though, the format did play a part in making *Watchmen* and *The Dark Knight Returns* the successes they were. In 1986, regular comics cost 75¢. *Watchmen* was printed on higher quality paper and cost $1.50. With its glossy pages and square binding, the cover price of *Dark Knight* was $2.95. The marketing department at DC had found a way to quadruple their prices *and* increase their unit sales. Comics that had been intended as oversized regular editions (including Moore's *The Killing Joke*), were published instead in the new square-bound Dark Knight Format, which soon became known as Prestige Format. Rather than complain, comics fans lapped up these new books. Indeed, they proved willing to pay far more than cover price for comics – back-issue prices soared, and speculators hoarded copies of 'key issues' (the first issue, the first appearance of a new character, the first with a new creative team, most books in Prestige Format).

There is an episode of *The Simpsons*, 'Flaming Moe's', in which Homer comes up with the recipe for the perfect drink, which Moe the bartender then takes and sells at his bar. It becomes hugely successful and lucrative, and Moe refuses to give

Homer any credit or reward. When challenged, he counters: 'Hey, Homer came up with the drink, but I came up with the idea of charging $6.95 for it.' Alan Moore may have written a good comic, but DC's marketing department came up with the idea of doubling the price. They also had the ideas of getting people to pay for the buttons that had previously been given away, and selling the comic to them a second time as a hardback collector's edition. It was the marketing department who were planning to release the paperback graphic novel version; who pushed for *Watchmen* spin-off comics to be written and drawn by other creators; and who came up with 'Watchmen Month' to tie in with the release of the graphic novel, filling comic shops with art portfolios, T-shirts and smiley-face *Watchmen* watches.

But do the people at DC really credit the marketing department with *Watchmen*'s success? Paul Levitz has worked for DC for over forty years. He was executive vice-president when *Watchmen* was published, and rose to become publisher from 1989 to 2002, then president from 2002 to 2009. His 2010 book *75 Years of DC Comics: The Art of Modern Mythmaking* is, then, the nearest we can get to the party line on the company's history of the period. And the book's description of *Watchmen* spends three times longer discussing the format than it does the contents:

> As with *The Dark Knight Returns*, *Watchmen* set off a chain reaction of rethinking the nature of super heroes and heroism itself, and pushed the genre darker for more than a decade. The series won acclaim, including becoming the first comic to win science fiction's prestigious Hugo Award, and would continue to be regarded as one of the most important literary works the field ever produced.
>
> Arguably, though, *Watchmen* would not have continued to achieve such recognition (and certainly would not have reached most of its readers), if not for another important step DC took. For ten years, DC had explored formats to offer its best work for continuing sale, unlike its fading tradition of occasional magazine-format reprints like *80-Page Giants* and *100-Page Super-Spectaculars*.
>
> These experiments had failed, but in 1986, DC launched a line of trade paperback editions designed to be continually available for sale, as was typical of 'real' books. Beginning with *The Dark Knight Returns* (in a limited edition hardback and trade paperback), this line enabled these key titles to

> stay continuously in print, showing off the best comics DC ever published and attracting thousands of readers who didn't have a chance to read the initial publication. Initially reaching bookstores through a partnership with sister company Warner Books, and later on its own, DC became the unquestioned pioneer of what would be known as the graphic novel format. *Watchmen* would become the best-selling American graphic novel, and its original form as a periodical would become a footnote to the legend.

This version of events contradicts Len Wein's line that it's not DC's fault *Watchmen* continues to sell, instead attributing the comic's success to cunning marketing. Wein, though, another forty-year veteran at DC, made a very telling remark (my emphasis): 'I am aware of Alan's rewards for *being part of the original process* and I would happily trade with him.' Moore's position is that he and Dave Gibbons were more than merely 'part of the original process'. As he himself has noted, 'We got 8 per cent between us for *Watchmen*. That 8 per cent bought this house, the car, the worthless broken-down CD player in the corner and all the rest of it. For a while you're dazzled by this shower of money you find yourself in . . . you think "this is wonderful, I've got more money than I've ever had in my life! What kind people they are to give us all these royalty cheques." And then you think hang on, 8 per cent from 100 per cent leaves 92 per cent. And that, as far as we can see, DC have taken as payment for editing mistakes into *Watchmen* and getting it to the printer on time. In one instance they cut up balloons, leaving a word out so it no longer makes any sense. I don't want to get into an embittered rant, but we're barely getting anything from the merchandising. What we do get is a fraction.' Moore believes that DC marketing efforts during the late-eighties boom ended up damaging the comics industry by looking for the quick buck instead of developing a long-term strategy based on the quality of the product. When the first wave of 'graphic novels' were a success, DC 'could only see another fad to be exploited and effectively driven into the ground, milked dry'. That, in other words, the marketing department were causing problems, not solving them. It was a clash between the creator and marketing, philosophically, as a business calculation and, ultimately, at the personality level. As Moore put it, 'there was no longer any possibility of me working for DC in any way, shape, or form'.

For their part, DC offered several concessions. Notably, they ended the ratings plan in July 1987, replacing it with a simple 'For Mature Readers' label on standard-sized comic books that contained particularly violent or sexual content. And they stressed that this would not be imposed on creators ('we want to assure you that the determination to label a book "mature" will be made by an editor only after consultation with the creative team on the book'). Miller, Wolfman and Chaykin all agreed to resume working for the company. Alan Moore didn't, explaining that he hadn't been threatening to leave as part of a strategy to get them to drop the labelling scheme; he simply didn't want to work for a company that did things like impose one unilaterally, or that would sack Marv Wolfman for speaking against it.

The same month, Dave Gibbons reported that he and Moore 'now have a categorical assurance from DC that they won't do anything with the *Watchmen* characters unless Alan and I are the ones doing them' and that the prospect of the suggested *Minutemen* prequel was now 'more and more remote'. This was confirmed in a 1988 *Comics Journal* interview with Dick Giordano. Moore says he was also 'offered better financial deals', which would seem to mean DC promised a bigger slice of the pie for future projects, rather than revised terms for his existing publications. Perhaps unsurprisingly, he felt insulted by this, seeing the ratings issue and his other concerns as points of principle and entirely separate from his level of compensation.

He had, in any case, already burned his bridges. In an essay, 'The Politics and Morality of Ratings and Self-Censorship', that appeared in the *Comics Buyer's Guide* (13 February 1987) and was reprinted in *The Comics Journal #117* (September 1987), he writes that comics creators had been insulted as 'part of what I can only perceive as a politically motivated manoeuvre of the crudest sort . . . we have been accused of producing work that is negative, unwholesome, and likely to damage the mental well-being of children'. The position he sets out is essentially that 'it is an act of cowardice for any parents to expect creators or comic companies to do their moral policing for them', and that those behind the campaign to restrict comic books are the same people who ban books from school libraries: 'There is only one group which would ever call for the banning of *The Diary of Anne Frank*, and I don't care what they happen to be calling themselves these days.' The essay ends with an announcement: 'Since I cannot be a party to this kind of behaviour, with the conclusion of the work that I am actually contracted to do, I shall be producing no work in the future for any publisher imposing a ratings system upon its creators and readers . . . Looking like a shrill, over-reactive prima donna is something I can live with. Compromising my integrity to appease a bunch of political thugs is something I can't.'

Why, though, did DC allow Alan Moore to slip through their fingers?

Many commentators have treated the *Watchmen* contract as if it was written in stone, have and suggested that even if those at DC wanted to change it, their hands are tied because 'a contract is a contract'. This is not the case. Publishing agreements are routinely revisited. Ebook rights are not, for obvious reasons, usually included in contracts signed before the 1990s, and recently most publishers have gone back to their existing authors to renegotiate terms to include them. Publishers will also revisit early contracts with their major authors rather than lose those authors to a rival.

There was no company policy at DC that banned returning to a contract. Shortly before Moore's dispute, Frank Miller had a rights reversion clause retroactively added to his *Ronin* deal. Soon afterwards, the company would agree a sweeping renegotiation of Neil Gaiman's contract for *The Sandman*. If DC, Alan Moore and Dave Gibbons had all wanted to change the terms of the *Watchmen* contract, they could have drawn up an addendum to the original document, signed it, and the terms of the contract would change. This was apparently all Moore and Gibbons asked for when it initially became clear the plan was to keep a collected edition of *Watchmen* in print (attempts to paint the problems as stemming solely from Alan Moore's personality usually fail to take into account that Gibbons co-created *Watchmen* and was arguing for many of the same things). A couple of years later, Gaiman suggested to all parties that they should adopt the revised *Sandman* terms for *Watchmen* and *V for Vendetta*. Reportedly, Moore agreed but DC flatly refused.

While Dick Giordano said of Moore and Miller's departure in protest at the ratings sytem, 'We miss them as creative people . . . we're certainly going to miss the revenue that we won't have from Alan's projects, because everything that he did for us sold very, very well', it is clear that some at DC weren't so sorry to see him go. Alan Moore did not exist in a vacuum; he was by no means the only 'name' creator. *Swamp Thing* and *Watchmen* were not DC's biggest-selling comics. *The Man of Steel*, a 1986 miniseries that relaunched Superman, written and drawn by John Byrne, was released concurrently with *Watchmen* in the summer of 1986, and outsold it at least fivefold.

Byrne had been a star performer at Marvel, coming to prominence as the artist on *The X-Men*, then moving on to become the writer and artist on *Fantastic Four*. DC had poached him specifically to relaunch Superman, and Byrne was paid over $2 million for his work on the character. In 1985, DC's fiftieth anniversary, the company had taken the opportunity to revamp their entire line, bringing in new creators – and unceremoniously dumping a number of writers and artists who had freelanced for the company for decades. The comics industry was changing fast, and there were those who were not impressed by 'golden boy' Alan Moore. Byrne certainly had no love for *Watchmen*: 'I was not impressed. I loved Dave Gibbons' art, but I found the story (if it can really be called such) increasingly hard going, and when we came to the revelation that Rorschach had been crazy even before he put on the costume, I gave up. It was all too negative and nihilistic, and completely at odds with what superheroes are supposed to be. Like using a baseball bat to beat somebody over the head. Sure, you CAN do it, but does that mean you SHOULD?'

And as for another high-profile Moore project (my emphasis): '*The Killing Joke* is a self-indulgent piece of masturbation, in which a writer *who has risen above editorial control*, was allowed to bring his own "vision" to the characters without any consideration of their past or future. It added absolutely nothing to the Joker, and in fact subtracted a great deal.'

Byrne was neither on the staff at DC nor party to any of the editorial decisions, but it is not hard to infer that there were editors also worried that certain writers and artists were being ceded too much power, and taking established characters down the wrong path. Giordano had encouraged Moore to develop *Watchmen* and was happy to say *Dark Knight* was 'born in my office', but he was aware that he had more to worry about than keeping one creator onside. When asked why he had not consulted Miller and Moore before imposing the ratings system, he replied: 'If we're going to consult the creative community, [who] do we consult? [do we consult the] 300 that's on my list? Or do we just consult Frank Miller and two or three important ones, further alienating those people who feel as if we've already bestowed more attention and love on the Frank Miller and Alan Moores of the world?' Giordano went on to talk about having to manage 'middle-level creators' in an environment where star creators were getting the plum jobs.

Here there is a gulf between attitudes. Moore has edited publications where

he's the main creative force behind the project – *Embryo*, *AARGH!* and *Dodgem Logic* – but this is not the same job as being a staff editor at IPC or DC. Alan paid close attention when Steve Moore advised him about writing comics scripts, but consciously avoided the career path taken by his mentor. Alan Moore simply has no time for 'middle-level creators'. He believes what he said back in *On Writing for Comics*: 'if you want better comics, you need better writers.'

Even before he broke ties with DC, Moore was saying, 'It's no good whining about the stupidity of the general public in not accepting comics as a valid artform when the large majority of comics simply *aren't* any kind of artform whatsoever. Being honest, about 95 per cent of the titles currently on the market, while they might briefly satisfy a junkie, are nothing more than mass-produced rubbish churned out without a moment's thought on the part of anyone involved. This is fine for making money with minimal effort, but it only works in the short term . . . I think that a dozen really good writers, each able to handle say three good books a month, could totally transform the industry almost overnight. Can you imagine thirty-six *good comics, every month*?' He suggested looking to established authors like horror novelist Ramsey Campbell, noting that, 'Comics writing is admittedly quite a complex skill that has to be learned gradually, but if the current batch of chimps can manage it, I'm sure some of the greater literary intellects of our time would find it to be no trouble at all.' The way Moore would deal with 'middle-level creators' would be to winnow them out.

Whether or not DC continued 'to treat their creators as chattel' – as Moore put it – the publisher literally did own far bigger stars than any of their writers or artists. Although Miller's *Dark Knight* saw a huge surge in interest in Batman, the character has been perennially popular, with DC duly doing their best to satiate demand with more and more monthly comics, paperback collections, original graphic novels and guest appearances in other titles (Moore himself had contrived to get Swamp Thing to Gotham City). DC would never have a problem selling Batman comics, whoever wrote or drew them.

Ultimately, DC could afford to lose Moore because he had already shown them the path they should take. It was evident that the 'revisionist' approach Moore had used on *Marvelman* and *Swamp Thing* could act as a template to work from, and while he wanted to take the medium further, DC were keen to consolidate.

They had also raided the UK, headhunting creators from *2000AD*. The initiative was led by Moore's *Swamp Thing* editor, Karen Berger, who said, 'I found their sensibility and point of view to be refreshingly different, edgier and smarter . . . The British writers broke open comics and took the medium to a new level of maturity.' She quickly hit paydirt, hiring writers like Neil Gaiman and Grant Morrison, Alan Grant, Jamie Delano, Brett Ewins, Pete Milligan and Garth Ennis. The British writers, all of whom had keenly followed Moore's career, were now set the same task he had been given on *Swamp Thing*: take an obscure old character, completely reinvent it with a novelistic dollop of social conscience and adult psychology. The writers of the 'British Invasion' worked on titles like *Black Orchid*, *The Sandman*, *Animal Man*, *Doom Patrol* and *Shade the Changing Man*. Many of these writers were younger and less experienced than Moore had been – Garth Ennis was only twenty when he was first commissioned by DC. The older hands of the British comics industry, like Steve Parkhouse, Steve Moore, Pat Mills and John Wagner, typically picked up little work, although Marvel published Mills and Kevin O'Neill's *Marshall Law*, a vicious satire on superheroics. But with DC and Marvel also recruiting British artists like Ian Gibson, Alan Davis, Steve Dillon and Simon Bisley – and in the mid-nineties, a new wave of creators like Warren Ellis, Mark Millar and Bryan Hitch would continue the trend – a buyer of an 'American' comic was likely to be reading something at least partially created in the UK.

Berger tried her best to get Moore to reconsider, but although Moore liked and respected her, he was in no mood to listen. 'I was spitting blood and venom by the time I clawed my way out of the building. It got pretty bad over various things. Mainly about the fact that I created *Watchmen*, but DC owns *Watchmen*, they own *V for Vendetta* and all the work that I did, and that didn't please me.'

Could Moore have been won over? If the ratings issue had sparked off a year earlier, before the contractual disputes had led to bad blood between him and some members of DC's management, then perhaps both sides would have been more willing to listen to each other. By mid-1987, though, there seemed little chance of it. Moore said at the time, 'since quitting DC, I've put DC completely out of my mind, more or less, and have been thinking about other things that I'd like to do.'

There was to be a period of détente between Moore and DC around the year 2000, but it was short-lived. DC meanwhile continue to publish *Watchmen*, *V for*

Vendetta, *The Killing Joke* and *Swamp Thing*, along with *DC Universe*, a collection of Moore's shorter pieces for the company. Every single page of Alan Moore's published work for DC remains in print.

Despite his displeasure, Moore completed his contractual obligations with DC, even if this amounted to little more than finishing *V for Vendetta*, which took about another year, until the spring of 1988. Possibly the last piece he wrote for DC was the Introduction that appeared in #1 of the comic and was reused in the graphic novel. He also agreed to a UK publicity tour for the graphic novel edition of *Watchmen* – a week at the end of October 1987 during which he and Gibbons did two signings a day, one starting at noon, one at four, taking in Sheffield, Leeds, Nottingham, Birmingham, London, Glasgow, Edinburgh, Newcastle, Sheffield (for the second time, but at a different shop) and Manchester. At every event there were queues out of the door, and in the case of Forbidden Planet in London, they were around the block. Technically, this didn't involve DC, as the UK edition of the graphic novel was published by Titan Books, and Moore happily did publicity, including signings and British television interviews, for their editions of *Swamp Thing* and *The Killing Joke*, too. He also wrote an afterword for the limited edition of *Watchmen* in 1988, but again technically this wasn't working for DC as it was published by Graphitti Designs.

Speaking to *Comics Interview* around April 1987, just as he had finished his work on *Watchmen* and *Swamp Thing* and completed a second draft of *Fashion Beast*, Moore welcomed the opportunity for a break: 'I'm going to take a couple of months off and basically not have a single creative thought in my head for that entire period. I'm just going to sit and watch data on the television and vegetate and hang around with my family and sort of human, mundane stuff like that . . . it's been eight years of working weekends and working approximately a ten-, sometimes eleven-hour day, and I haven't had a holiday in that time, so this two months is going to be something quite spectacular.' He also had the chance to reflect on what he would do next. While the headline on the cover of that issue read 'Alan Moore bids farewell to comics – at least for now!', the interview itself said no such thing. Moore's thought was 'I think, at least for the time being, I'm going to steer away from superhero work . . . there's an awful lot of genres . . . I think I'd love to play the field a little more and just experience some of the genres that have been neglected for so long.' He mentioned romance, shock and crime suspense, humour, war and (after prompting, in a reference to *Watchmen*) pirates. But his opinion was clearly to evolve. A couple of years later, he was able to say: 'Most of the fiction that I'm doing now is an attempt to go beyond genre . . . comics previously have had nothing but genre. I think a lot of my reaction to genre is probably borne of the fact that I haven't had a choice up to now. I've always had to work in one genre or another.'

In September 1987, Moore attended UKCAC in London. Two years before, the inaugural United Kingdom Comic Art Convention had been attended by around 500 people; now it attracted possibly ten times that number. It was held only weeks after the last issue of *Watchmen* had been published, and Moore found himself at the centre of something akin to Beatlemania: 'At the last convention I was just held pressed up against a stairwell in a corridor for almost the entire convention. In two days I arrived at one panel late – that was the only panel I was on – and for the rest of the time I was just hiding in the hospitality room because I couldn't get out the door.' A comics industry legend has it that when Moore was at a urinal at UKCAC, he suddenly realised that the long queue behind him was of people wanting his autograph. He says of the story, 'No, it's charming. I may have had one person follow me into a urinal and say "can I have an autograph?" . . . there certainly wasn't a queue of people, so that's a piece of entertaining apocrypha.' Moore found the mass adulation unsettling and impersonal; he had experienced it before in San Diego, and that had left him with recurring nightmares about hands grabbing him. UKCAC would be the last convention he attended for over two decades.

In October 1987, Moore made his third and final visit to the US, this time accompanied by Debbie Delano, recording his visit in a one-page strip published in the magazine *Heartbreak Hotel*. He spent some time in New York, although he didn't visit the DC offices, and someone at Penn Station came up to him and asked if he was Alan Moore. The main purpose of his visit was as a guest of the Christic Institute in Washington DC, a public interest law firm seeking to expose events and individuals connected to a CIA 'secret team' responsible for assassinations and other illegal covert activities, including the Iran-Contra affair. The Institute had invited Moore to write a comic cataloguing the history of the secret team, and this would be published in early 1989 as *Brought to Light*.

Moore spoke in 1988 about the challenges facing the mainstream comics industry: 'If you would have asked me five years ago to describe my audience, I would have started by placing it between thirteen and eighteen years of age. Now I'd place it between thirteen and thirty-five or forty. It has expanded a great deal. If we're going to keep that audience we're going to have to be conscious of their interests, which aren't going to be the same as our captive audience. It's true that this new audience will occasionally enjoy a novel take on the superhero, but it won't want a steady diet of that.'

With perfect comic timing, his long-gestating Joker story, one of the very first projects Moore had discussed with DC, was published in March 1988. *The Killing Joke* epitomised everything that Moore had just walked away from. It was perhaps the quintessential 'dark' eighties comic, a better example even than *Watchmen* or *The Dark Knight Returns*, because it shares all the violence and pessimism of those books with virtually none of the satire or urge to subvert or deconstruct. It is a glossy, corporate product that features graphic scenes of the fun-loving former Batgirl being crippled and sexually assaulted. We see her father Commissioner Gordon stripped, degraded and forced to look at photographs of his daughter suffering. A pregnant woman is killed. It's morally empty, with a narrative that doesn't stand up to any form of logical or emotional scrutiny. *The Killing Joke* isn't some piece of pulp that accidentally transcends its humble origins to achieve a sort of kitschy grandeur, nor is it a raw yarn that manages to somehow tap into something primal and visceral. Its nihilism is calculated, carefully choreographed.

It is beautiful.

In 1988, most comics were still printed on greyish, flimsy newsprint paper where the colours bled and faded into each other, while every three or four pages there would be an advert. *The Killing Joke* had perfectly white paper, sharp colours, precision-engineered edges, no ads. It was like holding the Platonic ideal of a comic book. Brian Bolland's art makes every page look gorgeous: the scene where Batman roughs up a prisoner, the people punched in the face, shot through the head and doused in acid, the prostitutes, the potholes and litter, every set of mad, staring dead eyes. It is so seductive, the climactic fight scene so cathartic. Every panel is memorable and much-imitated, but they flow together to tell the story. It is an episode of the Adam West *Batman* TV show directed by David Lynch – every bit as misconceived and compellingly unpleasant as that implies. Even at the time,

Moore expressed his unhappiness with it, saying just before it came out: 'I think people have almost got themselves hyped up into believing that this is the next *Watchmen* and they'll be understandably disappointed.'

The Killing Joke was a huge success. Having been ordered in vast quantities, it sold out and was almost instantly reprinted, and reached its fifth printing by the end of 1990. Although not everyone was keen – Cefn Ridout's review in *Speakeasy* described it as 'a grave disappointment, this is Alan Moore at his most self-conscious and heavy-handed' – most comics fans lapped it up. It was massively influential on subsequent *Batman* projects, including Tim Burton's 1989 movie version, which adopted its forties retro look. It still sells strongly every month, with sales spikes whenever a new *Batman* movie is released.

DC had always published non-superhero books, usually in other action-adventure genres like westerns, war comics, horror or science fiction. In the late eighties the company understood it now had a keen, older audience and put in an extra effort to try new formats and subject matter. But the audience didn't bite. While 'grim and gritty' superhero stories like *The Killing Joke* and *Batman: Year One* have remained in print for a generation and been reissued in ever more luxurious editions, DC's Piranha Press imprint, which from 1987 to 1994 produced eclectic, creator-led graphic novels with titles like *Epicurus the Sage*, *Gregory* and *The Elvis Mandible*, has all but been forgotten. Its successor, Paradox Press, produced books like *Road to Perdition* and *A History of Violence* that have been adapted for cinema, but were ignored by the comics-reading audience before then. As one commentator notes: 'Although intended to be the last word on comic book superheroes, ironically *Watchmen* breathed new life into the genre, establishing the cynical comic book hero as a staple of superhero fiction, and leading to a succession of mostly inferior imitations that continue to this day.' Comic book readers were far more interested in seeing existing superheroes being given 'the *Watchmen* treatment' than in anything Piranha or Paradox had to offer. DC are in the business of selling comics, and had to follow the market.

Moore was now extremely disenchanted with the comic book industry, or at least with DC and Marvel, the dominant players. Having read the magazine articles proclaiming adult comics to be the next big thing and Alan Moore to be the figurehead of the movement, though, mainstream book publishers were suddenly very interested in 'graphic novels', and Moore was in contact with both Penguin and Gollancz around this time. Editor Faith Brooker at Gollancz commissioned from him a prose novel which had the working titles *Memory of Fire* and *The Buried Fires*, and would eventually be published as *Voice of the Fire* (1996). And both companies would go on to publish comics work from him in 1991: his short strip 'The Bowing Machine' appeared in Penguin's anthology *RAW* and Gollancz's VG Graphics imprint published his graphic novel *A Small Killing*. Moore's initial plan was simple enough: 'For my part, I might as well work with book companies and be treated as a proper author, so my ambition really is to write graphic novels for book companies, which will be going out to the book shops, with me owning the rights to my own creations, the company having the right to print the material once. This is a bit more reasonable and civilised. So that's my strategy: comics for book companies rather than comics for comic book companies.' Exposure to the world of book publishers had reaffirmed Moore's instincts about the comics industry.

As late as 1986, Moore had expressed surprise that good novelists who found it hard to make a living from their writing weren't flocking to comics; he said he would 'like to see a concerted campaign to demonstrate to "proper" authors that there are artistic and creative opportunities in comics that are even greater than the financial opportunities to be had'. But a couple of years later, he had come to understand why novelists weren't jumping at the chance to do work-for-hire at DC and Marvel: 'I've been content to work under those conditions for years – because those are the conditions that prevail and you have to go with them to get into the industry. I've now broken through to the real world of publishing and I can now see what it is I've been swimming through for the past five or six years. It certainly isn't lavender water.'

Moore was ready to move on artistically, and had a degree of financial security, saying in interviews that 'I'm not rich by any means, but I have a healthy bank balance' and telling Eddie Campbell 'it's nice not to have to worry'. He was able to turn down work that simply didn't interest him, like scripts for a *Robocop* sequel and the twenty-fifth anniversary story of *Doctor Who*.

His first major post-*Watchmen* work to appear was as editor and organiser of a response to Clause 28 of the 1988 Local Government Bill, which had been pushed by 'family values' Conservative backbenchers and actively supported by the Thatcher government. Their concern was, in the words of Conservative MP Jill Knight (now Baroness Knight of Collingtree), that 'it is wicked to tell children of five and six years old how to commit a homosexual act and encourage them to do so . . . it is malicious to approach young mentally handicapped girls with the idea that homosexuality is a good way to proceed.'

Moore saw this not just as some abstract issue, but as a direct assault on how he had chosen to live his life:

> At the time ... there was me, there was my wife and there was our girlfriend and we were all kind of living together quite openly as a different sort of relationship. It lasted for two or three years. At that time obviously we were a lot closer to the lesbian and gay scene and when we saw this legislation coming down we thought it was pretty alarming because there actually hadn't been any legislation that had specifically legislated against one particular sub-group before. This was Nazi legislation, especially when you'd got enthusiastic Conservative councillors talking about gassing the queers' being the only ultimate solution to the problem ... So what we decided to do was mobilise as many famous friends as I could dig up and put out a benefit book with all the money going to the organisation for lesbian and gay action.

Clause 28 was part of a long battle between the Conservatives and local authorities, many of whom were controlled by the left wing of the Labour Party. In support of the Conservatives' long-held belief that taxpayers' money was being used to push left-wing propaganda, the relevant clause stated that local authorities should not 'intentionally promote homosexuality or publish material with the intention of promoting homosexuality'. This is clearly not a provision for anything remotely like gas chambers, but lest we think Moore was being melodramatic, a few local politicians had openly called for just that:

> The Tory leader of South Staffordshire Council, Bill Brownhill, is in the centre of a political storm following his call for the mass extermination of gays. His comments followed a meeting of the council's Health Committee at which a government film on AIDS was shown. He said, 'I should shoot them all ... those bunch of queers that legalise filth in homosexuality have a lot to answer for and I hope they are proud of what they have done. It is disgusting

> and diabolical. As a cure I would put 90 per cent of queers in the ruddy gas chambers. Are we going to keep letting these queers trade their filth up and down the country? We must find a way of stopping these gays going round yet we are making heroes of some of these people and some are even being knighted.'
>
> He was supported in these views by the leader of the local Labour group Jack Greenaway, who said, 'Every one of us here will agree with what has been said'. The only dissenting voice was Liberal councillor John Chambers who argued that AIDS was originally a heterosexual disease originating in Africa, 'there is little point in queer-bashing other than making ourselves feel better.'

Moore's response was a 76-page protest comic titled *Artists Against Rampant Government Homophobia! – AARGH!* for short – an anthology that featured an enviable line-up of comic book creators and other artists, including Frank Miller, Robert Crumb, David Lloyd, Neil Gaiman, Kevin O'Neill, Garry Leach, Brian Bolland, Kathy Acker, Dave McKean, Bill Sienkiewicz, Posy Simmonds, Alexei Sayle, Oscar Zarate, Harvey Pekar, Bryan Talbot, Dave Sim, Dave Gibbons and Art Spiegelman. Moore's story was 'The Mirror of Love', a poetic survey of homosexuality with art by Steve Bissette and Rick Veitch. It was published by Mad Love – a company set up to produce *AARGH!* and consisting of Alan Moore, Phyllis Moore and Debbie Delano (Moore's lovers co-wrote the afterword). This was an energising introduction to the world of self-publishing for Moore. Either through raw subversive cunning or complete coincidence, *AARGH!* was published the same month – March 1988 – as *The Killing Joke*. Titan distributed the book for free, and Mad Love donated the profits – around £17,000 – to OLGA (the Organisation of Lesbian and Gay Action), one of the most prominent groups to oppose Clause 28.

To Moore's disgust Neil Kinnock's Labour Party voted for the Bill out of fear of the right-wing press, and it passed into law on 24 May 1988. While there were never any prosecutions under what was now Section 28 of the Local Government Act, the vague wording had the desired effect: a climate was created which led schools to err on the side of caution when teaching about homosexuality, and which made local councils wary of supporting gay organisations.

AARGH! and *Brought to Light* had been departures for Moore, in terms of his

writing methods as much as his subject matter. He liked the intensive research he had done for *Brought to Light* and 'The Mirror of Love': 'In the morning I'd be researching sodomy and heresy in early modern Switzerland, and in the afternoon I'd be researching heroin smuggling in Thailand during the seventies . . . I found that research was really enjoyable . . . in the case of *Brought to Light*, it was exhilarating . . . compiling all that information, making it fit and then finding a way to convey it to the readership in an interesting and entertaining way.' While he had always been a voracious reader and collector of books, Moore had typically described his research process by means of self-deprecating jokes. He confessed his total lack of familiarity with the Louisiana bayou where *Swamp Thing* was set, or explained how he'd slot some nugget of information from an article in that week's *New Scientist* into whatever he was writing, even though he only half understood what he'd read. Working on weekly or monthly comics, he simply hadn't had the time to acquire an in-depth knowledge of his subject matter. This new, immersive approach to research would become Moore's method of working on all his major projects. From now on, when he was interviewed, he would frequently go off on tangents about his opinions on philosophy, history, science, literature or current affairs, subjects he'd barely mentioned before.

None of his new interests comfortably fitted the superhero genre, and he 'no longer felt the superhero form was really the best way to tell important meaningful stories . . . if I wanted to do a story on the environment, I think it would be better without the swamp monster in it, if I wanted to do a story about politics, it would be better not to have a bunch of superheroes in it.' But he found himself still writing superheroes, under contract to finish his *Warrior* series, *V for Vendetta* and *Marvelman*. Returning to them, he faced the problem that not only he, but the superhero genre and the world too had moved on. He felt that Britain had lurched so far to the right politically in the five years or so since he had started writing *V* that the present was beginning to resemble the dystopian future he'd imagined, and the Introduction to the collected *V for Vendetta* (written in 1988) indicates his level of alarm:

> My youngest daughter is seven and the tabloid press are circulating the idea of concentration camps for persons with AIDS. The new riot police wear black visors, as do their horses, and their vans have rotating video cameras mounted

on top. The government has expressed a desire to eradicate homosexuality, even as an abstract concept, and one can only speculate as to which minority will be the next legislated against. I'm thinking of taking my family and getting out of this country soon, sometime over the next couple of years. It's cold and it's mean spirited and I don't like it here anymore. Goodnight England.

He was unhappy with his superhuman lead character now – 'I'd rather do it without the strong guy who kills in the centre role' – and changed the ending because he felt it was unrealistic: 'Originally, I had intended to have V instigate an anarchist utopia at the end of the third book.' Instead, the story ends with the fascist regime in tatters and Evey taking on V's role after the man himself is killed.

Continuing *Marvelman* presented a different challenge. Thanks in no small part to Moore himself, the idea of treating superheroes 'realistically' was no longer, as it had been in 1982, a shocking departure from the norm. Now it was pretty much what the audience expected. Moore quickly wrapped up the small-scale story he had been telling and launched into a new phase, *Olympus*, which saw Marvelman gaining a pantheon of superhuman allies and travelling into space, though at heart *Marvelman* retained its mission of treating superheroes realistically. Indeed the central action sequence of the final act is a virtual re-run of the fight between Superman and General Zod in the movie *Superman II*, except that when cars are thrown and buildings collapse, tens of thousands of bystanders are killed and the city is left ruined.

Marvelman #16 (December 1989) ends with the title character taking over the world, using his great powers to instigate the utopia V couldn't. In a handful of pages, in single panels deliberately reminiscent of Superman's super-feats in the comic books of Moore's youth, Marvelman and his friends restructure the world economy into smaller units, depose Margaret Thatcher, teleport all weapons of mass destruction and nuclear power plants into the sun, lay soil in the deserts to feed the world, repair the ozone layer and stop global warming, legalise all drugs (ending most crime), release and rehabilitate the criminally insane and abolish money. Superheroes had always been power fantasies, and this was clearly Moore's dream of 'if I ruled the world' . . . but the tone is one of regret, not triumph. It's made clear that these are imposed terms. The human beings we see haven't striven for this, it's left them bewildered and angry. It's the dictatorial rule of elite super-fascists, however benevolent the outcome. By this point Margaret Thatcher was Moore's arch-nemesis as surely as Lex Luthor was Superman's, but when Marvelman gets rid of her, even here, Moore sounds a note of regret: 'The way she hung onto the minister beside her, voice too choked to speak, her eyes so dazed walking away, she looked so old so suddenly. I could not hate her.'

Moore was not looking to make every comic overtly about a specific political issue; there was something else at work here: 'I'm much more interested in exploring our own world rather than creating new alien worlds and such. There are so many areas of our own landscape that seem like the first outpost of Mars there is no need to create fantastic worlds.' Even while he had been writing *Watchmen*, Moore had become fascinated by the non-superhero characters. Many of the scenes in the book are set within a few blocks' radius of a New York intersection, and over the course of twelve issues, Moore and Gibbons had built up a recurring cast of New York natives. On casual reading, it's very easy to miss, but – mostly as 'sight dramatics' in the background as the main characters go by – they are seen arguing, making up, and living out all sorts of relationships with each other. Ultimately, we see virtually every single one of them lying dead in the streets, killed by Ozymandias.

Now he devised a story that brought a similar, intricate cast of ordinary people to the foreground. This was the series Moore himself considered to be 'the follow-up to *Watchmen*', and it started life with the title *The Mandelbrot Set*. Moore announced he was writing it in an interview published in May 1988, and that it was to be a twelve-issue series drawn by artist Bill Sienkiewicz, who was well known to comics fans for his work on *X-Men* spin-off *The New Mutants* and *Elektra: Assassin*, a series written by Frank Miller published hot on the heels of *The Dark Knight Returns*. This new series was going to feature 'shopping malls, mathematics, history and skateboards . . . the whole book is going to be about nothing more exciting than the building and accomplishment of the shopping mall'. At this point, Moore had a 21-page synopsis, and by the end of August he had drawn up an infamous poster-sized grid that plotted out every aspect of the series.

Moore had enjoyed the experience of self-publishing *AARGH!* and was pleased to demonstrate that comics could be put to serious purpose. A number of comics professionals, including *Cerebus the Aardvark* creator Dave Sim, a contributor to *AARGH!*, had spent the past few years trying to persuade other high-profile creators that self-publishing would allow them total creative and financial autonomy; now Moore, Phyllis and Deborah found themselves in charge of a small but successful and effective publishing company.

Even before *AARGH!* was released, Moore had decided that *The Mandelbrot Set* would be published by Mad Love. He invested his proceeds from *Watchmen* as start-up capital, while Phyllis and Debbie were responsible for the business, legal and marketing sides. Moore would have artistic control over every aspect of his book, 'from the ground up with no preconceptions'. In practical terms this meant a long planning and development phase, with even the physical size and binding of the book up for consideration. Nevertheless, Moore was soon speaking confidently about *The Mandelbrot Set* as his magnum opus: 'It's a way in which I can get what I want to say out to the public in an unaltered form, without compromising it to meet the demands of a marketplace or the demands of individual publishers. That's something that increases the purity of my message.'

Then, around 1989, Moore's marriage ended. For Alan, Phyllis and Deborah, living together had been an experimental relationship, and often an emotionally turbulent one. The two women left together, moving to Liverpool and taking Leah and Amber with them. The family home was sold, and Moore bought a new house about 150 yards down the road; he admitted fifteen years later, perhaps unsurprisingly, that this 'was not the best time in my short life'. He named his new house, in one of the most landlocked towns in the country, Sea View and set about renovating the interior so that it resembled a Moorish palace. Friends and family soon reported that he'd managed to clutter up the house as though he had been living there for many years.

Mad Love continued, with Phyllis and Deborah still in their marketing and administrative roles, sending out press releases and answering correspondence. *The Mandelbrot Set* was renamed *Big Numbers*, and two issues of the series came out in April and August 1990, before it ran into problems that had little or nothing to do with the breakdown of Moore's home life. The original plans for Mad Love had been ambitious, with Moore intending it to be the future home of his more personal projects, but in the event, the company only ever produced *AARGH!* and two issues of *Big Numbers*. Twenty years on, Moore would publish a magazine, *Dodgem Logic*, under the Mad Love imprint, but for a long time Mad Love was to exist in name only.

While contributing short pieces to small press comics and anthologies, Moore spent the remainder of 1988 and 1989 on a number of other projects that he hoped would demonstrate the potential of the comics medium and stretch him artistically. As he plotted out his more substantial work, he clearly started from a blank piece of paper, showing no interest in resurrecting, for example, the ideas from the Fantagraphics incarnation of *Dodgem Logic*, and declining Bryan Talbot's suggestion that they try to develop *Nightjar*, the series they had pitched to *Warrior*.

Moore did consider inviting Talbot to be the artist on a new project: a documentary comic about a murder and the subsequent investigation and consequences. 1988 was the 100th anniversary of the Jack the Ripper murders and, after initial reluctance, Moore realised this was a subject worth tackling, deciding on the title *From Hell* (after the address given in one of the letters sent to the authorities and allegedly written by the killer). Talbot's work on *Luther Arkwright* and a memorable steampunk sequence in *Nemesis the Warlock* demonstrated that he would be at home among Victoriana, while Moore also considered that the horrific nature of the murders might suit his *Swamp Thing* and *Miracleman* artist John Totleben. Once *From Hell* found a home in Stephen Bissette's new horror anthology *Taboo*, though, Moore settled on Eddie Campbell as the artist. Campbell, for his part, felt at first that his background, which was mostly in autobiographical comics, meant he would have been better suited for *Big Numbers*, but Moore and Bissette persuaded him that he was right for the story precisely because he wouldn't interpret it as a horror comic, with Bissette saying 'it was essential that the artist not be seduced by the violence inherent in the tale'. Campbell received the script for the Prologue and first chapter in December 1988.

Moore also said he would like to 'try my hand at doing an erotic comic and that possibly I might do one based on *Peter Pan*', but at this stage it had been little more than 'a vague, half-assed notion . . . I'd been thinking about the flying sequences in the work, and how from a Freudian perspective at least they could be seen as a symbol of sexual expression.' In 1989 he was invited to contribute an eight-page strip to an erotic anthology 'that I think was called *Lost Horizons of Shangri-La*'. The publishers had also invited a London-based American underground artist, Melinda Gebbie, to contribute – Moore had been aware of Gebbie's work for many years, and mentioned her in a 1983 article – but she could get no further than deciding that her story should involve three women. Their mutual friend Neil

Gaiman gave Gebbie Moore's number and suggested they collaborate on the strip.

Melinda Gebbie hails from the opposite of Northampton: Sausilito, California, 'just down from Hurricane Gulch, where the Golden Gate Bridge crosses a rainbow-painted tunnel and breaks through into golden sunlight from pearly fog on the other side of the bay'. She was avidly copying images from Archie Comics and *Mad* by the age of twelve, followed *Mad* editor Harvey Kurtzmann's *Little Annie Fanny*, and became a prominent member of the underground comix scene in San Francisco in the early seventies. As Moore said, 'She made an eloquent and good-humoured response to the actually rather jokey and harmless "misogyny" found in the work of male contemporaries like [Robert] Crumb and [S. Clay] Wilson.' (As well as eviscerating Wilson's work, Gebbie had dated him.) She had also seen one of her strips banned by British customs, and later moved to London, where she worked in animation.

Moore and Gebbie had met at conventions and had last seen each other a couple of years before at a meal for the contributors to a benefit comic, *Strip AIDS*. By combining their two vague ideas, they came up with a story for their collaboration: 'It was a fairly logical step from thinking if Wendy from *Peter Pan* was one of these three proposed women, who would the other two be? It was a fairly short step from that to thinking of Alice and Dorothy, and once we'd got those three names in place the idea just snowballed massively from that point very quickly. I think that probably within another week, or two weeks at the very most, I'd got the entire story roughly planned out and I knew that we weren't talking about an eight-page inclusion in an anthology.'

Moore's marriage had ended around a year ago, and Gebbie spent a couple of weekends at his house. Then, once *Lost Girls* was underway, she moved to Northampton, although they agreed it would be better if they didn't live together: 'I had to be able to keep that particular reverie that I needed, so, if we had been living together, I don't think that it would have worked like that . . . we got together several times a week and we were very close, but of the work, we lived apart, and I think that was a very important and functional thing: that was part of the reason why I think it was successful.' Like *From Hell*, *Lost Girls* would also find a home in *Taboo*. Both have clear origins in a time when Moore was still thinking in terms of 'working in other genres', splicing two genres together: *From Hell* is a crime story, marinated in horror; *Lost Girls* is an erotic comic that plays with children's literature.

*

The first major post-DC work Moore completed was less easy to pigeonhole. *A Small Killing* had art by Oscar Zarate, an artist originally from Argentina who now lived in London. The two men had met when they contributed to *Strip AIDS*, and Zarate had gone on to contribute to *AARGH!*. He had made it clear he would like to work with Moore, and offered the image of a man being followed by a small boy. This reminded Moore of a dream in which a man was stalked by his younger self. The book was commissioned by Gollancz and published in the UK in September 1991. Moore has said, 'I still think *A Small Killing* was one of the best things I've ever done.'

Like *Big Numbers*, *A Small Killing* sees a creative person – in this case advertising executive Timothy Hole (pronounced 'Holly') – returning to the comforts and frustrations of his working-class roots while struggling to come up with his next big project. It also follows *Big Numbers* in containing clear echoes of Moore's own experiences, such as Timothy's recollection of going home to his parents while coming down from an acid trip, and the story's central incident: burying a jar full of live insects (something Moore did as a child). Of course, Moore resists the idea that either work can be seen as thinly disguised autobiography, but he was clearly beginning to make conscious use of his own experiences in his writing. Even so, *A Small Killing* remains one of the more obscure and underrated of his books – although, in this context, that means there have been a couple of years in the past twenty when it was out of print, and that it had to wait two years (until its American publication) before Moore won an Eisner Award for it.

Moore would come to see the work from this phase of his life – *From Hell*, *Lost Girls*, *Big Numbers*, *A Small Killing*, 'The Mirror of Love', *Act of Faith* and *Voice of the Fire* – as 'one major personal cycle'. It came out of an extraordinary couple of years: he'd gone from living with two women, and raising daughters with them, to living alone. From golden boy at DC to self-exile. From believing his work might change the world to seeing as Prime Minister an immovable Mrs Thatcher who apparently – to use a comics analogy – was employing Bizarro Alan Moore to draw up every single policy.

One's reaction to *Big Numbers* may serve as a Rorschach test for how one sees Alan Moore's career once he left DC. After nearly two years meditating on the subject, and with a free hand, Moore concluded that the best direction after *Watchmen* was to self-publish a black-and-white comic in a peculiar square format that told the stories of ordinary people in Northampton who sat around making tea, following timetables and filling in surveys while a giant American shopping mall gradually imposed itself on the edge of their town. There's a stark choice between mutually exclusive alternatives: either *Big Numbers* marks a dramatic point of transition for Moore as an artist, and would have done likewise for the comics medium if only it had been smart enough to realise, or it marks exactly the moment he lost the plot.

8 I, MAGE

> *'At his fortieth birthday party, he declared himself a magician. He wasn't of course. He couldn't even do balloon animals. Not long after that, he started worshipping a snake. You can see how we might have worried about him.'*
>
> Leah Moore, Introduction to *The Extraordinary Works of Alan Moore*

On 18 November 1993, Alan Moore announced to his friends and family that he would be devoting his time to the study and practice of magic – and early the following year, he declared that he had become a devotee of the snake god Glycon. Since then, much of his work has been inspired by his exploration of magic, even 'subsumed within magic', while the art itself represents 'communiques from along the trail' of his progress.

Most interviews with Moore and articles about him have made a point of touching on the subject of his belief system. His pronouncements contain clear elements of showmanship and bullshitting – he once told the *NME* 'I am a wizard and I know the future', and fobbed off another interviewer with the reply 'since the Radiant Powers of the Abyss have personally instructed me to prepare for Armageddon within the next twenty years, this is all pretty academic. Next question' – but this theatricality is entirely consistent with his brand of magic, indeed is a vital part of the process.

Moore is a magician who is more than happy to explain what he is doing and what he hopes to achieve: 'I'm prepared to lay it on the line: if I do something

. . . I'm quite prepared for people to say "Well, that isn't magic". Or, "That isn't any good"," he says with a chuckle. 'I'm prepared to do it in the open, on a stage, in front of hundreds of strangers and they can decide whether it's magic or not. That seems to me to be the fairest way. Not to put yourself above criticism by only performing in darkened rooms with a couple of initiated magical pals. Do it in the open, where people can see what you have up your sleeve. Where they can see the smoke and the mirrors. And where they can see the stuff that appears authentic.' Regular revelations in interviews and essays along the lines that he had advanced so far as to be exploring the sixth of ten Sephira of the Tree of Life, or that he had on 11 April 2002 'acceded to the grade of Magus, the second highest level of magical consciousness' have led numerous critics, readers and colleagues (although, tellingly, few friends or family) to wonder if Alan Moore has gone at least a bit mad.

Since walking away from DC, Moore had worked on *Big Numbers*, *From Hell* and *Lost Girls*, all projects defined both by great artistic ambition and a vicious circle of massive delays and funding issues. He had been writing his prose novel, *Voice of the Fire*, but this was also proving to be slow going. Nothing came of his plan to illustrate Steve Moore's Victorian-set graphic novel *Endymion*. And though a book recommended to him by Neil Gaiman – Richard Trench and Ellis Hillman's *London Under London* – inspired plans for *Underland*, a graphic novel for older children set in a magical subterranean kingdom beneath London populated by weird fantasy characters, this was scuppered when Moore learned Gaiman himself had a very similar project underway, which became the prose novel and TV series *Neverwhere*.

As the publisher of *Big Numbers*, Moore had sunk his own money into the series, including $20,000 to the artist Bill Sienkiewicz, but its publication had ground to a halt after two issues. In an interview published in November 1993, Moore described it as 'a catalogue of misfortune from start to finish. I have written about 200 pages of it. Five episodes. Bill Sienkiewicz, after completing three episodes, felt defeated and was unable to continue it . . . Al Columbia stepped up. I believe Al completed one issue, but I'm not sure what happened to that . . . I seem to be leaving these artists as smouldering wrecks by the fire.' With nothing to sell, Mad Love could generate no money. This frustrated Moore: 'We were selling tons!

For a black-and-white book that isn't about superheroes, the first issue sold 65,000 copies, which is better than most DC titles, I believe. There was a potential there for establishing alternative comic publishers as a real force . . . but unfortunately the perception will be that *Big Numbers* isn't out anymore so it must have been a commercial failure. It was by no means a commercial failure. It was a massive success that earned me more money than any other comic I've ever done.'

From Hell and *Lost Girls* both featured in the horror anthology *Taboo*, published in America by Moore's friend and *Swamp Thing* artist Stephen Bissette. *Taboo* had begun publication in 1988, and attracted top talent from the worlds of both comics and horror like Ramsey Campbell, Moebius, Alejandro Jodorowsky, Charles Burns, Dave Sim, Clive Barker and Neil Gaiman. Yet it was soon mired in similar problems to *Big Numbers*, and only seven issues were published in five years. Moore had agreed to split a fee of $100 per page with his artists for his work on the anthology, but to pay even that Bissette and his family were forced to exist on a diet of macaroni and cheese.

To add insult to injury, the mainstream comics industry had boomed, and a lot of freelancers who had stuck to writing superheroes were making unprecedented amounts of money: there were rumours that *X-Men* writer Chris Claremont had bought his mother a private jet. The artist on that series, John Byrne, would later testify in court that Marvel had paid him around $5 million in the eighties, that he had made 'a couple million dollars doing *Superman*' and 'four or five million doing the *Next Men*' (a creator-owned series published through Dark Horse starting in 1991). Grant Morrison was another to benefit: he wrote *Arkham Asylum*, DC's first original hardback graphic novel, a Batman story with fully painted art by Dave McKean which came out in time for Christmas 1989, the year Tim Burton's *Batman* movie was the biggest summer blockbuster and then the best-selling videocassette. On the basis of pre-orders alone, DC were able to cut Morrison a cheque for $150,000, and royalty payments quickly bumped that up to half a million. It remains the best-selling original graphic novel of all time.

If not so awash with cash, the British comics scene was equally fevered. When Alan Grant, John Wagner and Simon Bisley signed copies of a *Judge Dredd/ Batman* comic at the Virgin Megastore in Oxford Circus, they proved to be the store's biggest ever attraction, beating the record set by David Bowie. Extra police had to be drafted in to manage the crowd. The big success story, though, was *Viz.*

A scatological parody of kids' comics like the *Beano* and *Dandy*, *Viz* had started life as a photocopied fanzine sold in Newcastle pubs and record shops. By 1985, 4,000 copies of each issue were sold and it came to the attention of Virgin Books, who began distributing the magazine in Virgin stores nationwide. Three years later it was selling half a million copies a month; by 1990 sales had doubled again and it was the fourth best-selling magazine in the country. It spawned many short-lived imitators like *Poot*, *Smut* and *Zit*, as well as *Brain Damage*, which used veteran underground comix creators like Hunt Emerson and Melinda Gebbie, and *Oink!*, a deceptively smart, rude children's comic. *Viz* was a true phenomenon, in the way *Mad* magazine had been in America in the fifties.

Watchmen acted as the spearhead that encouraged every bookshop to dedicate a shelf or two to comics, but Moore had failed in his attempt to define the 'graphic novel' in terms of technically complex, personal work like *Big Numbers* and *A Small Killing*. Instead, it came to refer to paperback albums collecting around half a dozen comic books, and comics companies adjusted their business plans – although not always their contracts – to factor in such reprints.

Thanks to deals that gave him royalty payments for *Watchmen*, *V for Vendetta* and *The Killing Joke*, all of which remained bestsellers, Moore did not suffer the fate of the comics creators of previous generations. He also benefited from the many comics shops which had opened, establishing a vast number of outlets for *Big Numbers* and *Taboo*, with almost every customer aware of Moore's name. And although he had sworn off appearing at comics conventions, Moore continued to be interviewed by both the booming comics press and the mainstream media. As one might, he grew increasingly resentful of other people's material success, especially as much of it was achieved by copying his methods (even John Byrne's *Next Men* had followed the lead of *V for Vendetta* and *Watchmen* in abandoning thought balloons and sound effects), but his main frustrations seemed to be artistic rather than financial: 'I could see stylistic elements that had been taken from my own work, and used mainly as an excuse for more prurient sex and more graphic violence . . . I felt a bit depressed in that it seemed I had unknowingly ushered in a new dark age of comic books. There was none of the delight, freshness and charm that I remembered of the comics from my own youth.'

Despite the money pouring into the industry from graphic novels, many creators working for the big comics companies continued to conclude that the terms on offer did not give them a fair slice of the pie or enough creative freedom especially in Britain. By failing to offer high page rates or royalties, *2000AD* had suffered a huge talent drain; as the eighties drew to a close, they were simply unable to retain even the services of new writers and artists unless they had a sentimental attachment to the magazine. Warren Ellis, for example, wrote one *Judge Dredd* story before beginning a lucrative career in US comics. Conversely, in America, some creators were able to thrive within the existing corporate structure. When his *Sandman* series proved to be a mainstream hit, writer Neil Gaiman managed to convince DC to extensively renegotiate his contract, retroactively granting him co-ownership of the characters and licensing rights, as well as improved royalty rates on the graphic novel collections of the series.

It wasn't lost on some commentators that this was exactly what Alan Moore had asked for and not received with *Watchmen*. Stephen Bissette drew a direct connection:

> Neil takes good care of himself. He's very pragmatic in his company dealings. Believe me, there were plenty of times in the past when DC crossed the line with Neil. He was always diplomatic; he did not give ground, but he would allow them room to 'save face', as he put it. Things went better for Neil and Dave McKean and Grant Morrison and Michael Zulli, who is now doing a lot of work with Vertigo. I think DC learned an important lesson with Alan. When Alan walked, they couldn't quite believe it. I think pressure came down from Warner on some level. This is all supposition on my part, but there had to be a point at one of those board meetings where somebody upstairs said 'When's the next *Watchmen* coming out?' and they had to admit that they had lost Alan.

Bissette would later quote Gaiman as saying: 'I saw an interview with Ice-T . . . and he pretty much summed it up by saying something like "If a creative person is a whore, then the corporation is the pimp and never think your pimp loves you. That's when a whore gets hurt. So just get out there and wiggle your little bottom" . . . I'm a whore and a very good one at that. I make my living selling myself . . . DC doesn't love me and I don't love them. So we work together just fine.'

The contrast with Moore's attitude could hardly be starker. With a career that has neatly segued into novels, movie scripts and television, Gaiman has stated that he learned the art of writing comics from Alan Moore, but it seems just as

fair to say that when it comes to the business side, he's thrived by doing the exact opposite. Or, as Gaiman put it, talking about his dealings with the movie industry, 'You can learn from your experience, but you can also learn from your friends' experience, because your friends are walking through the minefield ahead of you and you go, "Ah-ha, don't tread on that".'

When the revolution came, though, it was not fomented by British writers with literary ambitions. It didn't lead to the dismantling of the corporations in favour of small press, black-and-white anthologies and creators keen to eschew musclebound spandex-clad clichés for more personal, difficult work. Instead, a group of 'hot artists' who'd been working for Marvel left to create their own superheroes.

While DC were winning awards and encouraging readers to send in their poetry, Marvel were selling a lot of monthly comics in which superheroes beat up bad guys and lived sprawling science fiction soap opera lives. A new generation of artists was now drawing some of Marvel's most successful books, including *Spider-Man* (Todd McFarlane), *The Amazing Spider-Man* (Erik Larsen), *X-Men* (Jim Lee), *X-Force* (Rob Liefeld), *Wolverine* (Marc Silvestri) and *Guardians of the Galaxy* (Jim Valentino). They shared a broadly similar style, derided by older fans for its single-panel pages, contorted anatomy, speed lines and snarling faces, but it was dynamic and distinctive and by 1991, such comics were selling in vast quantities. The artists were young – only Valentino was over thirty and Liefeld was twenty-four; Lee was drawing *X-Men* comics while still at medical school – and barely had a professional credit between them five years before. Yet the first issue of a new *Spider-Man* series, written and drawn by McFarlane, sold 2.5 million copies in 1991, and a few months later, Lee was co-writer and artist on *X-Men* #1, which became the best-selling comic of all time with over 8.1 million copies sold. Even without these crazy numbers, regular monthly sales of the top books were in the high hundreds of thousands.

So the artists came to a familiar conclusion: although Marvel paid better page rates than DC, the company wasn't giving the creators enough credit for their contributions, or a fair share of revenue for merchandise like posters. It was clear that in the nineties superheroes would become multimedia properties, the subjects of movies, television series and cartoons. Superheroes were a natural fit for videogames, in particular. Marvel were not only slow and poorly positioned to exploit this, the existing contracts would not reward the artists when they got round to it.

An unintended consequence of assigning books featuring D-list superheroes to the young British writers had been that when those books did well, DC couldn't argue that it was just because people wanted to read about the character. *Sandman*'s success was inarguably down to Neil Gaiman, people bought *Doom Patrol* because Grant Morrison was writing it. Even though just as many people – more – were buying *Spider-Man* because Todd McFarlane was drawing it, Spider-Man was a perennially popular character, and both Marvel and McFarlane knew that however 'hot' an artist was, he was replaceable. This limited the artists' bargaining power. The solution was a radical one: the six left Marvel to set up Image Comics, an umbrella organisation within which each of them ran their own company, or 'studio', sharing marketing, printing and other costs. The creators would retain all the rights to their characters and would aggressively seek to license their intellectual property. There was a certain inbuilt rivalry between the creators, but also a huge amount of creative energy. Liefeld's *Youngblood*, Lee's *WildC.A.T.S.*, McFarlane's *Spawn* and Larsen's *The Savage Dragon* debuted in the first half of 1992, and sold in huge numbers. The canniness of the operation can be extrapolated from those titles – racked alphabetically, McFarlane's and Larsen's comics sat just before *Spider-Man*, the Marvel character they had been most associated with. Meanwhile, *WildC.A.T.S.* and *Youngblood* bookended the best-selling *X-Men* comics.

Very soon, however, a critical consensus emerged that the Image books tended to have striking art but terrible stories, thin characters and poor dialogue. *Spawn* had been an instant hit – the first issue had sold 1.7 million copies – but the book's creator Todd McFarlane hoped he'd created a superhero who would endure as long as Superman or Batman. He understood he would need to find ways to sustain interest in the character. The solution was simple enough for a company awash with money: in the summer of 1992, McFarlane phoned up the top comics writers and made them offers they couldn't refuse. He signed deals to write a single issue of *Spawn* with Neil Gaiman, Frank Miller, Dave Sim . . . and Alan Moore. The issues appeared between February and June 1993, and the writers were paid staggering sums for writing a single comic book: $100,000 up front, plus royalties.

Signing Moore to Image was a significant coup, but McFarlane had not been the only partner to approach him. The first had been Jim Valentino, who'd promised him a miniseries, with only one proviso: it had to be about superheroes. Moore had begun planning out a storyline encompassing superheroes (a Captain Marvel archetype called Thunderman) and horror (Golem, an 'urban Swamp Thing'), as well as a 'Lynch meets Leone' western with a cast of characters all implicated in a murder. Moore had always liked David Lynch's movies, but was particularly enamoured of the television series *Twin Peaks* (1990–2). His proposed series included the character Major Arcana, a mystic serving in the US military like *Twin Peaks*' Major Briggs. Collaborating with his *Swamp Thing* artists Rick Veitch and Stephen Bissette, he whittled these ideas down until he had *1963*, an arch parody of the Marvel comics from the sixties he had loved so much as a boy, with characters like Mystery Incorporated and Horus standing in for the Fantastic Four and Thor. The pastiche was so complete it saw Moore adopting an 'Affable Al' persona in captions, editorials and interviews akin to that of 'Smiling Stan Lee' back in the day. Recruiting Moore was a triumph on Valentino's part, says Bissette:

> the other Image partners wanted a piece of that action, which would also trump Jim Valentino's initial coup. There was apparently more than just a healthy collegiate rivalry involved. Some of it seemed pretty cutthroat from where we sat . . . Todd McFarlane trumped everyone by inviting Alan to write for *Spawn*, which led to the whole four-issue Moore/Gaiman/Sim/Miller arc on *Spawn*. His first issue and miniseries with Alan was already coming out before *1963* #1 hit the stands in April 1993, making it appear Todd had landed Alan.

According to Bissette, 'Rick Veitch and I found ourselves caught in the crossfire between the Image partners' pissing contests. We didn't grasp what was going on at the time – we thought everyone was eager to work together, we didn't realise the Image partners were in competition with one another . . .'

In the event, *1963* was not what the audience were expecting from an Image comic – or for that matter from an Alan Moore comic – and reviews were decidedly mixed. In post-*Watchmen*, post-*Dark Knight* comics, superheroes were troubled figures who enforced justice by throwing rusty hooks into the bad guys. Moore's appeal to a more innocent, colourful era was either poorly framed or poorly timed – the problem may simply have been that the new audience Image was carving out just wasn't au fait with the old Marvel comics, and so was ill-equipped to get the jokes. Moore was building up to a finale in the *1963 Annual* which would have pitted the *1963* characters against the 'grim and gritty' stars of the Image range, like Spawn and Youngblood, but in the event, disputes and delays between the Image partners meant the *Annual* was never published – leaving the series as a set-up without its punchline.

The first issue of *1963* sold around 660,000 copies, more than six times the sales of *Watchmen*, and represented the biggest payday of artist Stephen Bissette's career. Despite that, it was seen as something of a flop at Image, a company used to million-sellers. Frustrations over the *Annual* led to considerable rancour between the creators, and as a result *1963* is one of very few Alan Moore projects that has never been collected as a graphic novel.

Moore stuck around though. Over the next couple of years, he went on to write more *Spawn* spin-offs, as well as one-offs for two other Image books, *Shadowhawk* and *The Maxx*. *Spawn* had enough momentum now that McFarlane could license a movie, an animated series and computer games. In 1994, he founded Todd McFarlane Toys, a company that launched with a line of Spawn action figures but which soon exploded into an operation that brought out wave after wave of toys based on horror movie icons, basketball and baseball players.

Moore was, by any reckoning, a terrible fit for the crassly commercial, art and merchandising-led Image books. For three or four years he had been loudly declaring that he was done with superheroes and, now comics had a vast new audience of adult readers, he was primarily interested in exploring the outer limits of the medium's potential in 'serious' work like *Big Numbers*:

Yet, here, he was writing comics like *Violator v Badrock*:

One reason – obvious to everyone at the time – that Moore had chosen to work for Image was financial. An interview in comics news magazine *Overstreet's Fan* framed it perhaps over-bluntly, and Moore responded in kind: 'Contrary to what some may believe, Alan's continuing work with Image is not just for the money . . . "the money that comes from *WildC.A.T.S.* or *Supreme*, that's very handy. It's useful to have a source of income that enables me to carry on doing the projects that are dearest to my heart like *From Hell*, *Lost Girls*, the CDs that I'm doing; the more obscure and marginal projects, which is where my real interests lie."'

Nonetheless, he would often find himself batting away the allegation that he had become a pen for hire: 'I have never done anything purely for the money. If I couldn't find a way to enjoy the project, then I wouldn't do it.' In some of his justifications he sounded uncharacteristically as if he was wriggling to find a loophole in his previous statements: 'The biggest element for me was the world of imagination that comics opened up! . . . It was the wonderful concepts, not the superhero's muscles, which gave me the biggest charge'; 'I have no desire to be hip in comics. I have no desire to really be part of the comics industry. I have a great interest in the medium . . . I'm trying to create an interesting realm of the imagination for teenage, adolescent, or even younger boys. And that seems valid.' But there were other reasons, perfectly consistent with the various stances he had taken: 'all of a sudden it seemed the bulk of the audience really wanted things that had almost no story, just lots of big, full-page pin-up sort of pieces of artwork. And I was genuinely interested to see if I could write a decent story for that market that kind of followed those general directives'; 'Although my aesthetics are different from theirs, I admire what the people at Image are doing. They've shaken up the industry in a very brutal way and probably shaken it up for the better'; 'All I really knew about Image was that they're the opposite of DC and Marvel and that sounded pretty good to me, you know?'

The problem Moore faced was that the Image work was his only new material to see the light of day in this period. He would state in interviews, 'I've nearly finished *A Small Killing*, after that the next book I finish in about a year's time will be either *From Hell* or *Lost Girls*, and then I will finish *Big Numbers*', but only a trickle of this work actually appeared. In 1992, *Comic Collector* not only called an interview with Moore 'Out of the Wilderness', it began: 'Five years ago, Alan Moore was the most lauded and feted star in the comics firmament. Times change and times move on apace and in 1992 newer advocates to the comics' cause might be forgiven for asking "Alan who?'" The dream of a world of sophisticated graphic novels for adults was over, leaving work like *Big Numbers* that was meant to be the vanguard of the revolution high and dry. As Grant Morrison (who'd 'managed to write three issues of *Spawn* in 1993 as the result of a misunderstanding') later put it, 'when [Moore] returned to the superheroes he'd made such a show of leaving behind it was clear that he needed money . . . it was easy to tell that he'd rather be somewhere else, stretching his wings, but even the stentorian Moore had capitulated to the Image juggernaut.'

No one blinks when a successful actor chooses to balance prestigious work for the theatre or in arthouse films with a lucrative appearance as the villain or mentor in a summer blockbuster. While there were undoubtedly people who smirked at Moore for 'lowering himself' to work for Image, he was receiving a large amount of money and a high profile for relatively little work, and had struck a deal that granted him far more rights than working for Marvel or DC ever had. If Moore had surrendered, he'd done so on remarkably good terms.

Moore's bank balance received another significant boost when, in 1994, he sold the movie rights to *From Hell*. He remained a proud Northampton resident, but around this time he and Melinda Gebbie bought at auction a three-acre farm in Wales, and began the long process of renovating the ruined farmhouse. But Moore hadn't abandoned his principles to make a buck. In 1996, even Marvel found Image an irresistible force, subcontracting some of their biggest titles – *Fantastic Four*, *Thor*, *Iron Man*, *Captain America* and *The Avengers* – to Image's Jim Lee and Rob Liefeld and relaunching the titles under the banner 'Heroes Reborn'. Lee offered Moore the chance to write *Fantastic Four*, but Moore turned down what would have been another huge payday, still unwilling to work (even indirectly) for Marvel. Indeed, despite Morrison's assertion, the problem might actually have been that Moore was enjoying himself a little too much at Image: '*1963* has been a great deal of fun. It's given me a great burst of energy that has been very refreshing in the midst of more demanding projects. It's a bit like customarily working in a symphony orchestra, but playing in a bubblegum band on weekends.' Moore's work for Image certainly represented his most blatant attempt to write 'something commercial' and 'fit in' since his very earliest days as a freelance comics writer. His private life was about to become far less conventional.

Alan Moore's personal situation had changed beyond recognition. He had become famous enough to be a 'cultural icon'. After years when Mad Love – and presumably the breakdown of his marriage – had absorbed much of his DC income, Image had stabilised his finances. His daughters had moved to Liverpool with his exes Phyllis and Debbie, but they remained on good terms. Moore had also moved, albeit to another house in Northampton, with Melinda Gebbie living nearby and had delighted his parents by buying them a large greenhouse with some of his *Watchmen* money. (The Chinese whispers of comics fandom transformed this into a 'large, green house', evidence of Moore's fabulous wealth.)

Ironically, Moore was also literally playing – or at least singing – in a bubblegum band at the weekends. He had met guitarist Curtis E. Johnson, who set Moore's lyric 'Fires I Wish I'd Seen' to music, and they recruited Chris Barber of Bauhaus (bass) to record it at the Lodge studios in Northampton under the name the Satanic Nurses. The three were then joined by Peter Brownjohn (drums) and Tim Perkins (viola) as The Emperors of Ice Cream, the name Moore had wanted to call his band in the mid-seventies. Moore wrote over a dozen more songs for the group. As Johnson remembers:

> We did about three gigs with that line-up and at each gig our girlfriends were all sitting at a table near the stage, I thought they should have as much fun as we are having and so the 'Lyons Maids' were born, comprising Ros Hill – who accompanied 'Murders on the Rue Morgue' with some wonderful contemporary dance – Sarah Parker and Melinda Gebbie. It was very visual, the entire backcloth was white nylon and various early cartoons were projected onto it – *Dreams of a Rarebit Fiend, Little Nemo, Gertie the Dinosaur*. During the song 'London', huge ultraviolet lights flooded the stage and the ultra-white suit Alan was wearing [handmade by Hill and Gebbie] and the backdrop lit up in ultraviolet whilst the Lyons Maids threw ultraviolet gris-gris in the air.
>
> We did about eight or ten gigs. Alan did the posters for all of them. At one, the backdrop and the side fills were hand-drawn comics of a future cityscape by Dick Foreman, Alan Smith and several other talented comic artists. The gigs were noisy, good fun affairs. We did covers of 'White Light' and 'Children of the Revolution', there was also a pastiche of 'Aquarius' from *Hair*, sung to the same tune in a *Mad* magazine opera style that began 'when the goons come crashing

down your doors, or drag you off in unmarked cars'. My favourite gig was the UFO Fair in Abington Park. We played the Rocking Horse (the back room of the Racehorse pub in Northampton), we played Chequers in Wellingborough which is also a pub, we played a couple of outdoor local festivals and we had a fantastic time.

Moore took obvious pleasure crafting lyrics that often feel a little reminiscent of his old *Future Shocks*: simple, funny, high-concept narratives such as 'Trampling Tokyo' (sung by a mournful Godzilla, who's 'tired of Trampling Tokyo . . . Bored to death / When my every breath / Sets the boulevard on fire') and 'Me and Dorothy Parker' (in which the narrator and the noted wit go on a Bonnie and Clyde-style crime spree: 'We went out with both lips blazing, and a pen in either hand'). Little of this material was released at the time, but fifteen of Moore's lyrics from various projects, including The Emperors of Ice Cream, were published in *Negative Burn* between 1994 and 1996, illustrated by a number of comics artists. Moore drew the posters for all the gigs, with Johnson remembering that 'the one for Easter 93 was my fave. It featured the Pillsbury Dough Boy on a cross and the heading said "rejoice for he has risen"'.

Even with his Image commitments, Moore had time to work on his 'more demanding' writing projects. According to a progress report he issued in the November 1993 issue of *Wizard* (the best-selling comics news magazine, rather than the trade journal of his future vocation), he'd just finished Chapter Eight of *From Hell* and the first book of *Lost Girls*. It would be a 'long time' before *Voice of the Fire* was completed, but he had it all mapped out. As for *Big Numbers*, Moore asserted: 'It is the most advanced comic work I've ever done in terms of the storytelling. I'm committed to it – I've never left a project unfinished yet, although I can't draw it myself. If I thought I could I would go for it . . .' The interview was conducted just before Moore's fortieth birthday, and there's no trace of an interest in magic in it. He describes *Voice of the Fire* in conventional genre terms – 'it's not quite fantasy, but there are certain fantastical elements in it' – and volunteers to the interviewer that what 'excites me as an artist' is 'the sense that you can make a difference in comics'.

The announcement that Moore had become a magician took even those who knew him best by surprise. Yet by his own account it had been brewing for at least a couple of years.

In a long interview for *The Comics Journal* conducted by Gary Groth in 1990, Moore had taken the opportunity to talk about politics and philosophy at some length. Confessing, 'I've got a very, very broad, almost functionally useless, definition of art: just as anything which communicates creatively . . . but I think you've got to have a broad definition . . .' he had concluded, 'there is only one organism that is human society or human existence. We've divided it up in our reductionist way into different areas of spirituality, sexuality politics, religion, all of these things, but essentially, we're talking about one thing, one organism.' While that sounds a little New Agey, he had little time for mysticism as commonly practised, but understood the impulse: 'New Age mysticism seems to me to be quite dippy and stupid a lot of the time . . . there are numbers of people out there who in however a muddled and woolly a way are looking for something of substance in their lives.'

Moore was working on the script for *Big Numbers* #4 at the time. One theme of that book was that people's lives are controlled by numbers, from everyday things like phone numbers and timetables, via demographics and high finance, right through to the mathematical structures that govern reality. Immersing himself in research, he read books like James Gleick's *Chaos*, Rudy Rucker's *Mind Tools* and *The Fourth Dimension and How to Get There*, and Douglas Hofstadter's *Gödel, Escher, Bach* and *Metamagical Themas*. The early nineties saw a vogue for fractals and chaos theory, and both fascinated Moore, as well they might: his work had always relied on pattern, symmetries, echoes, interwoven narratives, entangled events that only appeared to be random. Now he found that much of his work already conformed to the concepts described in the books he was reading, such as the emergence of deep complexity from very simple processes and the huge, unforeseeable consequences of tiny events. Fractal mathematics, Moore felt, dictated that 'there is order in the world, but it also says that that order does not care about us . . . we can't regulate chaos, we can't impose our will upon the world in the way that we've been previously trying to . . . it's simply not true that the world is there for man to impose his will on'. He felt that society could be described using this new maths, that we were approaching 'a boiling point and what comes after the boiling point will be radically different to whatever came before'.

Moore was also working on *From Hell*, and finding the research equally immersive. He and his artist, Eddie Campbell, would frequently uncover some odd coincidence: 'There were an awful lot of surprises. They were strange little things that probably wouldn't mean anything to anybody who hadn't been obsessively absorbed in all this stuff for the past eight years.' He noted that one Ripper murder had been carried out close to both Brady Street and to an establishment called Hindley's – resonant names because Ian Brady and Myra Hindley were notorious serial killers from the 1960s. 'Like I say, if those first initial impressions are accurate enough, then everything that you subsequently discover will fit in, in some way. It's quite an eerie process, but it's one that I've found on numerous occasions and in *From Hell*, that was very definitely true. So there were no real surprises.' The last sentence of that quote contradicts his opening comment, but not irrevocably. As Moore said, he was immersed in the material, engaging his imagination and looking for patterns. As he had learned with *Watchmen*, the deeper his research, the more odd pre-existing connections and facts he found to support his instincts. It wasn't, in other words, a surprise that he found surprises. 'I was constantly unnerved and amazed by the amount of confirming "evidence" that turned up to support my "theory", precisely because I knew it wasn't a theory: it was a fiction. This is a much more strange and wonderful phenomenon than simply being able to say, "I was right all along! William Gull was Jack the Ripper!"'.

While writing Chapter Four of *From Hell* in early 1991, Moore had found himself putting in the mouth of a man of science, William Gull, words about the divine:

Writers often talk about how their characters or stories become independent of them, saying or doing things that hadn't occurred to their creator, and this was an example. When Moore read it back to himself, he found that 'Having written that and been unable to find an angle from which it wasn't true, I was forced to either ignore its implications or change most of my thinking to fit around this new information.' That the words were coming out of the mouth of the man *From Hell* identifies as Jack the Ripper seemed to inspire rather than concern him. As Moore saw it, Gull was 'quite aware that he is going mad, but that was what he wanted to do. He saw madness as a gateway to a different sort of consciousness'. When Gull talks to himself later in the chapter, 'Gull the doctor says "Why, to converse with Gods is madness" . . . And Gull, the man, replies, "Then who'd be sane?"'

Back in 1988, Moore had started with the idea of simply writing 'some sort of reconstruction of a murder as a graphic novel' and alighted on the Jack the Ripper case. Now he began to understand that the power of the Ripper story came from the mystery, the legend, the historical context, the conspiracy theories – above all else from a quest to impose meaning on it. One of his inspirations was the title of Douglas Adams' novel *Dirk Gently's Holistic Detective Agency* (1987). When, like Adams, he realised that a holistic detective would have to take *everything* into account, every 'trivial' nugget of fact and 'incidental' detail, the scope of his enquiry into the murders expanded considerably:

> we start out with the murder of five people in London. A well-known murder that took place in the late 1880s in London. Now from that we find that there are threads of meaning that stretch back as far back as say the Dionysiac architects of ancient Crete, that stretch into the architecture of London and London's history. That stretch into all these different areas of society and privilege that run all the way up to the twentieth century . . . the whole system is connected and you can start at any point and from there you will find this radiant web of connections that sort of spans everything.

From Hell Chapter Four was written in the first half of 1991, so more than two years were to pass between Moore's initial insights and the declaration that he was a magician. Having already become fascinated by the question he, along with every other creator, was asked most frequently – 'where do you get your ideas from?' – his natural instinct, in line with Brian Eno's philosophy, was not to be scared of examining his own creative process, but instead to interrogate it: 'Brian Eno is one of my biggest influences. He had no respect at all for all that precious mystique of music. He's got a purely mechanical approach to art and craft. He said, in effect, "There are hard scientific principles at work here. If you look at them you can work out what they are and you can use them".'

He had already undergone such a process of self-examination in 1985, in his essay *On Writing for Comics*, where he had given a prosaic answer: 'I'd probably say that ideas seem to germinate at the point of cross-fertilisation between one's artistic influences and one's own experience.' A couple of years after that, he had been scathing of anyone who wasn't equally pragmatic: 'I really have no time for this big mystique of art. I think that's a lie. I think that a lot of artists will try to pretend that they exist in some state of cosmic crushing misery that the rest of the human race can not possibly appreciate and that is just simply bullshit. Art is the same as being a car mechanic. It is just purely a matter of application. There is nothing mystical about it at all.' Now, though, he began to make connections between the mathematics he was researching for *Big Numbers* and the study of the occult he was making for *From Hell*. Reading up on linguistics allowed Moore to see that both were systems attempting meta-analysis of the universe – languages. Language was clearly essential to creativity and to consciousness itself.

There's a fact that Alan Moore recognised sooner than most of his readers: his work in the late eighties was in danger of being stuck in a rut, of becoming sterile, over-calculated. He needed 'a new way of looking at things, a new set of tools to continue. I know I could not carry on doing *Watchmen* over and over again, any more than I could carry on doing *From Hell* over and over again.' Now he found a name for this different approach, one that would extend his analysis of his working method into a more general theory of how the creative process worked: 'Beyond the boundaries of linear and rational thinking, a territory that I came to label, at least for my own purposes, as *Magic*.'

Moore's interest in magic did not arrive out of the blue. He remembers being fascinated by myths and legends as a child, and recalls that the first book he borrowed from the library, aged five, was called *The Magic Island*. He often dreamed of gods and the supernatural, and as a teenager this developed into an interest in the occult and Tarot. Back then, he'd written poetry and drawn pictures inspired by H.P. Lovecraft. Moore had later, of course, created the 'blue collar' magician John Constantine in *Swamp Thing*, and *Nightjar*, the abandoned series for *Warrior*, had been about a secret war fought between modern-day magicians; he had also experienced a number of odd coincidences and occurrences which he had tended to dismiss – although he was fond of telling the 'strange little story' of how he had once 'met' his creation Constantine in London. But, until this point, magic had not featured heavily in his professional work – Maxwell was a magic cat in name only.

Steve Moore, however, had long practised magic, and had edited the *Fortean Times*, a magazine dedicated to reporting the spectrum of strange phenomena (Alan read the magazine and occasionally contributed reviews and

letters). Friends like Neil Gaiman were well-read on the subject. While writing *From Hell*, Moore had begun studying the history of magic and ritual and either discovered or reacquainted himself with mystical artists like Arthur Machen, David Lindsay, Robert Anton Wilson, Austin Osman Spare and Aleister Crowley.

For Moore, 'magic' is the name he gives to instances where language can be seen to affect reality; it's how human consciousness and imagination interact with the world. The principal way in which human beings do this is through art: 'writing is the most magical act of all, and is probably at the heart of every magical act.' Fittingly, the most ornate elaboration of his belief system to date has come in comic book form. In the 32-issue series *Promethea* (1999–2005), with art by J.H. Williams and Mick Gray, the main character, Sophie Bangs, is initiated into the secrets of magic, and her story depicts all sorts of elements that we know are part of Moore's own experiences.

The artistic unfurling is an essential part of the explanatory process, which means that a quick summary of Moore's magical belief system can only sell it short. That said, it is possible to break it down into three key components: psychogeography, snake worship and ideaspace.

Psychogeography, as Moore practises it, is a deep exploration of the landscape and history of a specific location – in his words, 'a means of divining the meaning of the streets in which we live and pass our lives (and thus our own meaning, as inhabitants of those streets)'. The chapter of *From Hell* that furnished Moore with the line 'the one place gods inarguably exist is in our minds' represents a good example of the technique. William Gull directs the cab driver Netley on a tour of London, drawing attention to a number of sights. Some are familiar tourist traps like the Tower of London, St Paul's Cathedral and Cleopatra's Needle, and we're reminded how odd those landmarks are. Gull shows that many of the same symbols, including the Sun and the Moon, recur in the most unlikely places. They complete a circuit of the striking London churches designed by architect Nicholas Hawksmoor in the early eighteenth century. At the climax of his tour, Gull reveals that if you draw lines between the Hawksmoor churches on a map, you construct a 'pentacle of Sun Gods, obelisks and rational male fire, wherein unconsciousness, the Moon and Womanhood are chained'.

In his annotations, Moore makes no secret that his main source was the poem 'Lud Heat' (1975) by the British writer and avant-gardist Iain Sinclair. He was also heavily influenced by Sinclair's examination of Gull, the novel *White Chappell, Scarlet Tracings* (1987). Sinclair's work had been recommended to him by Neil Gaiman, whereupon Moore got in touch with Sinclair and the two men become fast friends. In 1992 – a year before he announced he had become a magician – Moore made an appearance 'typecast as an occult fanatic' in *The Cardinal and the Corpse*, a film made by Sinclair for Channel Four. In the story, he plays a man (in a leather jacket and Rorschach T-shirt) searching for a book by Francis Barrett that he says 'is a key to the whole city, it's called *The Magus* . . . the key to the city, the Qabalah.'

Moore – unlike Gull – has made it clear he does not believe he is uncovering some existing code put there by some other being, natural or supernatural. The lines exist, but as lines of information:

> That is a pattern I have drawn upon existing events, just as a pentacle is a pattern that I've drawn over real sites in London. It's a meaning that I've imposed. I suppose what I was trying to say is that history is open to us to cast these patterns and divine from them, if you want. I mean, no, there is no pentacle over London by design. There is no secret society of Freemasons that actually put these sites into a pentacle shape, but those points can be linked up in a pentacle, that means that those ideas, the ideas that those ideas represent can be linked up into a pattern as can events in history, like the events of the Ripper murders.

But there's an ambiguity when Moore says he is 'divining', or when Sinclair talks of 'dormant energies' and a 'grid of energies' in the London landscape. Is this meant as a figure of speech, or more literally? Sinclair wants it both ways: 'it was reinvented into London with people like Stewart Home and the London Psychogeographical Association, who mixed those ideas with ideas of ley lines and Earth mysteries and cobbled it together as a provocation, and I took it on from that point.' In his 1997 performance *The Highbury Working*, Moore gives a tongue-in-cheek description of the practical work undertaken by his Moon and Serpent group of magicians: 'think of us as Rosicrucian heating engineers. We check the pressure in the song-lines, lag etheric channels, and rewire the glamour. Cowboy occultism; cash-in-hand Feng Shui. First you diagnose the area in question, read the street plan's accidental creases, and decode the orbit maps left there by coffee cups, then go to work.' Whatever the status of this energy, there's a purely materialist point being made. Like Sinclair, Moore uses psychogeography to draw attention to the history of an area, to map the deep roots of history and culture.

Sinclair's work continues that of the Situationist movement which flourished in the sixties and has inspired many British radical groups since. Situationism encouraged the exploration of the terrain of a city as an act to reappropriate the landscape from the demands of consumerism and commodification. It's a conscious response to the process, accelerated in the Thatcher era, of redeveloping old, proud working-class areas into office space and yuppie flats. Sinclair concentrates mainly on the gentrification of the East End of London, Moore on redevelopment in his native town of Northampton. Sinclair would agree with Moore's line from *The Birth Caul* that the recent burst of property development represented the 'final wallpapering of England'.

Psychogeography has also provided the basis for Moore's prose novels. *Voice of the Fire* (1996) was built up from short stories, all set in Northampton at various periods from the Neolithic to an autobiographical chapter set the day Moore wrote it. *A Grammar*, an abandoned novel that was in its 'early planning stages' in 1997, followed 'a sheep track between Northampton and Wales. It's a drover's track that existed probably since the Bronze Age and it crosses through a lot of fascinating territory: Shakespeare Country; Elgar Country; the territories of Pender, the last pagan king of Britain; Alfred Watkins, the ley-line visionary'. The forthcoming *Jerusalem* is in a similar vein.

Moore first publicly declared that he was now worshipping the snake god Glycon in a February 1994 interview with D.M. Mitchell in *Rapid Eye*, a magazine described by style bible *I-D* as a 'heavyweight periodical devoted to documenting apocalypse culture'. An article in *Fortean Times* stated that Alan Moore 'was introduced to Glycon by Steve Moore . . . whereupon they decided to form the Grand Egyptian Theatre of Marvels'. Other accounts have implied, either accidentally or through ambiguous language, that the encounter with Glycon was an unplanned occurrence during a magic ritual and that Moore only subsequently learned the fascinating, and extremely apt, history of Glycon worship. This is not the case. For at least fifteen years Steve Moore had enjoyed contact with the moon goddess Selene, as Alan would outline in some detail in *Unearthing*: 'I found Steve Moore's relationship with the goddess – largely conducted through ritual and dream – to be both interesting and potentially instructive.' Alan wanted his own supernatural guide. Although it was unintentional on his part, it would be Steve Moore who found Alan's god for him. When Steve showed him pictures of a statue of the moon goddess Hecate that had been excavated in Tomis, Alan's eye was caught by another statue that had been found with it. 'I can best describe it as love at first sight. This unutterably bizarre vision of a majestic serpent with a semi-human head crowned with long flowing locks of blonde hair seemed in some inexplicable way familiar to me, as if I already knew it from somewhere inside myself, as pretentious as that probably sounds.' The two then researched this snake god, which they learned was called Glycon.

The name means 'sweet one' in Greek (it's from the same etymological root as 'glucose'). A snake that uttered prophecies, Glycon was the focus of a second-century cult which attracted the attention of Emperor Marcus Aurelius. The satirist Lucian was personally acquainted with the man running the operation, Alexander of Abonoteichus, and felt him to be as villainous as his namesake, Alexander the Great, was heroic. Lucian goes into great detail about the formation of the cult, describes at some length how Alexander's prophetic utterances were faked and what he charged people to hear them, and explains that the snake god Glycon was a simple ventriloquist's puppet. Rather than being discouraged by such fakery, though, Moore embraced it, feeling it would 'pre-empt the inevitable ridicule by worshipping a deity that was already established as historically ridiculous'. It was only after Glycon passed this thorough background check – if 'passed' is quite the right word – that Moore sought contact. 'If, as I believed, the landscape that I hoped to enter was entirely imaginary in the conventional usage of the word, then it seemed to . . . not make sense, exactly, but to be appropriate . . . that I should enlist an imaginary playmate as my guide to it.'

Late on the night of 7 January 1994, Alan Moore and Steve Moore took magic mushrooms, and as they talked about magic, they came to share the experience of meeting the snake god Glycon. Alan had a conversation with the god that lasted 'at least part of the evening':

> the first experience I had, and this is very difficult to describe, but it felt to me as if me and a very close friend of mine, were both taken on this ride by a specific entity. The entity seemed to me, and to my friend, to be . . . this second-century Roman snake god called Glycon. Or that the second-century Roman snake god called Glycon is one of the forms by which this kind of energy is sometimes known. Because the snake as a symbol runs through almost every magical system, every religion . . . At least part of this experience seemed to be completely outside of Time. There was a perception that all of Time was happening at once. Linear time was a purely a construction of the conscious mind . . . There were other revelations.

A poem Moore would write soon afterwards, 'The Deity Glycon', describes an encounter with this 'last created of the Roman gods . . . and the idea of a god, a real idea . . . his belly filled with understanding, jewels and poison'.

'Alan Moore's private magical workings with Glycon are, of course, private', but we can glean some sense of the form his magical activities take from articles Steve Moore has written about Selene, including the publication of a detailed 'Selene Pathworking' designed to engineer an encounter with the goddess. Preparation involves 'relaxation by any preferred method', 'deep breathing and mantra', then the visualisation of a detailed scenario not unlike those found on self-hypnosis tapes ('all you can see is blackness. Now you visualise a small glowing disc of silver-white light'), but written by the participants beforehand to give a sense of structure, ritual and purpose to the occasion. At first Alan used magic mushrooms as his 'preferred method' of relaxation, but he no longer does so:

> Back when I was starting out in magic, I probably did an awful lot more mushrooms. I don't think I've done any actual mushroom-based rituals since . . . end of last year? [1999/2000] . . . I find that whereas once I would have used drugs to explore all of the various spheres that I explore in *Promethea*'s Qabalah series – I mean, indeed I did use drugs to explore the lower five sephirot, but above that, I'm using my own mind, I'm using I suppose it's what you'd call meditation, although it's exactly what any writer does when they're trying to get into a story, it's just that the story in these instances is deeply concerned with these qabalistic states, so getting into the story is almost the same as getting into the state.

A reference by Leah Moore to the postman seeing her father 'covered in blood and feathers' was, as we might guess, facetious. Moore has stated, 'I'm in the unfortunate position of being a diabolist and vegetarian, I'm afraid living sacrifices were out of the question . . . I have burned objects of meaning and significance to me.' At various times he has conducted rituals alone, with Steve Moore, with 'a musician' (in fact Tim Perkins) and with 'other magicians'. Moore once showed Brian Bolland his cellar and told him demons had manifested there, but he's also conducted workings in his living room. Once the ritual is underway, Moore has said he enters a 'fugue state' where a 'disorientating, overwhelming, even terrifying' amount of information is presented to him and he has to find a path through it. The only way to do that is to lose a sense of 'self', so that once the ritual is over 'recollection of the experience is necessarily non-linear, fragmentary . . . It's not that I have any reservations about discussing these matters clearly and lucidly; it's just that I can't.'

As for specific encounters, we know that in January or February 1994, Moore 'had a moment which was right on the very cusp of madness, in which I thought I was Jesus, that I thought I was the messiah and had come to lead the world out of darkness and into light. I thought "well, it's hardly surprising. I always knew I was a special, lovelier-than-average person. It only makes sense that Jesus would turn out to be someone fabulous like me.' Then, luckily, a more sane part of me moved in and said "Focus, you cunt! You're not Jesus – this energy is Jesus – the Christos".'

A line in *Promethea* #12 (February 2001) that 'initiation may be a dark and dangerous ride, a journey through the land of shade required before progress is made' suggests Moore's early experiences were not all pleasant. We know that something of the kind happened 'about a month' after the initial encounter with Glycon (again, then, February 1994):

> I also had an experience with a demonic creature that told me that its name was Asmoday. Which is Asmodeus. And when I actually was allowed to see what the creature looked like, or what it was prepared to show me, it was this latticework . . . if you imagine a spider, and then imagine multiple images of that spider, that are kind of linked together – multiple images at different scales, that are all linked together – it's as if this thing is moving through

> a different sort of time. You know Marcel Duchamp's *Nude Descending a Staircase*? Where you can see all the different stages of the movement at once. So if you imagine that you've got this spider, that it was moving around, but it was coming from background to foreground, what you'd get is sort of several spiders, if you like, showing the different stages of its movement.

Moore noted that Asmodeus spoke 'with great politeness and charm'. Unlike Glycon, Moore says, he only did his research into Asmodeus *after* encountering him, although we know he was previously at least aware of the name, as it had appeared in one of his very first published pieces. The third stanza of the poem 'Deathshead' in *Embryo* #2 (December 1970) runs:

> *I told you the words*
> *That might call up Asmodeus*
> *I wrote out the score*
> *For the ghosts of Japan*

He would later depict Asmoday in *Promethea* as a malevolent, fearsome force.

These early magical experiences inspired a burst of creativity from Moore as he attempted to assimilate and describe them. He created a picture of Glycon, which he named *The Garden of Magic; or, the Powers and Thrones Approach the Bridge* (see next page).

Within a week of his first encounter with the god, he had written two songs, 'The Hair of the Snake That Bit Me' and 'Town of Lights'. The first of those begins 'Step up now, Gentlemen and Ladies, come this way here in the Moon and Serpent Grand Egyptian Theatre of Marvels', and soon afterwards, an actual organisation of that name 'tumbled into existence, a fictional freakish sideshow alluded to in the song lyric that somehow seemed to be begging to be brought to some kind of peculiar life'.

The Moon and Serpent Grand Egyptian Theatre of Marvels consists of Alan Moore, Steve Moore, Tim Perkins, David J, John Coulthart and Melinda Gebbie, but it's an extremely loose 'organisation' and doesn't have initiation rituals or, indeed, any formal structure, to the point that it 'doesn't actually exist in the conventional sense'. The participants came up with a fake history for the society dating back centuries, a parody of secret societies such as the Rosicrucians and

Masons which are associated with similar claims. The 'moon' and 'serpent' are, respectively, Selene and Glycon.

When the journalist D.M. Mitchell interviewed Moore in February 1994, he managed to capture some of Moore's initial disorientation at his experiences: 'This is all very new to me. I've been receiving some kind of bargain basement apotheosis, and my head's still spinning. Probably in a few months I'll be able to talk about this more calmly and more coherently.' Mitchell knew Moore had begun a new book, *Yuggoth Cultures*, a collection of poetry and prose pieces based on the works of H.P. Lovecraft, because it had grown from a short story commission for Mitchell's anthology *The Starry Wisdom*. Though Moore had been interested in Lovecraft since he was thirteen, he told Mitchell: 'I have recently seen him in a different light.' This was surely because Moore had been reading the works of Kenneth Grant, the occultist appointed – at least according to Grant – by Aleister Crowley as his successor. Grant asserted that Lovecraft's tales of Great Old Ones 'represented valid channels of magical information'. But Moore claims to have abandoned writing *Yuggoth Cultures* after he left the manuscript in a taxi, and there's supporting evidence that this is more than just a tall tale: he mentioned the book in his *Rapid Eye* interview, and it was advertised and assigned an ISBN number. In the event, the surviving fragments, barely a few hundred words long, were printed in the anthology itself titled *Yuggoth Cultures*.

The two songs Moore had written became the opening and closing numbers of the new group's first performance piece, also called *The Moon and Serpent Grand Egyptian Theatre of Marvels*, which was staged around seven months after his first magical encounter, on 16 July 1994. It was intended as a one-off: as a child, Moore had seen the comedian Ken Dodd perform, and had been struck during the performance that Dodd performed the same jokes night after night, that the spontaneity and intimacy with the audience was an illusion, and that he could have almost exactly the same experience again just by going back the next night. Each of the Moon and Serpent's workings has in contrast been specific to the time and location: in this case, it was the night the comet Shoemaker-Levy impacted Jupiter, one of the more spectacular astronomical events of the twentieth century. Moore and his colleagues intended it as a public magic ritual, taking the form – in a clear echo of his old Arts Lab days – of a multimedia performance that would engage the audience in an immersive, rich blend of music, monologues, dance and poetry.

The piece laid out the basics of Moore's cosmology, sketched in some background details, and depicted magical experiences which were presumably very close to his own. The performance began with the 'roll up, roll up' call of 'The Hair of the Snake That Bit Me', moving on to 'The Map Drawn on Vapour (I)', where Moore set down some of the basics of the associative nature of Ideaspace, and related it to his own experience with Iain Sinclair and psychogeography. This was continued in 'Litvinoff's Book', which discussed East End gangsters, before segueing into 'A Map Drawn on Vapour (II)', virtually a recap of Gull's tour of London in *From Hell*. From there, Moore moved to a more transcendental realm. 'The Stairs Beyond Substance' discussed quantum physics and the limits of knowledge, then 'The Spectre Garden' plunged into three poems about encountering gods: 'The Enochian Angel Of The 7th Aethyr', 'The Demon Regent Asmodeus' and 'The Deity Glycon'. The final act was 'The Book of Copulation', a long poem that built to a crescendo, asserting that we are all – every person, every supernatural entity – aspects of one being. The song 'Town of Lights' was a coda, telling us that there are angels within us and Jerusalem is in sight.

It was performed as part of a three-evening event hosted by Iain Sinclair which attracted a 'surprisingly small' audience. A backing tape composed by David J and Tim Perkins played in the background. Perkins didn't attend, but 'David J mimed, mummed and performed enigmatic symbols at the stage periphery – Ariel to Alan's Prospero'. Melinda Gebbie provided the voice of an angel. Moore left the stage to applause from the audience, then circulated to gauge reaction, which was positive.

A transcript was published in the fanzine *Frontal Lobe*, and the lyrics for a number of the songs appeared over the next few years in *Negative Burn*. Shortly afterwards, Moore rerecorded his part in a studio and it was mixed with the existing backing tapes by David J and Perkins for eventual release on CD (2001). A photograph taken during rehearsal that apparently showed a spectral figure standing behind David J, beaming energy or ectoplasm at Moore, was published in *Fortean Times*, alongside the *Rapid Eye* interview and on the CD sleeve.

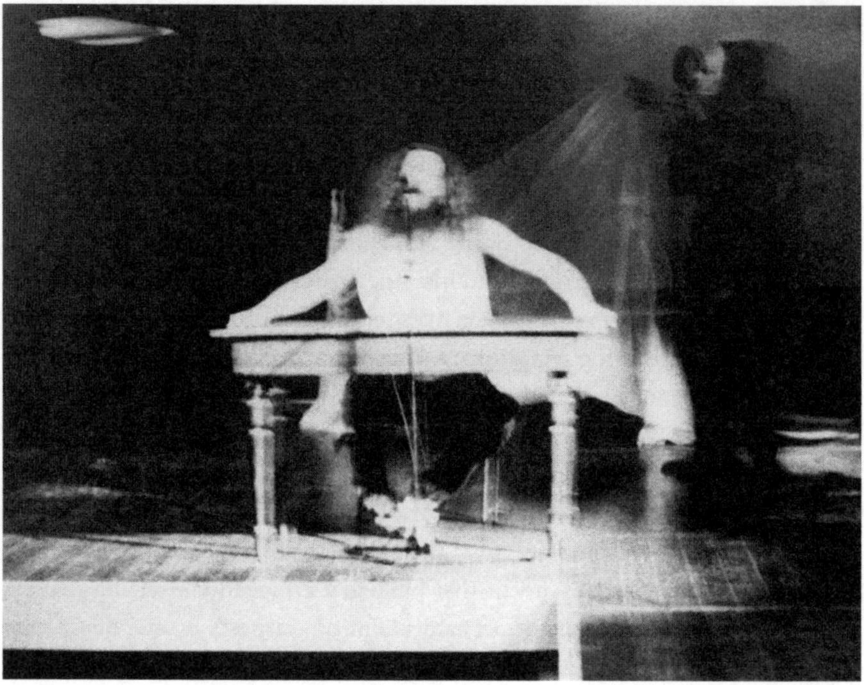

A little dissatisfied with that first 'working' and painfully aware he was finding it difficult to describe his experiences, Moore 'switched to a more analytical mode' and began to assemble a large library of books about magic and the history of the occult, as well as grimoires and artefacts of magical significance.

But does he really believe that Glycon and Asmodeus exist? Inarguably, we have to accept that they exist inside Alan Moore's head. And once we've accepted that, we can move on to the meat of his argument: psychogeography and veneration of Glycon are methods Moore uses to explore Ideaspace.

When he first started his research, Moore had been surprised to discover that there wasn't 'much of a theory to make sense of any sort of consciousness'. Moore is committed to the scientific worldview. He believes that magicians and occultists have tended to make a fundamental mistake in seeing magic as a rival scientific system with strict 'laws'. Magic, for Moore, is an art, albeit a 'meta-art' akin to psychology or linguistics, and, in his view, virtually all great art has been created by artists with magical beliefs of one kind or another. Science, however, has at least one serious limitation: it 'cannot discuss or explore consciousness itself, since scientific reality is based entirely upon empirical phenomena', and so 'if I wanted a working model of consciousness that would be of any use to me personally or professionally, it became clear that I'd have to build it myself'.

The entire middle section of *Promethea* is an extended journey into Ideaspace – called the Immateria in the comic – the 'magical realm'. The series is essentially a lyceum lecture in which Moore reports on some of the places he's explored. In #11 (December 2000), the title character's words can easily be imagined as an echo of Moore's own thoughts back in the early nineties: 'I feel a need to take a long journey soon, to find someone. A journey into magic. I've read a lot of books, I understand the ideas intellectually, I suppose, but I don't really feel them . . . I need to understand it from inside.' Promethea carries a staff, a twin-snake-headed caduceus (Moore had taken to carrying a walking cane topped with a carved snakehead). The snakes start to talk to her. They are Mack and Mike (short for 'macro' and 'micro'), and she consistently fails to tell them apart. They talk in rhyme, and paint a picture that Moore's regular readers would recognise from 'The Hair of the Snake That Bit Me':

> *to enter magic, in a sense,*
> *means entering our intelligence.*
> *That record-breaking smash-hit show,*
> *the theatre of what we know,*
> *where thoughts parade in fancy dress*
> *upon the stage of consciousness*

The next issue, *Promethea* #12 (February 2001) is one of the most extraordinary entries in Moore's canon. It is a survey of how the history of the universe is underpinned by magic, with an emphasis on the development of human culture. Each page is a variation of the same ornate single panel and each depicts Promethea considering a different Tarot card, each card being drawn as a cartoon character. Mack and Mike give their interpretation of the cards, still talking in rhyme. Scrabble tiles spell out apt anagrams of the word 'Promethea' (so the chapter as a whole is called 'Metaphore', and on the page where sex is discovered, the tiles read 'Me Atop Her'). Running along the bottom of the pages, Aleister Crowley takes the whole issue to tell a joke, while we see him age from embryo to skeleton. There are recurring design elements, including a chessboard pattern across the top of each page and a cartoon devil and angel that appear on alternate pages. Moore is never afraid to make it clear how clever he's being, or of deploying puns. At one point, Promethea is overwhelmed by the mass of information, and in her confusion comments on the joke Crowley is recounting instead of the Tarot card: '"railway carriage", are you sure that's part of this train of thought?' – I'm sorry, I'm having trouble keeping the different threads separate. I'm not even sure which of you two is which.' The snakes on her staff inform her (and us), 'it's like a fugue, you have a choice of following a single voice, or letting each strand grow less clear, the music of the whole to hear'.

Subsequent issues are equally elaborate. As comics critic Douglas Wolk notes, Moore was clearly 'emboldened by the fact that Williams and Gray's hands hadn't strangled him'.

Moore interprets the universe as a four-dimensional solid containing past, present and future which we explore using our consciousness. Within our heads, we have an individual mental landscape – Ideaspace – that fits together associatively. An example Moore is fond of giving is that Land's End and John O'Groats are close together in Ideaspace – they are conceptually close precisely because they're proverbially far apart. Ideaspace is organised into areas governed by certain principles, such as Judgement. The first explorers to discover the 'shifting contours' of Ideaspace were shamans, who used hallucinogenic drugs to enter the realm of the imagination and so were able to guide the rest of early humankind. This tradition has continued and developed; in more recent times occultists have drawn up maps like the Tarot and Qabalah which, if used correctly, can function as allegories for the entire possible range of human experience. Moore believes magic is central to art, indeed that language itself was originally a system of signs and symbols designed to explain what the shamans were encountering.

Some of these symbols frequently recur. The Serpent is one: the 'lifesnake', Will, male principle, or phallus – the 'snake energy' known to many of the world's belief systems in the form of snake gods (including Glycon). This symbol is often associated with gold, and is ultimately a representation of the double helix of DNA. Another symbol is the Moon: the imagination, dreams, the feminine principle, often personified as a goddess (like Selene), and associated with silver.

The dream world, the underworld and the land of the dead are all the same place, and governed by the Moon. The joining of the male and female principle – will and imagination – is the origin of creativity. Sex is a metaphor/avatar/example of this. The interplay between life and imagination originates the Theatre of Marvels: the universe.

Moore's personal experiences have led him to believe his Ideaspace is connected to that of others, so it may be something like Jung's collective unconscious. Ideaspace is not neutral or inert, there are clear indications it has awareness, an agenda, and a sense of humour. The gods live in Ideaspace, Ideaspace is contained within our minds, so we all contain gods. Angels are our highest drive, devils our lowest impulses. 'There are angels in you.'

Moore makes no secret of the fact that his worldview is a synthesis of his research and experience. In *Promethea* #10 (October 2000), Sophie is given a pile of books to read before her entry into the Immateria ('Crowley's *Magick Without Tears* and *777*, plus some other stuff. Eliphas Levi'). Broadly speaking, he is offering a reinterpretation of Crowley's cosmology, with reference to author and philosopher Robert Anton Wilson, and artist and occultist Austin Osman Spare. This is counterbalanced by insights gleaned from a voracious reading of books about quantum physics, genetics, mathematics and computer science by writers like Rudy Rucker, Stephen Hawking and Richard Dawkins. The conclusion of the *Moon and Serpent* performance is almost a direct quotation from Joseph Campbell, who asserted (via Jung), 'All the gods, all the heavens, all the worlds, are within us. They are magnified dreams, and dreams are manifestations in image form of the energies of the body in conflict with each other. That is what myth is. Myth is a manifestation in symbolic images, in metaphorical images, of the energies of the organs of the body in conflict with each other.' It's clear from *Moon and Serpent* that the basics of this belief system had been worked out/revealed to Moore in his first few months as a magician. That said, he has also picked up new ideas along the way. As he wrote in one essay, 'The Serpent and the Sword', the idea that snake symbolism in mythology represents DNA came from *The Cosmic Serpent*, by the anthropologist Jeremy Narby (first published in English in 1998). Moreover, he accepts Narby's theory that DNA stores information, and believes some DNA – possibly so-called 'junk DNA' – acts as a storehouse of ancestral knowledge which can be accessed using ritual.

*

Although Moore might have claimed that his initiation into magic represented (my emphasis) 'a major *sea change*. It has opened up different sorts of perceptions. I still have access to all my old perceptions, but I have a range of new ones now as well,' it's hard to find anything truly new in his work after his encounter with Glycon. Moore's Road to Damascus moment didn't lead to a radical rethink. He did not wake up the next morning, embrace the material, shave off his hair and decide to see the world. Everything that followed can be seen as an extension of his previous beliefs and concerns. His narrative techniques remain similar. The grand survey of human history we see in *Promethea* is reminiscent of V's televised address or *The Mirror of Love*. He's still telling stories full of symmetries and creating comic strips where the last panel leads neatly back to the first, he's still making heavy use of puns and similar wordplay, and his writing still has the same distinctive rhythm, what Douglas Wolk called 'an iambic gallop: da-*dum*, da-*dum*, da-*dum*'. For that matter, the tone of 'Fossil Angels', a 2002 essay exhorting existing magicians and followers of the occult to abandon their twee clichés, is very similar to the articles he wrote in the early eighties bemoaning the laziness of comics creators who still relied on Stan Lee's template. Once again, he sees untapped potential in the medium, held back by nostalgia and by unimaginative people who've forgotten the original, primal power of the stories modern practitioners merely ape.

The message he drew from contact with higher powers wasn't quite 'steady as she goes', but it did act as a reaffirmation of his existing beliefs, giving him new energy to pursue the themes he was already exploring.

There are also very similar concepts present in his earlier work. *Promethea*'s Immateria, a glittering web of interconnected life and shared consciousness, strongly resembles depictions of 'the Green' in *Swamp Thing*, both in terms of their conception and in the way Moore represents them on the page. And in *Snakes and Ladders*, Moore wrote of a second encounter with John Constantine: 'Years later, in another place, he steps out of the dark and speaks to me. He whispers: "I'll tell you the ultimate secret of magic. *Any cunt could do it.*"' Moore clarified in the documentary *The Mindscape of Alan Moore* that this encounter took place during a magic ritual; he either hasn't noticed, or has chosen not to draw attention to, a scene from the beginning of Book Two of *The Ballad of Halo Jones*, written fifteen years before, around the time he created Constantine. In it, we learn details of Halo Jones' epic journey out into the universe (some of which foreshadow events beyond the end of the published series) – 'she saw places that aren't even there any more!' And we learn her most memorable quotation: 'Anybody could have done it'.

There's more. When Moore says, 'I think that if magic is anything, it's about realising the *unbelievable supernatural magic*' – those words being spoken in a stage whisper – 'is in just the fact that we are thinking and having this conversation. Realising just how magical every instant is, every drawn breath, every thought. Just how astronomical the odds are against it. How wonderful. And following through these kinds of beautiful chains of symbols that can lead to some interesting revelations,' it's hard not to hear an echo of Dr Manhattan:

> thermodynamic miracles . . . events with odds against so astronomical they're effectively impossible, like oxygen spontaneously becoming gold. I long to observe such a thing. And yet, in each human coupling, a thousand million sperm vie for a single egg. Multiply those odds by countless generations, against the odds of your ancestors being alive; meeting; siring this precise son, that exact daughter . . . until your mother loves a man she has every reason to hate, and of that union, of the thousand million children competing for fertilization, it was you, only you that emerged. To distill so specific a form from that chaos of improbability, like turning air to gold . . . that is the crowning unlikelihood. The thermodynamic miracle. . . . but the world is so full of people, so crowded with these miracles that they become commonplace and we forget . . . I forget. We gaze continually in the world and it grows dull in our perceptions. Yet seen from another's vantage point, as if new, it may still take the breath away.

Moreover, Moore's observation that 'if there is truly no linear time as we understand it, then the events that make up the vast hyper-solid of existence can be read with as much validity from back to front as from front to back', is a lesson Dr Manhattan had already learned. And when he goes on to say 'our lives are as "true" if we view the film in reverse. In this reading of the world, our inert bodies are dug up from the ground or magically reassembled in the inferno of a crematorium oven', he is echoing precisely the sequence of events depicted in a *2000AD Future Shock*, 'The Reversible Man'. Back in 1985, he'd even described a method of plotting a story that sounds like Promethea navigating the Immateria: 'establish your continuum as a four-dimensional shape with length, breadth, depth and time, and then pick out the single thread of narrative that leads you most interestingly and most revealingly through the landscape that you've created, whether it be a literal landscape or some more abstract and psychological terrain.'

There is, too, a distinct sense of landscape in *Swamp Thing*'s Louisiana, and even something psychogeographical in Rorschach's declaration 'This city is afraid of me . . . I have seen its true face.' But Moore's ahead of us: 'One of the perceptions I had bore relevance to my previous work; especially to *Watchmen* (the Dr Manhattan chapter) and a couple of the time travel stories I wrote for *2000AD*. In the burning white heart of the experience, I thought I had a revelation that those stories were premonitions of the state that I exist in now. Time can be seen just as effectively one way as another. The Dr Manhattan material was a "memory" of the state I'm in now in 1994 – a "memory" which persisted until 1985.'

So, what are we to make of all this? It's paraphrasing only very slightly to say that Alan Moore has consulted the contents of his own head and concluded that everything in our culture, including language and art, arose from bearded shamans who were fond of magic mushrooms and expressed their message in obscure, coded picture writing. Indeed, the world would be a much more chilled place if everyone would just listen to their modern-day equivalents. Oh, and those guys give *really* great orgasms. Whatever else it is, Moore's view of the world is inescapably self-indulgent.

Moore the Magus alienates some of his readers, and it's not fair to dismiss them all as snarky arrested-development types who'd prefer him to be writing *Watchmen* /*Batman* crossovers where Rorschach goes after the Joker for crippling Babs Gordon. Douglas Wolk, writing about the stories in *Promethea*, notes that 'their ratio of profundity to claptrap varies with the reader's openness to semi-digested Crowley, and occasionally Moore threatens to sprain an eyelid from winking so hard', while Moore himself has said that *Promethea* 'lost several thousand readers' over the course of the Immateria sequence, and that people who stuck with it 'are either dedicated in their resolve, or else have had their cerebral

cortex so badly damaged by the last four or five issues that they are no longer capable of formulating a complaint'.

There's no way of knowing what percentage of his readership think Moore's beliefs are 'true', but when the subject is raised, it's often framed in terms that presuppose he's either mad or that even he doesn't really believe a word of it. While his journey is personal and spiritual, the fact he has made it so public is also clearly, at least in some degree, intended as provocation on Moore's part. There is a whole spectrum of ways to take all this, and it boils down to the inferences readers make about Moore's own motives, judgement and psychological state. It involves a decision about where he stands in relation to 'the truth', and – as he has been at pains to point out – 'truth' is a surprisingly slippery word. It's natural enough, though, for readers who become aware of Moore's belief in magic to seek some form of rational explanation.

Moore has been expansive about his magical experiences, practices and beliefs. He has said that 'what you see is what you get'. Detailed interviews about his magic add little to what you would know if you'd paid attention during *Moon and Serpent* or *Promethea*. We don't have to take him at face value, but if we don't, then – ironically – we have to enter a personal realm of speculation and imaginative engagement.

There are a number of obvious, dismissive explanations. If you take a hallucinogenic drug, the chances are you will hallucinate. Alan Moore would not be the first person to smoke funny cigarettes with his mates and have an evening where he thought he had discovered the profound secrets of the universe. Moore has admitted this is a possibility ('bearing in mind that this could be just the product of a lot of psycho-active drugs', he said in *Rapid Eye*).

Nor would he be the first public figure to make headlines after a declaration that he had adopted an eccentric spiritual belief system. Moore was horrified in the late nineties that celebrities like Roseanne Barr and Britney Spears were adopting the Qabalah.

There are more cynical interpretations. Is it an act? Well, yes. Moore has never done anything but put his cards on the table when it comes to that question. It's a 'theatre of the mind'; it's all a way for him to practise his art. A more precise question is whether Moore is sincere. Some people have suggested he's not, that it's a form of publicity stunt. One of the Image partners, Rob Liefeld, said for example:

'He once called us up to tell us that he had just been in the dream realm and talking to Socrates and Shakespeare, and to Moses, dead serious, and that they talked for what seemed to be months, but when he woke up, only an evening had passed, and he came up with these great ideas. And I'm tellin' ya, I think it's shtick, dude. I think it's all shtick. I'm gonna start saying that stuff. Cuz you know what? It makes you instantly interesting. Like "O yeah, last night I was hanging out with Socrates. Came to me in a dream. We played poker. We dropped acid." That's the kinda stuff Alan would say all the time.' Moore laughs off the suggestion that either conversation took place: 'I've never spoken to Rob Liefeld at all in my life . . . I don't ever remember ringing the Image office. I have had some conversations with [Image partner] Eric Stephenson, er, but I never had conversations with Socrates, Shakespeare and Moses.'

Moore's initial declaration, and his explorations of magic, inarguably came at an oddly schizophrenic time in his professional life, when highly personal work that was difficult to pigeonhole had been put on the backburner in favour of the most lightweight material he would ever produce. It's very tempting to see the magician persona as a reaction against that. It might have been for public consumption, a ploy, to mark him out in a crowded marketplace, or to demonstrate that there was more to Alan Moore than superhero comic hackwork. More insidiously, becoming a magician might have been a way of convincing *himself* that there was more to him than telling thirty panel stories about demonic clowns.

But such cynical interpretations can be dismissed by noting that, twenty years on, Moore's still a magician. Drugs wear off. Publicity stunts have very short shelf lives: when Moore started on this path, Madonna was wearing her cone bra; since then she's engineered dozens of controversies (including her own declaration of interest in the Qabalah). To put things in perspective, Moore has now been a magician five times longer than he wrote for DC. He's continued to write about magic and continued to practise it. His worldview is clearly elaborate and consistent, not a random outpouring of provocative statements.

Then there's the most obvious explanation: has Moore just gone a bit mad? It was something that worried him, just as it had worried Steve Moore after his first encounter with Selene. In February 1994, Moore described the process as 'going completely insane, and at the same time hopefully doing something a little more constructive . . . if, in five years time, I'm shot full of thorazine and wearing a vest

that ties up at the back, then obviously this declaration of magickal intent is going to sound pretty silly.' He understood how it all sounded: 'I should imagine that, very reasonably, most would assume that all of this I've just spoken of is nothing more than the ramblings of a disintegrating mind, or that it's just some sort of glorified New Age way of talking about the work that I do, that's what I would assume if I had heard it.'

When *Voice of the Fire* was published in 1996, he said again, 'I continually monitor the possibility that I might be going mad'; reminded of this in 2002 by *Times* journalist Dominic Wells, he noted, 'Oh, I've gone much madder in the last six years, though my ideas have become more sophisticated. Yes, I was a mere amateur in lunacy then . . .' Describing his magical experiences, he'll say things like 'I'll admit to you, this is looked at from an increasingly mad perspective on my part', and when asked whether the right term for what had happened to him was 'magical awakening,' he replied with a laugh, 'That'll do. "Mental breakdown" will do if you want. It's all the same to me.'

As far as Moore was concerned at the time, though, magic had actually helped him psychologically, allowing him to reconcile the various roles he found himself in. 'I couldn't think of another system which would get all of my various energies running in the same direction . . . It struck me that, as an individual, I had too many components in my life that weren't unified.' Three years later, he was able to say: 'These days, after a great deal of hard work, I have refined the Hydra down to one head. I'm Alan Moore when I'm talking to my daughters, or to my eighty-nine-year-old aunt, or to my readers, or to myself.'

And as so often in Moore's life, it needs to be stressed that however weird or exceptional what he's doing looks, he's rarely the first or only person in his circle doing it. Steve Moore, his best friend, had been in personal contact with a divine being years before Alan encountered Glycon. Researching *From Hell* led Moore to take a fresh look at William Blake, a self-publisher who merged pictures and words and told of 'demigods with grandiose and punning names that can be viewed as having much in common with . . . Jack Kirby', while H.P. Lovecraft was in Moore's view 'a visionary – a prophet. He was an American William Blake.' Moore is aware that science fiction author Philip K. Dick had very similar transcendental experiences to his own, involving ancient Rome, time as a solid state and Asclepius, and that Dick was trying to articulate those experiences in his later work while seeing his earlier efforts as containing 'pre-echoes' of subsequent revelations. Golden Age *Superman* and *Batman* writer Alvin Schwartz believed he had repeated encounters with a tulpa, or spirit form, of Superman.

It's equally possible that Moore was looking even closer to home, and was envious of his fellow comic book creator Dave Sim, whose sprawling *Cerebus the Aardvark* project started at roughly the same time as *Roscoe Moscow* and in much the same vein of crude parody. After Sim had a transcendental religious experience during a drug trip, however, it mutated beyond all recognition into a 300-issue single narrative that took a quarter of a century to create and served as a map of every one of Sim's idiosyncratic beliefs, prejudices and preoccupations. According to Moore: '*Cerebus*, as if I need to say so, is still to comic books what hydrogen is to the periodic table.' Rather than thinking it made him unique, or even peculiar, Moore may well have sought out divine help to make his work more personal, subsume his art into his mystical beliefs, because . . . well, that was the standard career path of so many of the artists he admires.

Moore's personal and professional lives are in radically different places to where they were twenty years ago. His magical experiences have had a permanent effect on him. It is clearly something he takes profoundly seriously. His friends and family have consistently told us that he believes what he says; in fact, you sense a little to his chagrin, they were completely relaxed about his new calling:

> My mother listened to the first *Moon and Serpent* CD and that seemed to really affect her. She was saying 'Ooh, I could have gone'. Gone into the music, something like that, gone into the words. The odd thing was that when I announced I was a magician, it didn't faze my family at all. My mother really, really liked the picture of Glycon I gave her. And my devoutly Christian Aunt Hilda, her sister, who had a little shrine of religious items in the corner of her living room, she asked if she could have a copy to put on her shrine . . . I think they recognised that this was something benign. My mother, on the other hand, didn't want a copy of the Asmodeus picture in the house.

Reading interviews with him, seeing his new work, it's clear he's sticking to his story.

In the end, Moore came up with a simple test: did practising magic have 'demonstrable utility', did it make him a better writer? Tim Perkins, who has worked with Moore on many of his recent musical endeavours, describes the magical practices as 'off-the-wall concepts to get your fat arse down the brain-gym'. Likewise, Moore believes magic gave him 'a new set of eyes to look at this planet through'. He has concluded that 'as long as the results are good, as long as the work that I'm turning out either maintains my previous levels of quality or, as I think is the case with a couple of those magical performances, actually exceeds those limits, then I'm not really complaining.'

Moore's '*Watchmen II*' phase in the early nineties had almost been sunk by highly personal, immersive projects which required him to bite off more than even he could chew. He could toss off scripts for *Spawn*, but no one could possibly have thought his heart was in it. His options seemed limited either to complex work that would never be finished or commercial work which held little personal interest. Moore had needed *something* to get him out of the rut, to introduce more vitality into his work, and in 1996 he was given the opportunity to put his new methods into action.

Rob Liefeld, one of the founding partners of Image, asked Moore to take over as writer on *Supreme*, a series featuring an 'edgy' Superman-style character who killed his opponents and was generally something of a bully. Moore was not terribly impressed with the core concept and when he took over *Supreme* with #41 (August 1996), he retasked Thunderman, one of the many ideas he'd had while brainstorming *1963*. Moore wanted to tell *Superman*-type stories set in the present day, but also include flashbacks to earlier adventures that would pastiche the carefree comics of the Silver Age. But, where *1963* had played the parody so straight that many readers hadn't spotted the joke, *Supreme* was framed in such a way that readers couldn't avoid seeing Moore winking at them.

Although sales rose, they didn't shoot up, but Moore's *Supreme* was an instant critical success, jointly winning the Eisner Award with *From Hell* in 1997 (Moore had won in both 1995 and 1996 on the strength of *From Hell* alone). He would 'have a lot of fun' working on *Supreme* and clearly found it rather therapeutic. He was even able to link it to his new worldview. 'I could parody the various ills of the comic industry and I could play with wonderful ideas, you know? Which was always the thing that Superman represented to me as a child . . . wonderful ideas, ideas that to me at that age were certainly magical. Where, to me, they provided a key to the world of my own imagination.'

In one of the later issues, *Supreme: The Return* #6 (published June 2000, written two years before), Moore steered Supreme to a strange realm populated by a diverse set of characters who look remarkably like those created by Jack 'the King' Kirby. The comics legend had died in February 1994 and by way of tribute Moore had Supreme meet the ruler of the realm, the Monarch – Kirby himself:

> **MONARCH:** You gotta know something about the world of ideas. It's like, y'know, where do they come from? Where does the idea of anythin' come from? See what I mean? It's a tough question.
>
> **SUPREME:** I think I may understand a little of what you're saying: I myself have access to a realm called 'Ideaspace'. . .
>
> **MONARCH:** Yeah, yeah, that's good. 'Idea Space'. Only the name should be punchier. Something like, I don't know, the Psychoverse, or the Cognitive Zone, or whatever. Me, I call it home.
>
> **SUPREME:** Home? You mean you're a native of imaginary space, like some of the demons, gods and angels I've encountered?
>
> **MONARCH:** Nah, I'm just, like, this guy who commuted to Idea Space when he went to work every day.

Shortly after Moore started work on *Supreme*, Liefeld fell out with the other Image partners. He immediately set up a new studio, Awesome Comics, to publish his existing titles and hired Moore to revamp the whole line. Moore wrote his customary long discussion documents and scripts for existing series *Glory* – a Wonder Woman style character – and *Youngblood* – a team of teen superheroes akin to the Teen Titans or X-Men. The first few issues scripted by Moore appeared at the end of 1997 and the beginning of 1998, along with *Judgment Day*, a series designed to widen out the fictional universe that they and Supreme inhabited. Moore also worked on two other series, *War Child* and *The Allies*.

In March 1998 he received a phone call from Scott Dunbier, who he had known since meeting him in San Diego in 1986. Dunbier was now an editor at Wildstorm, the Image studio owned by artist Jim Lee, and he asked if Moore was interested in working for them. Moore said he was happy at Awesome . . . at which point Dunbier broke the news that Awesome had hit serious financial problems after losing its main backer. Publication schedules had slipped. Moore had written six issues of *Youngblood*, which was meant to be a monthly publication, but only three

were ever published, in February and August 1998, and August 1999. The books received glowing reviews, but the erratic schedule made it hard for comic shops or readers to maintain their enthusiasm. By April 1999, Liefeld had resorted to publishing *Alan Moore's Awesome Universe Handbook* – the pitch documents for *Glory* and *Youngblood*.

Moore told Dunbier he would draw up a proposal. A couple of years before, he had come up with an idea for a series initially called *The League of Extraordinary Gentle-Folk*, a 'Justice League' style super-team of characters from Victorian adventure fiction, such as Allan Quatermain, the Invisible Man, and Jekyll and Hyde. In late 1997 he approached Kevin O'Neill, a *2000AD* veteran who'd worked with him on *Green Lantern Corps* (and an abortive *Bizarro World* series) when Moore had been at DC.

Moore decided to create a whole comics line from scratch. Searching his old notebooks, he found a string of names for characters he had forgotten writing, including Tom Strong, Promethea, Cobweb and Greyshirt. He'd given them no previous thought, but quickly came up with an idea of what characters with those names would be like. In each case, it was a question of matching the name to an existing superhero archetype – Tom Strong was Superman; Promethea was Wonder Woman; Top Ten would be a super-team. It occurred to Moore that now Awesome had gone under, a lot of the artists he had been working with would also be looking for new assignments, and he had devised the characters with those illustrators in mind: Tom Strong for his *Supreme* artist, Chris Sprouse, Promethea for *Glory*'s Brandon Peterson, Top Ten for *Youngblood*'s Steve Skroce.

In the event, Peterson had been snapped up for a variety of *X-Men* projects by Marvel . . . as had (somewhat to Moore's relief, given their history) Dunbier's next choice, Alan Davis. Bruce Timm and Alex Ross also turned *Promethea* down, though Ross suggested J.H. Williams, who was delighted to accept. Skroce was also busy, working on storyboards for the movie *The Matrix* (he would later work with its directors, the Wachowskis, on storyboards for the *V for Vendetta* movie). Moore further extended the community he was building by coming up with characters for some of his oldest friends in the industry (they'd all also worked with him on *Supreme*): Cobweb would be a sexy crimefighter, drawn by Melinda Gebbie; Greyshirt would be similar to The Spirit, drawn by Rick Veitch; *The First American* would feature art by Jim Baikie. All of these projects would be developed by Moore and his artists, who would be credited as co-creators. Wildstorm jumped at the chance to publish what was now titled *The League of Extraordinary Gentlemen* and four monthly books by Moore: *Tom Strong*, *Promethea*, *Top Ten* and the anthology series *Tomorrow Stories*, which featured *Cobweb*, *The First American*, *Greyshirt* and *Jack B Quick*. They were branded America's Best Comics, which Moore liked because 'if it turned out to be crappy then I could claim that it was ironic'.

But Rob Liefeld was not happy:

> Much of the ABC line is made up of poorly masked Awesome characters and story outlines he prepared for us. If I was as sue-happy and litigation driven as some suggest I be, I believe I could draw direct connections to many of the ABC characters and their origins coming from pages of Awesome work we commissioned from him. In short order, *Tom Strong* is *Supreme* mixed with his *Prophet* proposal. *Promethea* is *Glory* and the rest I honestly don't pay much attention to. Don't have the time or interest. Simply put, there is no ABC without *Supreme* and the Awesome re-launch.

There's an element of truth to this: *Tom Strong*, particularly, is drawn by the same artist as *Supreme* and has the same basic concept, that of a long-lived Superman archetype who we see in a complex present day, as well as in flashbacks to a more carefree past that act as homages to old comics. Strong, though, was more like the earliest incarnation of Superman, who was tough, but couldn't fly or fire heat rays from his eyes. Siegel and Shuster had based their creation on pulp magazine hero Doc Savage (a character with a Fortress of Solitude and the first name Clark), and Tom Strong looked a lot more like Doc Savage than Supreme. Other series diverged further: *Top Ten* changed beyond recognition from a superhero teambook into a *Hill Street Blues*-style police soap opera set in a city where everyone – police, criminals and bystanders – has superhuman powers (we see a billboard advertising a movie with the tagline 'You'll Believe A Man Can't Fly'). Most people would have assumed, like Liefeld, that *Promethea* was where Moore was going to reuse his ideas for *Glory* (Awesome Comics had only published a short preview issue before going under), but in fact it became one of Moore's most personal, difficult mainstream comics. Most of Moore's *Glory* notes are simply concerned with coming up with close analogues for *Wonder Woman* characters and concepts like Steve Trevor, the Holiday Girls and the invisible

plane; while the pitch had mentioned the Qabalah, it was only as a framework for mythological stories that would be 'flexible enough to take the whole spectrum of possible gods, demons and monsters and still [remain] clear and coherent'.

There was a twist in the tale. By the end of August 1998, Jim Lee had decided to sell Wildstorm to DC Comics. He knew Moore had vowed never to work with DC again, and rumours of the sale broke on the internet while Moore was on holiday at his Welsh farmhouse. Lee and Dunbier jumped on a plane, wanting to give him the news face to face before he heard it from anyone else. Moore met them at the railway station: 'I remember getting out of the cab with my customary snake-headed walking cane, and apparently Jim thought that I'd already heard the news and brought the stick to inflict some kind of physical damage upon him.' Moore was suspicious that DC had bought Wildstorm specifically to co-opt the America's Best Comics line, and it was true that the company had made their move very soon after the ABC contracts had been signed; as the *Daily Telegraph* put it, 'When he fell out with the largest comics publisher in the world, the New York-based DC, he found a home with an American independent publisher, Wildstorm. DC dealt with this defection in a remarkably straightforward way – they bought Wildstorm in order to get him back (an experience Moore describes as like having "a really weird, rich stalker girlfriend").' Around the same time, DC tried to buy out *1963* but Moore and the other creators unanimously rejected the offer.

There were, however, other reasons DC might want to buy Wildstorm. The studio was a pioneer in the use of digital colouring of comics, while Jim Lee himself was a popular artist who had managed to steer Wildstorm through the collapse of the comics market in the nineties, attracting top talent and publishing successful titles like *The Authority*, *Astro City* and *Danger Girl*. But despite Paul Levitz's assertion to the *New York Times* that 'we did the deal on the assumption that Alan would be gone the day it was signed', gossip site Bleeding Cool sums up the industry consensus: 'it was generally agreed they wanted [Wildstorm] for three things. The colourists. Jim Lee. And Alan Moore.'

Moore was keen on the ABC project and 'decided it was better to forego my own principles upon it rather than to put a lot of people who'd been promised work suddenly out of work.' So Lee had Moore list his concerns, then came to an agreement: Moore would have no contact whatsoever with DC. A new company, Firewall, was set up so that DC's name didn't even appear on his cheques. Dunbier would edit the books and be the only person to contact Moore about them. But amid all this wrangling, Moore made a decision that was oddly at variance with his views on creators' rights. As Don Murphy, a movie producer who'd optioned a number of Moore's books, put it: 'Jim Lee showed up with a contract that bought everything from Moore for a slightly higher page rate. Alan was happy to have it. Later Paul Levitz would actually be stunned that the grand complainer Moore would have made a stupid deal for himself again. But because the film rights for *League* were tied up with Fox and me they didn't include that in the ownership package. So for all the hate Alan feels about Hollywood and me, he would have sold *League* to Jim Lee for an extra $20 a page, too.'

Moore understood the deal and knew he was in a good position – the project could not go ahead without him. Jim Lee and Scott Dunbier had shown up willing to negotiate. Why then did he sign work-for-hire contracts for Tom Strong, Promethea and the other properties? Moore admits,

> Yes, I can see that does seem a bit puzzling. At the time, I was largely doing these scripts with Jim Lee's company and I was mainly doing them for my collaborators, after the collapse of Awesome Comics. At the time, it seemed to me that, without knowing what the strips were, there would probably be more money for my collaborators with a deal like that, and I felt at the time that dealing with Jim Lee had never been any problem, he seemed to be an agreeable and amenable man, and it struck me if there were serious disparities that arose from any of those strips, he would probably be amenable to a renegotiation. I wasn't worried about the strips while the deals were made purely with Jim Lee. It was after I signed those deals that Wildstorm was bought by DC Comics. So, yeah, it was probably a stupid thing to do, but that was the reason why I was doing a stupid thing. For what that's worth.

The extra money, even accumulated across all the books, would have little effect on Moore's personal finances. It would, though, be a significant, immediate boon to his artists. The Wildstorm contracts of the late nineties were more accommodating than the old work-for-hire arrangements and other ABC co-creators, like Rich Veitch and Chris Sprouse, weren't rubes; they signed the contracts with their eyes open, seeing them as a relatively good deal. Ultimately, both sides must have understood that the whole point of the ABC line was that Alan Moore was the guiding creative force behind it, that DC had to keep him on side and had no incentive to produce ABC books he disapproved of. Likewise, Moore was not going to find another publisher with deep enough pockets to put out the whole range of comics he envisaged, then turn them into lavish collected editions that stayed in print. In fact he became immersed in ABC, saying it 'required more work than I've ever turned out even back when I was in my twenties and early thirties . . . I'm smugly proud of having been able to do that.'

Alan Moore's belief in magic has provided, for twenty years now, a framework within which he's been able to create complicated, difficult and soaring works. There is an element of calculation, an element of showmanship and more than a whiff of folly about it, but it all makes sense if it's seen primarily as a way in which Moore can both spark his own creativity and explore the creative process in his art.

If we're inclined to credit Moore's productivity to his magical beliefs, we have to balance the explosion of output in the first ten years after declaring himself a magician with the caveat that the *second* ten years saw a marked decline in the quantity of work produced. Most of his creative energy was consumed by his magazine *Dodgem Logic* (2009–11), as well as two big projects that haven't yet been completed, the vast novel *Jerusalem* and the grimoire *The Moon and Serpent Bumper Book of Magic*. Although Moore clearly hasn't been slacking off – a couple of projects fizzled out through no fault of his own, like the libretto of an opera about Elizabethan magus John Dee for the Gorillaz, the 'virtual band' created by Blur's Damon Albarn and *Tank Girl* co-creator Jamie Hewlett – those who only keep track of his comics were not kept busy from 2003 to 2013. This period saw the winding down of the ABC line, a handful of *League of Extraordinary Gentlemen* sequels; *Neonomicon*, and a giveaway with the second issue of *Dodgem Logic* called *Astounding Weird Penises*. The performance art slowed down, too, with no major activity in the period, though Moore did write the screenplay to a movie, *Jimmy's End*.

As for the *quality* of this output, that's always going to be subjective. *From Hell*, *Lost Girls*, *Voice of the Fire*, *Tom Strong*, *Supreme*, *The League of Extraordinary Gentlemen*, *The Birth Caul*, *Promethea*, *Dodgem Logic* and *Unearthing* are clearly all 'major works', and they run the gamut from ultra-accessible action-adventure comics to idiosyncratic and resolutely uncommercial spoken pieces, from deeply serious to colourful romp. Judgement is made all the more difficult by the knowledge that Moore is most proud of his performance art, which by its very nature is his least accessible work. Some of that is simply a matter of logistics: the performances themselves are designed as one-offs, tailored to the date and location they are performed. The recordings may represent the soundtrack, but not the entire immersive, hypnotic experience – and in any case, they are very hard to come by. *The Birth Caul*, for example, was issued in a limited edition of five hundred copies. These are never going to be widely available, mass-market products in the way even small-press novels and comics have the potential to be, and there has to be some suspicion that this is precisely why Moore is so proud of them.

Moore is not attempting to convert us to his snake cult ('Glyconism . . . there's only me and I'm not looking for members') Many of his recent works talk directly about the occult, others do so indirectly, but it's not the only thing Alan Moore is writing about. You can acknowledge the magnificent technical achievements represented by *Promethea* or *Lost Girls* even if you find the subject matter baffling, just as you can with *Watchmen*. His work in the past twenty years has been diverse, but is all clearly created by the same author. Moore may very well not be a 'real magician', but using magic has meant he's done what he set out to achieve. As he put it himself: 'I was saying to my musical partner a while ago, that actually if we continue to get material like this, it doesn't really matter whether the gods are there or not.'

9 PICTOPIA

> 'Do we need any more shitty films in this world? We have quite enough already. Whereas the $100 million could sort out the civil unrest in Haiti. And the books are always superior, anyway.'
>
> **Alan Moore, *Total Film***

There is an urban legend in Northampton – a tale the details of which change a little depending on who tells it – that Johnny Depp once showed up unannounced at Alan Moore's house, but no one was in. The movie star sat patiently on the doorstep for three hours, signing autographs, before Moore eventually returned home carrying his shopping, and the two of them went for beers at the White Elephant.

This is only the most literal example of Hollywood beating a path to Alan Moore's door. Depp was the lead actor in the movie version of *From Hell*, the first of four adaptations of Moore's work to reach the screen in the first decade of the twenty-first century. *From Hell* (2001) was followed by *The League of Extraordinary Gentlemen* (also known as *LXG*, 2003), *V for Vendetta* (2006) and *Watchmen* (2009). Moore was not involved in the production of these adaptations. He says he has never seen any of the movies, a claim corroborated by all his friends and family. Latterly, he has refused to take any money from the projects, and has arranged for his share of the revenue to be sent to the artists of the original comics instead. Yet he was not always so hostile to movie versions of his work. His attitude has evolved almost exactly in parallel with his approach to the comics industry: initial excitement has given way to indifference, eventually hardening into suspicion and now open antipathy.

When Moore was starting his career in comics in the early eighties, the prospect of a cinema version of a British comic book character was a pipe dream. A few TV cartoons were based on children's comics and newspaper strips, such as *Fred Bassett* and *Bananaman*, and there had been talk of a *Dan Dare* film for many years, although it never materialised. David Lloyd says that he and Moore put some effort into getting *V for Vendetta* on to television: 'The only thing that me and Alan thought about that might make us rich was if we could sell it as a TV series or a movie, and we were actively involved in trying to do that.' Both he and Moore sent out a variety of proposals, but 'There was never any possibility of it happening . . . We never had any approaches.'

In America, the situation was a little rosier: there was a long roll call of Saturday morning cartoons based on comics, while the *Superman* movies had been a success and there were TV shows like *Wonder Woman* and *The Incredible Hulk*, which tended to be camp and colourful. But the *Superman* franchise stumbled with a noticeably cheaper third movie (1983) and a disastrous *Supergirl* spin-off (1984), and though a handful of filmmakers and producers knew the comics readership was getting older and the storytelling more sophisticated, they found it impossible to convince the studios. It did not help that a major movie based on a 'grown-up' comic, *Howard the Duck* (1986), proved a huge flop which critics almost unanimously declared to be one of the worst movies of all time. Other films, while not officially based on comic books, took their cues from the more sophisticated examples of the medium, but even here the results were mixed – *Robocop* (1987), unmistakably influenced by *Judge Dredd*, was a big success, despite an R-rating that – in theory at least – barred children and teenagers from seeing it, but *He-Man and the Masters of the Universe* (1987), a covert homage to Jack Kirby's *Fourth World* comics, lost a lot of money.

The *Watchmen* movie had been optioned in August 1986 by Lawrence Gordon, producer of *48 Hrs*, *Brewster's Millions* and *Jumpin' Jack Flash*. Within the next few years, Gordon would go on to produce the *Predator* and *Die Hard* movies and *Field of Dreams*, as well as comic book adaptations *The Rocketeer*, *Timecop* and *Hellboy*. Moore was reportedly offered the chance to script the *Watchmen* movie; the offer may have been made face to face when he met producer Joel Silver, who remembers, 'I had lunch with Alan and Dave Gibbons at the time and he was an odd guy. But he was very intrigued and interested in the process. He was game to be involved.' But Moore declined the opportunity, citing a heavy workload, and instead Sam Hamm was assigned to the job, having delivered his script for a big-budget *Batman* movie in October 1986. He impressed Moore when they met: 'His reason for doing *Watchmen* was that if someone's going to fuck it up he'd rather it was someone who cared about it. He said, "I realise I'm defeated before I've started so I've got to take a Samurai attitude to it: that I'm already dead, so I'll discharge myself with honour." I couldn't ask for a better attitude.'

Hamm's main task was to condense twelve issues of the comic into a feature-length story, which he achieved mainly by ditching all hints of the Minutemen, the earlier generation of superheroes. This means the disappearance of the suggestion in the comic that Nite Owl is following in the footsteps of an earlier crimefighter by the same name; more significantly, the removal of an entire backstory involving the Comedian and Silk Spectre's mother (there is nothing in the script to say that the Comedian is any older than his team-mates). In the new story, all the superheroes were formerly part of a team called the Watchmen, which was forced to disband in 1976 after they accidentally blew up the Statue of Liberty while thwarting a terrorist attack. There are some nice touches: for example we catch sight of a war memorial commemorating those 'who gave their lives to achieve victory in Vietnam. Below it are the names of the American dead. There are almost four hundred of them'. And the script is keen to emphasise the slight differences between our world and that of the film, with details like self-lighting cigarettes. In part, this is because the changed ending depends on it: in this version, Ozymandias plans to save the world from nuclear holocaust by changing history to prevent the creation of Dr Manhattan (whose presence, as in the comic, has affected the course of the Cold War). At the end, he succeeds and the surviving Watchmen find themselves in our world, looking distinctly out of place in their superhero costumes.

Terry Gilliam was appointed to direct, and the movie went into pre-production. Rumours began to fly that Robin Williams was keen to play Rorschach, Jamie Lee Curtis would be the Silk Spectre, Richard Gere Nite Owl, and that Arnold Schwarzenegger was happy to shave his head and be painted bright blue to play Dr Manhattan. Moore was even able to see the sunny side of that last rumour, reminding fans that Dr Manhattan had originally been Jon Ostermann, the son of a German immigrant. Gilliam, though, was not happy with Sam Hamm's script. It missed very few of the story beats from the present-day sequences of the comic, but failed to get under the skin of the characters: 'He had made some very clever jumps, but killed it. He made it into a movie, but what did you end up with? You ended up with these characters, but they were only shadows of the characters in an adventure. And I didn't think the book was about that.'

Gilliam set about a rewrite, sitting down 'with Charles McKeown, my writing partner on *Baron Munchausen* and *Brazil*, to squeeze out a script. Time passed. Frustration increased. How do you condense this monster book into a 2 to 2½-hour film? What goes? What stays? Therein lies the problem. I talked to Alan Moore. He didn't know how to do it . . . I suggested perhaps a five-part miniseries would be better. I still believe that.' A second draft was completed, credited to Gilliam, Warren Skaaren and Hamm (but not McKeown). It's essentially a redraft of Hamm's script, with certain elements, including Rorschach's voiceover, restored from the comic. Gilliam was still unhappy to lose so much material from the original, but in the event, that was not the main problem. As he explained: 'Joel Silver said he had $40 million to do it, but he didn't have $40 million, he had about $24.25 million, and we talked about the fact that I had just made *Munchausen*, which was a huge flop that had gone over budget, and he had just made *Die Hard 2*, which had gone way, way over and had been less successful than hoped. So the two fools were running around Hollywood trying to raise money for this thing that's darker than anything.' Long after the project collapsed, Gilliam continued to field questions about *Watchmen*, and he was approached to direct again in 1996, when a new version of the script had been written.

V for Vendetta was also optioned in the late eighties, with Joel Silver again set to produce. A dystopian science fiction story was a far more bankable prospect than a superhero movie at the time, and nothing in the original comic demanded a vast budget, so it would seem eminently more 'filmable' than *Watchmen*. Despite this, the project never really seemed to pick up momentum. One reason might be that the studios felt *V for Vendetta* was too parochially British. Moore remembers an early attempt to rectify this:

> Now in the first screenplay that I got for *V for Vendetta*, because this anarchist dresses up in a Guy Fawkes costume, of course people in America have no idea who Guy Fawkes is, so they were going to change it to Paul Revere, and it wasn't going to happen in London, 'cos that's just gonna confuse Americans who can't remember that there's more than one country in the world, so perhaps it's going to be set in New York. And that political stuff about fascism, that doesn't really play, so we'll have an America that's been taken over by the commies. So you've got this true American dressed as Paul Revere fighting against the commie takeover. Eventually I think they realised that was a stupid idea.

Hilary Henkin, author of the screenplay for *Road House* (1989), and who would go on to receive an Oscar nomination for co-writing *Wag the Dog* (1997) with David Mamet, wrote a second *V for Vendetta* script around 1990. This shifted the action into a more generic science fictional landscape, so that Bishop Lilliman oversaw a newly manufactured state religion and the Fingermen (simply plain-clothes policemen in the comic) were half-goat mutants operating from a building in the shape of a giant finger. In this version, Evey is tortured by the government, her captivity isn't faked by V, and at the end, she learns V was her father. Yet it's not quite the travesty that those details suggest. It positions the story in the same sort of New Wave SF idiom as work by long-time influences on Moore like Michael Moorcock and William Burroughs, and is clearly informed by works like Harlan Ellison's '"Repent Harlequin," Said the Ticktockman' and Ray Bradbury's *Fahrenheit 451*, stories that Moore had always cited as influences on *V*. This version nonetheless baffled Moore: 'As I said at the time, if you wanted to do a film about goat policemen, then why the fuck didn't you just buy the option to *Rupert Bear*?'

One movie based on Alan Moore's work *was* released in the late eighties: *Return of the Swamp Thing* (1989). Subject to the deal struck before Moore began working on the character, the filmmakers had the rights to use characters and situations from any *Swamp Thing* comics, including Moore's run on the book, without him or his artists being consulted, credited or compensated – a situation that naturally irked Moore, but which by that point was a long way down the list of his grievances against DC Comics. So, the film's title sequence was a montage of comic book panels and covers, many from Moore's run, Swamp Thing had some of the powers

Moore granted him, like the ability to grow new bodies and control plant life, and the story featured the romance between the protagonist and Abby introduced by Moore; producer Michael Uslan told an interviewer, 'that, to me, is a wonderful Beauty and the Beast/Phantom of the Opera love story'. There's even a short sequence where, like *Swamp Thing* #34, Abby eats a tuber from Swamp Thing's body and the couple are able to make love – the episode, depicted in the comic with pages of LSD-trip imagery set to poetry, becomes in the movie a soft-focus dream sequence in which, for the duration, Swamp Thing has a human body. At the end of the movie Swamp Thing and Abby walk off into the bayou together, the scene fading to an image reminiscent of the cover to Moore's final issue.

The project was not aiming to be a horror film: the poster promised 'a cross between *Little Shop of Horrors* and *The Incredible Hulk* with a light spritz of *Hairspray*', while Uslan admitted at the time, 'This is a general audience Swamp Thing . . . we cannot do a movie that's on the plane of philosophy of the Alan Moore comic. We cannot reach the kind of audience we need to reach by going into a line-by-line adaptation of the kind of work they've produced so well in the comics.'

Moore was surprised to read this: 'I thought, well, that is an astounding admission. What do you mean "it's only a movie"? Isn't it supposed to be "it's only a comic"? This is the field that gave us *Citizen Kane* and *Battleship Potemkin* and all the rest of it, you're telling me you can't reach the same philosophical depth as I can in a copy of *Swamp Thing*?'

Even as Uslan was being interviewed, work was concluding on another movie he was producing. *Batman*, scripted by Sam Hamm and directed by Tim Burton, proved to be a dark, complex comic book adaptation that audiences flocked to in the summer of 1989. The year after that, the indie comic *Teenage Mutant Ninja Turtles* became a bona fide phenomenon. Studios were now very open to the idea of making 'comic book movies' and a raft of titles based on comics, old and new, began to appear. Superhero movies, though, remained a highly unpredictable prospect. *Dick Tracy* (1990), lavish, stylised and starring Warren Beatty, was hyped, but underperformed. *The Rocketeer* (1991) and *Spawn (1997)* barely proved profitable. *Tank Girl (1995)*, *Judge Dredd* (1995), *Barb Wire* (1996) and *Steel* (1997) all made back only a fraction of their production budgets. On the other hand, *Batman Returns* (1992) did well, and its critically derided sequel

Batman Forever (1995) actually did better. Two of the biggest movies of the nineties, *Men in Black* (1997) and *The Mask* (1994), were also based on obscure comic books.

As the options for *Watchmen* and *V for Vendetta* expired, they were renewed, and Moore and his co-creators received a fresh round of payments. In February 1994 Don Murphy, co-producer of Oliver Stone's *Natural Born Killers* (1994), written by Quentin Tarantino, optioned *From Hell* on the strength of the first Tundra issue. As the graphic novel hadn't been finished, Moore wrote a 5,000-word synopsis of the remaining chapters. Murphy was a fan of Moore's work, while Moore described Murphy as 'a nice bloke who phones me up and asks if I've got any more projects that could be turned into films, any laundry lists that I might have forgotten about.' Murphy met Moore about half a dozen times. They discussed *Fashion Beast*, as well as ideas for an original movie featuring Nic Cage as a magician. Murphy optioned *The League of Extraordinary Gentlemen*, in Kevin O'Neill's words 'before I'd finished drawing the first issue' – before it even had a publisher, in fact – saying he'd bought the rights when 'it was only a three-page idea sheet. It was amazing.' Murphy was also a fan of Moore himself: 'He is a big personality and very smart and charismatic. I really thought he was a great person – a genuine genius and eccentric. I discussed the deals with him, got him an ICM agent for *League*, made sure he was well represented.' The optioning of his work was lucrative for Moore: Murphy claims Moore was paid '$800,000 for *From Hell*, $1 million for *League*'. Eddie Campbell was able to use his *From Hell* option money to quit his day job as a metal fabricator and set himself up as a publisher.

Throughout the nineties, various rumours and tentative announcements of *Watchmen* and *From Hell* movies would surface from time to time, but all the projects remained in the early stages of pre-production. The experience allowed Moore to spot a pattern: 'I was under the illusion that the way that films worked was that you got a lot of option money and then after a couple of years they decided that they weren't going to make the film, which was a perfect result.' Around 1998 even *Big Numbers* was optioned by Picture Palace Productions. Producer Alex Usborne saw it as a twelve-part TV series along the lines of the BBC's 1996 political saga *Our Friends in the North*. Moore was more enthusiastic about this prospect, seeing it as a good way to complete the *Big Numbers* project, but in the event nothing came of it.

*

In the late nineties studios finally managed to crack the nut of the superhero movie formula. The first picture to do so featured a C-list Marvel character, *Blade* (1998) in a fast-moving, mid-budget film that did far better than anyone expected. It encouraged the development of other projects based on much more prominent Marvel characters, *X-Men* (2000) and *Spider-Man* (2002), which between them made well over $1 billion at the box office and became lucrative franchises. The trend was too much for Barry Norman, the most prominent British film reviewer, who announced his retirement in April 2001 explaining that he wasn't enjoying his job anymore because 'the film industry has changed and I find it slightly depressing that almost all the big movies coming out of Hollywood next year are based on comic books.' The next ten years or so would do nothing to change Norman's decision. Indeed, alongside dozens of superhero movies, there were many that were less obviously adapted from comics, including *A History of Violence*, *Road to Perdition*, *Ghost World*, *30 Days of Night*, *Art School Confidential* and *Whiteout*.

Academic discussion of movie adaptation has evolved over time. In the introduction to his influential book *Literature and Film: A Guide to the Theory and Practice of Adaptation* (2005), New York University professor Robert Stam warns, 'The conventional language of adaptation criticism has often been profoundly moralistic, rich in terms that imply that the cinema has somehow done a disservice to literature. Terms like "infidelity", "betrayal", "deformation", "violation", 'bastardisation", "vulgarisation" and "desecration" proliferate in adaptation discourse, each word carrying its specific charge of opprobrium.' He suggests that we should be wary about simply listing what's been added or subtracted from the book, or talking in terms of what's been 'lost' in translation between media. This is a shame, for while the directors and stars tend to laud Moore in the press pack and DVD extras, the decisions they make have usually moved their film away from the source material, almost always making the movie version less successful artistically than the original comic.

From Hell serves as a textbook example of how the Hollywood system takes a long, difficult book and turns it into an action thriller that's designed to play well in multiplexes. The most fundamental change is that while the comics version shows us that Jack the Ripper is William Gull within the first few pages, the movie version reveals it only as a twist towards the end, and the main character is Johnny

Depp's detective, Abberline. Producer Don Murphy explained, 'There's just no way you're going to convince a studio that Jack is the main character. Y'know it would be very fascinating, it would be very interesting to watch Jack, but that's not a popular commercial film and there was never, ever a discussion. Right after I became friendly with Alan Moore and hung out with him and talked to him, it was like you understand that this is immediately going into Abberline's story, it's really going to be about the guy who we as an audience – we're going to have Johnny Depp in the film – we're going to follow and although Jack should be prominent, Jack should be a major character, it's not Jack's story, it's Abberline's story. And that's the major departure.'

Moore and Campbell had, of course, deliberately chosen to avoid the conventions of the murder mystery genre, and of all previous Ripper fiction's portrayal of the murderer as a top-hatted silhouette. Eddie Campbell says of being told that the movie would be a whodunit, 'they put it to me almost as though it was a good idea. I remember they said, "Eddie, look, we've got this great idea." They said, "Look, you don't know who the Ripper is until right at the end!". That was the first thing we kicked out, because Alan absolutely detested the idea of turning murder into a parlour game.'

A number of critics felt that the movie was a 'Disneyfied' version of the original. As Iain Sinclair noted in his *Guardian* review, '*From Hell* returns to source, as a penny-dreadful, a shocker; a distortion of place and time. An industrial product crafted to stand alongside the wave of predatory development that maligns history and treats the past as the final colony in the American world empire.' The project had started at Miramax – a division of Disney – who had clearly wanted a more family-friendly movie about the serial murder of prostitutes. The directors, the Hughes Brothers, read the comic only after they had read the first version of the script, and when they had done so came up with a new draft that tried to recapture at least some of the original's spirit.

Campbell remembers, 'there was an earlier version of this script, where [Abberline] escapes, he goes into Special Branch and he steals a file, or he looks at the file, gets the information he needs. Then he hears somebody coming along the corridor. And there's no way he can get out that room and out the building without being caught. So he turns and he sees a window open, and it's overlooking a railroad track. He quietly climbs out of the window onto the

ledge, jumps onto a train that's passing below, lands on the roof . . . At the time, we first read this 1995, 1996, I'm trying to picture our Abberline jumping onto a moving train. Our fat guy . . . So they'd obviously changed that by the time the movie got made. I didn't like the original script. The script was certainly improved, I will say that.'

But the movie was released to lukewarm critical reception and box office. Some reviewers unfamiliar with the source material thought they had diagnosed the problem: 'When I walked out of the movie theater after watching *From Hell*, I had one thing on my mind. What the Hell were they thinking? Only later when I discovered that the movie was based on a graphic novel did it sink in just where the movie was coming from. Because like a graphic novel, this movie is beautiful to look at, but has little substance.' It's an analysis that's particularly galling to Alan Moore, who has championed the medium and constantly tried to come up with new ways of telling stories within it: 'And I have gotten tired of lazy critics who, when they want to insult a film, they'll say it has "comic book characters" or a "comic book plot" – using "comic book" as code for "illiterate" . . . I'm not going to claim all comic books are literate – there's a lot of rubbish out there. But there have been some very literate comic books done over the past twenty years, some marvellous ones. And to actually read a comic, you *do* have to be able to read, which is not something you can say about watching a film. So as for which medium is literate, give me comics any day.'

The critical consensus was perhaps best summed up in a conversation between Eddie Campbell and interviewer Dirk Deppey for *The Comics Journal*:

DEPPEY: I was of two minds about the film version of *From Hell*. I saw it with our news editor, Michael Dean. Driving back, we were discussing the film, and we basically came to the conclusion that it wasn't in any way close to the quality of the book, but on the other hand, if you were somebody who had never read the book and had no interest in it, and you just went to it expecting a slasher film, then you probably got something a little more high-minded than you were expecting. Does that make any sense?

CAMPBELL: Yeah, I would agree with that. And that's what I was expecting. They did a fine job at that level.

Moore never saw *From Hell* and had no strong feelings one way or the other, either before the movie came out – when *Uncut* stated that 'reports from Prague, where the Hughes Brothers (*Menace II Society*, *Dead Presidents*) are currently adapting his hugely acclaimed Jack the Ripper strip, *From Hell*, for the big screen, are met with complete indifference. Johnny Depp's in it, you say? Nigel Hawthorne? Heather Graham? He doesn't care. It's not comics. "I'd be quite happy if they made *Carry On Ripping*. It's not my book, it's their film"' – or subsequently. He did not exist in total isolation from the movie: he had read the scripts, and Iain Sinclair reported in his review for the *Guardian* that Moore 'was staggered' when he saw photos from the set. He researched the Hughes Brothers, and was delighted to learn that Heather Graham was in the movie, because she had played Annie in *Twin Peaks*, 'so with me she merits a particular kind of sainthood'. So his comment that 'I haven't seen the *From Hell* movie yet. I might see it when it comes out on video' clearly goes beyond mere neutral incuriosity. Don Murphy says, 'He told me that from the day he optioned it. I thought that was odd but not that big a deal. He was invited to the set and the premiere. I can't recall – he might have sent his daughter to a screening, but he had no interest. Eddie and his daughter came to the film premiere and had fun.'

Moore had known at an early stage that the movie would bear little resemblance to the comic, and this prompted him to keep his distance. At this stage, it wasn't because he thought the film would make him angry. He wasn't disowning the movie or being hostile, it was genuine disinterest: 'As far as I know, the *From Hell* movie – while it really is nothing like my book, apart from a couple of scenes here and there – was probably a decent attempt at trying to film a book that is, when you think about it, pretty much unfilmable. I believe that they did probably as good a job as anybody could, the Hughes Brothers . . . which is to say, that they probably still shouldn't have bothered, in that the end result would have so little resemblance to anything that I wrote that they might just as well have made their own Jack the Ripper film, with their own story.'

Unlike *From Hell*, the first volume of the comic *The League of Extraordinary Gentlemen* is a straightforward action-adventure. And for the movie, as with *From Hell*, virtually everything from the comics was ditched apart from the 'high concept', a few ideas and specific scenes, some design work and most of the character names. As Moore noted:

> There was a time I would have said that if any of my books could work as films, it would have been that first volume of *The League*. It was pretty much structured so it could have been made straight into a film, and it would have been as powerful as it was in the original publication. But that is to overlook the proclivities of contemporary Hollywood, where I really simply don't believe that any of my books could be benefited in any way by being turned into films. In fact, quite the opposite.

The script for *LXG* was written by James Dale Robinson, a writer well regarded for his *Starman* and *Justice Society of America* comics at DC. Sean Connery was cast in the lead role of Victorian adventurer Allan Quatermain – a coup, but one that meant there was little budget left for any other star names. The story was no longer an ensemble piece but was largely about Quatermain and, as with *From Hell*, paths deliberately not taken in the original comic became features of the movie; thus Mina Harker is a subordinate of Quatermain's rather than being the nearest thing the team have to a leader (Harker, a character from *Dracula* who was bitten by the Count, is also explicitly shown to be a vampire in the movie, something the comic never quite rules out but remains deliberately coy about). And there were more concrete problems: Connery and director Stephen Norrington clashed repeatedly – to the point that reports appeared in the press suggesting they had almost come to blows, and some cast and crew members took steps to prevent the two from ever being alone together. By the time the movie had wrapped, both had vowed never to make a Hollywood film again. The standing sets in Prague were destroyed in severe floods.

LXG was released in July 2003 to terrible notices ('Even if, per Wilde, all art is quite useless, it need not be quite as useless as this,' said Ed Park in *The Village Voice*). A number of reviewers, such as Charles Taylor of the *Salon*, were careful to absolve Moore of blame:

> After this movie and *From Hell*, Moore fans might start to take comfort that the movie version of his *Watchmen* has never come to fruition. His stories seem tailor-made for the movies, but his dark sensibility and the creepy pleasure

he gets in playing with historical what-ifs don't fit with the mindlessness most mainstream blockbusters exhibit right now. The irony of *The League of Extraordinary Gentlemen* is that it has the most literate pedigree of any action movie you're likely to see this year or next – and it's been made by people who seem to have no sense of how to tell a story.

The movie made over $100 million dollars more than it cost, and its release saw a spike in sales of the comic in May which put the book comfortably at the top of the graphic novel chart. But there was no appetite from the makers or the audience for a sequel. Alan Moore barely said anything about *LXG*, except to note the irony that in *From Hell*, they had changed the character of Abberline to make him 'an absinthe-swilling, opium-den-frequenting dandy with a haircut that, in the Metropolitan Police force in 1888, would have gotten him beaten up by the other officers. On the other hand when I *have* got an opium-addicted character, in Allan Quatermain . . . Sean Connery didn't want to play him as a drug-addled individual. So the main part of Quatermain's character was thrown out the window on the whim of an actor.'

By September 2003, it seemed like *LXG* had been and gone. At the end of the month, though, writers Martin Poll and Larry Cohen sued Fox Entertainment Group, Twentieth-Century Fox and Fox Filmed Entertainment claiming that their script, *Cast of Characters*, had been stolen to make the film. Their lawsuit named Moore as party to this, and made some very specific allegations about his conduct. To head off the obvious defence that *LXG* was the adaptation of an existing comic book, it was claimed that '[President of Twentieth-Century Fox Film Group Tom] Rothman, or others at Fox under his direction, provided Moore with ideas from *COC* that are protected under state and federal law. Thus, Moore could write a graphic novel to provide a smokescreen behind which Fox could hide when plaintiffs inevitably saw *COC* being misappropriated as *LXG*.'

The League of Extraordinary Gentlemen was hardly the first story to take characters from Victorian fiction and team them up. Philip José Farmer's fictional biography *Tarzan Alive!* (1972) was only the first of his books to play with the 'Wold Newton Family' concept that many of the heroes of popular fiction – Tarzan, Sherlock Holmes, James Bond and countless others – were descendants of people who'd been present in a Yorkshire village the night a radioactive meteorite hit the ground nearby. There's a whole subset of modern Holmes pastiches that pit him against his real life and fictional contemporaries, including Jack the Ripper, the Phantom of the Opera, Freud, H.G. Wells and the Martians from *The War of the Worlds*. It wasn't even the first time Alan Moore had done it – he has said that '*The League of Extraordinary Gentlemen* actually conceptually grew out of *Lost Girls* because we'd had so much fun doing three fictional characters in a sex context that I thought maybe this could work as an adventure book'. In fact he'd alluded to the concept earlier still, in the introduction to the first *Swamp Thing* collection (1987), where he'd explained superhero crossovers by analogy: 'For those more familiar with conventional literature, try to imagine Dr Frankenstein kidnapping one of the protagonists of *Little Women* for his medical experiments, only to find himself subject to the scrutiny of a team-up between Sherlock Holmes and Hercule Poirot. I'm sure that both the charms and the overwhelming absurdities of this approach will become immediately apparent.'

Both *The League of Extraordinary Gentlemen* and *Cast of Characters*, then, are part of an enduring literary tradition. Any lawsuit had to be about specifics, not just the idea of literary mash-up. On the face of it, some of the changes made from the comic for the movie version, such as the addition of Dorian Gray and Tom Sawyer, did bring it closer to *Cast of Characters*. So had the makers of the *LXG* movie started with Moore and O'Neill's comic and then incorporated some ideas from an earlier pitch for a similar story, *Cast of Characters*? Don Murphy's answer is categorical: 'I knew it existed as a script because several persons had said "Oh, League is like that." But I never read it. Still haven't.'

Then there's the question of whether Alan Moore might be complicit in such a scheme. Anyone familiar with Moore would, to put it mildly, find it difficult to imagine he would be a Hollywood movie studio's first choice as a tame stooge. It's unclear, though, whether the plaintiffs *did* know anything about Moore or the comics field. While the document was keen to stress their credentials as 'well-known and respected figures in the film industry', it didn't mention Moore's stature in the comics world. There was no mention that he was a UK resident who didn't even have a passport or an internet connection. It didn't refer to Kevin O'Neill, co-creator of the series, or note that *The League of Extraordinary Gentlemen* was creator-owned and so it had cost Fox a substantial amount of money to acquire the rights. Besides, it is a matter of record that Moore had first mentioned *The League of Extraordinary Gentlemen* in an interview carried out on 8 July 1996, nearly two full years before June 1998 when the lawsuit alleged he had been briefed to write it. Don Murphy says 'the claims were beyond insane. They had Moore conspiring with the then head of the studio, who was somebody Alan never met or would even talk to.'

The case proceeded anyway, and Moore was called as a witness. In the words of the *New York Times*, 'Mr Moore found the accusations deeply insulting, and the ten hours of testimony he was compelled to give, via video link, even more so. "If I had raped and murdered a schoolbus full of retarded children after selling them heroin," he said, "I doubt that I would have been cross-examined for ten hours." When the case was settled out of court, Mr Moore took it as an especially bitter blow, believing that he had been denied the chance to exonerate himself.' But Fox's lawyers decided to settle the case on 29 December 2003, before it went to trial. As Don Murphy explains,

> the lawsuit was settled for a pittance because the studio insurance company didn't want to pay for a trial. That's it . . . I took the whole thing personally. The movie had taken $200m worldwide but because we opened against *Pirates of the Caribbean* the US total was lacklustre. Then these clowns come along and sue . . . somehow it got settled. That was crap. Alan's reaction I never understood. My Scottish wife says that Brits aren't used to lawsuits. Fair enough. But the litigants were alleging malfeasance on his part and his signed contracts provided he be available to testify that he had not stolen the ideas. He did that and did that brilliantly – and then went nuts on everyone, cursing Hollywood and swearing off it forever. I became the latest in the long list of friends banished forever. It's a shame really, but nothing that can be done about it.

Moore blamed Murphy, having learned during the deposition that Murphy had sent a prank email to the plaintiffs saying that Moore had been given the ideas by someone at the studio. Murphy admits that 'in a fit of pique I sent an anonymous email – it said basically "No, it wasn't the head of the studio, it was the guy who got the coffee". It turned out they went crazy trying to figure out who sent this, it was the only evidence they had which meant they had nothing.' But Moore didn't see the funny side. His encounters with legal affairs – the 'Marvelman' title, the *Watchmen* contract and now this – reinforced his belief that legal decisions had very little to do with right and wrong, and everything to do with corporate shenanigans. He had made a conscious choice to keep out of the way of the movie versions of his work, but found himself dragged into court anyway. He couldn't just ignore them, after all. 'I've decided that I don't want anything more to do with films at all . . . I thought if I'm going to react, I may as well overreact, y'know. So, I said, right, that's it, no more Hollywood films. And if they do make films of my work, then I want my name taken off of them and I want all the money given to the artists. I thought, God, that sounds principled and almost heroic!'

Then, the next Monday, he received a phone call from DC's Karen Berger:

> She said, 'Yeah, we're going to be sending you a huge amount of money before the end of the year because they're making this film of your Constantine character with Keanu Reeves.' And I said, 'Right, OK. Well, take my name off of it and distribute my money amongst the other artists.' I thought, well, that was difficult, but I did it and I feel pretty good about myself. Then I saw David Gibbons who I had done *Watchmen* with and he was saying, 'Oh Alan, guess what, they're making the *Watchmen* film.' And I said, with tears streaming down my face, 'Take my name off of it David. (sniffles). You have all the money.' Then I got a cheque for the *V for Vendetta* film. It was just, this was within three days!

Moore had no control over these projects, all of which were based on his DC Comics work, and they came at a time when his relationship with the company was breaking down over, as he saw it, editorial interference in the ABC line. So he found it easy to elide the problems he was having with Hollywood and those with the comics industry, particularly as DC and Warner Bros, the studio behind all three movies, were both part of the Time Warner multimedia empire.

There had been a period of détente between DC and Alan Moore. From 1999, DC had published the America's Best Comics line while keeping out of Moore's way, as agreed, and both parties seemed determined to get their non-relationship to work. Relations had in fact thawed to the point that in the summer of 2000, DC announced at San Diego Comic-Con that they would be celebrating the fifteenth anniversary of *Watchmen* (the following year) by publishing *Absolute Watchmen*, a $100 slipcased hardcover edition for which the original story would be recoloured and a second volume included containing the full scripts and other behind-the-scenes material. There would also be a range of *Watchmen* action figures, with four prototypes displayed at the convention. This was all being done with Moore's blessing, and a new documentary he recorded with Dave Gibbons was shown by DC at conventions that summer.

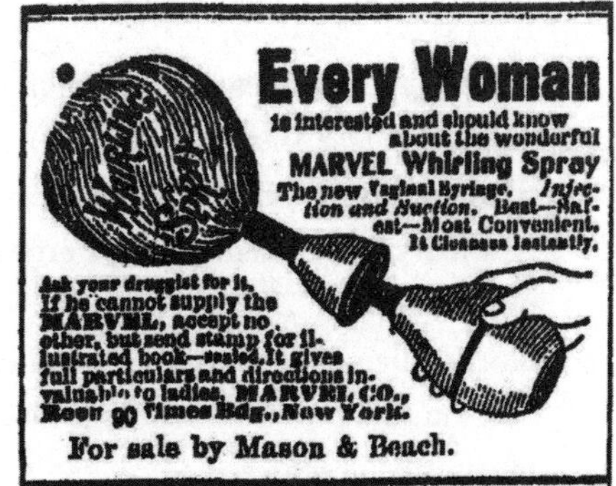

At the same time, though, DC stepped in to block the publication of two ABC titles. The first was *The League of Extraordinary Gentlemen* #5 (June 2000), which reproduced a genuine Victorian advertisement for a 'MARVEL whirling spray syringe, the new injection and suction vaginal syringe'.

DC publisher Paul Levitz felt that this was an insult to DC's arch-rivals, Marvel, so the original print run was pulped and a new edition, containing an identical advert except with the brand name altered to AMAZE, appeared within weeks. The same month, Levitz also blocked a *Cobweb* strip, due to be published in *Tomorrow Stories* #8, that recounted a true story involving L. Ron Hubbard, the founder of Scientology, and his involvement with occultism. Moore told Newsarama:

> the DC lawyers seem to be very sane, practical people. As a creator, I've heard for a long time what lawyers are like, but actually speaking to Lillian Laserson, she was practical, sane, responsible, professional and logical. We went through it for an hour, talking about this six-page story, and the reference book that I'd taken most of the story from, how it's all in the public domain and is all over the Internet, and it's been in two or three magazines and a book. This is stuff that there's no possible threat of litigation, which I think Lillian pretty much agreed with, and then Paul Levitz apparently said, even so, he didn't want it to go out, which I think was the case all along. I think Lillian was a bit perplexed as to why an hour of her and my time had been wasted . . .

This was exactly the sort of editorial interference that had always rankled with Moore, but his contracts gave him little room for manoeuvre except to spit feathers. With his opinion of Levitz now little better than his attitude towards Dez

Skinn when *Warrior* had been on its last legs, Moore disowned the *Watchmen* anniversary project, saying 'there's just been a lot of stuff recently where I've been trying to cooperate with DC and be friendly, but this has not been reciprocated'. Editor Scott Dunbier was able to smooth the waters and Moore continued to produce regular scripts for the ABC range.

On 17 September 2002, Top Shelf, publisher of the US editions of *From Hell*, *The Birth Caul* and *Snakes and Ladders*, announced a slate of new and reprinted work by Alan Moore. They would be publishing *Lost Girls* in 2004 (in the event, it took two years longer than anticipated), and were also to publish new editions of *Voice of the Fire* and *The Mirror of Love*. With the *Cobweb* story that Paul Levitz had blocked being included in an anthology, *Top Shelf Asks the Big Questions*, Moore had found a publisher happy to work with him, one who would put out even his most difficult material.

Even before the second volume of *The League of Extraordinary Gentlemen* had been completed (the final issue was published in November 2003), it was known that Moore and O'Neill planned a third six-issue miniseries, with each issue focusing on a different League prior to the 1898 version. Moore wanted a break before starting work on Book Three, but was aware that Kevin O'Neill was keen to continue. So they devised a stopgap, a sourcebook which a Wildstorm press release on 28 December 2004 said was 'due in late 2005' and was to be called *The Dark Dossier* – though this was news to Moore, who notes that 'right from the first outline it was called *The Black Dossier*. Me and Kevin were a bit surprised when DC kept referring to it as *The Dark Dossier*. We didn't know whether they were having one of their periodic anxiety attacks about the use of the word "black". We put them right.'

Moore grew more and more enthusiastic about the project, describing it in May 2005 as 'not my best comic ever, not the best comic ever, but the best thing ever. Better than the Roman civilisation, penicillin. The human brain? Yes and the human nervous system. Better than creation. Better than the Big Bang. It's quite good . . . It will be nothing anyone expects, but everything everyone secretly wanted.' The book showed all the signs of Moore enjoying himself, getting a little carried away and ultimately more than a little self-indulgent – as well as a 3D section, sections on different paper stocks and a mini comic, he also recorded two songs to appear on a vinyl record that came with the book. What had begun as a straightforward, rather dry guide to the history of the League became a massive exercise in literary mash-up. Among many other things, Jeeves faced off against Cthulhu, there was a porno comic written in George Orwell's 'Newspeak' and a pastiche Shakespeare play which saw Prospero form the original League. As the book became more ambitious, it also became clear it would take a little longer to produce.

The Black Dossier did not appear in 2006, but the movie of *V for Vendetta* did. It's fair to say fans of Moore's work had low expectations. A press release stating that Evey 'begins to develop feelings for V' and a trailer that emphasised slow-motion knife fights, explosions and the fact that the film was from the makers of *The Matrix* did little to change that. By now it was widely reported that Moore wanted nothing to do with cinema adaptations of his work and had asked for his name to be removed from any future projects. When the movie was finally released, though, a number of critics wondered if he had been too hasty. Joe Lozito wasn't the only reviewer who felt: 'it's no wonder Mr Moore would be a bit wary. But he needn't have removed his name from director James McTeigue's refreshingly faithful but maddeningly uneven adaptation. While it contains none of the brilliance or immediacy of the source material, for any fan of Mr Moore's original, there are moments of pure bliss.'

Moore reports that Karen Berger had said something similar to him, that 'maybe I'd want to reconsider taking my name off this, because actually it was very faithful to the book'. But he was highly sceptical and made it clear he would not reverse his position. When Lana Wachowski, one half of the writer/producer team, telephoned him, he reiterated his standard line: he wasn't interested in being involved, but that didn't mean he wished the producers ill.

However, at a press conference on 4 March 2005 – transcribed in a press release the same day – producer Joel Silver was asked about Moore's involvement and stated that Moore was 'very excited about what Larry had to say and Larry sent the script, so we hope to see him sometime before we're in the UK [to start filming]. We'd just like him to know what we're doing and to be involved in what we're trying to do together.' Exactly why Silver said this is unclear. The pair had met back when *V for Vendetta* was first optioned, and Moore had been excited at the time – but nearly twenty years had passed.

It's been suggested that Silver heard an account of the phone conversation with Wachowski that was a little more optimistic than was warranted. The fact that director James McTeigue could tell an interviewer, 'I don't know whether [Moore] really doesn't want it made. I mean, obviously, the rights are out there for the film to be made so at some point he wants the film to be made,' might suggest that some of the key people making the movie hadn't been made entirely au fait with the situation. Whatever the case, when Moore found out about the press release, he was furious. He called Scott Dunbier and informed him that unless a retraction was issued, he would pull all future *League of Extraordinary Gentlemen* projects from DC. To avoid loss of face, Moore would be happy for the retraction to blame 'a misunderstanding', although he considered it to be 'a flat, knowing lie'. After five or six weeks, when no such retraction had appeared, Moore made public his antipathy towards the film. In a May 2005 interview for the online comics gossip column Lying in the Gutters, he revealed he had seen the shooting script:

> It was imbecilic; it had plot holes you couldn't have got away with in *Whizzer and Chips* in the nineteen sixties. Plot holes no one had noticed ... They don't know what British people have for breakfast, they couldn't be bothered. 'Eggy in a basket' apparently. Now the US have 'eggs in a basket', which is fried bread with a fried egg in a hole in the middle. I guess they thought we must eat that as well, and thought 'eggy in a basket' was a quaint and Olde Worlde version. And they decided that the British postal service is called FedCo. They'll have thought something like, 'well, what's a British version of FedEx ... how about FedCo?' A friend of mine had to point out to them that the Fed, in FedEx comes from 'Federal Express.' America is a federal republic, Britain is not.

While Alan Moore takes great pride in building up his fictional worlds from meticulously thought-through telling details, and so any carelessness in that area must have irked him, getting angry at 'FedCo' does seem like an overreaction – for the record, the final version of the film replaced the name with the British Freight Company (and it is never spoken, it only appears on some prop boxes). Moore's confession, in a later interview, that around the same time he had dumped his entire consignment of contributor's copies of a new edition of *V for Vendetta* in a skip because he had spotted a spelling error on the back cover added to the impression that he was spoiling for a fight but was struggling a little to find ammunition.

In fact, the movie version is recognisably *V for Vendetta*, one touchstone being that the Valerie sequence, in which Evey reads a letter from a lesbian inmate of Larkhill concentration camp, is retained almost word for word. (So faithfully, in fact, that we're told Valerie sat the Eleven Plus exam – fine in the comic, where she was born in 1957, but in the movie she was born in 1985, long after the exam had been abolished.) Originally appearing in *Warrior* #24, Book Two, Chapter Eleven of *V for Vendetta* remains a highlight of Moore's writing, as well as a tour de force from David Lloyd, who's said: 'I'm often in this position where I'm defending the movie. I do support the movie, very strongly, despite some flaws. But the Wachowskis were big fans. They thought they needed to add their own creative input, that's just one of those things. They were fans of it, there was no question of them losing [the Valerie material]. They were committed to it. I don't think there was any question that was the core of it.'

When Moore says, 'If that book had ever been understood by the people publishing it in the first place, then they would not have told me that the scripts for the movie were true to my book. It wasn't. It hadn't got anything to do with my book,' he's not talking about FedCo, or disputing that the movie retains important material like the Valerie sequence. So what is Moore's real objection?

Despite the teaser poster's tagline that it's 'an uncompromised vision of the future', *V for Vendetta* is unmistakably a product of the Hollywood studio system and has been reshaped by that. The London setting is retained – although the movie was mostly shot in Berlin – and the supporting cast are almost all from the UK, but concessions, large and small, have been made to an American audience. To explain what a 'Guy Fawkes mask' is, the movie opens with a flashback to Fawkes' capture and execution. As with Sean Connery's presence in *LXG*, the casting of Natalie Portman as Evey has clearly led to rewrites. While the screenplay's first draft retained a sixteen year old so desperate she plans to prostitute herself, Evey in the finished movie is a runner at a television company who wants a promotion and faces the hardship of going to dinner with Stephen Fry.

The movie was being made because the studio wanted the Wachowskis' next project, and the Wachowskis wanted to make *V for Vendetta*. Even though they weren't directing, the posters and captions of the trailers made it clear this was a film 'by the creators of *The Matrix* trilogy'. Those films had been notable for their 'bullet time' slow-motion effects, and there are similar sequences in *V for Vendetta* involving V's knives. V throws multiple knives at once and they fly through the air to their targets in slow motion, trailing CG swirls of air, while we see their victims' faces reflected in the blades. In the comic, too, V has knives: we see him with at least three on his belt in the very first reveal of his costume in Book One, Chapter One – although he doesn't use them that night, when he rescues Evey. It's Book Two, Chapter Three, before we see one in V's hand, and the second and final time he uses one is when he stabs Finch's shoulder in Book Three, Chapter Seven. In the official script book, a comment by director James McTeigue encapsulates how the movie foregrounds and fetishises the weapons: 'The knives around his belt are like glistening teeth, roundabout where a cowboy's guns would be'. In the movie, violence is *cool*.

There's more going on, though, than adding a little Hollywood gloss to the original material. The political message of the book has also been Americanised, and it's this that's at the root of Moore's objection. Put simply, *V for Vendetta* was an early example of Moore's personal, political work, and the makers of the movie *changed the politics*.

The comic *V for Vendetta* is a political work in two distinct, even contradictory, senses. First, it is a product of its times. Moore has said, 'When I wrote *V*, politics were taking a serious turn for the worse over here. We'd had Margaret Thatcher in for two or three years, we'd had anti-Thatcher riots, we'd got the National Front and the right wing making serious advances.' Some critics, particularly Americans, see the book in broader strokes. James R. Keller, in *V for Vendetta as Cultural Pastiche: A Critical Study of the Graphic Novel and Film* – which despite its subtitle is mainly concerned with the movie – asserts that the AIDS panics of the eighties 'serve as the backstory of Moore and Lloyd's graphic novel' and Chapter Nine of his book, '"V for Virus: The Spectacle of the AIDS Avenger and the Biomedical Military Trope", examines *VfV*'s not so subtle allusions to the AIDS panic of the 1980s, the period in which Moore and Lloyd conceived and composed their viral avenger'. In fact, *V for Vendetta* began publication in 1982, before the term AIDS had been coined, when the condition was barely known outside medical journals (there had only been seven reported cases in the UK by the end of the year). That was to change rapidly – by 1983 the British tabloids and US right-wing Christians were talking about 'the gay plague', by 1987 the UK government had launched massive

public health campaigns and there were 1,200 cases in the UK, and by 1988, when Moore finished the series, the Conservative government was eliding medical and moral health as a pretext to introduce Clause 28. Many existing elements of the story had clear resonance with the real-life demonisation of homosexuals, and the AIDS crisis certainly came to inform Moore's work, but *V for Vendetta* simply couldn't have initially been conceived 'as a response' to something that hadn't yet happened.

V for Vendetta is a 'response to Thatcherism', but Thatcherism changed radically between 1981 and 1988. When Moore started writing the strip, Margaret Thatcher was leader of a divided government that was singularly failing to end a deep recession. The backstory Moore developed was premised on the idea that the Conservatives would lose the next election . . . in real life, they won by a landslide. The political left fractured, the Falklands War had been won, the recession had ended. Thatcher had steered the country to the right, and she hadn't needed anything as outré as nuclear war – she had done it by selling off council houses, thereby transforming council tenants into homeowners who were suddenly very concerned with mortgage rates and property prices.

When he was writing *V for Vendetta*, Moore was not assessing this situation twenty years on, from a different country. He had grown up in council houses. Having entered exactly the type of 'unconventional lifestyle' that was under attack, he was directly affected by gay rights issues. As he finished *V for Vendetta*, he was also assembling the anti-Clause 28 benefit comic *AARGH!*. In many ways, *V for Vendetta is* a parochial story, or at least is a nuanced, personal response to a specific period of British political life. When an academic watches the movie and describes V as 'the artistic embodiment of the AIDS avenger' or the director sums up Clause 28 as 'a law that banned any homosexual expression – art, music, anything that was deemed homosexual', it oversimplifies the British political landscape to the point of being an active misrepresentation.

Of course, any retelling of the tale twenty years on would seek to recontextualise it, to address modern concerns. The *V for Vendetta* movie tries, but loses a lot in translation. As Moore says: 'Now, in the film, you've got a sinister group of right-wing figures – not fascists, but you know that they're bad guys – and what they have done is manufactured a bio-terror weapon in secret, so that they can fake a massive terrorist incident to get everybody on their side, so that they can pursue their right-wing agenda. It's a thwarted and frustrated and perhaps largely impotent American liberal fantasy of someone with American liberal values [standing up] against a state run by neo-conservatives – which is not what *V for Vendetta* was about.'

The movie's account of the rise of the right-wing regime boils down to a slight rebranding of the 'Truther' conspiracy theory that accuses President Bush's government of instigating the 9/11 attacks as part of a grand plan to increase the power of the state, at home and abroad, under the pretext of protecting its citizens from future terrorist attacks. Moore is fond of grand narratives, and not fond of American right-wingers. So, does that mean he buys into 'Trutherism'? As a reader of *Fortean Times*, Moore is familiar with countless conspiracy theories: *From Hell* is based around one; *Brought to Light* dramatised countless CIA plots and cover-ups, drawing attention to the people and organisations connecting them; *Watchmen* revolves around a plot to fake an attack on New York that will cause mass slaughter. Moore's conclusion: 'The main thing that I learned about conspiracy theory is that conspiracy theorists actually believe in a conspiracy because that is more comforting. The truth of the world is that it is chaotic. The truth is, that it is not the Jewish banking conspiracy or the grey aliens or the twelve-foot reptiloids from another dimension that are in control. The truth is more frightening, nobody is in control. The world is rudderless.' Moore has been asked specifically about 9/11 and has written two pieces on the subject for benefit comic books. He has consistently stressed that he sees 9/11 as tragic but unexceptional:

> The thing is that the public, in the rest of the world, we have kind of got the idea by now. Ever since Guernica, probably almost everywhere else in the world, apart from America, have been relatively used to being bombed. And yes it is upsetting. Of course it is. But at the end of the day, without wishing to appear brutal, on September the eleventh 2001 you lost a couple of buildings and a few thousand people. There's other people who've had it far worse, and sometimes at the hands of America.

For Moore, the Truther analogy doesn't work because it's *not* unthinkable that such atrocities might occur.

As he laid out his objections to the movie, Moore even managed to slip in a sly reference to its very first draft, from the late eighties: 'It's been turned into a

Bush-era parable by people too timid to set a political satire in their own country . . . perhaps it would have been better for everybody if the Wachowski Brothers had done something set in America, and instead of a hero who dresses up as Guy Fawkes, they could have had him dressed as Paul Revere.'

V for Vendetta, though, had never simply been Moore's projection of where British politics might head after 1982. The second sense in which it is 'political' is that, for him, it explores a more universal struggle: '*V for Vendetta* was specifically about things like fascism and anarchy . . . Those words, "fascism" and "anarchy", occur nowhere in the film.' The comic was about his personal politics, far more than he had planned when he began creating it with David Lloyd. Moore has long believed we face a relatively simple binary choice, as individuals, to be either self-determining or controlled by others. *V for Vendetta* dramatises this, but it also problematises it. At heart, there's quite a simple scheme to the comic: the character we're meant to identify as the 'hero' (the one who espouses what we know to be Moore's personal politics, and who is the apparent protagonist of the story) is a masked killer who is at the very least traumatised, and possibly insane; his opponents are fascists, but they are also ordinary people with jobs and families – they're policemen, broadcasters, civil servants. V is fighting fascists, but Moore never lets us forget that he's also leaving a trail of widows and orphans. The film all but ignores this, with McTeigue saying V has a 'bipolar nature, he has this great idea for altruistic social change, but on the other hand, he's murdering the people he thinks have done wrong by him'. While Alan Moore called the first chapter of the comic 'The Villain', McTeigue was happy to refer to V as 'a superhero'.

Moore started *V for Vendetta* in 1981 as a young writer fresh from the dole queue trying to prove himself. He completed it in 1988 as a wealthy celebrity in a polyamorous relationship who was assembling a benefit comic by roping in his showbiz pals. The Alan Moore of the twenty-first century is an older man, one who has increasingly drawn the distinction between the comics medium, 'a grand tradition rooted in its healthy scepticism with regard to rulers, gods or institutions; a genuine artform of the people, unrestricted by prevailing notions of acceptability', and the comics mainstream, 'a critically-accepted and occasionally lucrative component of the entertainment industry'. He's an author who's used his work to challenge the imposition of US corporate values on the

world. A Hollywood movie is, by definition, incapable of dissent: it is a product *of* American cultural imperialism.

A number of reviewers familiar with the source material picked up on the movie's lack of depth:

> This movie simply doesn't add much to the gallery of dystopian art – where Moore's book already hangs quite prominently – aside from an embittered topicality that will look rather dusty in a decade or so. It's capably acted – Stephen Rea sags expressively as the inspector on V's trail; Portman carries off Evey's arc from naïf to radical with aplomb. But the film shouts when it should sing. Bombastically insecure, it treats the audience like V treats Evey, preaching condescendingly and instructing us to watch the fireworks. But, as it has been translated and condensed for multiplex consumption, it really has no deeper meaning beyond the fireworks.

The 'political' message of the movie version of *V for Vendetta* is equally undemanding: totalitarianism is bad, rounding people up and sending them to death camps is bad, government censorship of the media is bad; romantic individualism is good, self-determination is good. These are not provocative or challenging positions, and it's not surprising that some of the movie's most vocal supporters were right-wingers: supporters of libertarian Republican Senator Ron Paul, and the Tea Party, an offshoot of the Republican Party, saw the movie as championing their own political stance of small government and Ayn Rand-style selfishness.

The movie of *V for Vendetta* has attracted a cult following among young political activists, and there were commentators who saw a story that focused on a terrorist opposing a right-wing government as 'edgy' in the George W. Bush years. But some of the material audiences responded to was purely from the movie, not Moore and Lloyd. The line 'People should not be afraid of their governments, governments should be afraid of their people' is often quoted on social media, credited to Alan Moore. But it's not in the original comic. First appearing on the movie's teaser poster, issued over the Fourth of July weekend in 2005, it's an adaptation of a well-known Thomas Jefferson quote – although fittingly, a fake one. And the long alliterative monologue that V uses to announce himself to Evey – also oft-quoted online – is entirely the work of the movie:

> Voilà! In view, a humble vaudevillian veteran, cast vicariously as both victim and villain by the vicissitudes of Fate. This visage, no mere veneer of vanity, it is a vestige of the vox populi, now vacant, vanished, as the once vital voice of the verisimilitude now venerates what once they vilified. However, this valourous visitation of a by-gone vexation, stands vivified and has vowed to vanquish these venal and virulent vermin vanguarding vice and vouchsafing the violently vicious and voracious violation of volition. The only verdict is vengeance; a vendetta, held as a votive, not in vain, for the value and veracity of such shall one day vindicate the vigilant and the virtuous. Verily, this vichyssoise of verbiage veers most verbose, so let me simply add that it's my very good honour to meet you and you may call me V.

It's the story's ending that changed the most in the film. At the end of the comic, the fascist regime is toppled, but nothing has emerged to replace it. V has anointed Evey as his successor, knowing he is too violent to be the architect of a peaceful future, but Evey's first act is to destroy 10 Downing Street. While the comic opens up knowing ambiguities, however, the movie often appears simply incoherent. At its climax, the tyrant Sutler (disliking the name of the fascist leader in the comic, 'Adam Susan', the Wachowskis simply conflated 'Susan' and 'Hitler') is toppled, an occurrence that takes little more than the threat of a large public demonstration, but there's no hint of what happens next. It might simply be the restoration of parliamentary democracy . . . in which case the destruction of the Houses of Parliament at the end is something of a mixed message. Evey delivers her last line in a voiceover: 'No one will ever forget that night and what it meant to this country. But I will never forget the man and what he meant to me', which suggests the makers intend it to mean we're watching a happy ending.

Giving *V for Vendetta* the 'Hollywood treatment' did the material a disservice. Moore had come to see Hollywood movies as inevitably compromised: 'I've developed a theory that there's an inverse relationship between money and imagination.' He found some suggestions baffling: 'We had one particularly dense Hollywood producer say, "You don't even have to do the book, just stick your name on this idea and I'll make the film and you'll get a lot of money – it's . . . *The League Of Extraordinary Animals*! It'll be like *Puss In Boots*!" And I just said, "No, no, no. Never mention this to me again"." He did not feel 'honoured' that people wanted to adapt his comics for the cinema:

> The idea that there is something prestigious about having your work made into a film, that is something which infuriates me because it seems to be something that everybody else in the industry absolutely believes. Which to me sells out the entire reason why I worked all those years in comics, which was to advance the medium. All of the people that I was talking to during those years, they told me that that was what they wanted, too. It turned out, however, that at the first hint that their work could be made into a film, their attitude changed. It would seem that having a film made of your work is what validates it, that before that it was just a comic but now it's a movie.

It was clear by now that no movie would be given Alan Moore's approval, but was it possible to create a film truly 'faithful' to one of his books? There was a further barrier. An 'Alan Moore comic' is nothing of the sort: it's a collaboration. The first three major movies based on his work did little or nothing to emulate the art of the comic beyond restaging the occasional iconic panel. As he said of *The League of Extraordinary Gentlemen*:

> If you continue to, say, 'remain faithful to my story or my dialogue' – I mean, that is so unlikely as to be absolutely impossible, but say that that was to happen. What about Kevin's artwork? Kevin's artwork is so integral to the whole feel of *The League* that it couldn't be done with anyone other than Kevin ... Kevin has always had an absurdist, grotesque British undercurrent to his work ... In a film, it's not a Kevin O'Neill drawing. I don't care how much CGI there is in it. It's not a Kevin O'Neill drawing. When I am thinking about *The League of Extraordinary Gentlemen*, it's Kevin's drawings that I want to see, Kevin's storytelling, or the storytelling that is the combination of both of our efforts. These are the things that are important to me about *The League*.

Ironically, though, Moore's absence from the movies has pushed the artists into the spotlight. It's they who appear on promotional materials, like DVD extras and video diaries on the movies' websites, while Moore is barely mentioned. Eddie Campbell, Kevin O'Neill, David Lloyd and Dave Gibbons have all trodden a line where, while admitting to reservations with the finished result, they have been happy to go on set visits and to premieres, and to be quoted in press releases expressing delight at seeing their drawings brought to life. Kevin O'Neill got to share a whisky with Sean Connery while *LXG* was being filmed, and noted, laughingly: 'People obviously ring up Alan all the time. They go to him first, but if they can't get Alan, they end up talking to me . . . I did visit the movie set in Prague. They've spent a phenomenal amount of money, and there's an incredible amount of craftsmanship going into it. All the cast members I met were fans of the book, and they all wanted to meet Alan, of course. Steve Norrington, the director, is a big fan of the book, and wants to do the best job possible.'

In 2009, over twenty years after it was first optioned, the *Watchmen* movie was released. When asked about it, Moore told the *Los Angeles Times* that he would be 'spitting venom all over it for months to come'. But although he was interviewed a number of times in the run-up to its release, he barely mentioned it unless prompted, in which case he would offer the same basic answer: he and Terry Gilliam had agreed it wasn't filmable decades ago, he didn't even have a copy of the comic in his house because he resented the way he had been treated by DC. Yet the *Watchmen* movie was, as *The Atlantic* put it, 'as devout and frame-by-frame a reworking as could be imagined'. Director Zack Snyder had thrown out all the innovations of the previous drafts, preferring a reverent adaptation. The story was streamlined, which changed the ending, but in the post-*Lord of the Rings* era, blockbuster movies were now allowed to run far longer, and could be reissued in immense extended DVD versions (*Watchmen: The Ultimate Cut*, the DVD release, is just over three and a half hours long, and even finds room for an animated version of the *Tales of the Black Freighter* pirate story). The *Los Angeles Times* called *Watchmen* 'nothing less than the boldest popcorn movie ever made. Snyder somehow managed to get a major studio to make a movie with no stars, no "name" superheroes and a hard R-rating.'

The climate, though, was favourable for a 'faithful' *Watchmen* movie. Studio heads were now aware that superhero movies had the potential to earn back the hundreds of millions they often cost to make, and that 'adult superhero' was not a contradiction in terms. A new generation of filmmakers was emerging that consisted of proud comic fans. They had adopted Moore's strategy of reinventing superheroes – and other fantasy properties with nostalgic appeal – along more grounded, cynical lines. *Watchmen* had been the obvious Ur-text for two big hits: the gloomy suspense movie *Unbreakable* (2000) and the colourful family film *The Incredibles* (2004). There had been a solid decade of mainstream superhero movies, so just as the comic was able to subvert the tropes of the genre, the movie had its own clichés to play with. Special effects technology had advanced to the point that Moore's 1988 suggestion 'for Dr Manhattan to be played by a computer graphic' was now feasible. The graphic novel of *Watchmen* was on university reading lists, it could be found in any bookstore, and it's noticeable that mainstream reviewers who hadn't read the comic felt the need to justify their illiteracy. Fanboy culture was now utterly mainstream, comic book geeks could be seen swapping obscure references in the American sitcom *The Big Bang Theory*. When Moore visited the San Diego Comic-Con in 1985, he had found 5,000 fans gathered in one place an overwhelming number. By 2009 the same event hosted 126,000, and had mutated into a vast entertainment industry trade fair where studios sent their biggest stars to wow the early adopters.

In the summer of 2008, Warner Pictures released *The Dark Knight*, the second of Christopher Nolan's *Batman* movies, which pitted the caped crusader against the Joker. Unmistakably influenced by the late eighties take on the character, it made over $1 billion at the box office internationally. The film also saw the beginning of a year-long publicity drive for the *Watchmen* movie, with a lengthy preview trailer running before every screening. The stars had aligned . . . and the *Watchmen* movie flopped.

Watchmen eventually eked out $107 million at the box office, less than the reported $130 million it cost to make. It proved to be a hard sell in foreign markets. With an R rating in the US (an 18 in the UK), it was never going to be as lucrative as *The Dark Knight*, but benchmarked against it, *Watchmen* was a disaster. Its $55 million opening weekend was a third of *The Dark Knight*'s total and it quickly fizzled out, making less in its fourth weekend than *The Dark Knight* did in its tenth.

It's possible to hold an inquest. The main problem is that no *Watchmen* movie was ever going to have the same relative status as the original. The trailer declared *Watchmen* to be 'the most acclaimed graphic novel of all time'; the movie was never going to be equally acclaimed. The central conceit of the comic had been that it would be unusual to see 'realistic' superheroes, but for twenty years moviegoers had

seen little else. The film also failed to sell the premise that the superheroes were past their prime by casting actors who were noticeably younger than the middle-aged characters they were playing – Matthew Goode (Ozymandias) and Malin Akerman (Silk Spectre) were both under thirty. Zack Snyder is much more interested in creating moments of visual impact, or recreating them from the comic, than in the psychology of people who'd want to be superheroes, so while Patrick Wilson (Nite Owl) and Jackie Earle Haley (Rorschach) in particular are trying to get under the skin of their characters, the movie doesn't leave them enough room.

A number of reviewers took issue with the pace, noting that 'Snyder unwinds every bone-splintering blow with copious slo-mo combined with concussive shifts in frame rate. Truth is, he leans too hard on that slo-mo button' and 'we're left with a movie that feels overlong and incomplete at the same time, a frustrating combination'. Terry Gilliam, who must have put more thought into how to make a *Watchmen* movie than just about anyone else, came to the same verdict:

> There are great sequences in there, but the overall effect is kind of turgid in a certain way . . . in the comic book, or graphic novel . . . It's like the Comedian's coffin is going into the grave with the stars and stripes on top of it and reading it in the comic book it's three panels: boom, boom and boom. On film hhhhhhhhhhmmmmm . . . The pace is wrong. I think *Watchmen* really bothered me, because I thought it should be better. It was all there. It looked right, but to me it was pace. It didn't have pace. It needed a bit more quirkiness in there. Dr Manhattan was getting boring, frankly, and then Ozymandias by the end I thought 'Oh, come on!' They lost me by the end, frankly, but it was certainly looking better than what I was going to do!

Alan Moore sees the pacing issue as one that affects cinema in general: 'You are trapped in the running time of a film – you go in, you sit down, they've got two hours and you're dragged through at their pace. With a comic you can stare at the page for as long as you want and check back to see if this line of dialogue really does echo something four pages earlier, whether this picture is really the same as that one, and wonder if there is some connection there.'

J. Michael Stracynski is the creator of early nineties science fiction soap opera *Babylon 5*, and was nominated for an Oscar and BAFTA for his screenplay of *The*

Changeling. He's written comics including *Superman: Earth One* and *The Twelve*. He also wrote a number of the *Before Watchmen* prequel comics published by DC in 2012, and declares himself to be a fan of Moore's work; he once said, 'Alan is the best of us. I've said repeatedly, online and at conventions, that on a scale from one to ten, Alan is a full-blown ten. I've not only said it, more importantly, I've always believed it.' When asked why the *Watchmen* movie failed at the US box office, he answered:

> On an emotional level the *Watchmen* book is fairly cool to the touch; it's thoughtful, intellectual, with great characters, but nonetheless on the cool side. Film and television are hot mediums, in that they rely on passion and extreme emotions to reach across the darkness of a theatre to affect the audience. Granted that there are some of those moments in the book, they are not what makes for a successful film, and in being so literal in the director's transferral of the story from print to screen, that coolness was preserved, and the film became emotionally distant.

Moore himself had dismissed the idea that *Watchmen* was cinematic: 'It's almost the exact opposite of cinematic . . . I didn't design it to show off the similarities between cinema and comics, which *are* there, but, in my opinion are fairly unremarkable. It was designed to show off the things that comics could do that cinema and literature couldn't.' He now has an absolutist line on the concept of adaptation:

> I think that adaptation is largely a waste of time in almost any circumstances. There probably are the odd things that would prove me wrong. But I think they'd be very much the exception. If a thing works well in one medium, in the medium that it has been designed to work in, then the only possible point for wanting to realise it on 'multiple platforms', as they say these days, is to make a lot of money out of it. There is no consideration for the integrity of the work, which is rather the only thing as far as I'm concerned.

But Moore may have diagnosed the real problem with the *Watchmen* movie before the comic had even been published. In 1985, in his essay *On Writing for Comics*, he discussed the 'cinematic' techniques of comics: 'Cinema in comics

means Welles, Alfred Hitchcock and maybe a couple of others, all of whom did their best work thirty years ago. Why is there no attempt to understand and adapt the work of contemporary pioneers like Nick Roeg or Altman or Coppola, if a true cinematic approach is what we are aiming for?' He goes on to discuss Peter Greenaway's *The Draughtsman's Contract*, and how it's been designed to be seen several times. Stephen Bissette saw the influence straight away:

> I'm a huge fan of Nicholas Roeg, the director who did *Performance*, *Walkabout*, *The Man Who Fell To Earth*. Brilliant seventies filmmaker. And Alan loved his work too. Alan's first script that I drew was *Swamp Thing* #21, *The Anatomy Lesson*, and it was structured like a Roeg film. And I recognised it, and I immediately wrote to Alan, 'This is fucking brilliant. I love this stuff where you tell a story from the middle out, and by fragmenting it, you reveal more about the narrative than you would have if you had presented it in a straightforward, linear fashion'.

The *Watchmen* movie does include a couple of nods to Roeg's *The Man Who Fell to Earth*, but only in the set design, not the style of direction or editing. A 'faithful' adaptation of *Watchmen* would resemble the eighties arthouse cinema of Roeg or Greenaway, not the sort of popcorn action movie that the most successful superhero movies have been – and it's hard to imagine such a film making more for the studio than Snyder's version.

Although Moore has distanced himself from them, the movie adaptations of his work have inevitably affected his reputation. Movies have multi-million-dollar international advertising campaigns designed to raise awareness of the title and the iconography, they are routinely reviewed in newspapers and magazines, they enjoy an afterlife on DVD and casual viewers will bump into them when they are shown on television. The least successful movie will reach more people than even the most successful comic. That said, none of the movies based on Moore's work was a blockbuster. They were all number one at the US box office in their week of release, except *The League of Extraordinary Gentlemen*, which opened the same weekend as the first *Pirates of the Caribbean* movie at #2. *LXG* went on to be the most lucrative of the four adaptations. *V for Vendetta* is the only one of the movies that can be argued to have had a lasting cultural impact.

Nevertheless, the films have served both to introduce Alan Moore's work to a wider audience and to reframe it for the existing comics readership. Somewhat counter-intuitively, the movie industry's appropriation of his work, generally against his wishes, has tended to empower Moore. While the internet harbours a broad spectrum of critical opinion on every subject, it's hard to find many people who think any of the movie versions outshine the originals – the comparison has only reinforced the critical consensus that books like *Watchmen*, *From Hell* and *V for Vendetta* are 'classics'. Moore had previously been seen as the master of taking existing concepts and reinterpreting them, to the point that one critic had suggested 'Moore's fiction is like yoghurt – he needs a bit of a starter to get his own batch going.' The movies have increased the profile of Alan Moore's own creations.

One demonstrable fact is that the Hollywood versions have led new readers to the comics that they're based on. The best example was probably the earliest movie, *From Hell*. The comic was dogged with production and distribution problems. It took three and a half years for the story to reach the first murder, and ten years passed between the publication of the prologue and that of the epilogue. The issues put out by Kitchen Sink, the last of *From Hell*'s four original publishers, had print runs of only around 4,000 copies. Kitchen Sink went bankrupt in 1999, making it impossible to order back issues from the publisher. *From Hell* was expensive and difficult to collect, and a relatively obscure part of Moore's body of work. Even the movie production team couldn't find enough issues to go around and had to make photocopies. The first collection of *From Hell* in November 1999, self-published by Eddie Campbell, received fewer than 6,000 orders, and so was 'made on the cheapest possible materials'. However, pre-publicity for the movie sparked interest from bookstores in the US and UK. By the time *From Hell* opened in theatres, the book had sold 110,000 copies and within a few years that total had doubled. *From Hell* was a book waiting to be rediscovered, but it was the catalyst of the movie that elevated it into the top flight of Moore's oeuvre.

The same pattern was repeated with every movie: anticipation sent people to the source material, and although sales settled down after the movie's release, they remained steady at a higher level than before. This applied even when *Watchmen* was adapted, despite the fact that the book had already sold in the millions and was Moore's most acclaimed and discussed work. DC boasted that they had printed a million copies of the graphic novel to keep up with the demand generated by the trailer that went out in front of *The Dark Knight*.

Moore's public denunciation of the movies – and rejection of the money – handed mainstream journalists a simple narrative about a maverick concerned only with his art raging against the corporate machine. It has led to the incongruity of dozens of newspaper stories and magazine profiles about how he is reclusive and not interested in celebrity. The articles find the idea of Moore the Magus irresistible, and tend to have titles like 'The Wonderful Wizard of . . . Northampton' and 'Could it be Magic?' One clear benefit to Moore is that such coverage has tended to contrast his more difficult, personal current work – such as *Lost Girls*, *Unearthing* or *Jerusalem* – with the slick Hollywood product based on his old comics, giving that new work a great deal more attention from British broadsheet newspapers than any DC superhero comic would get.

It also allows him to publicise issues local to Northampton – protesting the closure of St James's Library or the council's decision to sell off an ancient Egyptian statue. Moore gives an example of the 'loud voice' he now enjoys:

> After a visit to the museum by some fundamentalist Christians, the evolution display had been completely covered up by the cowardly county council. So Norman [Adams, a local activist] phoned me up on the Saturday night and said: 'Look, this has just come up. I'm gonna be organising a small protest group outside the museum tomorrow at one o'clock. Any chance of you coming down and saying a few words?' I said sure, because that's something I do feel strongly about. Anyway when I got down there, because Norman had announced that I would be coming, the council had been out overnight and had removed the cover. Not that it did a lot of good, because by the time it happened, it got reported that I'd spoken at this thing, and it got on the midweek news. I had Radio 4 programmes driving up to Northampton to interview me about it. So that's the way that I can be most useful. I have been given this kind of unasked for clout, in terms of people who know my work. It's not something that I've ever sought, but it is there, and if it's needed in some way to help stem the tide of idiocy, then I can do that.

It also gives him a way to counter DC's marketing efforts that's so effective that it almost looks like symmetrical warfare. Moore was able, for example, to appear in newspapers in both the UK and US to criticise the publication of *Before Watchmen*, a 2012 spin-off series he didn't write and Gibbons didn't draw, and which Moore did not want DC to make. The prevalent story became one of Moore's disappointment and the poor standing of writers and artists in the comics industry. Moore is unsympathetic to DC's plight: 'It's so unfair when you think about it, isn't it, that you've got a barely educated thug from the English Midlands picking upon this huge multinational corporation. You know, I ought to be ashamed of myself.'

10 WHATEVER HAPPENED TO THE MAN OF TOMORROW?

> *'When I was a teenage boy I came up with a ridiculous, poorly thought through, fantasy image of the kind of figure I might want to be when I was older. And horrifically, this seems to have come completely true down to the last detail.'*
>
> **Alan Moore, *The Art of Dismantling***

July 2006 finally saw the publication of *Lost Girls*, Alan Moore and Melinda Gebbie's pornographic epic. What had started as a vague idea for an eight-page short story by two people who 'barely knew each other' ended up as a four-inch-thick, three-volume work by a couple who were engaged to be married. As Moore noted, 'I'd recommend to anybody working on their relationship that they should try embarking on a sixteen-year elaborate pornography together. I think they'll find it works wonders.' Moore thought he and Gebbie were staking out territory on the extreme edge of culture and he was ready for a fight, but instead found that a work that featured – among many, many, many startling images – Wendy giving Peter Pan a handjob while her brothers look on, masturbating, had earned him academic attention and serious literary respectability. *Lost Girls* received enough mainstream press on both sides of the Atlantic to delight any novelist, and the coverage was unprecedented for a *graphic* novelist. The release of a project originally 'meant to fill in time between *Big Numbers* issues' had become a publishing event, heralded as the debut of a new major work by, as the *Independent on Sunday* put it, 'the first great modern author of comics in the English language'. A *Channel 4 News* item went further, declaring, 'Alan Moore isn't just a comic writer but a spiritualist, a performance artist, even a magician, and to his many fans an anarchic visionary.'

Like *The League of Extraordinary Gentlemen*, *Lost Girls* brought together characters from different Victorian and Edwardian novels – in this case, *Alice in Wonderland*, *Peter Pan* and *The Wizard of Oz*. In *Lost Girls*, three women meet as guests on the eve of the Great War at an isolated hotel, where they describe their sexual experiences and engage in erotic exploration with each other and various guests, in pretty much every possible permutation, depicted frankly and with utter explicitness. These are not technically 'the characters' from the original books, but they have processed their formative sexual experiences in terms we recognise from those stories. So, for example, the Dorothy of *Lost Girls* was not literally swept up in a tornado to find herself in Oz; it's a metaphor for the new realm of experience she found herself in following her first orgasm. The three main characters represent different ages and social classes – Alice is old and upper class, Wendy middle-aged and middle class, Dorothy young and rural. It's a simple framework for an episodic story which allows Moore and Gebbie to engage in increasingly complex exercises in literary and artistic pastiche (there are sequences in the styles of Aubrey Beardsley, Alfons Mucha and Egon Schiele), and a growing contrast between the 'pornotopia' of the isolated hotel and the war brewing beyond its walls.

The main significance of *Lost Girls*, surely, is that it is a major work by Alan Moore produced in collaboration with the woman who would become his wife. They would marry on 12 May 2007; the ceremony, at Northampton's Guildhall, was attended by friends, family and artists including Neil Gaiman, Dave Gibbons, Todd Klein, Kevin O'Neill, Iain Sinclair, Chris Staros, Jose Villarrubia and Oscar Zarate. Moore wrote his own vows, Gebbie illustrated the invitations. On the day, Moore wore a bowler hat, Gebbie arrived in a horse-drawn carriage and guests were treated to a Bonzo Dog Doo-Dah Band tribute act, the Gonzo Dog-do Bar Band. The couple honeymooned in Edinburgh. In terms of *Lost Girls*' place in Moore's career, though, while it was published in 2006, it might best be thought of as a holdover from the late eighties or early nineties, the same period as *From Hell*, *Big Numbers* and *The Mirror of Love*, projects conceived in the years after Moore had left DC, when he was developing elaborately structured, ambitious comics for adults.

Working for mainstream US publishers had meant working within Comics Code Authority guidelines that decreed: 'Nudity in any form is prohibited. Suggestive and salacious illustration is unacceptable.' In practice, by the mid-eighties, comics – and not just those by Alan Moore – catered for an older audience, and no longer existed in a prelapsarian world. Even a Code-approved comic could get away with the occasional bare bottom, or a hint that characters were post-coital. In any case, Moore had soon divested himself of his CCA seals. Many of his books for DC featured a scattering of panels where a woman's nipples were visible – still relatively tame compared with other media – and *Watchmen* broke the taboo of full-frontal male nudity (albeit full-frontal, fluorescent, blue post-human male nudity).

Far more controversially, and from early in his career, Moore had frequently incorporated sexual violence into his stories. Interviewed by *Rolling Stone* in 2012, Grant Morrison remarked: 'I was reading some Alan Moore *Marvelman* for some reason today. I found one in the back there and I couldn't believe it. I pick it up and there are fucking two rapes in it and I suddenly think how many times has somebody been raped in an Alan Moore story? And I couldn't find a single one where someone wasn't raped except for *Tom Strong*, which I believe was a pastiche. We know Alan Moore isn't a misogynist but fuck, he's obsessed with rape. I managed to do thirty years in comics without any rape!' It may be colourfully put, but Morrison's observation is not entirely unfair. Nor is he the first to make it. All of Moore's best-known work for DC features sexual assault (or the threat of it) at crucial dramatic moments: *The Killing Joke* sees Batgirl abused by the Joker; *V for Vendetta* starts with Evey being rescued from rapists by V, who later performs a cavity search on her as part of a fake captivity; and perhaps most controversially, in *Watchmen* the Comedian attempts to rape Silk Spectre (although the two are reconciled and later have a child together).

In 1988, there was controversy over the violence in *The Killing Joke* . . . and not a word about *The Fear*, a two-part story that ran in the Code-approved *Detective Comics*, in which Batman tracks down Cornelius Stirk, a serial killer who kidnaps his victims from the streets, then terrifies them to death and eats their hearts. *The Killing Joke* inflicts its violence on a long-running character who was a strong role model for girls, whereas Stirk's victims are created to be killed off, explaining why readers were more disturbed by the former. Even so, superhero comics intended for young readers routinely include spree killing, mutilation, armed robbery, beatings, stabbings and shootings, and depict people being drowned, burned, electrocuted or doused in acid. Moore's work navigates fictional universes predicated on violent conflict. His inclusion of sexual violence is clearly, in part, consistent with the idea of treating the action-adventure genre 'realistically'. No one is surprised when the Joker commits murder, but in a world with violent super-criminals, wouldn't there be sexually violent supervillains? Moore is intentionally trying to shock his audience, and when challenged that his work has tended towards the dark and grim, he has conceded that 'I've probably done more comics about the horrors of nuclear power than I've done about the delights of windmills.'

There are, of course, Alan Moore adventure stories that don't involve sexual violence. But many others do, and he does not always treat the subject with high seriousness. When we meet the Invisible Man in the first volume of *The League of Extraordinary Gentlemen*, the character is loose in a girls' school, and the comic plays rape for laughs. Moore noted, 'I know technically it was rape. I still thought it was funny, just because – it's a funny idea, people floating in space with their legs wrapped around nothing, gasping in rapture.' And for the record, there *is* a rape in *Tom Strong*, again treated lightly – in #6, the title character is drugged and raped by Nazi scientist Ingrid Weiss, who goes on to have his son, Albrecht. More recently, particularly brutal, lengthy and graphically depicted rape scenes have provided defining moments in both *Century 1910* and *Neonomicon*.

Any analysis has to acknowledge that Moore *has* written about the delights of windmills, too. He has dealt with positive aspects of sex and sexuality as often as he's depicted rape. In *Swamp Thing*, Moore's only ongoing series for DC, he was able to explore the subject of sex from a number of angles, including the issue-long, joyous sex scene that is #34, 'The Rite of Spring'. Moore reasoned, 'if you could fill comic book after comic book every month with fights, then surely you could fill at least one comic book with a sexual act. Surely that was as interesting as a fight.'

Freeing himself from DC allowed Moore to address the topic of sex far more openly. In early interviews about *Lost Girls*, he was keen to stress that he was working within the traditions of the comics industry. There had been porn comics before *Lost Girls*, such as the Tijuana Bibles, which – as Moore had informed readers of *Watchmen* – usually featured famous cartoon characters like Betty Boop or Dick Tracy. During the thirties and forties, these circulated in their millions in all-male environments like barracks and barbershops. Invariably eight pages long, they were therefore known as 'eight-pagers'. As Moore said, 'The great appeal of showing thoroughly non-sexual figures such as Blondie, Jiggs or Popeye taking part in pornographic skits lies in the greater contrast, with the sexual content seeming dirtier when in the context of some previously spotless cultural icon. There is also the subversive pleasure that is to be had in puncturing the anodyne and sexless vision of society presented by the Sunday funnies.' The basic premise of *Lost Girls* was the same: characters from children's fiction having explicit sexual encounters. The critic Annalisa Di Liddo and *Onion* reviewer Noel Murray independently concluded that it's no coincidence its chapters are eight pages long.

There was, too, a radical impulse: Melinda Gebbie had a fine pedigree in underground comix, and Moore was keen to remind people of the role the counterculture had played on both sides of the barricades during the sexual revolution: 'Of course, both sex and sexual expression are political and always have been, but it wasn't until the late sixties and the seventies that they were widely seen as such. Sprung up from the same sixties counterculture that had given rise to Robert Crumb came feminism to provide the artist with his fiercest critics.'

Almost from the beginning, underground comix had appropriated existing cartoon characters. When Dan O'Neill and his colleagues showed Mickey Mouse behaving like an underground comix character – dealing dope, swearing, leering and giving Minnie an STD caught from Daisy Duck (on finding out, Minnie yells 'you dirty duckfucker') – in their 1971 *Air Pirates Funnies* anthologies, it was a protest against the safe world of Disney, an assertion that free speech applied to corporate-owned characters, too. O'Neill was embroiled in an eight-year legal case for his trouble, and used the trial to express the opinion that freedom of speech should allow a cartoonist to parody cartoons. He also noted that 'wholesome' Disney cartoons routinely traded in ethnic and gender stereotypes. The *Air Pirates* case became a cause célèbre among the comics community, with Disney winning vast damages they knew they could never collect from an artist who listed the sum total of his assets as $7 and a banjo.

The British equivalent was the *Oz* obscenity trial, which ran for six weeks over the summer of 1971. The underground magazine was routinely full of lewd images and swear words, but the trial somehow came to centre on the inclusion of an image of Rupert the Bear with an erection. This led to memorable exchanges in court: the prosecution claimed that as Rupert was a child, the images therefore qualified as obscene images of children – a far more serious charge than doodling

a cock onto a cartoon bear. The defence was led by barrister John Mortimer (author of the *Rumpole* novels), who called the psychologist Dr Michael Schofield to offer expert opinion that the images were not harmful and would not corrupt the intended audience, leading to the following memorable exchange under cross-examination:

> **BRIAN LEARY (prosecution):** What sort of age would you think Rupert is, to your mind? What sort of aged bear?
>
> **SCHOFIELD:** Oh, I'm very sorry. I'm not up to date with bears.
>
> **LEARY:** You don't have to be, because he doesn't change, Rupert, does he?
>
> **JUDGE ARGYLE (interrupting):** I think the question is 'what age do you think Rupert is intended to be: a child, an adult or what?'
>
> **SCHOFIELD:** It is an unreal question, you might as well ask me 'how old is Jupiter?'

Moore has alluded to this a couple of times in stories – a flashback image in *Big Numbers* #2 that shows baffled parents discovering a teenager's copy of *Oz*, complete with the offending image of Rupert, feels at least semi-autobiographical. And towards the end of *Lost Girls*, Wendy is horrified to find a book containing a story in which a pair of young children have sex with their parents – we see the illustrations. The man who gave her the book offers a defence that's a clear allusion to the *Oz* trial, but he soon sort-of snatches away the get-out clause he's just drafted:

> Incest, c'est vrai, it is a crime, but this? This is the idea of incest, no? And these children: how outrageous! How old can they be? Eleven? Twelve? It is quite monstrous . . . except that they are fictions, as old as the page they appear on, no less, no more. Fiction and fact: only madmen and magistrates can not discriminate between them . . . I, of course, am real and since Helena, who I just fucked, is only thirteen, I am very guilty. Ah well, it can't be helped.

In the early nineties, *Lost Girls* had been one of many forthcoming projects from Moore, who described it as 'almost symmetrical' with *From Hell*: 'In some ways *From Hell* – what I hope it to be – is a painfully meticulous examination of the disease, whereas *Lost Girls* offers some tentative suggestions towards a possible cure.' Unfortunately, the parallels didn't end there, the two series also sharing a patchy publication history. Like *From Hell*, the opening chapters of *Lost Girls* appeared in *Taboo* in 1991–2, and Kitchen Sink published two magazine-sized volumes of the series in 1995–6. Even without a publisher, though, Moore and Gebbie continued to work on the project. Moore remained 'sure that a major work of mine is going to be published sooner or later. I've been able to maintain my sangfroid concerning the various ups and downs in the publishing status of the books. I'm convinced that the work is the main thing to concentrate on, and when it's ready to be published there'll be a publisher there to do it.'

It would take over ten years, but *Lost Girls* did find its publisher. This was Chris Staros at Top Shelf, who announced in September 2002 that he was committed to publishing the book exactly to Moore and Gebbie's specifications. Top Shelf pulled out all the stops to make the final product as lavish as possible. *Lost Girls* was to be a slab-like slipcased set containing three volumes, each one a hardback with its own dust jacket, on thick paper that Moore said 'to my mind smells better than the finest Chanel, you can really bury your face in *Lost Girls*, and it's such a great quality paper, it adds to the experience'. The delays in completing the book only improved the quality of the final product: 'If we'd finished it a little earlier there would not yet have been the reproduction techniques that would have been capable of reproducing Melinda's artwork with the kind of fidelity that we see in the Top Shelf volume.' The original art was photographed at a specialist printer's in London, the only place in the country they could find which was up to the technical challenge of duplicating Gebbie's delicate pastels. The finished product would retail for $75 at a time when a standard comic book cost $2.95.

Not only did the printing and other costs represent a commitment of around $350,000 for Top Shelf – an immense financial risk under any circumstance for a small press – but *Lost Girls* presented a whole new set of potential problems. Due to its content, it was unclear that consignments of the book would be allowed through customs in a number of countries (as it was printed in Hong Kong, there was no guarantee it would even leave the printers' warehouse). There are places where any depiction of underage sex, even in drawings, is banned and merely possessing a copy of a book containing them is a serious criminal offence. And in the UK there came another challenge: London's Great Ormond Street children's hospital, who were bequeathed the rights to *Peter Pan* by its creator J.M. Barrie, blocked sales in Moore and O'Neill's home country on more straightforward copyright grounds. The initial print run of 10,000 looked extremely optimistic.

When asked 'are you worried about bankrupting Top Shelf?' Moore's answer didn't rule out the possibility:

> I'm incredibly proud of the way Chris is standing behind this book. Chris knew what the book was when he decided to do it, and we've been completely honest about what this book contains during the whole sixteen years we've been working upon it. Of course we don't want anybody to be disadvantaged or bankrupted by this book. At the same time, what are our alternatives? If you're living in a politically repressive time where you have this seemingly fundamentalist-directed agenda percolating down not only through America but through all of those countries who are fortunate enough be in the shadow of America, you've really got no option other than to make your statement as you see fit, or shut up.

As the publication date approached, Staros began a careful marketing campaign: 'We really worked the press hard on this book, for several reasons. One, it's such an expensive book to produce, it had to launch big or it would have killed us financially. Secondly, it was very important for a book this controversial to be sort of pre-approved by the public at large as a work of art, rather than come out cold and start getting detractors from the beginning . . . I've made sure the book is legitimised as a work of art. That's why we've packaged it the way we have . . . So, there's no confusion that it has literary merit, which in this country means it's not obscene.' Neil Gaiman – who, lest we forget, was the person who put Moore and Gebbie in touch in the first place – wrote a review for *Publishers Weekly* that, by accident or design, was perfectly on-message:

> As a formal exercise in pure comics, *Lost Girls* is as good as anything Moore has written. (One of my favorite moments: a husband and wife trapped in a frozen, loveless, sexless relationship, conduct a stiff conversation, laced with unconscious puns and wordplay, moving into positions that cause their shadows to appear to copulate wildly, finding the physical passion that the people are denied.) In addition to being a masterclass in comics technique, *Lost Girls* is also an education in Edwardian smut – Gebbie and Moore pastiche the pornography of the period, taking in everything from *The Oyster* to the *Venus and Tannhauser* period work of Aubrey Beardsley. Melinda Gebbie was a strange

> and inspired choice as collaborator for Moore. She draws real people, with none of the exaggerated bodies usual to superhero or porno comics. Gebbie's people, drawn for the most part in gentle crayons, have human bodies. *Lost Girls* is a bittersweet, beautiful, exhaustive, problematic, occasionally exhausting work.

The biggest gun in the marketing battle, though, was Alan Moore himself. *Lost Girls* would be published a few months after the release of the *V for Vendetta* movie, and there were many articles in the mainstream and comics press about his disputes with Hollywood and the comics industry. Moore was able to contrast such matters with his work on *Lost Girls*. As ever, he was not afraid to explain how clever he was being, and his approach to writing pornography was characteristically thoughtful as he brought his revisionist, deconstructionist techniques to bear: 'Even porn's most uncompromising and vociferous feminist critic, Andrea Dworkin, has conceded that benign pornography might be conceivable, even if she considered such a thing highly unlikely. Given that we don't want "bad pornography" and can't have "no pornography", it's in this mere suggestion of the possibility of "good" pornography that the one ray of light in an intractable debate resides.'

Moore wanted to create such 'good pornography', work with genuine artistic merit and a degree of technical accomplishment. There was a grand purpose to the endeavour, and he was keen to position *Lost Girls* as a political statement:

> I think if you were to sever that connection between arousal and shame, you might actually come up with something liberating and socially useful. It might be healthier for us, and lead to a situation such as they enjoy in Holland, Denmark, or Spain, where they have pornography all over the place – quite hardcore pornography – but they do not have anywhere near the incidence of sex crimes. Particularly not the sex crimes against children that we suffer from in Britain, and that I believe you suffer from in the United States. It seems at least potentially that pornography might be providing an essential pressure valve in those countries, which we do not have access to here. Rather than being able to have a healthy relationship with our own sexual imagination, we're driven into some dark corners by shame and embarrassment and guilt, and those dark corners breed all sorts of monsters. Things that cross the line between the kind of pornography Melinda and I are doing, which only occurs in the realm of the mind, to the very unpleasant things that can occur in real life.

In a long essay, 'Bog Venus v Nazi Cock Ring', Moore summed up, with his tongue mostly in his cheek, what he believed to be the simple choice: 'Sexually open and progressive cultures such as ancient Greece have given the West almost all of its civilising aspects, whereas sexually repressive cultures like late Rome have given us the Dark Ages.'

This was nothing new. Moore has contrasted 'sex' and 'violence' from his earliest work. In *Miracleman #13* (November 1987), an eternal cosmic war between two galactic civilisations is ended following this exchange between the leader of one side and Miraclewoman:

KINGQUEEN:	Are both cultures forever doomed, then, to an unproductive war's dull toil?
MIRACLEWOMAN:	Excuse me . . . but couldn't you have sex instead?
KINGQUEEN:	Have sex?
	. . .
MIRACLEWOMAN:	If two organisms or two cultures are forced into contact, it can be thanatic and destructive, or erotic and creative.

It boils down to the old hippy mantra: 'make love, not war'. But Moore, true to character, sees it not as a suggestion, but as a description of fundamental universal forces, with history representing the Manichean struggle between them.

In *Promethea* #22 (November 2002), Moore describes 'godsex' as 'This chaotic animal force. It's the primal scene. It's mom and dad doing it, humping towards the moment of conception, but it's the conception of the universe. The universe. All the male and female energies pounding in the binary throb of being. On and off. Back and forth. In and out. Gravity. Electromagnetism. The weak nuclear force. The strong nuclear force. Earth, air, water, fire. This phosphorous angel copulation . . . building like music, building to a crescendo. Building to its outburst.' It's a coming together that creates the universe.

Indeed, Moore sees sex as the ultimate union and creative act. He's often described it in similar, psychedelic terms as a great journey upwards. *Promethea* #10 (October 2000) includes the passage 'This is heart, and soul . . . this is the Sun, this is the Gold in us and you are almost me and I am almost you. Oh love. Love . . . and we become each other . . . become hermaphrodite . . . as we climb . . . towards the godhead'. *Snakes and Ladders* (1999) reaches a transcendental climax:

'we climb on . . . the he and she of us become a limitation to our pleasure, sloughs away in favour of a more erotic possibility: the limitless horny intimacy if we could become each other.' And there's the sex scene in *Swamp Thing* #34 (March 1985): 'I am no longer certain where I end . . . where he begins . . . I feel my own hand like he feels it [. . .] we . . . are . . . one creature . . . and all . . . that there is . . . is in us . . . Together we know the light, exploding upward in a birdcloud.'

That *Swamp Thing* story, 'The Rite of Spring', was named after the Stravinsky ballet which holds an important place in Moore's worldview. For Moore, the original *Rite of Spring* represents truly revolutionary forces in its unbottling of great passion. Such energies can be channelled in one of two directions: war divides and destroys; sex unites and creates. While he has been dismissive of Freud, once telling *The Onion*, 'Sigmund Freud, frankly, I've not got a great deal of time for, because I think he was a child-fixated cokehead, to be perfectly honest', Moore's model is practically identical to Freud's theory of Eros and Thanatos. As he explains: 'Control sex and death, and controlling populations becomes simple. Death's easily subjugated: William Burroughs observed that anyone who can lift a frying pan owns death. Similarly, those owning the most pans, troops, tanks or warheads own the most death, and can regulate the supply accordingly. Death's a pushover, but how do you control desire?'

This is the question at the heart of *Lost Girls*. In the story, the main characters leave the hotel to attend a performance of *The Rite of Spring*. While they are carried away sexually by the pagan rhythms, the majority of the audience becomes violent and a riot ensues. In 2006 Moore was able to make a case for the contemporary relevance of the book, saying 'This has taken us sixteen years. We didn't know it was going to come out in 2006, in the middle of George Bush's second administration, with the world plunged more thoroughly into war than it's been in a couple of decades. It could just have easily come out nine years ago, when Clinton was in office, and it might've seemed irrelevant, and not particularly shocking in a time of [Andres Serrano's] "Piss Christ". And if we'd done this forty years ago, there would've been people asking us if we hadn't gone a bit far by portraying homosexuality.'

The regularity with which Moore is interviewed means that when he's asked the same question by different journalists, naturally enough he will give broadly the same answer, and tends to use similar examples or anecdotes. With the round of

Lost Girls interviews, though, he gave almost word-for-word answers to MTV, the *Independent*, *Onion*, *Patriot-News* and other media outlets. He was clearly girding his loins for a fight, aware he needed to choose his words carefully.

Moore was ready for anything . . . except what actually happened. Soon, the *Independent on Sunday* was able to report:

> In spite of worries that *Lost Girls'* explicit imagery might prove controversial or even actionable in America, the book received glowing press, even in the normally conservative *USA Today*, and sold out there of its 10,000-copy first printing in one day. Already going into a third printing of 20,000, their distribution to Britain has been delayed because of correspondence to the publishers, Top Shelf, from Great Ormond Street Hospital – which was given the copyright to *Peter Pan* in J.M. Barrie's will – possibly until January 2008, when its rights expire. This has not stopped the book hitting the Top 20 on Amazon.

The first print run sold out on the day of release, Wednesday 30 August 2006. Two weeks later, Chris Staros announced, 'since the back orders in the Diamond system were already greater than the second printing of 10,000 we had ordered in anticipation of higher demand, we had to go ahead and order a third printing of 20,000 copies. So in a period of four days, we went through the first, second and part of the third printing.' By 9 November, Top Shelf announced that 17,000 of the following month's third printing were already back ordered. *Lost Girls* was not banned by any store or (for any length of time) by any jurisdiction, and remains available from any retailer of graphic novels, latterly in a single-volume edition. American bookstore chain Borders insisted the book be shrinkwrapped, but that was just as likely done in an effort to protect a $75 book from grubby-fingered customers as to protect the customers from the contents of the book.

Challenge after challenge fell away. Moore said, 'We got back a wonderful letter from the Canadian Customs Authority, basically saying that, even though there were scenes that were tantamount to bestiality or incest, this could in no way be considered obscene, and even though it did appear that there were underage people taking part in some of the sex scenes, this could in no way be considered as child pornography, and that it was a work of great social and artistic benefit.' There was no tabloid outrage. When Moore was interviewed on BBC Radio 4's *Today* programme on 22 June 2006, the encounter started out confrontationally, but Moore soon turned

the subject around from child abuse to the joys of free speech and the exchange ended up almost playful. He could hardly have had a more respectable or prestigious platform – his interview followed a discussion with Al Gore about climate change. And on New Year's Eve 2011, he was invited back to *Today* to deliver the Thought for the Day homily; he chose to extol the virtues of worshipping a glove puppet, ending with: 'Anyway, thank you very much for listening and from both me and Glycon, a very happy new year to you all.'

The coverage of *Lost Girls* was by no means all fawning or even positive, but the criticism it received was concerned less with its subject matter and more with its merits as a comic. For some time the work became the focus of heated back-and-forth debates in both the venerable *The Comics Journal* and the online academic comics forum InterText.

It also attracted broad scholarly attention. Moore and Gebbie had managed to encompass many of the hot button topics of contemporary English Literature courses – gender studies, queer theory, identity politics, Victoriana, the fin de siècle, constructions of childhood, the First World War, children's literature, sex, rape and censorship – as well as offering rich meat for those looking simply to examine formal aspects of comics storytelling. It seemed there was much to discuss; the introduction to the collection *Sexual Ideology in the Works of Alan Moore* went as far as to assert '*Lost Girls* has become a sort of Rosetta Stone for understanding Moore's career'. When Leah Moore was at university in the late nineties, both she and her father had been a little surprised to find his work on her reading lists; since then, a number of books have been published solely dedicated to his life and work, ranging from slim paperbacks to coffee-table books. There are book-long interviews with Moore, collections of old interviews, and a growing weight of academic papers. By 2010 Moore was such a focus of scholarly attention that on 28–29 May, the University of Northampton organised *Magus: Transdisciplinary Approaches to the Work of Alan Moore*, an event that included papers with titles like 'Big Numbers: Comics Beyond Referentiality and Reinvention', 'Chaotic Criminality: The Villains of Alan Moore' and 'V Versus Hollywood: A Discourse on Polemic Thievery'. Subjects ranged from Moore's mainstream comics, through his connection to Northampton, to his performance art and magic. Efforts were made to link his work to broader literary movements, such as postmodernism and

the Gothic, and there was considerable discussion of his influences and influence. There were also screenings of Moore rarities like *Don't Let Me Die in Black and White*, before the conference culminated with a panel appearance by Moore and Gebbie themselves.

Whether or not *Lost Girls* was really the keystone to Moore's career it was presented as by some journalists and critics at the time, it is a useful landmark. Its publication came in 2006, the year when Moore made a conscious and very public effort to distance himself from the entire comics industry. Thanks to tension over editorial decisions at ABC and Moore's anger about DC's handling of the *V for Vendetta* movie, he had decided to wind down his involvement in the ABC range, shelving plans for new series *Comet Rangers* (with art by Jim Lee), *Pearl of the Deep* (John Totleben), *The Soul* (John Coulthart) and *Limbo* (Shane Oakley), and an anthology series called *Cascade* which he hoped would involve Dave Gibbons, Brian Bolland and Bryan Talbot.

There was, as Moore put it, one 'slender thread' connecting him to DC: *The League of Extraordinary Gentlemen.* Moore reiterated that he and Kevin O'Neill would not accept any further editorial interference. By mid-2006, the one-off *Black Dossier* was nearly ready, and it was slated for release in October that year, but the complex nature of the book saw it slipping into early 2007. Just as *The Black Dossier* was completed, there was to be one further delay, as O'Neill explained:

> A Hollywood film producer insisted on seeing the book, long before publication, in the early part of the year it was finally published. He was putting a lot of pressure on DC, and if I understand the story correctly – I'll try to keep names out of this – someone important at DC flew out, showed the assembled book to the guy, who was flicking through the pages going, 'Oh fuck, oh fuck, oh fuck, you guys are going to be sued out of existence, oh my God, what are you doing, what are you thinking?' . . . then, unfortunately, the same producer was at a book fair in New York, and met someone from DC and said, 'Jeez, you're not still publishing that thing?'

While O'Neill didn't name names, he was clearly referring to *LXG* producer Don Murphy, who explains that he had asked to read *The Black Dossier* in case there was potential for a movie sequel:

> By this point Alan was done with Hollywood ... John Nee brought it to the studio and stayed while I read it. It was not really a coherent story, but very fun. It seemed clear to me that there were dozens of modern copyright violations, like with James Bond and Jeeves, that were outrageous. But remember, I'm not a lawyer, I make movies. I'm fairly good at rights, but DC and Warners have the best lawyers in town. If DC scuttled the book because I said something, that's crazy? Who am I? On the other hand, later on O'Neill, in an interview slagging what I said, mentioned that he felt that Warners should have given them the rights to Jeeves because a sister company owned it. They played fast and loose on later editions of the *League* with copyrights and certainly felt entitled to other people's creations.

Because *The Black Dossier* was set in the fifties, everyone involved always knew that it would contain characters who might still be trademarked or in copyright. Moore, O'Neill and their editor Scott Dunbier had been careful throughout the process of putting the book together to discuss and work through the legal issues this might entail. Nevertheless, Paul Levitz, DC publisher, recommended that *The Black Dossier* only be sold in the US (the given reason being that an intended pastiche of P.G. Wodehouse would fall foul of UK law). It was also decided that one of the two songs on the vinyl record, 'Home With You', was too close to the song it was parodying, the theme tune to Gerry Anderson's sixties puppet series *Fireball XL5*, and so the record would not be included with the book.

Publicly, ever since Moore's first falling out with DC in 1987, Levitz has never been anything other than complimentary about him in interviews, while a number of people have credited Levitz with blocking all attempts to publish a *Watchmen* sequel or otherwise exploit the property – in the event, the only new *Watchmen* material published until 2012 was in a 1987 role-playing game module created in co-operation with Moore, and a 2009 videogame that tied into the movie (Levitz vetoed the creation of any new material for the game). After Levitz stepped down as president and publisher of DC Comics in September 2009, this would quickly change.

For Moore, though, Levitz's intervention over *The Black Dossier* was already a bridge too far, and he concluded that he had finally had enough. 'At that point, we had decided we'd switch publishers. Because even if we changed things, they could always come back with one more petty alteration – it was like having a boot on our neck.' The obvious place to take future volumes of the *League* was Top Shelf, publishers of *Lost Girls*, who were keen to pick up the series. In the UK, it would be handled by venerable underground publishers Knockabout, with whom both Moore and O'Neill had separately worked on numerous occasions in the past.

Moore explained why he was leaving mainstream comics in an eighty-page interview with journalist Bill Baker, published at the end of the year as the book *Alan Moore's Exit Interview*. It was another exercise in bridge burning, during which Moore accused DC's management of being more interested in movie deals, corporate politics and their own egos than in making comics. After more than a quarter of a century as a writer, he claimed he barely owned a single thing he had written, and, from his perspective, the business practices of comics publishers routinely involved lying, blackmail and fraud. Moore still loved the medium, but had come to believe the industry was institutionally incapable of respecting writers and artists: 'It treats them as a resource. It treats them as fuel rods. It has no respect for them as individuals. It will work them to death in the hope of getting a few more books out of them. And then, when they're dead, it can publish fulsome obituaries and release all their work in commemorative editions and continue to make money out of them.'

Though the American comics industry has been around since the thirties and seen its share of peaks and troughs, it's clear that it currently faces a big problem. The internet has radically altered the market for newspapers and magazines, and ultimately comics are just another form of printed periodical. Like the music industry, the comics companies were caught out by internet piracy and slow to offer a legitimate alternative. They are insulated from the worst ravages – collectors fetishise physical comics, thinking of them as investments, and there's some basis for that belief. The first issue of *The Walking Dead*, for example, came out in 2003 and cost $2.95; in November 2012, a mint condition copy sold for $10,000. The direct sales distribution system essentially means comics are print-to-order and non-returnable, and so the publishers take on very little risk. But comics have relied on existing readers for too long. In the eighties, industry professionals were surprised to learn that some of their readers were old enough to go to college; nowadays they would be surprised to learn they had many readers that young. In 2012 Grant Morrison, then writing both Superman and Batman for DC, told

Rolling Stone: 'comics sales are so low . . . It's just plummeting. It's really bad from month to month. May was the first time in a long time that no comic sold over 100,000 copies, so there's a decline . . . There's a real feeling of things just going off the rails, to be honest. Superhero comics. The concept is quite a ruthless concept, and it's moved on.'

Moore had been saying for years that the industry was doomed. In an interview for podcast Panel Borders, he offered the following suggestion:

> The thing which I think might really save the comics industry, what we really need, is a good insurance fire. I think that if we actually burned the industry down to the ground, and we could probably lock the fire exits on all the big companies before we did that, then what we'd have would be scorched earth, which is rich in nitrates and which green shoots can blossom from. That perhaps sounds a bit apocalyptic, but I think that would be really healthy to actually bust the comics medium back down to the ignored state that it used to blissfully enjoy before people like me came along and spoiled everything.

There is a comics community, one in which most professionals started out as fans – Moore, of course, being no exception – and it's a network with very few degrees of separation. Comics, like every other creative industry, has its fair share of feuds, splits, factions and grudges, but it's broadly fraternal. So when Moore offers a critique, he inevitably provokes a reaction – from the creators, who feel personally slighted, and from the fans who champion the work of those writers and artists he is seen to be criticising. In September 2010, Moore remarked that if 'they have got these "top-flight industry creators" that are ready to produce these prequels and sequels to *Watchmen*, well this is probably a radical idea, but could they not get one of the "top-flight industry creators" to come up with an idea of their own? . . . Just simply get some of your top-flight talent to put out a book that the wider public outside of the comics field find as interesting or as appealing as the stuff that I wrote twenty-five years ago. It shouldn't be too big an ask, should it?' Such comments are incendiary, and quickly spread online, but it's a one-way process: while virtually all comics creators now have a blog and Twitter account, Moore genuinely still does not have an internet connection (although, based on comments he's made, he clearly gets reports from friends and family).

Even when silent, his voice is heard. Every comics fan knows Alan Moore

wrote *V for Vendetta* and *Watchmen*, so when the credits on the movie versions read 'based on the graphic novel illustrated by David Lloyd' and 'based on the graphic novel co-created and illustrated by Dave Gibbons', it means they start their viewing experience with a jarring reminder of his disapproval. Many fans are now in early middle age and prefer Moore's early superhero work from their formative years to his more recent projects. They take Moore's criticisms as personal attacks, with various degrees of denial, bargaining, anger, depression or acceptance. Fans of the *V for Vendetta* movie can't comprehend why Alan Moore dismisses it.

All this has fuelled an image of Moore as reclusive and embittered, particularly, it would seem, among sections of American comics fandom. As Melinda Gebbie told the *New York Times*, 'Because he looks like a wild man, people assume that he must be one. He's frightening to people because he doesn't seem to take the carrot, and he's fighting to maintain an integrity that they don't understand.' Journalists often note their surprise on discovering that Moore is rather affable, the consensus being summed up by a profile in the *Guardian*: 'You could be forgiven for thinking he's a curmudgeonly old hermit, but in person he's genuinely warm, considerate and utterly unpretentious.'

Most sixty year olds, presumably, have lost touch with former pals, or aren't on the same good terms with every workmate they had in the eighties. Moore is no exception: he's fallen out with a number of his collaborators over the years, including people he used to be friends with. He has also maintained friendships with Northampton locals since childhood, retained friends from the world of comics like Steve Moore, Neil Gaiman and Eddie Campbell for many decades, and stayed on good terms with many of his artists, going so far as to marry one of them. He has, though, also consciously cut people out of his life. On occasions he's made it clear to publishers that he's only willing to speak to certain individuals – latterly at DC, for example, he would only take calls from his former *Swamp Thing* editor Karen Berger, and his only contact at ABC was Scott Dunbier. By the mid-eighties, he had stopped communicating with Dez Skinn to the point that the *Warrior* editor had to send letters to him by registered post to be sure Moore had received them. Moore only wants to deal with people he trusts. Skinn's response is: 'Trust? Unless one's paranoid, I'm not sure where that even factors in. I've never even stopped to consider whether I trusted my bosses at IPC, Marvel, *Mad* or anywhere. As long as they paid me, I worked for them.'

This goes beyond purely professional relationships; Moore has applied the same sort of all-or-nothing approach to his friendships. He and Stephen Bissette started out on very good terms, working together as writer and artist on *Swamp Thing*. When Bissette began self-publishing *Taboo*, Moore provided *From Hell* and *Lost Girls*, as well as other material; Eddie Campbell, clearly a little frustrated with the venue, says 'I always knew that *From Hell* was going nowhere as long as it was imprisoned in *Taboo* but Alan stuck loyally by his original agreement with Steve.' Bissette visited Moore in Northampton, staying at his house. Moore took an interest in Bissette's creator-owned dinosaur comic *Tyrant*. They worked together on *1963* for Image, enjoying at least the initial process, and both earning a lot of money.

But things were to change abruptly. Bissette told *The Onion* that Moore had fallen out with him over an interview in *The Comics Journal* #185 (March 1996): 'I sent copies to anyone I mentioned by name, of the transcript of the interview with a cover letter, saying "If anything upsets you, I will take it out. If there's anything I got wrong, I will change it. Please read this, go over it, and let me know." Alan, I never heard from. But when Neil [Gaiman] saw him, Alan . . . Actually, Neil called me before he left England, and I called Alan that night, and it was the last sentence he ever said to me. He said "Right, Steve? I'll keep this short. Don't call me, don't write me, as far as I'm concerned, it's over, mate." Click. That was it. All done. I don't know what offended him . . .'

Moore's recollection is that although 'the conversation wasn't a long one, it was slightly longer than Steve Bissette reports. I asked him why he had never raised *any* of these problems and complaints about my behaviour with me. When he did raise them, he decided rather than raise them to my face, to raise them in a comics fanzine. He didn't really reply to that. Also, that hadn't happened . . . he was talking about how working for Todd McFarlane had completely changed my head and I'd lost interest in *1963*, when as far as I remember I was still trying to write that last issue when Steve Bissette and Rick [Veitch] said they didn't want to do it any more – the project. I could understand their frustrations at dealing with Image, where every couple of weeks it seemed to be another part of the Image partnership wanted to handle the book and it was just hopeless.'

The final issue of *1963*, the *1963 Annual*, was due to feature a few pages of art each from most of the Image partners, but there was no editorial team to coordinate or sort out the paperwork. Bissette picked up many of these duties, feeling that those involved – including Moore – were prioritising other projects at Image. But the straw that broke the camel's back for Moore would seem to be when he read Bissette saying:

> I really didn't think, when push came to shove, that Alan would abandon us so readily. We built the bridge with him to Image, but I suppose we were just his porters in the eyes of the Image 'aristocracy'. Alan became 'Affable Al.' It took me a little time to recover from that. It surprised me that money would be that motivating a factor. But, you have to understand how long Alan had been scraping. At the same time, his life was moving in another direction, away from the exclusive focus on comics, into really amazing creative avenues elsewhere.

Moore says, 'When he called up I went through all this with him, I explained to him what had happened, that when I got this package, after *The Comics Journal* was already on the stands, I got halfway through it and I was in tears. My daughter took it out of my hands and put it in the trash bin . . . up until that moment, I had thought he was one of my closest friends. And, yeah, that was very, very upsetting.' The relationship between Moore and Bissette had changed over the years. It meant 'a phone call to Alan that used to be a friendly, peer-level co-creator chat was turning into more and more business. And Alan hates doing business. And it was becoming more and more of an intrusion in his life.'

A dozen years later, it appears, a similar rift opened with Dave Gibbons. Gibbons was enthusiastic about the *Watchmen* movie, Moore wasn't. Each knew and respected the other's view. Gibbons had been party to all the discussions and disputes in the mid-eighties and so, while the rest of us can only speculate, he understood the reasons Moore had fallen out with DC. He, like Moore, was keen to ensure that DC didn't water down the original book. His attitude to *Watchmen* spin-offs was only a hair more generous than Moore's: 'As far as I'm concerned, what Alan and I did was the *Watchmen* graphic novel and a couple of illustrations that came out at the same time. Everything else – the movie, the game, the prequels – are really not canon. They're subsidiary. They're not really *Watchmen*. They're just something different.' In 2011, he did provide a quote for the *Before Watchmen* launch, but it sounded so lukewarm many commentators were surprised DC used it: 'The original series of *Watchmen* is the complete story that Alan Moore and I wanted to tell. However, I appreciate DC's reasons for this initiative and the wish of the artists and writers involved to pay tribute to our work. May these new additions have the success they desire.' Gibbons remained on good terms with the publisher overall, though, and has continued to work for them.

As DC geared up for the release of the movie of *Watchmen*, they wanted to market a one-off *Black Freighter* comic that took the panels of the pirate comic-within-a-comic interspersed throughout *Watchmen* and wove them together into a complete comic book. Moore said that he didn't like the idea, but as long as his name wasn't on it he didn't mind if Gibbons approved. When Gibbons remarked, 'DC said that they expected you to be quietly compliant', Moore's hackles were raised; he had become convinced that the publisher had begun using his friends against him.

Steve Moore had not worked for DC for two years, and felt he had been blacklisted. He was surprised, then, to be offered the chance to write the tie-in novel for the *Watchmen* movie (he had previously novelised *V for Vendetta*). He was nursing his dying brother at the time, and the book would represent useful income. But shortly after Alan had refused to put his name to the *Black Freighter* comic, Steve received a letter from Warner Books saying they had decided not to publish a novelisation. Alan Moore believed he saw a connection: 'At that moment I suddenly understood what they had meant by "We expect Alan to be quietly compliant". Of course it's all deniable. That is the marvel of these people, they always have complete deniability, but I know what I think and what I think is that they, knowing that Steve had got a terminally ill brother decided that this would be the thing that would put pressure upon me so that I could not refuse.' News website Comics Alliance reported this under the headline 'Alan Moore Goes Beyond Paranoid in His Latest Crazy Old Man Rant'.

Certainly there were more innocent – and perhaps more plausible – explanations. When anyone except Alan Moore wrote ABC comics, Steve Moore included, orders dropped dramatically. And a number of sources have stated that the *Watchmen* novelisation was cancelled at the request of director Zack Snyder, specifically because he assumed publishing it would offend the comic's author. For Moore, however, 'the only perceptions that were important in this were mine.

This was what I perceived had happened ... short of an explanation of what "We expect Alan to be quietly compliant" meant, which I've never received, that still is the only scenario that makes any sense to me. So I said to Dave Gibbons, "For the sake of our friendship, Dave, I think it would be better if you and I did not discuss *Watchmen* ever again." Obviously, it was something that both of us felt a little upset about, but it was the only way that I could stop Dave from ever being used to pass on creepy little messages to me, with or without his knowledge.'

Moore was engineering a situation whereby even indirect communication with DC was cut off. *From Hell* and *LXG* producer Don Murphy saw a pattern: 'There are some people who aren't happy if they aren't complaining. It suits them to be able to blame other people, blame companies and blame the world because that means they don't have to look in the mirrors and be responsible.' He cited the example of the 'twisted logic' with which Moore had attacked Dave Gibbons, and said the same applied to 'Steve Bissette, the lovely Karen Berger, Scott Dunbier who ate his crap for years, Marvel, DC, me and many many others. He's an unhappy person, and that's a real shame because he is talented as hell.' Independently, Dez Skinn had reached much the same conclusion: 'One internet wag said: "Someday the world will run out of bridges, because Alan Moore will have burnt them all." It would be a terrible waste of talent were that to happen, but unlike say the more politically savvy Neil Gaiman, he does seem to be running out of artists and publishers. Even his audience is far smaller than in the old days.'

Are Murphy and Skinn right? Moore's most recent comics work has come from Top Shelf and Avatar, established publishers, but small fry. Avatar, the larger of the two, averages something like a 0.8 per cent share of the retail market, while DC and Marvel each have about a third. That said, Top Shelf were able to place *Nemo: Heart of Ice* at the top of the graphic novel charts in a busy month that also saw new *Batman*, *Walking Dead* and *Adventure Time* titles and a *Doctor Who/Star Trek* crossover, all of which did well. *Watchmen*, *The Killing Joke* and *V for Vendetta* are perennial sellers, but his new work does better still: Moore's only new release in 2011, *Century 1969*, ranked third in the annual charts, after two *Walking Dead* collections, and the following year's *Century 2009* was the only graphic novel in the top ten that wasn't a *Batman* or *Walking Dead* title. Moore can still shift more comics than most.

People in the comics industry sometimes have a skewed view of where the

'mainstream' is. The best-selling comic in August 2006, the month *Lost Girls* was released, was *Justice League of America* #1, a relaunch of a title teaming up DC's most popular superheroes, written by thriller novelist Brad Meltzer. It sold 212,178 copies. This was an exceptional number (number two on the chart, Marvel's *New Avengers* #12, sold 153,970). Nevertheless, at $75 a copy, the dollar sales of the first two print runs of *Lost Girls* added up to $1.5 million, while *Justice League* #1 made $846,590. Even in terms of unit sales, *Lost Girls* outdid the last regular comic books Moore had written for DC the previous year, *Promethea* #32 (15,833 copies) and *Tom Strong* #36 (12,193 copies). And it was *Lost Girls* – and its creators – that got the critical attention. Moore had produced exactly the sort of comic he had been hoping to create as far back as *Warrior*: daring, personal and utterly uncompromised, with high production values – a showcase of storytelling techniques that couldn't work in any other medium, and which raked in acclaim while being profitable for all concerned. The fact that there was no chance whatsoever that anyone would ever option the movie rights wasn't a drawback, it was the icing on the cake.

So whatever happened to Alan Moore?

For most of his career, Moore has been physically distinctive, but it would be a serious mistake to think that he was any kind of outsider. He's best thought of as encapsulating what was going on around him in the comics industry. He wasn't the only person writing more worldly British comics in the post-*2000AD* era; or dark superhero comics that appealed to sixth-form boys in the mid-eighties; or who came a cropper self-publishing in the nineties as the market crashed; or who became a demigod to sections of the fanboy population which inherited the Earth in the internet age. Even being a comic book creator who saw movie studios run off with his creations made him part of a crowd; he wasn't being singled out. Moore wrote landmark comic books that were hugely influential, but if he had stuck to his office job processing invoices for Pipeline Constructors Ltd, Frank Miller would still have written *Daredevil* and *The Dark Knight*, Art Spiegelman would still have written *Maus*, DC would have revamped their line. Karen Berger may not have had the impetus to seek out British writers, but there was a whole cohort of creators at *2000AD* who would have built careers for themselves. Batman would still be a major character if *The Killing Joke* hadn't been written (though it's possible the Joker wouldn't be *quite* so popular). And for all that *Watchmen* is an important, beautifully crafted book, and extremely influential, there would still be graphic novels if it had never existed, just as there would still be movies if *Citizen Kane* had never been made.

There are many other 'name' comic book writers besides Alan Moore. A list limited to British writers often mentioned in the same breath would include people like Neil Gaiman, Grant Morrison, Mark Millar and Warren Ellis. All have creative autonomy, distinctive voices and enough of a following that they can switch publishers, even media, and take a large chunk of their fanbase with them. There are movie versions of their comics, they've made efforts to write more than superhero stories, they have done experimental work, they have a satirical streak. Ten years ago, it would have been easy to say Moore was in the same category as these creators, albeit one who came to prominence a couple of years earlier, and whose disputes with his editors were noisier.

Now, though, Moore really is sui generis. His contemporaries have embraced what wealth and status they can. They'll be flattered if a senior editor at Marvel or DC headhunts them for a high-profile superhero project. They'll take transatlantic flights to meet movie producers or attend Comic-Con. There is nothing wrong with this – most freelance writers would envy them such opportunities. What marks Moore out is his wilful rejection of playing that game. He stays in Northampton and self-publishes a magazine with articles about bus lanes and how to make trifle. Without an agent or an attempt to find a publisher, he's spent seven years (so far) writing a novel that, when finished, will be about the same length as the Old and New Testaments put together, and which he's admitted may not be readable, conceding that 'certainly the last chapter, the Lucia Joyce chapter, nobody is going to get through that, it's brilliant but it's completely unfathomable'.

Has Moore been forced into the position in which he finds himself? Not by others. He and DC may have had their differences, yet, according to Moore, the publisher offered him 'probably a couple of million dollars' to work on *Before Watchmen*. Recently Marvel bought the rights to Marvelman, and it's hard to imagine they would do anything but bite Moore's arm off if he wanted to return to the character. But there's little either company can offer him, and he evidently has no interest in Hollywood. He works only with people he wants to work with. He carefully reads his contracts with Top Shelf and Avatar, but admits 'I still don't get a lawyer to look at things, because that seems to me mistrustful. Yes, I know that sounds stupid, given that it's obviously an industry I mistrust, but I do really prefer to be working with people on the assumption everyone's being honest with each other. I'd rather not work with people than be in a continual state of mistrust.'

So is his situation the result of a quirk of personality? At the end of 2012, Moore recounted a little family history to the *Observer*:

> He hates being coerced, whatever the financial incentive, and it may well be something in the blood. His great-grandfather Ginger, the hard-drinking cartoonist, was at the turn of the twentieth century offered the chance to become the director of a glass company in town, Moore claims. He was told: 'You'll make millions! The only condition is that you stay out of the pub for two weeks.' The answer, inevitably, was no; and Vernon spent the rest of his life walking past the mansion of the man who took the job. 'But I'm immensely proud of that. Turning something down because *it wasn't what you wanted to do*. This stuff . . . it's probably in the genes.'

Moore sees the rejection of money as virtuous: 'You can't buy that kind of empowerment. To just know that as far as you are aware, you have not got a price; that there is not an amount of money large enough to make you compromise even a tiny bit of principle that, as it turned out, would make no practical difference anyway. I'd advise everyone to do it, otherwise you're going to end up mastered by money and that's not a thing you want ruling your life.'

It's easy to talk about not selling your soul to the corporations if you don't have to worry about money. Moore's first professional sale was an illustration of Elvis Costello, who sang of John Lennon (in 'The Other Side of Summer'), 'Was it a millionaire who said "imagine no possessions"?' It's an awkward fact that Moore has been financially secure, and able to work on long-term or uncommercial projects, thanks in large part to the income he's had over the years from his DC work like *Watchmen*. Lennon lived in an apartment overlooking Central Park with a refrigerated wardrobe for his fur coats; Alan Moore does not. 'I've got enough money to be comfortable. I live comfortably, I can pay the bills at the end of every month.' It's true that he has *chosen* not to be rich by turning down 'millions', but he's not sitting on a miser's hoard. When he finds himself with a surplus of cash, Moore has used it to donate Christmas hampers to poor residents of the Boroughs,

and he sponsors the Northampton Kings basketball team, made up of kids from the same deprived area of the town.

Alan Moore is in a position now to do what he wants. So the question becomes whether what he wants to do is worthwhile, and – perhaps easier to judge – whether he's succeeding in the terms that he's laid out for himself.

When America's Best Comics started out, Moore was prolific, imaginative and versatile; it's a range that includes some of his most baroque formal work, but also some of his most enjoyable action-adventure romps. But it failed in at least one of the terms Moore set for it. In April 2000, he told *Tripwire*, 'What I'd really like in an ideal world would be for me to be able to continue doing ABC for another few years and establish it as a thriving, vital comic line.' After falling out with DC, however, Moore chose to end the ongoing story in an event that saw all the other ABC characters team up but fail to prevent Promethea from ushering in the Apocalypse. DC have since shown little enthusiasm for continuing the line without him, and have cancelled a couple of follow-up titles by the series' co-creators mid-series. They have kept all Moore's material in print, but taken the ABC branding off later reprints, so *The League of Extraordinary Gentlemen* and *Promethea* have joined *V for Vendetta* under the Vertigo banner. ABC feels a little like ancient history.

So if Moore is not a comics writer now, what is he? Any answer to that has to tackle the issue of Moore the magician. Even if 'magic' is thought of simply as an oblique strategy Moore uses to improve his creative output, the problem remains that his concept of magic is broad enough to allow him to claim kinship with any creative person he chooses to: 'If you start looking beyond the confines of self-declared magicians, then it becomes increasingly difficult to find an artist who wasn't in some way inspired either by an occult organisation or an occult school of thought or by some personal vision.'

In practice, he has identified a fairly narrow artistic, mainly literary, magical tradition. In an introduction to a comics adaptation of William Hope Hodgson's *The House on the Borderland*, Moore praises the novel for 'the aura and charisma that surround it, evident before the book is even opened. The mad whirlpool of fantastic imagery and wildly, apocalyptic notions it contains.' He declares it to be part of 'a buried treasure seam of literature which might immeasurably enrich our current largely moribund cultural landscape, if only it were not buried, had not been ruthlessly buried alive in the first instance', and goes on to name Poe, Lovecraft and Stoker as belonging to this tradition, as well as the less well-known Hodgson, Lord Dunsany, Clark Ashton Smith, Arthur Machen, M.P. Shiel, Algernon Blackwood and David Lindsay, and more recent exponents Angela Carter, M. John Harrison, Jack Trevor Story, Mervyn Peake and Maurice Richardson. Elsewhere, he's described Robert Anton Wilson, Iain Sinclair and Michael Moorcock in similar terms, and talked of 'Dee, Machen, Blake, Dunsany, Hodgson, Bunyan, the Duchess of Newcastle. Stenographers of the apocalypse'.

Academics have also attempted to locate Moore within an existing tradition. Annalisa Di Liddo concludes her study of Moore's work, *Comics as Performance, Fiction as Scalpel*, by placing him alongside Angela Carter (Di Liddo wrote her thesis on Carter), Iain Sinclair and Peter Ackroyd, with honourable mentions for Michael Moorcock and Kathy Acker, all of whom have 'a significantly shared artistic terrain, the main focus of which ultimately is reflection on the idea of identity: hence the recovery of tradition through new codes and modalities of representation; the focus on gender, ethnic and class trouble; the consideration of otherness and its contribution to the evolution of the UK; and the examination and reassessment of the locations of Englishness'.

This makes for a long list, but the artists on it have many shared characteristics and literary interests. More relevantly, an examination of their lives and work allows us to triangulate a sense of what Moore now aspires towards.

In 2002, Moore wrote an introduction for an edition of one of his favourite books, *Voyage to Arcturus* by David Lindsay (1876–1945), a phantasmagorical allegory about a man transported to an alien world. He 'demands that David Lindsay be considered not as a mere fascinating one-off, as a brilliant maverick, but as one worthy and deserving of that shamanistic mantle; of the British visionary and apocalyptic legacy'. Again, he seeks to place an apparently outlying author firmly within an existing tradition. After mentioning Henry Treece and Nicholas Moore, he invokes 'the Britannic honour roll of seers and suckers and transported ranters, in that noble foam-flecked crew with Bunyan, Moorcock, Bulwer-Lytton, Machen, Lord Dunsany, Robert Aickman, Iain Sinclair, M. John Harrison, Hope Mirrlees and William Hope Hodgson, and there is David Lindsay, one that almost got away'. He goes on to describe the qualities that he feels make Lindsay's book noteworthy:

> There is more to this than run-amok fantasy trilogies turning the marvellous into the irritatingly ubiquitous, that carpet every bookchain. There is more to this than fiction. These are crystal-gazings, reconnaissance missions, unmanned camera-drones to map the dreamtime from high-altitude, to overlook the Overworld. This is Revelation as a cottage industry, a local craft tradition. Burning, screaming angels at the bring-and-buy . . . In *A Voyage to Arcturus* it is not difficult to glimpse the heavily-masked blueprint for an idiosyncratic, beautifully deranged utopia. Civilisation suddenly illuminated by an understanding of its own enslavement in the Empire of the Senses. Men and women made free from the limits and restrictions of their psyches, their identities, able to grow new spiritual appendages or apertures to counteract the vagaries of their existence, of Crystalman's treacherous and endlessly refracting mirror-maze dominion . . . There are other tentative utopian suggestions in the text, occasions when one might conclude that Lindsay is attempting to float his own scientific theories in the guise of fantasy.

Needless to say, Moore is describing himself as efficiently as he is Lindsay. Moore often stresses his kinship with the lives led by the authors on his list, not just the contents of their books. Most (although not all) were writers of genre stories rather than great literary works, but to Moore that's a strength. Comparing himself to H.P. Lovecraft (1890–1937), he's said, 'We're both pulp writers trying to express our vision of the truth . . . you tend to work faster as a pulp writer and you're absolved of literary obligations and pretentions. Your vision is purer'.

In recent years, he has produced a number of projects based on Lovecraftian themes. The first was a prose story, 'The Courtyard', set in the present day (and later adapted for comics by Antony Johnston). Moore decided to write a sequel, *Neonomicon*. Freely admitting that he took the job because he needed the money, thanks to a combination of late royalty payments and an unexpected tax bill, he was nevertheless keen to create a work that depicted the horrors Lovecraft only alluded to in his stories, 'to actually put back some of the objectionable elements that Lovecraft himself censored, or that people since Lovecraft, who have been writing pastiches, have decided to leave out. Like the racism, the anti-Semitism, the sexism, the sexual phobias which are kind of apparent in all of Lovecraft's slimy phallic or vaginal monsters'. The result is suitably nasty, although the metatextual criticism of Lovecraft's prejudices is overshadowed by a brutal, explicit rape scene that takes up almost a whole issue. Moore, who had once said 'there isn't a Too Far. And if there is, it's absolutely the place to be seen', now admitted to an interviewer, 'Looking back, yes, maybe I have gone too far – but it's still a good story.' In late 2012 it was announced that Moore would be writing a longer series, *Providence*, based around the life of Lovecraft himself.

He has also become a prominent advocate for the artist Austin Osman Spare (1886–1956), writing an introduction to the brochure for an exhibition commemorating the fiftieth anniversary of Spare's death, and appearing on *The Culture Show* in 2010 to argue that 'not only was he an incredible artist, he was also in my opinion possibly the greatest English magician of the twentieth century'. While Spare during his lifetime enjoyed a strong reputation as a portrait painter and for his nudes, he also produced works of occult significance, often inspired by dreams or produced using automatic drawing techniques. Moore – who has a nude by Spare hanging in his front room – praises him because 'He kind of completely eschewed the gallery art scene and his middle-class upbringing and just said "I am going to move to Brixton amongst prostitutes and crooks, because I trust them and I am never going to exhibit other than in the back rooms of pubs." And he excommunicated the whole of the human race and even he said later perhaps that was going a bit too far. You have got to admire the man, wonderful artist, brilliant magician.' This, of course, mirrors Moore's own resistance to moving out of the working-class areas of Northampton.

Moore sees the 'magical' writers on his list as having a political purpose, or at least a practical, positive effect on society:

> I find myself very attracted to the Apocalypse school of poets, who are completely forgotten these days, and in fact nobody can understand why they were called Apocalypse poets when all they talked about was nature: little birds sitting in trees, and flowers . . . The big totem of Apocalypse poets was Dylan Thomas. [The movement] would have included people like Henry Treece and a lot of other forgotten names. But what they were, what they meant by 'apocalypse', was simply revelation. And that other thing in the world is

> kind of pregnant with revelation if you're somebody who comes equipped with the right kind of eyes and the right kind of phrasebook, if you like, for decoding . . . At the moment, I feel that hopefully in some of the pieces that I'm doing, I might be providing attitudes, mental tools, ways of looking at things, that could actually be of use in these otherwise turbulent times. That's the plan.

Virtually everything Moore has produced in recent years has at least an echo of his belief that the world is on the verge of a transition to a new state. He has clarified when he feels the apocalypse will occur: 'The time that I'd heard, and this is both from conventional sources and from imaginary friends when I was in my more extreme magical states, (that's not to say there's any validity to them at all, just feelings that I got), is that there is probably some sort of event looming between 2012 and 2017.' And in *Snakes and Ladders*, he described what it would feel like: 'As species or as individual, we approach the moment when the lights go on, the point of comprehension and of revelation. Of Apocalypse. The sum of human information doubles ever faster, every fifteen months and counting. The reaction at the core of us tips over into critical. Our crisis is approaching, though it may be in the late-Victorian pornographic sense. Pulse racing, human history convulses, nearing orgasm.'

Moore's work has often dealt with apocalyptic themes. When, in 2005, the magazine *The End is Nigh* drew up an 'Alan Moore Apocalography – the complete apocalyptic works', they found thirty-two stories that qualified. When Promethea ushers in the Apocalypse, in Moore's most positive depiction of what he envisions might be coming, the happening represents a welcome shift. As Promethea explains: 'Don't be frightened. Our lives are all a story we've been telling to ourselves. Whiling away the long afraid night of our human ignorance. But now we are grown. Now the night is over. Now there is light.' Moore is, however, keen to stress that he thinks 'there is great change likely to occur, but whether that's for the better or not, I really don't know'. Elsewhere, he's suggested the human race may not survive this apocalypse.

But for all this talk of global transformation, the artists Moore identifies with often have a strong sense of place. Likewise, much of his recent work has been about his home town of Northampton. In practical terms, this means he has come full circle, back to the sort of community activism he was involved with when he began his career working for *ANoN* and *The Back-Street Bugle*. Consistent with that, he resurrected the Mad Love imprint to produce a magazine called *Dodgem Logic*, using the same title as the fanzine he had not been 'together enough' to compile in 1975. Debuting in December 2009, *Dodgem Logic* looked like an old school underground fanzine, albeit one with exceptionally high production values. Its contents included an essay from Moore about the underground press that began by quoting journalist H.L. Mencken's assertion that 'freedom of the press is limited to those who own one', as well as cheap recipes, a how-to guide on guerilla gardening, illustrations by Kevin O'Neill and comedian Josie Long, and articles about feminism by Melinda Gebbie, Northampton's notable rock concerts by Gary Ingham and Twitter by comedy writer Graham Linehan. The issue came with a CD of tracks by Northampton musicians.

It was a print magazine in the internet age, a deliberate decision: 'I see a chasm opening between the information-rich and information-poor and, possibly because of my own background, age and prejudices, I believe that something funny, lovely and informative that is available to everyone without the need for a device or internet connection is the option which, to me, makes most sense both emotionally and ethically.' Moore was internet-savvy enough to spot that by assembling an eclectic selection of items he found personally interesting, he had basically invented 'a new form of blog that avoids the internet altogether'. *Wired* were impressed, declaring that '*Dodgem Logic*'s spirit of triumphant creative individualism celebrates Moore's individualist philosophy, delivering a perfectly timed message for a world filled with failing states and superpowers.'

It was a tough sell, though, and while Moore hoped other people might create local offshoots of the magazine, replacing the Northampton content with material from their own towns, these failed to materialise. Moore planned to fund six issues, until it got on its feet; the magazine lasted only a little longer, eight issues, until spring 2011. Moore announced in the editorial for #8 that he had had 'some of the best fun that I can remember having in my career', but 'our initial strategy of paying contributors, high production values, no stinking capitalist advertising and an affordably low cost cover price (basically "let's do everything backwards and see what happens") seems not to have worked'.

Dodgem Logic #5 spoofed a *Vanity Fair* cover by featuring a picture of Spring

Boroughs resident Phil, 'a bad lad and a bad dad', holding an albino ferret in one hand and a hatchet in the other, and captions enticing us to read about 'Brian, Dougie, Frankie, Claire, Rosalind, Marion, Warren, Charlie and George'. Does this demonstrate a witty satire on the priorities of celebrity culture, or does it indicate that Moore's concerns are now meaningless to anyone who doesn't live within sight of the National Lift Tower? How are we to take a statement like: 'I've travelled very little, I have never lived anywhere else other than Northampton. Consequently, this is my microcosm. The entire of the human world seems to me to boil down to these streets, to this history, these anecdotes.' Moore doesn't have a passport; he's left the UK only a handful of times. He has said of his second novel, *Jerusalem*, 'My earlier book *Voice of the Fire* was set within Northampton/ Northamptonshire, but this book is a lot less cosmopolitan and far reaching'. Even acknowledging that such remarks are meant lightly, there's a sense of agoraphobia within them, rather than empowerment.

One of the main characters in *Halo Jones*, Rodice, always panics at the thought of going outside. But perhaps we see a clearer echo of Moore in the character Brinna, a rich old lady who lives with Halo and Rodice. In 1986, Moore said: 'Brinna is someone who is too rich to need to live in the Hoop but who is emotionally trapped there by her basic *nostalgie de la boue*, which roughly translates as "nostalgia for the mud". It's like when rich people go and live in Greenwich Village because they like the atmosphere and liveliness that poverty often brings with it. In her way, Brinna is as helpless to escape the Hoop as anyone else is, despite her money, and it is this which eventually kills her.' Is Moore's nostalgia for the mud of Northampton an indication he's 'helpless'? Moore clearly doesn't think so, and this sequence from *Big Numbers* #1 (1990) is evidence it was his position when the world was his oyster.

Moore is attempting to make a point that *wherever* we live is important. For

him it's Northampton, for us it should be where *we* live: 'They're all wonderful. And rather than berating them or complaining about them, we should actually appreciate the things that are mythical and powerful about them.'

Meanwhile, without any intervention on his part, Moore was having a very visible impact on the face of political activism around the world:

> From New York, to London, to Sydney, to Cologne, to Bucharest, there has been a wave of protests against politicians, banks and financial institutions. Anybody watching coverage of the demonstrations may have been struck by a repeated motif – a strangely stylised mask of Guy Fawkes with a moustache and pointy beard.

With CCTV cameras and police videotaping of demonstrations now routine, protestors began wearing *V for Vendetta* masks to render themselves anonymous. Fittingly, it was members of a group called Anonymous, a collective of computer hackers, who were the first to adopt the V masks, outside offices of the Church of Scientology in March 2008. Moore admitted to *Entertainment Weekly*, 'that pleased me. That gave me a warm little glow,' and he told Laura Sneddon of the *Independent*: 'Obviously I couldn't say that I am universally behind everything that they might do in the future, you know? But sort of so far at least I've got a huge amount of admiration for the stuff that Anonymous and LulzSec and people like that have been doing. They are, they seem to be, genuinely frightening authority in general because they're very hard to root out or track down and they seem to be very efficient in digging up information that we are entitled to know.'

The use of the mask became more widespread in 2011, during the 'Occupy' protests against governments, banks and corporations implicated in the global banking crisis. The BBC reported that 100,000 masks were being sold a year, and by November 2012, the United Arab Emirates had banned them from being worn during National Day celebrations, while security forces confiscated stocks from shops. Many journalists have noted that the anti-corporate demonstrators are channelling money to one of the world's largest entertainment corporations, Warners, who own the rights to the masks – it's reported less often that the creators, including Dez Skinn, are also entitled to their cut (in David Lloyd's case, a reported £50,000 a year).

Reporting on the V mask's 'inescapable presence at the anti-capitalist protests around the world', Britain's *Channel 4 News* sent Moore to the Occupy demonstration outside St Paul's Cathedral, from where he declared, 'It's a bit surprising when some of your characters who you thought you'd made up suddenly seem to escape into ordinary reality . . . I'm amazed, I'm very impressed and I'm rather touched. The people here are amazing. I think that this is probably the best-organised and most forward-thinking protest that I've ever had experience of.' He later told the *Observer* that the mask

> turns protests into performances. The mask is very operatic; it creates a sense of romance and drama. I mean, protesting, protest marches, they can be very demanding, very gruelling. They can be quite dismal. They're things that have to be done, but that doesn't necessarily mean that they're tremendously enjoyable – whereas actually, they should be . . . I think it's appropriate that this generation of protesters have made their rebellion into something the public at large can engage with more readily than with half-hearted chants, with that traditional, downtrodden sort of British protest. These people look like they're *having a good time*. And that sends out a tremendous message.

'If there's one quality in Alan Moore that I envy more than any other,' Eddie Campbell said in 1986, 'it is simply his understanding of the temper of our times.' Is it possible for Moore to be in tune with a generation of protesters who organise via social media, when the nearest he has ever got to a hashtag is the sticker on a large tin he keeps half-hidden in his kitchen? When protestors wear the V mask, are they proclaiming their sympathy for Moore's political positions?

There's some evidence that representatives of Anonymous are familiar with the philosophy behind *V for Vendetta*. The nature of the group is anarchic: they don't have 'an official spokesman' or leadership, and they've issued videos highly reminiscent of V's video address to the nation. This is not, however, always the case with the street protests. Many journalists covering the Occupy protests asked protestors why they wore the V masks; the BBC quoted one as saying, 'It's a visual thing, it sets us apart from the hippies and the socialists and gives us our own identity. We're about bypassing governments and starting from the bottom.' And the net effect of the Occupy movement, a coalition of various political positions,

THE MOVIE V FOR VENDETTA IS BASED ON A GRAPHIC NOVEL (BOOK SIZED COMIC BOOK), A POWERFUL WORK OF ART WITH REVOLUTIONARY IMPLICATIONS. IT'S A SHAME THAT THE ESSENTIAL POINT OF THE STORY--THAT FREEDOM AND GOVERNMENT CAN NEVER CO-EXIST--HAS BEEN WATERED DOWN TO MAKE V SAFE FOR A BIG HOLLYWOOD RELEASE.

WHY GUY FAWKES?

V WEARS A GUY FAWKES MASK-- A SYMBOL OF A MAN WHO TRIED TO BLOWUP PARLIAMENT, THE SEAT OF BRITISH GOVERNMENT. WHY? BECAUSE V KNOWS THAT THE GOVERNMENT HE FIGHTS CANNOT BE REFORMED OR REPLACED BY A DIFFERENT GOVERNMENT.

THE TRUTH

WE DO NOT LIVE IN A TRUE DEMOCRACY. CRUCIAL DECISIONS THAT DIRECTLY AFFECT OUR LIVES HAVE BEEN LEFT UP TO FIGURES OF AUTHORITY TO DECIDE FOR US.

THE CRISIS

WAR...TORTURE CAMPS...POWER IN THE HANDS OF AN UNACCOUNTABLE FEW...A POPULATION NUMBED, DECEIVED, FRIGHTENED INTO SUBMISSION. CONSTANT SURVEILLANCE BY AN EVER-GROWING POLICE STATE.

SOUND FAMILIAR?

THIS ISN'T JUST THE MOVIES! OUR SOCIETY, OUR PLANET, IS APPROACHING CATASTROPHE UNDER THE CAPITALIST SYSTEM OF EXPLOITATION AND PLUNDER. WE ARE AT A TURNING PONT IN HISTORY. THE ELITES ARE EXTENDING THEIR SYSTEMS OF CONTROL AND DOMINATION BECAUSE THEY EXPECT RESISTANCE. AND THEY'RE DAMN WELL GONNA GET IT.

WHAT IS ANARCHY?

ANARCHY IS THE IDEA THAT INDIVIDUALS HAVE THE CAPACITY AS WELL AS THE RIGHT TO THINK FOR THEMSELVES, MAKE DECISIONS THAT DIRECTLY AFFECT THEIR OWN LIVES, AND ULTIMATELY, SELF-GOVERN. IT IS EACH PERSON'S RESPONSIBILTY TO REALIZE THIS FREEDOM AND LIVE IN BALANCE WITH OTHERS, AS WELL AS THE EARTH. THERE ARE ANARCHISTS IN YOUR CITY. WE'RE WORKING TO BUILD A NEW WORLD EVEN AS WE FIGHT TO DISMANTLE THE OLD ONE. FIND US!

FOR MORE INFORMATION: VISIT AFORANARCHY.COM

was perhaps closer to the movie's rather vague protest against Bush-era policies than the comic's specific alternative of anarchism; the Channel 4 reporter noted that Moore maintained a diplomatic silence when protestors he talked to mentioned the movie. While the V of the comic is rebelling against an oppressive government, the book stresses the roles of individuals, rather than any mass protest. V's technique is one of targeting individuals for assassination or political indoctrination. There's not even a near equivalent in the book to the movie's scenes of a crowd of protesters all wearing V masks. At least one anarchist was moved to circulate a pamphlet exhorting people to seek out the original (see facing page).

Perhaps as a similar corrective, Moore has contributed articles and interviews to Occupy publications such as *Occupy Comics* (2013), offering general advice and historical context. He suggests that psychogeography might help root the protests, as it is

> derived at least in part from Situationist conceptions of the city, is a means by which a territory can be understood and owned, an occupation in the intellectual sense. Those able to extract the deepest information from a place are those most able to assert some measure of control on that environment, or at least on the way it is perceived. At the same time, by mining seams of buried or excluded information, it is possible to reinvest a site with the significance and meaning which contemporary town planning and commercial vested interests have removed from it.

When pushed, Moore can easily justify it in more accessible terms: 'Illuminate your little patch of ground, the people that you know, the things that you want to commemorate. Light them up with your art, with your music, with your writing, with whatever it is that you do. Do that, and little by little it might gradually get to be, if not a better world, then a better understood world.'

Moore's most affectionate work in this vein takes as its subject his friend and mentor Steve Moore. *Unearthing* was originally a prose piece commissioned by Iain Sinclair for the psychogeographical anthology *London: City of Disappearances*. Lex Records produced a lavish boxset containing Moore's reading of the piece (2010), and three years later an illustrated book was issued. The release of the box set led to some glowing coverage in the mainstream press. The writing is unmistakably Alan's, but the story is charming in a way that's rare for his work.

Steve Moore himself 'thought the piece would disappear as one of Alan's "minor works". Obviously it didn't happen like that!'

Much of Moore's recent output seems to be a conscious summation of his life and art to this point. The most explicit example has to be the long-promised *Moon and Serpent Bumper Book of Magic*, co-written with Steve Moore and illustrated by artists such as Kevin O'Neill, Melinda Gebbie, John Coulthart and José Villarrubia. It's a 'how-to' guide for the Moores' brand of magic, but also a playful history of the occult that Alan and Steve Moore have painstakingly researched, and have been working on in its current form since at least 2007 (it started life as a magazine called *Atziluth* three or four years earlier). Steve Moore has linked the projects: 'Alan and I tend to see all this as an ongoing process, somehow. *Somnium* [and] the non-fiction Selene book [both by Steve Moore], *Unearthing*, Alan's forthcoming novel *Jerusalem*, *The Bumper Book Of Magic* . . . they all seem to be part of some sort of vague, barely defined *Moon and Serpent* project to provide an alternative view to simple materialistic reality.'

Moore continues to write *The League of Extraordinary Gentlemen*, but acknowledges that the project has evolved: 'I don't think either Kevin [O'Neill] or I see that in the context of comics anymore. For me, it's one of the things I do, like the new novel, or the music I intermittently work on, or the book of magic. These are all things I do. I don't think of them in the context of the different media that I do them in. I still do think of new things to do with the comic medium, but now they're all pretty much sublimated into the *League*.'

The early volumes of *The League of Extraordinary Gentlemen* are among Moore's most accessible stories. Even if you've not read *King Solomon's Mines* or can't immediately recall that Mina Harker is a character from *Dracula*, Moore spends the first couple of issues introducing his cast and efficiently defining their personalities and capabilities. The comic itself tells a linear story, with the most baroque narrative technique in the first twelve issues being a single flashback. There's no need to understand the history of the comics industry, Northampton or the Qabalah. It's a comic that anyone, even if they've never heard of Alan Moore or ever read such work before, can pick up and enjoy.

The Black Dossier was always intended to be a little more convoluted, and Moore was concerned at the time that the way DC marketed it as a straight continuation of the series would confuse people. The third volume, *Century* (2009–12), shifts the premise of the series away from a crowd-pleasing steampunk literary mash-up to something more difficult to explain and which needs to be framed for its audience. It's composed of three 80-page issues, set in 1910, 1969 and 2009, each of which is self-contained but forms part of an overarching story about an attempt by a group of occultists to create a Moonchild, an Antichrist-like being who will usher in the Apocalypse. The series has an elaborate continuity of its own, but not one you'd know even if you'd read the main comic strip: the two surviving members of the League from Volume One, Quatermain and Mina, are now immortal – a fact revealed only in a text story in the back of Volume Two – and are joined by Orlando, introduced in a sequence for *The Black Dossier*.

Throughout *Century*, Moore is playing an ornate game about art imitating life imitating art. The occultists are not simply famous fictional practitioners of the arcane arts, they're also stand-ins for real-life occultists, mostly members of Aleister Crowley's Order of the Golden Dawn. *Century*'s 'Oliver Haddo', for example, is from Somerset Maugham's 1908 novel *The Magician*, a character Maugham used to parody Crowley, though Moore's Haddo perhaps tacks more closely to Crowley himself. In real life, Crowley wrote a critique of *The Magician* as Haddo for *Vanity Fair*, and accused Maugham of cobbling together his book from a variety of other people's novels . . . which, of course, is what Moore is openly doing.

There are also echoes of Moore's own life. Mina, like her author, goes to a free concert in Hyde Park in 1969 and has an acid trip. She, Quatermain and Orlando have a fractious polyamorous relationship, and our heroes mourn that the optimism of the sixties has given way to a dreary dystopian future. The book's touchstones are those that loom large in Moore's own understanding of twentieth-century literature, rather than an attempt at a general survey – he finds key roles for William Hope Hodgson's Carnacki, Captain Miracle (a superhero created in 1960 by Mick Anglo, who'd been responsible for Marvelman), and Iain Sinclair's Andrew Norton. Carnacki and Norton are portrayed as affectionate parodies of their original authors. All three books are about notions of the apocalypse, about the cheapening of art in the name of entertainment and the nature of fiction. With *Watchmen*, the more you know about the history of superhero comics, the more you'll get out of it. To best understand *Century*, you need to have some grounding in the life and beliefs of its writer. Reviewers with no sense of the subtext were clearly bewildered, and happy that the next League project, *Nemo: Heart of Ice*, returned to a more straightforward action-adventure narrative.

Those reviewers would presumably be equally baffled by *Jimmy's End*, a project written by Moore and located in the heart of the Boroughs and even deeper in his imaginative world. The series of five linked short films centre around the St James Working Men's Club in Northampton, and have a seedy, unsettling feel that's reminiscent of David Lynch's work. Moore features in a supporting role (in gold facepaint and silver suit) as the magical – we might dare venture 'heavenly' – Mr Metterton, who deals cards with DNA codes on them and makes pronouncements on the nature of reality. The series is directed by Mitch Jenkins and produced by the production company Orphans of the Storm set up in 2010 by Moore and Jenkins. It's a conscious attempt on Moore's part to create the sort of film he would like to see instead of adaptations of his superhero work. Moore did not need to put much money where his mouth is: the budget of the first part, *Act of Faith* was £11,000, which he suspected was less that the coffee budget for the *Watchmen* movie: 'This is it: I am horrified by the budgets of these films, almost as much as I am by the films themselves.' In 2013, Moore and Jenkins launched a successful Kickstarter appeal, squaring a circle that allowed them to fund the project without compromising it.

Since the beginning of 2005, though, Moore's main creative efforts have been directed towards his second prose novel, *Jerusalem*. Most reports have concentrated on its size, and Moore has estimated it will be 750,000 words long when completed (the length of the book you have in your hand plus *War and Peace*). The *Observer* reported in December 2012 that Moore was 'delighted if not a little concerned that having typed it all with single digits he has worn away the tips of his index fingers'.

Jerusalem will be a novel that maps out territory familiar from Moore's recent work: the history of Northampton (including Moore's family history), an exploration of fiction and imagination, and a discussion of magic and transcendence. The book consists of three parts, and each part has a different setting. As he explains: 'All three parts of the book have got elements of fantasy to them. The first part is about the Earthly domain of the Boroughs, and indeed the first part is called *The Boroughs*, and this is about eleven chapters that are all set in the material realm in Northampton, but it's not a straightforward realistic depiction, it has elements of quite outrageous fantasy as well. The second part is called *Man's Soul* and that entirely takes place on a higher plane above the Boroughs

in a fourth dimensional afterlife of sorts. The third part is a . . . it's very difficult to describe, it all gets a bit modernist, but in some ways it's a summary, a conclusion.'

That first part draws on anecdotes about local characters and an exploration of the town's history. Real life historical figures pop up, including Victorian fairy painter Richard Dadd, Lucia Joyce, Charlie Chaplin, William Blake and John Bunyan. There's a sequence involving a magic ritual in which Asmodeus is invoked, causing 'screaming pandemonium'. Some names have been changed or thinly disguised – there seems to be a Vernall family with a similar history to Moore's ancestors the Vernons. One main character, Alma Warren, is an illustrator, and appears to be a Moore analogue along the lines of Christina Gathercole in *Big Numbers*. She, like Moore, has a younger brother called Michael. There will be extracts, or possibly the full text of an imaginary children's book, *The Dead Dead Gang* illustrated by Alma that would seem to be the route into the second setting, a fictional realm 'brightly decorated with painted motifs'. Moore's description of the place as being 'constantly in flux, with details of the landscape metamorphosing and shifting like the details of a dream' suggests this is Ideaspace, or the Immateria. Above that is the third realm, a transcendental location akin to heaven.

The three realms are linked, containing echoes of each other. The Archangel Michael is a recurring character in the book, and manifests in all three realms. He has won a bar brawl in which golden blood was spilled, and is one of 'four master builders . . . crowbars of creation'. Moore has given a public reading of Chapter 24 of the book, 'Clouds Unfold', which is told from the point of view of the statue of the Archangel Michael atop Northampton's Guildhall. Consistent with Moore's belief that time is a solid structure, the Archangel experiences his entire life history simultaneously (unavoidably, there are echoes of *Watchmen*'s Dr Manhattan). It builds to a similar climax to *Snakes and Ladders*, in a moment where identities and experiences, good and bad, merge to create a perfect whole.

Moore's first novel, *Voice of the Fire,* was published soon after he had declared himself to be a magician, and it received little attention, let alone acclaim. He had made a conscious decision to avoid making it a superhero or science fiction story – although that was clearly what his fanbase wanted at the time. Moore's readers have since had twenty years to digest Moore the Magus. *Jerusalem* is a novel that only Alan Moore can write, both thematically and practically:

> I can take unfair advantage of my position. Only I could do this, only I could spend eight years of intense work on it, only I could actually recount what happened in that neighbourhood with those people, and only I am in a position where I could do that without worrying about getting it published. I don't need to go with a big publisher, they don't really have anything to offer me. It's not a big, popular book or a beach read, I'd much rather have a small publisher who had some understanding of what I was doing.

When *Jerusalem* appears, it will receive the level of attention that a major work by Alan Moore can now expect. After exploring his magical beliefs in comics, music, painting and performance art, Moore might have discovered that, ironically, it's unadorned prose that best gets across the worldview he has been developing and articulating all his life. It's unlikely to be his last major work, and it's foolish to judge a novel before it's even finished, but it clearly has the potential to be one of the larger landmarks in the terrain of his oeuvre . . . and at least a little baffling to the uninitiated:

> This is exactly the novel I wanted to write. I am really proud of it, I think it's sensational. That is, of course, just my own opinion. I am aware that conventional criticism will probably say that it's about ten times too long, that it's difficult in places, that some of the passages are deliberately alienating . . . it's going to be a very forbidding book in terms of its sheer size and because it's about the underclass. There is no better way of ensuring that you don't get a readership of your book than making it about underclass people . . . The only ambition I have for *Jerusalem* is for it to exist. I'm under no illusions that anybody is going to say this is the greatest book of the centuy. No, no, it's probably far too difficult for that. It's just an accurate expression of part of my life and part of my being that also includes lots of other subjects that have become part of that.

The endings of many of Moore's stories are neatly symmetrical. They loop back to the beginning, the threat of the apocalypse looms large, and as the narrative draws to a close, it's not always clear whether the protagonists are heroes or villains, whether they won or lost.

As above, so below.

On the face of it, Alan Moore has ended up almost exactly where he was before he sold his first professional drawing. He lives with his wife in Northampton, keenly aware of his roots in the town and of the modern world's encroachment in ways that promise great progress but often deliver upheaval, particularly to the poorest residents. He has sprawling writing projects underway, and rails against right-wing politicians and Northampton Council. Instead of tiny children, he has tiny grandchildren. (His eldest daughter, Leah, is now a successful comics writer in her own right.)

Many things have changed, of course. A young and hungry writer who sought out every opportunity and exploited it to the full has grown into someone defined more by who he won't work with. The man who thought he had landed his dream job when Dez Skinn was paying him £10 a page to write *Marvelman* now chooses not to make phone calls to New York or Hollywood that could earn him millions. Moore has a devoted audience, those who will lap up everything he releases and queue round the block to see him at an event. Again, there are two edges to that. Is a three-LP/three-CD reading of a short story about *Steve* Moore's life that comes with a dot matrix transcript and art prints and costs £50 the work of a man who's decoupled himself from the shackles of mere commerce to produce uncompromised art, or one who knows his fanbase will show up for anything and is just taking the piss?

Comics fans have a nostalgic streak. Moore's deconstruction of the superhero genre in the eighties is now as fondly remembered – and longer ago – than Lee and Kirby's revolution at Marvel was then. But Moore outgrew his personal warmth for superheroes. He has the advantage of a childhood that resists romanticisation. Where his nostalgic streak kicks in, his Rosebud, would seem to be the Arts Lab. Throughout his career, Alan Moore has clearly hankered for another place where he and his mates just get on and make art. *Warrior*, DC, Mad Love, ABC . . . Moore seems to have started out seeing each one as an Arts Lab with a marketing arm. He agrees that 'Arts Labs thinking has been an underlying factor in a lot of my subsequent work, it is how I do tend to organise projects: let's have fun, let's experiment. . . I'm basically still at the Arts Lab, it's just an incredibly enabled Arts Lab with whatever contributors I want. With the Arts Lab all of my needs to express myself, all my urges, had an outlet.' With *Moon and Serpent* – and Top Shelf, Knockabout, Avatar, the revived Mad Love and Orphans of the Storm – Moore has finally found a way to do his own thing, enjoy doing it and pay the bills.

Moore's as 'famous', however that's measured and whatever it's worth, as any living British writer who isn't J.K. Rowling. He has a continuing cultural impact. His – as he puts it – 'toxic influence' is reflected in many of today's comics, television shows and movies. Will his work endure? It has already, beyond any reasonable expectation – the year of his sixtieth birthday saw new editions of *Watchmen* and *Halo Jones* and *Unearthing* and . . . many others, even his *Empire Strikes Back Monthly* back-up strips. Will future generations sing his praises? It's notoriously difficult to predict. Moore's body of work is large and varied. It's of its time, while speaking to archetypes. It's accessible and usually fun to read, and there's much about the man and his art to discuss. With those qualities, there's every chance he'll make the same transition that, say, Philip K. Dick has from pop culture to the literary canon. Judging by university syllabuses, *V for Vendetta* may already have done so.

Although Moore disdains the cult of celebrity, his work now exposes far more of himself: his family history, his thoughts on sex, his deepest personal beliefs. This hasn't made it easier to decide whether Moore is cannily playing the game or has disqualified himself from it. Yes, when he says, 'The other end of the living room is a bit of a foreign country where they do things differently and have different stamps and passports and currency. I'm not interested in travelling. I'm all over the world in my head, I'm everywhere. I'm not very often where I actually am, so I don't really have to move,' it sounds like he's succumbed to a kind of insularity usually seen as harmful – even fatal – to a writer. But his *imaginative* horizons are wider than they've ever been. When he was starting out, Moore's literary interests were confined to the world of comics, with a few forays into other strains of fantasy fiction. Once a writer who soaked up various pieces of pop culture and reflected them back at the world, his curiosity now extends – albeit somewhat haphazardly, it feels, at times – over the realms of science, history and philosophy. Yes, much of his work today is now inflected by his magic, but the fact is that you don't have to welcome Glycon into your heart as your personal saviour to accept that 'consciousness', 'creativity', 'history', 'sex', 'language' and 'how our environment affects us' are weightier topics for an artist to engage with than 'what sort of person would put on a bright cape to fight crime?'

There would seem to be two possible interpretations of Moore's recent work. The first is that he has cut himself off from most of his former friends, and hurt only himself by adopting stubborn, naïve points of principle instead of making sensible business decisions; that he's not listening to the right people, and has become bitter to the point of paranoia. That both he and – crucially – his work are now increasingly insular and opaque. That he has, in short, lost it.

The alternative is that the comics industry is in a death spiral, that it's become the worst of all worlds: soulless corporate product that barely breaks even. The industry needs Alan Moore more than he needs it and should have listened to him when it had the chance. He's escaped to fashion for himself a unique position where he enjoys critical acclaim and commercial success by combining experimental storytelling in multiple media not only with a bold political flavour but also with a complex personal cosmology. Moore's a writer who loves posing questions but keeping his endings ambiguous, leaving the conclusion in the hands of his readers.

So . . . which one is Alan Moore?

'I'm a lot stranger than what I've just said. I'm just giving you the quick, commercial, acceptable outline. I've still got me secrets.'

Alan Moore, interviewed for Mania, *2007*

REFERENCES

INTRODUCTION

p2 **still buy** – Douglas Wolk, *Reading Comics* (Da Capo, 2008), p229 [Wolk]

p2 **centre of the universe** – DeZ Vylenz, *The Mindscape of Alan Moore* (Shadowsnake, 2005) [*Mindscape*]

p3 **horrendous hitchhiking** – AM, 'Behind the Painted Smile', *Warrior* #17 (March 1984) [Painted]

p5 **fancied** – bauhausgigguide.info/gig.php?gid=1671

p5 **communal narrative** – smoky man and Gary Spencer Millidge (eds), *Alan Moore: Portrait of an Extraordinary Gentleman* (Abiogenesis, 2003), p41 [Portrait]

p5 **extent of my unease** – Eddie Campbell, 'Alan Moore interviewed', *Egomania* #2 (2002) [Egomania]. Reprinted in *A Disease of Language* (Knockabout, 2005)

p5 **keeping a low profile** – *Culture Show*, BBC2 (9 March 2006)

p5 **a doddle** – Daniel Whiston, 'The Craft', *Zarjaz* #3–4 (2002) [Zarjaz]. Eric L. Berlatsky, *Alan Moore: Conversations* (University Press of Mississippi, 2012), reprints a number of interviews: *Hellfire*, *Zarjaz*, CI65, *Idler*, AV01, Craft, Nevins, Mautner, *Mustard*

p6 **boring existences** – Neil Gaiman, 'MOORE about Comics', *Knave* Vol 18, #3 (March 1986), p41 [*Knave*]

p6 **you'll use everything** – Steve Hanson and Christian Martius, 'An interview with Alan Moore', *Eclectic Electric* (8 March 1996). 'The next thing' is a reference to *The Birth Caul*

p7 **they were like** – *The Ballad of Halo Jones*, Book One, p18

p9 **second-wave** – Maggie Gray, 'Transcript: Interview with Alan Moore' (unpublished, conducted 28 November 2007 to support Gray's PhD thesis) [Gray]

p9 **I was special** – George Khoury, *The Extraordinary Works of Alan Moore: Indispensable Edition* (TwoMorrows, 2008), pp20–1 [*Works*]

p9 **biographical accounts** – see Victoria A. Elmwood, 'Fictional Auto/Biography and Graphic Lives in Watchmen', in Michael Chaney (ed.), *Graphic Subjects: Critical Essays on Autobiography and Graphic Novels* (Wisconsin Studies in Autobiography, 2011)

p10 **unavoidable political element** – Bill Baker, 'Alan Moore's Exit Interview', *Airwave* (2007 – conducted 8 May 2006), p46 [Exit]

p10 **10 Easy Ways** – Vaneta Rogers, '10 Easy Ways to Piss Off a Comic Book Reader', Newsarama (8 August 2011)

p11 **take out all the leaders** – Margaret Killjoy and Kim Stanley Robinson, *Mythmakers and Lawbreakers* (AK Press, 2009), pp43–4 [*Mythmakers*]

p11 **all about anarchy** – David Lloyd, telephone interview for this book, 25 March 2012 [Lloyd]

p11 **possibly unpopular** – Norman Hull, *Monsters, Maniacs and Moore* (Central, 1987) [*Monsters*]

p12 **going to be blunted** – Gray

CHAPTER I

p14 **three generations** – Paul Buhle, *The Art of Harvey Kurtzman: The Mad Genius of Comics* (Abrams, 2009)

p15 **Coming Attractions** – Eddie Stachelski, 'An Interview with Alan Moore', *Fantasy Express* #5 (January 1983), p7 [FE5]

p16 **load of the Ballantine** – Pádraig Ó Méalóid, *The Poisoned Chalice* (serialised at comicsbeat.com in 2013) [*Chalice*]. 'Superduperman' was reprinted in *The Mad Reader*

p17 **Big brave uncles** – *Chain Reaction*, S01E05 (BBC Radio Four, 27 January 2005; Stewart Lee interviews Alan Moore) [*Chain*5]

p17 **Completely infatuated** – *Works*, pp31–2. *Fantastic Four* #3 is cover dated March 1962, so Moore would have been eight. Somewhat ironically, the title of the story is 'The Menace of the Miracle Man'

p17 **written by Stan Lee** – This may be the most contentious statement in this book. Jack Kirby (and his heirs) vociferously asserted that he had done the lion's share of the work in his 'collaborations' with Lee. The Marvel Method is discussed further in Chapter IV, but a full discussion of the Lee/Kirby dispute is beyond the scope of this book. See, for example, Jack Kirby's interview in TCJ (The Comics Journal) #134

p17 **actual character trait** – *Chain*5

p17 **omnipotent losers** – AM, *Unearthing*, in Iain Sinclair (ed.) *London: City of Disappearances* (Hamish Hamilton, 2006); adapted as spoken word performance piece (2010) and illustrated book (2013) [Unearthing]

p18 **loopiest thuggee** – AM, 'Blinded by the Hype' (two-part article in *The Daredevils* #3/4, Marvel UK, March/April 1983) [Hype]

p19 **this chutzpah** – Michael Chabon, *Manhood for Amateurs* (HarperCollins, 2009)

p19 **exotic as Mars** – *Mindscape*

p20 **small the world** – In the sixties, Kinney Parking Company – a car parking company with mob connections – bought both *Mad* and DC as part of a swathe of acquisitions that would end up including Panavision and Warner Brothers. Following a financial scandal, the entertainment arm was spun off in 1971 as Warner Communications. As the media conglomerate grew, it acquired the intellectual property of its rivals. In 1972, DC licensed the rights to Captain Marvel, buying them outright in 1991.

As another example that there's always a connection to be made, the first American comic Moore wrote was *Swamp Thing*, and the colourist on that book was Tatjana Wood, the first wife of Wally Wood, the man who drew 'Superduperman'

p20 **722 issues** – see Kimota and Chalice for detailed histories of Marvelman

p20 **older Mickey Moran** – Kurt Amacker, 'Alan Moore Reflects on Marvelman', *Mania* (September 2009) [*Mania*09]. See also George Khoury, *Kimota! The Miracleman Companion* (TwoMorrows, 2001) [*Kimota*]. There's also an account in 'Miracleman: It's

a Miracle' in *Speakeasy* #52 (1985) [*Speakeasy*52]

p21 **tidied up** – AM always says he saw his story as a 'Kurtzman' style piece, but in some places that means a parody (e.g. *Speakeasy*52), in others something more poignant (e.g. *Works*, p77, 'a Kurtzman-type comic, but done seriously and for dramatic effect rather than for comic effect', and see the 'twist a dial' quote in the main text). There are big discrepancies between AM's various accounts of his age when this happened. AM was born November 1953, so would be twelve in summer 1966. In interviews, he has said: 'I was about twelve or thirteen . . . in about 1966' (*Speakeasy*52); 'It was 1968, and I was 15 years old' (essay in *Miracleman* #2 (1985), where there's no mention of 'Superduperman'); 'I'd probably been about eleven . . . around the same time I picked up one of the Ballantine reprints of *Mad*' (*Kimota* p11); 'I also picked up a copy of one of the Ballantine paperbacks of Harvey Kurtzman's brilliant *Mad*. It was the one that had "Superduperman". Since I picked up these two things on the same day – and bearing in mind that I was twelve' (*Mania*09); 'I was only thirteen or something at the time, or possibly even younger, twelve or thirteen, and it might well have had Don Lawrence art, but I wouldn't have known about that at the time. The main thing was, it was just this purely chance conjunction of events, really, that they were selling a *Young Marvelman* annual that I hadn't seen before, so I picked that up, and they'd also got a load of the Ballantine *Mad* reprints' (*Chalice*). The balance of evidence is for 1966, when AM was twelve. It's only in later interviews where AM states that he bought the *Mad* reprints on exactly the same day, so this is possibly a conflation for the sake of a better story

p21 **Percolated** – *Chalice*

p21 **Turn the dial** – *Kimota*, pp11–2

p22 **same house** – *Don't Let Me Die in Black and White* (Phrontisterion Films, 1993) [*B&W*]

p22 **employed as a foetus** – AM, 'Brasso with Rosie' in the *Knockabout Trial Special* (Knockabout, 1984) [Brasso]

p22 **£18** – *Works*, p15

p22 **Ginger Vernon** – David Sim, 'Dialogue From Hell', *Cerebus* 217–20 (1997) [*Cerebus*]

p23 **Victorian matriarch** – *The Comics Journal* #138, p58 [TCJ138]

p23 **five or ten miles** – *Works*, p13

p23 **upbringing** – *B&W*

p23 **morality** – Sridhar Pappu, 'We Need Another Hero', *Salon* (18 October 2000) [*Salon*00]: '"I got my morals more from Superman than I ever did from my teachers and peers," he says. "Because Superman wasn't real – he was incorruptible. You were seeing morals in their pure form. You don't see Superman secretly going out behind the back and lying and killing, which, of course, most real-life heroes tend to be doing."'

p23 **insidiously and invisibly** – Jeremy Seabrook, *The Unprivileged* (Longmans, 1967), pp36–7 [*Unprivileged*]

p23 **Counter-Juju** – *Brasso*

p23 **rigidly fixed pattern** – *Unprivileged*, pp157–9

p23 **Far Cotton and Jimmy's End** – Seabrook email correspondence for this book, 16 June 2012 [Seabrook]

p24 **shoe people** – Seabrook

p24 **sons of immigrants** – It's no coincidence that so many of the early comic book creators – including Joe Shuster and Jerry Siegel, creators of Superman, were Jewish, as well as Will Eisner and Harvey Kurtzman –

were Jewish. Danny Fingeroth's book *Disguised as Clark Kent: Jews, Comics and the Creation of the Superhero* (2008) spells it out: American Jews routinely had secret identities – Bob Kane, creator of Batman, had been born Bob Kahn, Stan Lee had been born Stanley Lieber, Jack Kirby and Joe Simon, co-creators of Captain America, had been born Jacob Kurtzberg and Hymie Simon

p25 **Kirby self-caricature** – Mark Evanier, *Kirby – King of Comics* (Abrams, 2008), p22

p25 **recognised my uncle** – TCJ134

p25 **very happy childhood** – TCJ138, p59

p25 **grim as it sounds** – *Works*, p48

p25 **sad about the working class** – Alex Musson and Andrew O'Neill, 'The Mustard Interview', Mustard 2.4 (March 2009, which edits together interviews from 2005 and 2009 and is reprinted in *Conversations*) [*Mustard*]

p25 **encouraging him** – Bill Baker, 'Alan Moore Spells It Out', *Airwave* (2005), p17 [Spells]

p26 **The Magic Island** – There are a number of books called *The Magic Island*. The one AM borrowed is most likely to be Ethel Talbot's 1930 children's book, which was reissued in 1955, when AM was two

p26 **knew where the library was** – TCJ138, p59

p26 **Omega Comics** – Gary Spencer Millidge, *Alan Moore: Storyteller* (Ilex Press, 2011), p26 [*Storyteller*]

p26 **smothering black dirt** – AM, *The Birth Caul* (1995 – originally a performance piece, it has been issued on CD and adapted for comics by Eddie Campbell) [*Caul*]

p26 **miniature god** – *Works*, p17

p27 **Call me naïve** – *Mindscape*

p27 **unacknowledged curriculum** – Seabrook

p27 **proper little gentlemen** – *Unprivileged*, p144

p28 **enthusiasm for sports** – In an uncredited interview with *Leftlion* (7 August 2012) [*Leftlion*], AM stated 'I have no interest in sports at all . . . competitive sports are one of the few things in culture that don't seem to derive from Shamans. Most of the art and most of the actual consciousness in society – is almost certainly derived from Shamanic roots. With sport, I can only assume that it was when the hunters wanted to show off'

p28 **impersonal and cold** – TCJ138, p61

p28 **twenty-seventh in the class** – '27th' in *Works*, p17, '25th' in *Mindscape*

p28 **genuine intellectual light** – *Works*, p17

p28 **sulky children** – *Mindscape*

p29 **Stan Lee achieved** – *Hype*

p29 **so we applauded** – *Exit*, p43

p30 **ruining my existence** – AM, Ecology, Cosmos and Consciousness lecture (October Gallery, London, 26 October 2010)

p30 **bewildered** – Pádraig Ó Méalóid, 'Lunar Man', Forbidden Planet International website (11 November 2011)

p30 **sixty or seventy** – Alex Fitch, 'Panel Borders: Alan Moore interview Pt 3', Resonance FM (2008)

p30 **undeniably a performer** – *Portrait*, p83

p30 **Obama** – Jon Swaine, 'Barack Obama: The 50 facts you might not know', *Daily Telegraph* (7 November 2008)

p31 **absolutely formative** – Gray

p32 **proto-hippies** – *Exit*, p43

p32 **Cyclops** – *Works*, p46

p33 **hell of a long time** – Paul Duncan, Alan Moore interview pt 1 in *Arkensword* #10 (April 1984) [*Arkensword*10]

p33 **Firebowels** – Reprinted in *Works*, *Storyteller*.

p33 **eleven-word letter** – Reprinted in

Works, it reads: 'Aspect was incredible. I'm overwhelmed. I have whelms all over me'

p33 Androgyne – Gray

p33 breast-beating things – *Works*, p33

p33 friend's motorbike – TCJ138, p61

p34 funny wonder – Moore, PC

p34 motherfuckers – *Embryo* #2 (circa December 1970 – the editorial advertises the poetry reading on 16 December and wishes readers Merry Christmas)

p35 art department – *Works*, p32

p35 growing his hair – Compare *Storyteller*, p39; *Works*, pp32, 35

p37 great clearances – Seabrook

p37 bothersome people – *Works*, p14

p37 two weeks after the death of his grandmother – *Caul*. Tom Lamont, 'Alan Moore: Why I Turned My Back on Hollywood', *Observer* (15 December 2012) [*Observer*12] dates this to 1969, when AM was sixteen. In a telephone interview for this book (July 2013 [Moore, PC]), Moore confirmed he misspoke on that occasion and was seventeen

p37 various reasons – TCJ138, p60

p37 woolly hat – Uncredited, 'Alan Moore interview', *Ptolemaic Terrascope* #8, 1991 [*Ptolemaic*] Moore, PC

p37 most inept – Nic Rigby, 'Comic Legend Keeps True to His Roots', BBC News website (21 March 2008)

p38 drugs squad – *Observer*12

p38 hearsay – Moore, PC

p38 upset and disappointed – *Works*, pp18–9

p38 being my parents – *Monsters*

p38 ideological reasons – *Works*, p19

p38 purple pills – *Works*, p19

p38 an incredible experience – *Works*, pp19–20

p39 rather harsh – *Mindscape*

p39 I was a monster – *Works*, p21

p39 £6 a week – *Salon*00

p39 antimatter – *Mindscape*

p39 scary dog – Moore, PC

p40 caustic dye – *Caul*

p40 there two months – *Storyteller*

p40 downward progression – TCJ138, p64. AM makes the same joke in *Mindscape*

CHAPTER II

p41 miserable jobs – TCJ138, p63

p42 supernatural powers – Gray

p42 I was living for – *Works*, p34

p43 chief occupation – Chris Welch, *Melody Maker*, September 1969

p43 Dave Thompson – email to author. See Thompson's *Your Pretty Face is Going To Hell* (Backbeat, 2009)

p44 soup of sensations – Gray. In TCJ138, p61, AM notes, laughingly, 'the Northampton Arts Lab, for four or five years, just basically decided that we didn't want any government support. Then somebody decided to try to get some just in case they were going to offer any. We wrote them a 50-page summary of our activities over the past five years and they offered us five pounds'

p44 I first started writing – TCJ138, pp62–3

p45 playing an instrument – John Doran, 'Hipster Priest', *Stool Pigeon* (Summer 2010)

p45 decent performer – Moore, PC

p45 Principal Edwards – Tony Palmer, *Observer* (8 February 1970); AM quote *Works*, p34

p45 Ashby – TCJ138, pp62–3

p46 Dutch customs – *Works*, p35

p46 Tom Hall – Moore, PC

p46 general disillusionment – Editorial, *Myrmidon* (1973), credited to 'Gary, Diane, and Dominic'

p46 eighteen months – TCJ138, p63. All material from the Arts Group is dated 1973

p46 **we're helped by** – *Myrmidon* editorial, which states there are 'around twenty' members and that about sixty people attended their first poetry meeting. The magazine lists thirteen group members: Carl [Bush], Fitz, Chris Barber (Music); Gary [Dudbridge], Diane [Thornton], Dominic [Allard], Jamie [Andrew James, aka Jamie Delano] (Words); Clive [Green], Paul [Bliss], Phil [Laughton], Dave and Pete [Billingham?] (Props, advertising, organising, looning etc); Sue. It lists five occasional members Alan [Moore] and George [Woodcock] (words and music), Richard Ashby (light and sounds), Pete Spencer and Herb [Bob Matcham] (Music). The gig report names Jerry Sears and Nick Tomkins as performers. In addition to many of those people, the three magazines published by the Arts Group also list Ian Bailey, Andrew Boddington, Glyn Bush, Shirley Casey, Carol Clark, Ian Fleming, Barbara Lovelady, Mu MacRobert, Norman Pridmore and Nina Steane as contributors

p47 **Pilgrim Zone Two** – both appear in *Storyteller*, dated to 1973

p47 **Lester the Geek** – *Myrmidon* editorial; neither piece has ever been published

p48 **The Doll** – Painted; AM says he was '22'

p48 **Old Gangsters** – in 1983 the song was released as the B-side to the single 'March of the Sinister Ducks'. The sleeve included a fold-out comics adaptation of the song (art: Lloyd Thatcher), and this was revised and reprinted in Paul Gravett (ed.), *The Mammoth Book of Best Crime Comics* (Running, 2008), as well as *Works*. One line, 'don't let me die in black-and-white', would become the title of the 1993 documentary about Northampton featuring Moore. A second comics version of the song followed in 2003 when the songs from *Another Suburban Romance* were adapted by Avatar

p48 **pinnacle** – Moore, PC

p48 **long friendships** – TCJ138, p63

p48 **Hitler lookalike** – AM, 'The True Story of the Rise and Fall of the Sinister Ducks', *Critters* #23 (April 1988) [*Critters*]

p49 **tone of the times** – TCJ138, p63

p49 **cultural and political wings** – Gray (who goes on to argue against seeing the split as being so clear-cut)

p49 **featuring trade unions** – ANoN #2, reprinted in *Works*, p21

p49 **inflammatory** – Gray

p51 **Eno** – *Chain*6

p51 **surrealist drama** – press release at avatarpress.com/anothersuburbanromance/

p52 **Peyton Place** – uncredited, Interview with Alex Green, *ApolloX* (1995) [*ApolloX*]

p52 **Another Suburban Romance** – AM recorded the song in 1992 with The Emperors of Ice Cream, which is on the *Storyteller* CD

p52 **Cutting himself shaving** – Lugosi died of a heart attack

p53 **album's worth** – Antony Johnston's 'The Musical Mystery Moore', in Avatar's *Alan Moore's Magic Words* (2002), puts the band's output at 'half a dozen songs', although Alex Green says it was 'a dozen' (*ApolloX*). The original band never recorded or publicly performed. AM formed a new incarnation of The Emperors of Ice Cream in the early nineties (see p403), with the later band performing a few songs originally written for the original. 'Another Suburban Romance' was definitely from the seventies, 'The Murders in the Rue Morgue' and 'Positively Bridge Street' also seem to be

p53 Moore did not meet – *ApolloX*: David J 'did not in fact, meet Alan until years later', but the two both attended the Deadly Fun Hippodrome, so presumably met there

p53 Dream band – *Works*, p235

p53 Summer of 1979 – Ben Brownton of the Shapes thinks it was 'circa 1978' (trakmarx.com/2005_02/15_bybus.htm) but this would have been before AM met David J, so AM's 'around 1979' (*Critters*) would seem more accurate. The ultra-comprehensive Bauhaus Concert Guide lists it as 1979: bauhausgigguide.info/artist.php?bid=8

p53 literally, dozens – *Critters*. Not to be left out, AM would use a pseudonym, Translucia Baboon, for the early eighties relaunch of The Sinister Ducks

p54 Barda – Chabon, p185

p54 if anything interesting – Gray

p54 becoming obsessed – FE5

p54 Olsen – Modern comics fans might not appreciate *Jimmy Olsen* was one of the top ten comics at the time, selling far more than any Marvel title, so represented a serious promotion

p54 Daredevil – *Chain*5

p55 slobbering hysteria – AM, 'Too Avant Garde for the Mafia' in *Infinity* #8 [Mafia]. The three comics are *Mad*, *Fantastic Four* and *Arcade*

p55 ranks as one – Monte Beauchamp (ed.), *The Life and Time of Robert Crumb* (St Martins, 1998), pp78–9. AM also singles out Stalin in *Mafia*

p56 Tally ho; not too distant past – *Mafia*; 'Griffy' is Bill Griffith

p57 Action – For more, read Martin Barker's *Action: The Story of a Violent Comic* (Titan, 1990). In the *From Hell* edition of *Panel Borders*, Moore cites Action when he's discussing the art styles of horror comics, noting when the art on *Hookjaw*, a series about a killer shark, was toned down and became 'quiet and unassuming', rather than gory, it was 'ten times' more horrifying because it was hard to dismiss as preposterous

p57 Bolland's cover – *Storyteller* identifies it as #11, 7 May 1977. (see p58)

p57 I recognised them – *Vworp*

p59 Ballerina – *Chain*5

p59 imploring eyes – *Chain*5. Elsewhere (e.g. *Works*, p35), AM has said that he'd already handed in his notice before Phyllis learned she was pregnant, and was offered his job back. Whatever the case, the choice AM faced between a dull office job and attempting an artistic career remained essentially the same

p60 £42.50 – *Works*, p36

p60 *Sun Dodgers* – Moore. PC

p60 Lord of the Rings – *Works*, p35.

p60 never going to finish it – *Chain*5

p61 Something Nasty in Mega-City One!! – Reprinted in *Works*, pp50–2

p61 the long way – *Warrior* #15, p12

p61 gritted teeth – Moore, PC

p61 over the fence – *Knave*, p39

p62 dirty doings – Gray

p62 stippling – FE5

p64 ageing hippies – 'Roscoe Moscow's St Pancras Panda' in *Back-Street Bugle* #30 (August 1979)

p64 Lex Loopy – *Warrior* #2, p12

p64 Rip-Off – alteredvistas.co.uk/html/steve_moore_abslom_daak_interv.html [*Alteredvistas*]

p65 Chandlerese – TCJ138, p64

p65 250,000 copies – *Warrior* #2, p11

p65 Vile – Contrary to a number of listings, AM used his own name for most work in this period. Curt Vile is credited for *Dark Star*, *Talcum Powder* and *Three Eyes McGurk* – co-created with 'Pedro Henry' (Steve Moore), as well as art in *Sounds* (*Roscoe Moscow*, *Ten Little Liggers*, *The Stars My Degradation* and spot illustrations). Some of AM's music journalism in *Sounds* was credited to Vile, some to AM. Curt Vile was credited for illustrations in *Back-Street Bugle* #34, #42 and #43. The Mystery Guests single 'Wurlitzer Junction' has the sleeve note 'featuring Curt Vile'. 'Nativity on Ice' is credited to 'Kurt Vile' [sic]. Curt Vile did two interviews – Eddie Stachelski, Curt Vile interview, *Cerebro* Vol 3, #15, July/August 1982 [*Cerebro*]), and *Warrior* #2. AM did little to hide his secret identity: *Kultural Krime Comix* features 'Curt Vile' creation Roscoe Moscow among AM characters like Anon E Mouse and St Pancras Panda. *Cerebro* freely discusses work credited to AM and *Back-Street Bugle* #30 had an article discussing AM's work for *Sounds*

p65 **simple objects** – *Storyteller*

p66 **solidly rooted** – 'Alan Moore's Yuggoth Cultures and Other Growths' (*Avatar*, 2007) [Yuggoth], p38

p66 **wasn't terribly popular** – *Comic Art Profile 3: Dave Gibbons & Alan Moore* (CA Productions, 1987) [*Profile*]

p66 **sub-underground** – Alan David Doane, ADD Weblog, 3 March 2004

p66 **glaring flaws** – uncredited, 'The Honest Alan Moore Interview' (*Honest*, 1 December 2011)

p66 **poorly executed drivel** – Ian Blake, 'Drawing Up Sides' (*ZigZag*, June 1984)

p67 **repulsive bilge** – TCJ138, p65

p67 **out there on the 'net** – A wealth of early Moore material appears on Ó Méalóid's site, glycon.livejournal.com

p67 ***Nutter's Ruin*** – Reprinted in *Maxwell the Magic Cat Volume One* (Acme Press, 1986) [*Maxwell*1] and *Works*

p67 **a little cat** – *Ptolemaic*

p68 **idle notions** – Eddie Campbell, 'Forward' (sic) in *Maxwell*1

p68 **a friend to all the people** – The original letter was in the 3 May 1980 edition of *Sounds*, the 'Curt Reply' followed on 17 May

p69 **space opera** – *Alteredvistas*. Steve Moore notes: 'in the third episode of Stars I suddenly found he'd parodied the courtroom scene from Abslom Daak. Well, you can imagine how outraged I was by the fact that later, when he asked me to write Stars for him, I said "yes" straight away. He was paying me £10 a week, after all!'

p69 **Hawkwind** – uncredited, 'Cult Heroes: Alan Moore' (*Uncut*, January 2000) [*Uncut*]

p69 **Shadow as a teenager** – *Works*, p33

p69 **meat and potato; two pages isn't a lot; a gothic costumier** – Gareth Kavanagh, Alan Moore interview in *Vworp Vworp* #3 (2013) [*Vworp*]

p71 **gesture of support** – *Alteredvistas*

p71 **might be acceptable** – *Spells*, p22

p71 **robots giving the thumbs up** – *Works*, p38. In FE5, AM says once he was invited to write a Future Shock he was 'accepted straight away'; in *Comic Book Artist* #25 (April 2003) [CBA] he says he wrote the Judge Dredd script, was invited to write *Future Shocks*, wrote 'one more' that was rejected, then 'The Killer in the Cab', which was accepted after he altered the ending (p14) and that he was commissioned for *Doctor Who Weekly* before *2000AD* (p15)

p72 **best possible education** – *Spells*, p22

p72 **more commercial** – *Spells*, p15

p73 **what the artist wants** – *Portrait*

p73 **mercenary** – *Vworp*

p73 **SSI** – Lloyd

p74 **Status Quo** – Eddie Campbell, 'Alec: How to be an Artist' (*Top Shelf*, 2001) [Alec], p27. 'Status Quo' looks like David Lloyd

p74 **coffee evening** – *Kimota*, p12

p74 **inch of ground** – *Works*, p78

CHAPTER III

p75 May 1981 – David Lloyd, 'From the Writer's Viewpoint', *Society of Strip Illustration Newsletter* #40, May 1981 [SSI] Reprinted in *Conversations*

p75 twice as many copies – Sales were regularly over 200,000 a week and were occasionally nearer 300,000, according to *Look-In* editor Colin Shelbourn (animus-web.demon.co.uk/lookin/colin3.html). For an interview with Allan, see animus-web.demon.co.uk/sapphireandsteel/angus/angus1.html

p75 how brilliant he was – Lloyd

p76 staggeringly easy – SSI

p77 roly-poly – *Portrait*, p83

p79 remarkable coincidence – *Works*, p73

p79 Bernadette Jaye – all Jaye quotes from email correspondence for this book, June 2013 [Jaye]

p80 April 1981 – 'Freedom's Road', editorial in *Warrior* #1

p80 so instead of – *Kimota*, p38

p80 too busy – Email correspondence with Dave Gibbons for this book, June 2013 [Gibbons]

p81 He's Back! – *Dark Star* #23 was published in March 1980, *Warrior* #1 in March 1983

p81 kill for the chance – *Kimota*, p40

p81 must have seen – *Kimota*, p12

p81 suggested me – *Painted*

p82 David suggested – email exchange with Dez Skinn for this book May 2012 [Skinn]. The reference to the 'script' must refer to the initial pitch document

p82 already said yes – Lloyd

p82 *Frantic* – *Kimota*, p73 versus p39

p82 purely historical – Skinn

p82 eight-page pitch document – reprinted in *Kimota*

p84 nothing like the depth – Lloyd

p84 we don't really remember – *Painted*

p84 Laurel and Hardy – Dave Itzkoff, 'The Vendetta Behind V for Vendetta' (*New York Times*, 12 March 2006) [NYT]

p84 *pssst!* – Lloyd. *pssst!* ran for ten issues from January to October 1982, but made massive losses. In FE5 AM said that he was working on two ideas for *pssst!* with artists Lloyd Thatcher and Steve Dillon. Neither of these ever saw light of day

p86 only a first draft – Reprinted in *Kimota*. *Ace of Shades* might be a play on the title of the 1921 Lon Chaney film *Ace of Hearts*, about an anarchist group dedicated to assassinating the rich and powerful

p87 established in my head – Yuggoth, p32

p87 work out the entire world – David Roach, Andrew Jones, Simon Jowett and Greg Hill, Garry Leach and Alan Moore, *Hellfire* #1, 1983, (reprinted in *Conversations*), p15 [*Hellfire*]

p87 word-heavy – Reprinted in *Kimota*

p87 stunning – *Kimota*, p39

p88 too dense to read – *Kimota*

p89 The big breakthrough – *Painted*, p89

p89 so British; – *Comics Britannia*: 'X-Rated: Anarchy in the UK' (BBC Four, 24 September 2007) [*Britannia*]

p89 Zara – Pádraig Ó Méalóid suggests this might refer to Zara's Kingdom, from Gilbert & Sullivan's Utopia Limited

p90 Heidelberg; – *Britannia*

p93 satisfactory revelation – *Painted*

p93 never had any intention – Lloyd

p93 apart from Evey – TCJ128, p27

p93 introducing Falconbridge – Lloyd

p94 spin entire plotlines – Yuggoth, p32

p94 warts and all – Introduction to *V for Vendetta* #1

p95 absolute accident; – Lloyd

p95 explore and exploit – *Works*, p75

p95 up the ante – Skinn

p95 editorial bullpit – *Portrait*, p85

p96 urban mass – *Knave*, p41

p96 very surrealistic – *Works*, p60

p98 few comedy strips – *Knave*, p41

p99 full potential – 2000adreview.co.uk/features/interviews/2004/parkhouse/parkhouse3.shtml
p99 interest in reviving – *Works*
p99 Adam Ant – Bryan Talbot, *The Art of Bryan Talbot* (NBM, 2007), p22 [Talbot]
p99 *Nightjar* – AM's script for *Nightjar*, the letter, completed first instalment and an article by Talbot appear in *Yuggoth* pp15–42
p101 hated the name – Skinn
p101 comics landscape – AM's introduction to Bryan Talbot, *The Adventures of Luther Arkwright*, Book Two (Valkyrie, 1987)
p102 sleeper hit – Skinn
p103 been an accountant – *Kimota*, p43
p103 120,000 copies – Talbot, p41
p103 print run of around – Skinn: 'Oh, we never got anywhere near the 40,000 on print run let alone sales. But these things needed hyping up to get IPC, Marvel UK and the like to believe such projects could work, an encourage them to do similar.' Initial estimates were that *Warrior* could break even on 16,000 sales
p103 festering – *Kimota*, pp53–4
p103 *Vignettes* – Letter from AM to Skinn, August 1982. *Kimota* reprints the fictional timeline

Chapter IV

p106 auto-plant workers – Chris Dahlen, 'Interview: Steve Bissette', *Onion* AV Club (23 July 2009) [AV09]
p106 it falls short – Alex Fitch, 'Panel Borders: David Lloyd' (10 July 2008)
p106 opera – *Profile*
p107 *Annual 1981* – Mark Salisbury (ed.), *Writers on Comic Scriptwriting* (Titan, December 1999), p60 (Ellis), p75 (Ennis)
p107 planning stages – *Works*, p68
p107 there isn't one – *Spells*, p57
p108 hard fascist people – Comicon 1984, transcript in TCJ #106, p43
p108 people's presence – Melinda Gebbie in Blake Bell (ed.), 'I Have To Live With This Guy', (*TwoMorrows*, September 2002), p158 [Guy]
p108 the phone rings – *Spells*, p57
p108 Harold Budd – *Mania*09
p108 *On Writing for Comics* – *Fantasy Advertiser* #92–95 (1985–6), reprinted in TCJ #119–121 (1988), and again, with a new afterword, in Alan Moore's *Writing for Comics* (Avatar, 2003 – page references from that edition). [*Writing*]
p108 all that is required – *Writing*, p19
p109 Enoesque – *Spells*, p27
p109 must be solved – *Writing*, p6; 15 words wide – *Writing*, p24; banes of the industry – *Writing*, p24; wading through mud – *Writing*, p29; useful in some way – *Writing*, p2
p109 golden rut – *Spells*, p27
p109 transform the medium – *Profile*
p110 high-altitude – *Cerebus*
p110 morbid dread – *Spells*, p42
p110 environmental reality – *Writing* p20;
p110 going on holiday – *Writing* p21
p111 order of events – *Writing* p34
p111 nut and bolt – *Spells*, p39
p111 structure – *Writing* p14; panel **progression** – *Writing* p9; element of time – *Writing* p30; broad mechanisms – *Writing* p13; elliptical – *Writing* p15
p112 re-reading – Iain Thomson, 'Deconstructing the Hero', in Jeff McLaughlin (ed.), *Comics as Philosophy* (University Press of Mississippi, 2005), p103
p112 Near Mint – See for example milehighcomics.com/information/grade.html
p112 gold sedan – Alex Fitch, 'Panel Borders: Looking for Lost Girls' (podcast 14 February 2008) [Panel08]

p112 giant grid – *Spells*, p39. The grid is reprinted in *Storyteller* and dated 28 August 1988, when the series was still called *The Mandelbrot Set*
p113 bareback – *Spells*, p40
p113 tricks and devices – *Writing* p16
p113 mugger's balls – Grant Morrison, *Supergods* (Spiegel & Grau, 2011), p201 [*Supergods*]
p113 how long – *Writing* p18
p114 scribbles – *Writing* p41
p114 method acting – Paul Duncan, Alan Moore interview pt 2, *Arkensword* #11 (October 1984) [*Arkensword*11]. AM was filmed getting into character as the Demon for Monsters.
p114 biro – *Spells*, pp46–8
p114 eleven chapters – *Spells*, p50
p114 first draft – *Spells*, p51
p115 hired hand – Talon, Durwin S, 'Panel Discussions: Design in Sequential Art Storytelling' (*TwoMorrows*, 2007), p41
p115 60's70's80's – Howard Mackie, 'Marvel Method vs Full Script', Byrne Robotics website, 28 November 2007 at 2.33pm
p116 huge balloon – *Hellfire*, p16
p116 May 1985 – jimshooter.com/2011/09/chris-claremont-face-down-in-his-mashed.html
p116 Claremont had won – 'Moore and Claremont Speak Out On Writing', *Speakeasy* #54 (May 1985) [*Speakeasy*54]. Claremont tied with Dave Sim in 1983 and won outright in 1984. AM would go on to win in 1985, 1986 and 1987. Claremont in 1988, 1989 and 1990. cbgxtra.com/knowledge-base/for-your-reference/cbg-fan-award-winners-1982-present
p116 cheap shots – *Warrior* #2
p117 cinema that doesn't move – *Spells*, p58
p117 Bullpen – Jim Shooter, 'Bullpen Bulletins' in Marvel comics cover-dated May 1982. Moore visited the Bullpen on his first trip to the US in 1984
p118 day job – Les Chester, 'An Interview with Alan Davis', *Amazing Heroes* #85 (15 December 1985), p24 [AH85]
p123 91 pages – watchmencomicmovie.com/121409-watchmen-typescript-contest.php
p123 one at a time; windswept – *Egomania*
p124 wheat from the chaff – *Profile*
p124 hard to crack – blogs.ocweekly.com/navelgazing/ill-lyteracy/rob-liefeld-shoots-on-alan-moo/
p124 beetles – AV09
p125 nails everything down – *Kimota*, pp84–5
p125 one chunk – Lloyd
p126 it's Alan's book – TCJ273
p126 sound and reliable – *Writing*, p41
p126 my way of doing it – *Spells*, p47
p126 conveyor belt – SSI
p127 emotional temperature – eddiecampbell.blogspot.com/2007/02/in-thrall-to-cinematic-principle_21.html
p127 jolted – David Colton, 'Writer prefers porn label for his Girls' (*USA Today*, 30 August 2006)
p128 annoys me – Guy Lawley and Steve Whitaker, 'Writer: Alan Moore', *Comics Interview* #12 (June 1984), p25 [CI12]
p128 space opera – Lloyd
p128 embarrassed by – Daniel Dickholtz, 'M for Moore', *Comics Scene* #4 (July 1988), p27 [CS4]
p129 breadth of his – *Bill Sienkiewicz Sketchbook* (Fantagraphics, 1990), p5
p129 boring for him – Dave Dickson, 'Alan Moore: Out of the Wilderness', *Comic Collector* #3 (May 1992) [CC]
p129 Kubrick period – 'Bill Sienkiewicz Speaks About Big Numbers #3', originally written for *The Beat*, finally published 2 January 2011 on Padraig O Mealoid's website (slovobooks.blogspot.com/2011/01/bill-sienkiewicz-speaks-about-big.html)

p130 who cares about windows? – Alex Fitch, 'Panel Borders: The Magic of Alan Moore' [PanelMagic]
p130 five weeks – AV09
p130 eight pages – *Comic Book Artist* #25 (2003), p39 [CBA25], p21
p131 quite frustrating – sardinianconnection.blogspot.com/2008/08/melinda-gebbie-interview-2.html [Sardinian]
p131 schism – AV09
p131 far less complex – *Writing* p43
p132 Mycroft – *Arkensword*10
p133 given series work – *Works*, p68
p135 out of your pit – Skinn
p135 pop into Marvel – Jaye
p135 I wasn't IPC! – Skinn. Most sources suggest that the *Warrior* rates were half the *2000AD* rates
p136 lucrative – Quality Communications Internal memo, 24 June 1981
p136 I'd love to know – Lloyd
p136 blessing – Skinn
p137 Eagle Awards – *Warrior* also won Favourite Supporting Character (Zirk from *Pressbutton*). *2000AD* could only muster Favourite Artist (Bolland) and Character Most Worthy of Own Title (Judge Anderson)
p137 no indication – *Ptolemaic*
p137 right track – *Works*, p69
p137 royal wedding – *Nemesis the Warlock Book Six*, starting in *2000AD* #482
p137 Badlander – *Works*
p138 Blackstuff – Alan Davis reports in AH85 that AM watched the last episode with him.
p138 cos he's little – *Hellfire*, p18
p138 appetite – *Works*, p57
p139 superhero direction – Jaye
p139 inaugurated – *Storyteller*
p139 not to compromise – Jaye
p139 out of place – *Arkensword*11
p139 prolific output; lifeblood – Jaye
p140 Westminster Hall – *Vworp*
p141 paucity – *Zigzag*, p28
p142 vacant throne – *Hype*
p142 four regular series – *Works*, p69
p143 *Herbie* – FE5. Elsewhere (goodcomics.comicbookresources.com/2012/01/06/comic-book-legends-revealed-348/), AM has said that Herbie was an influence on Rorschach
p143 *Thriller* – michelfiffe.com/?p=756
p143 wined and dined – Frank Plowright, *Comics Interview* #19 (January 1985), p25 [CI19]
p144 likenesses – Gibbons
p144 Martian Manhunter – *Works*, p109
p144 formally pitched – Gibbons

Chapter V

p145 optioned in 1979 – Will Murray, 'Scenes from the Swamp', *Comics Scene* #7 (April 1989) [CS7]
p145 17,000 – *Ptolemaic*
p146 covered in snot – *Chain*5
p147 fifteen-page document – *Works*
p147 *Tomb of Dracula* – CI12
p147 reality of American horror – *Profile*. In the video he says that Leah and Amber are six and three, therefore it was recorded in 1984
p148 phone directory – *Writing*, p22
p148 all-time favourite – *Portrait*, p217
p148 Pasko – TCJ34, p13 (1986) – AM was more generous: 'Marty Pasko had done some very good stories: he was obviously putting quite a lot of intensity into the writing.' (*Works*, p84)
p148 whole network – TCJ185
p149 hand grenade – artbomb.net/brainpowered.jsp?col=22
p150 *Sampler* – TCJ93, p70
p150 50 per cent – according to Karen Berger in *Profile*
p151 Frederick Wertham – *Knave*, p40
p151 Mengele – Mark Evanier, 'Wertham was Right' (*TwoMorrows*, 2003), p189

p151 nemesis – James E Reibman, 'The Life of Dr Fredric Wertham', in *The Fredric Wertham Collection* (Harvard University, 1990), p18, quoting a 1983 *Comic Buyers Guide* column

p151 depicts Wertham – Recent scholarship has reassessed Wertham. See for example Bart Beaty, *Fredric Wertham and the Critique of Mass Culture* (University Press of Mississippi, 2005)

p153 two different people – TCJ119, p73

p153 incestuous – *Works*, p90

p154 smugness – Paul Duncan, Alan Moore interview pt 3, *Arkensword* #13/14 (February 1986) [*Arkensword*13/14]

p154 Moore's memes – Douglas Rushkoff, *Media Virus!* (Ballantine, 1996) pp188–9

p155 unfettered – srbissette.com/?p=4479

p155 fill-in – *Works*, p92

p155 worst contract – Daniel Dickholtz, 'M for Moore', *Comics Scene* #5 (May/July 1988), p15 [CS5]

p155 $50 a page – srbissette.com/?p=4479

p156 they look funny – AH85, p26

p156 thermonuclear capacity – *Monsters*. American readers should note that AM is referring to the British character, who's appeared in the *Beano* since March 1951, not the American character who debuted in newspaper syndication the same month

p156 redeeming social value – TCJ138, p73

p157 triumphs and tragedies – *Monsters*

p157 small touches – *The Ballad of Halo Jones*, Introduction to Book One (Titan, August 1986) [*Halo*1]

p157 very fine tale – homepage.eircom.net/~twoms/halo1.htm

p157 their 24p – *Halo*1

p157 snake pit – *Kimota*, p71

p157 poisoned chalice – *Mania*09

p158 knowing deceit – *Mania*09 – the 'decision' here is a reference to the ownershp of the title

p158 lot of arguments – *Knave*

p158 editor's life hell – *Warrior* #16, p14

p159 offensively inoffensive – *Writing*, pp10–1

p159 tarnished; hangover – *Chalice*

p160 slightest qualm – *Arkensword*13/14. Refers to 'The Curse', a feminist werewolf story that first appeared in *Swamp Thing* #40 (September 1985)

p160 £20,000 – *Kimota*, p42 gives the figure as '$36,000'

p160 carrying the book – *Kimota*, p72

p160 enhanced, payscale – *Chalice*

p160 contentious – A Letter of Agreement dated 3 March 1982 allocated 40 per cent to AM, 40 per cent to Leach and 20 per cent to Skinn. As the quote indicates, Alan Davis believed the rights to be split evenly between AM, Leach and Quality (effectively, if not legally, Dez Skinn). In *Kimota!* (p46), Skinn says it started out as the three parties owning one-third each and he arranged a deal whereby AM and Leach would give Davis 5 per cent of their shares and Quality give him 18 per cent, so AM, Leach and Davis each ended up with a 28 per cent stake and Quality was left with 15 per cent

p161 Other artists had to – Lloyd

p161 Various people – *Kimota*

p161 heroic melodrama – *Chalice*

p161 early 1983 – *Warrior* #24

p161 bartering; invited to pitch; stumbling block – Skinn

p162 original pitch – reprinted in *Kimota*

p162 not prepared – CI12 (published June 1984, but the text says the interview was conducted in person on a 'wintry day')

p163 to see sense; cherry-pick – Skinn

p163 empty-handed – *Speakeasy*52

p164 serious aberration – Moore, PC

p164 returned his stake – comicbookresources.com/?page=article&id=567

p165 Jaye, had left the company – Jaye has confirmed this was for 'personal reasons' (Jaye)
p165 finished it off – TCJ106, p44 (a transcript of AM's panel at San Diego Comic-Con in March 1986)
p165 external, unconnected – *Chalice*
p165 golden boy – Paul Sievking, 'The Dave Gibbons Interview' (*Arkensword* #22, late 1987) [*Arkensword*22]
p165 *Bizarro* – CBA25, p71
p165 Metal Men – TCJ93, p85
p165 *Batman/Judge Dredd* – CI19, p29
p166 Joker – *Speakeasy*65
p166 promoted – TCJ106, p38
p166 faked alien attack – Gibbons says the alien attack was in the original proposal in *Arkensword*22, p59
p168 finalised the look – *Arkensword*22
p168 Dez Sez – *Chalice*
p168 the gang – Skinn
foggy – Lloyd
p169 bankruptcy – sandiegoreader.com/weblogs/bands/2008/apr/21/pacific-comics-the-inside-story-plus-indie-comic-h/
p169 Creation Convention – AM's account appeared in 'Comics USA – An Impossibly Rich Celebrity's Guide' in *Escape* #6 (1984). [*Escape*] He mentions the collapse of Pacific Comics
p169 my greatest mistake – *Exit*, p30
p170 baffled and shocked – Skinn
p170 divided neatly – As part of the initial agreement at *Warrior*, Dez Skinn got (and continues to receive) a 1 per cent cut of royalties for *V for Vendetta*, including film, DVD and merchandising rights. AM's 'far poorer deal' has ended up making far more money for Skinn than the deals Skinn cut in the US have for AM
p171 sympathy – *Kimota*, p44
p171 comparative trivialities – *Miracleman* #2
p172 *Liberators* – *Amazing Heroes* Preview Special 1985 [AHPS85], p125
p172 masterpiece – *Kimota*, p112
p172 March 1986 – *V for Vendetta* #6 had one chapter that hadn't been published in *Warrior*, but AM had written it two years before for *Warrior* #27.
p172 sticking point – TCJ95, p13
p172 no contracts – comicbookresources.com/?page=article&id=567Alan
p173 bottom of a drawer – *Exit*
p173 suggested by Moore – TCJ99, p26
p173 deserter – TCJ106, p45
p174 excited about – *The Ballad of Halo Jones*, Introduction to Book Two (*Titan*, October 1986)
p174 concessions – *Arkensword*13/14
p174 *Epic Illustrated* – Epic was a division of Marvel. AM had signed to write the story, with Rick Veitch as artist, by August 1984 (he mentions it in *Escape*). It was therefore commissioned before he vowed not to work for Marvel
p174 summer of 1985 – *Knave*
p175 £30,000 – Barry Kavanagh, 'The Alan Moore interview', *Blather* (17 October 2000) [*Blather*]
p175 turnaround – Craig Bromberg, *The Wicked Ways of Malcolm McLaren* (Harper and Row, 1989) [*Wicked*]
p175 walnut coloured – George Khoury, 'The Supreme Writer: Alan Moore', *Jack Kirby Collector* #30, p33
p176 *Superman* graphic novel is an odd way to describe *Superman Annual* #11, but this would seem to be what AM is referring to
p176 serious literature – AHSP85, p5
p176 *Dodgem Logic* – CBA25, p66. #1 was to feature 'Convention Tension', a 'very, very vicious' story set at a comics convention, #2 a biography of Aubrey Beardsley. This incarnation of *Dodgem Logic* would not materialise. Moore also pitched *Dodgem Logic* to First Comics,

including work involving *2000AD* artists Mike McMahon and Kevin O'Neill.

p176 ceased all contact – TCJ106, p44

p176 protests/refusals – 'Alan Davis talks Miracleman', *Comic Book Resources* (5 November 2001) [CBR01]

p176 hadn't bothered telling – Marvel had been reprinting Doctor Who strips in America. In *Doctor Who* #14 (November 1985), they reprinted AM's 'Black Legacy'. However – somewhat to the parent company's surprise – Marvel UK's contracts were not work-for-hire. AM retained copyright of the script (and Lloyd the artwork). TCJ102, p19.

p177 purposely avoided – Moore, PC

p177 95,000 – lh3.ggpht.com/--jhneWpXfcM/TsL7lEDsg6I/AAAAAAAAA1w/2eHFmZsAmPY/s1600/dc-sales-analysis.jpg

p177 intentions – Letter from Skinn to AM, dated 16 July 1985

p177 solid friendship – CBR01

p177 sold his share; sold out his rights – *Kimota*, p113 and p16 respectively

p178 legally bound – *Speakeasy*57

p178 safer long-term bet – Dezskinn.com

p179 whip up a storm – Skinn

p179 distraught – *Chalice*

p179 retrospect – Moore, PC

p180 short shrift – *Speakeasy*57

p180 August 1985 – *Kimota*, p45

p180 actually owed – *Kimota*, p55

p180 shabbily – graphicnovelreporter.com/content/looking-back-alan-davis-interview

p180 Dez, why don't you – This probably happened at UKCAC 1986, held in London in late August that year. Talbot, AM and Skinn were all in attendance.

p181 soured – *Kimota*, p16

p181 March 1985 – *Arkensword*22

p181 ninety-one pages – as reported in AHPS85, p125. In *Speakeasy*54 AM claims 164 pages. However, there's visual confirmation in *Watching* that the last page is p91

p181 six issues – TCJ106, p38

Chapter VI

p184 bloodsplattered – *Arkensword*22

p184 greetings card – *Mustard*, p16. The card slightly misquotes the start as 'life isn't divided into genres'

p185 gritty, grim – AH85, p125

p185 dark take – *Works*, p110

p185 jail sentence – *Works*, p120

p186 chuckle – Stanley Wiater and Stephen R. Bissette, *Comic Book Rebels* (Donald I. Fine, 1993), pp170–1 [*Rebels*]

p186 identity and magic – Annalisa Di Liddo, *Alan Moore: Comics as Performance, Fiction as Scalpel*, (University Press of Mississippi, 2009), p62. [DiLiddo]

p186 *Jack B Quick* – *Works*, p185

p187 I'm handsome – *Cerebro*

p187 nuclear warheads – Steve Moore wrote the last instalment of *The Stars My Degradation* and *Three Eyes McGurk*

p187 heavy irony – *The End is Nigh* #2 (2005) [*Nigh*]

p188 *Dredd* – forum.newsarama.com/showthread.php?t=1020

p189 black sense – Martin Barker and Kate Brooks, *Knowing Audiences: Judge Dredd* (University of Luton, 2005), pp206–7

p190 sight dramatics – *Works*, p110

p191 different meanings – *Nigh*

p191 musicians – Mary Borsellino, 'How the Ghost of You Clings: Watchmen and Music' (p24), in Richard Bensam (ed.), *Minutes to Midnight: Twelve Essays on Watchmen* (CreateSpace, 2011) [Bensam]

p191 supposed to be funny – robertmayerauthor.net/Page_2.html (quote has been amended on his website)

p192 subconsciously – Lance Parkin, *Alan Moore* (Pocket Essentials, 2002), p15

p192 untenable concept – TCJ119

p192 only a cloak – Afterword to the Graphitti edition of *Watchmen*

p194 afflictions – Daniel Dickholtz, Man and Overman, *Starlog* #114 (January 1987) [*Starlog*], p26

p194 staggeringly complex – NYT

p194 conventional Hollywood – *Supergods*, p204

p195 are not real characters – CBA25, p39

p195 sniggering – *Mustard*, p16

p196 'This Vicious Cabaret' – *V for Vendetta*, prologue to Book Two

p196 cruel man – User 'Matt' on bighollywood.breitbart.com/jjmnolte/2009/03/02/whos-watching-the-watchmen-reviewers/ on criticism of the meat cleaver scene in the movie: 'You mean, as opposed to try to understand the pedophile? I'll take the meat cleaver appoach. In fact, if the meat cleaver approach was more prevalent, I'll lay odds there would be far less pedophiles. The graphic novel was a masterstroke and I thought, pretty well balanced, as it takes shots at both sides of the aisle. Arguably, Rorsharch is the hero of the piece and his refusal to back down in the face of evil and compromise is inspiring.'

p197 distinctive views – *Works*, p113

p197 Manhattan is dark – *Works*, p121

p197 fascistic notions – *Starlog*, p26

p197 sexually assaulted – *Escape*, pp45–7

p198 'Son of Sam' – Christopher Sharrett, 'Alan Moore' (*Comics Interview* #65, 1988) [CI65]. Reprinted in *Conversations*

p199 crank file – *Watchmen* #10, p 24

p199 better dead – Ironically, the two staff members of the right-wing *New Frontiersman* newspaper are the only two New Yorkers who survive

p199 effeminate – Gene Phillips, 'Blotting Out Reality', in Bensam

p200 'Big Joke' – John Loyd, 'The Last Laugh', in Bensam

p201 stamp album – *Writing*, pp24–5

p202 'Dark Riders of Mordor' – John Coulthart, *Strange Things Are Happening*, vol. 1, #2 (May/June 1988) [Coulthart88]

p203 drug-addled – *Zigzag*, p29

p203 bad mood – Tasha Robinson, 'Alan Moore Interview', *Onion* AV Club (24 October 2001) [AV01] Reprinted in *Conversations*.

p203 lucidity – *Nigh*

Chapter VII

p205 finally came – Darrel Boatz, 'Alan Moore', *Comics Interview* #48 (1987) [CI48]. The interview was conducted after *Watchmen* #11 was published. AM: 'I finished *Watchmen* a little over a week ago, Dave Gibbons has finished the artwork.' Gibbons was drawing thumbnails for page 16 of #12 on 17 April 1987 according to TCJ116 (p101). In his afterword to the Graphitti edition, dated January 1988, AM says it is 'twelve months' since he finished the script for *Watchmen* #12. The discrepancy might be that AM finished the script in January but there was additional work for him to do on the project after he delivered the last script

p205 taxi – TCJ116, p101

p206 quintessentially – Neil Gaiman, 'Every Picture Book Tells A Story', *Today* (27 July 1986)

p206 fearsome – Don Watson, 'Shazam! The Hero Breaks Down', *Observer* (November 1986) [*Observer*86]

p207 Eisner – 2000adreview.co.uk/features/interviews/2006/goldkind/igor-goldkind.shtml

p207 doing well – Moore, PC

p208 I felt weird – *Ptolemaic*

p208 experimental relationship – newsarama.com/pages/Other_Publishers/Mirror_Love.htm

p208 undeserved adulation – *Knave*, p41

p209 Megastar – Roger Sabin, *Adult Comics: An Introduction* (Routledge, 1993), p95 [Sabin]

p209 a series called *Minutemen* – *Starlog*

p209 a fortune on *Watchmen 2* – CI65, p31

p210 *ownership position* – FA100

p210 1 per cent royalty – Sabin, p267

p210 Greenpeace – Maxwell1

p210 written in 1985 – Marv Wolfman reported (*Amazing Heroes* #135, February 1988) that he'd stayed at Bolland's house 'two years ago' and Bolland had begun drawing it by that point. In *Speakeasy*65 (1986), Bolland had said the project had started in 1985, but there had been 'a lot of tedious holdups, so the artwork wasn't started until quite a long way into this year'

p210 two-thirds – If Dez Skinn is correct that AM, Leach and Davis each had a 28 per cent share, with Quality owning 15 per cent, and Davis literally 'gave his share to Garry Leach', Leach would have ended up with 56 per cent. If, as Davis believes, he, AM, Leach and Quality each had 25 per cent, then Leach would have ended up with 50 per cent. What seems to have happened, formally or not, is that once Davis gave up his share, the deal reverted to the terms before Davis was involved – a third each for AM, Leach and Skinn. This is consistent with Clause 3 of AM's contract with Eclipse, which states that the Writer (AM) and Artist 'shall for the duration of their work on the series, jointly own one-third and Eclipse shall own two-thirds' of the characters and trademarks

p211 Crichton – See Jenette Kahn's letter of 1 July 1985 reprinted in *Watching*, p124

p211 no time pressure – *Arkensword*22

p211 revamped version – site. supermanthrutheages.com/History/end.php

p212 late 1986 – Moore's *Twilight* pitch: 'While I understand that Paul is attempting to sort out the Legion/Superboy problems over in LSH at the moment', a reference to Paul Levitz's story in *Superman* #8, *Action Comics* #591 and *Legion of Superheroes* #38 (August–September 1987). AM also speaks of *Legends* (August 1986–January 1987) as though it's current

p212 whatever we wanted – *Works*, p121

p212 necessarily my friends – *Works*, p123

p213 smiley button – DC also issued a four-button set (a radiation sign, an 'ego ipse custodes custodio', a Rorschach pattern, a doomsday clock) and sold them for $4.95, as a limited edition of 10,000. It's widely reported that DC tried to classify this set as a 'promotional item', but in *Watching* (p243) Gibbons states that while he and AM had no involvement in producing the set, they did receive the royalties due

p214 eventual resolution – *Watching*, p243

p214 sum equivalent to – Gibbons

p214 bits of meanness – *Works* p125. As a benchmark, the limited edition button set sold 10,000 units and retailed for $4.95. Moore and Gibbons split 8 per cent of that, so AM would have been paid roughly $2000 (around £1340 at 1987 exchange rates). That is comparable with what AM was getting for writing two issues of *Swamp Thing*, given Stephen Bissette's recollection (AV09) that Moore was paid around $50 a page

p214 lifespan – TCJ116, pp84–5

p215 rights to it forever – *Works*, p123

p215 received the contract – Gibbons

p215 competent business people – Kurt Amacker, 'Interview with Alan Moore', *Seraphemera* (March 2012) [*Seraphemera*]
p216 over 100,000 copies – George Gene Gustines, 'Film Trailer Aids Sales of Watchmen Novel', *New York Times*, 13 August 2008
p216 Bob Wayne – newsarama.com/comics/dc-vps-talk-november-2012-dc-sales.html – 'Our main focus, right now, is preparing the world of readers who wait for the trade, the collected edition readers, the people who bought over 2,000,000 copies of the *Watchmen* book over the years'
p216 hundreds of thousands – *Ptolemaic*
p216 earned millions – Coulthart
p216 $350,000 for the movie rights – CI48
p216 a fraction – Gibbons
p217 attrition – AV09
p218 *possibly get a lawyer* – Adi Tantimedh, 'Alan Moore Speaks Watchmen 2', *Bleeding Cool* (9 September 2009) [Tantimedh]
p218 creator-hostile – FastCoCreate, 2012
p219 raccoons – Kurt Amacker, 'Opening the Black Dossier', *Mania* (7 November 2007) [*Mania*07]
p219 entire occult – *Works*, p125
p220 not our fault – MTVWein
p220 recent comics – *Amazing Heroes* #71, p44
p220 Dystel – *Dreamer*, pp200–1. Exactly who coined the term 'graphic novel' (and what is meant by it) is contentious. There were prior uses of the term, but Eisner was unaware of this. *A Contract With God* is a short story collection, not a novel.
p222 punished – *Works*, p123
p223 attractive proposition – *Arkensword*13/14
p223 Gibbons revealed – *Arkensword*22
p223 editorial retreat – bleedingcool.com/2012/05/04/before-watchmen-nineteen-eighties-style/
p224 really miserable – Tantimedh
p225 dumping ground – TCJ117, p11
p225 lack of information – CS7
p225 common sense element – TCJ118, p71
p226 tooth and claw – TCJ118, p81
p226 surrender or truce – TCJ117, p36
p226 Tits and Innards – *Arkensword*11
p227 hotel lobby – Moore, PC
p228 breaking point – TCJ138, p68
p229 reconsidering things – *Works*, p126
p229 issue resolved – TCJ117, p12
p229 second-hand information – TCJ118
p229 *marketing device* – TCJ117, pp71–4
p230 Tolstoy – Works, p126
p230 'Flaming Moe's' – *The Simpsons*, S3E10 (writer: Robert Cohen, TX: 21 November 1991)
p231 explored formats – Levitz, pp563–4
p231 80-Page Giant – Paul Levitz, *75 Years of DC Comics: The Art of Modern Mythmaking* (Taschen, 2010)
p232 trade with him – MTV
p232 fraction – *Ptolemaic*
p232 milked dry – *Works*, p125
p232 shape or form – TCJ138, p68
p233 determination to label – TCJ117
p233 more and more remote – *Arkensword*22
p233 confirmed in – TCJ119, p84
p233 better financial – TCJ118, p62
p234 *Ronin* deal – TCJ119, p84
p234 We miss them – TCJ119, p78
p235 fivefold – Extrapolating from John Jackson Miller's research (www.comichron.com/special/watchmensales.html), *Man of Steel* #1 sold between 760,000 and 1.1m copies, while *Watchmen* #4 sold between 135,000 and 202,500. Note that *Watchmen* was only available in the direct market, priced $1.50, *Man of Steel* was 75¢. Given the higher price, the gap in revenue between the two would not be as pronounced as the gap

in unit sales, but would still greatly favour *Man of Steel*. In the overall sales charts, *Watchmen*'s twelve issues ranked 5th, 10th, 10th, 8th, 11th, 15th, n/a, n/a, 15th, 13th, 13th and 6th respectively

p235 masturbation – John Byrne. Byrne Robotics forum, byrnerobotics.com/forum/forum_posts.asp?TID=34515&TPN=4, 5 March 2010, 7:48am

p235 born in my office – TCJ119, p78

p236 chimps – *Arkensword*13/14

p236 chattel – CI65

p237 edgier and smarter – Dana Jennings, 'At House of Comics, a Writer's Champion', *New York Times* (15 September 2003)

p237 since quitting DC – TCJ118, p61

p238 quite spectacular; genres – CI48

p239 beyond genre – TCJ139, p81

p239 hospitality – TCJ138, p92

p239 charming – Moore, PC

p240 steady diet – CI65, p19

p240 sexually assaulted – Barbara Gordon is stripped and photographed by the Joker, a sexual assault. There has been a long debate about whether she was also raped. Fans debate too whether Batman kills the Joker at the end. DC integrated *The Killing Joke* into continuity, and Barbara Gordon became the wheelchair-bound hero Oracle. The sexual assault angle was consistently downplayed so, for example, *Booster Gold* #5 (2007) depicts the Joker taking photographs of a fully clothed Barbara Gordon. There is a good discussion of all these issues in Julian Darius' book *And the Universe So Big: Understanding Batman: The Killing Joke* (Sequart, 2012)

p240 Lynch – Bolland: 'even before he supplied me with a script, Alan said let's get a feeling of *Eraserhead* into this' *Speakeasy*65

p241 understandably disappointed – CS4, p27

p241 heavy-handed – *Speakeasy*85

p241 inferior imitations – Hughes, p148

p242 reasonable and civilised – CI65, p19

p242 proper authors – *Arkensword*13/14

p242 lavender water – Coulthart

p242 healthy bank balance – TCJ139

p242 worry – Alec, p73

p242 *Doctor Who* – *Doctor Who Bulletin* #46

p243 gassing the queers – Blather

p243 Brownhill – 'Gas Gays Storm', *In the Pink*, January 1987

p244 OLGA – Blather

p244 Kinnock – TCJ139, p88

p245 sodomy and heresy – *Ptolemaic*

p245 bunch of superheroes – *Chain*5

p246 anarchist utopia – TCJ139

p247 outpost of Mars – CI65, p23

p247 skateboards – Vincent Eno and El Csawza, 'Meet Comics Megastar Alan Moore', *Strange Things Are Happening*, Vol 1, #2 (May/June 1988)

p248 purity – TCJ139

p248 marriage ended – Matthew De Abautua, 'In Conversation with Alan Moore', *The Idler* (30 July 2005) [*Idler*]. Reprinted in *Conversations* – 'I was married when I was about twenty, and me and me wife split up in about 1989. I met Melinda a year later'

p248 short life – *Works*, p159. AM is vague on dates. In *Works*, he says he was 'about twenty' when he moved in with Phyllis and they were 'married thirteen years' (so c.1974–87). AM also says the split occurred 'some short time after' writing the introduction for *V* (dated March 1988). Leah Moore has said she moved to Liverpool when she was 'twelve' (her twelfth birthday was 4 February 1990). AM says he moved to Sea View in 1988 in an interview with Laura Sneddon, 'Superheroes are our dreams

of ourselves', *Independent* (20 November 2011) [Sneddon11]

p249 violence inherent – *Companion*, p11

p249 Peter Pan – IC1 (June 1992)

p249 flying sequences – Scott Thill, *We are All Complicit* (2006). Moore had recently written airborne sex scenes for *Miracleman* and *Act of Love*

p249 eight page strip – Tantimedh

p249 Lost Horizons – Jerry Glover, 'A Word with Alan Moore', *Headpress* #27 (2007) [*Headpress*]

p249 a 1983 article – AM, 'Phantom Ladies and Invisible Girls', *The Daredevils* #6 (June 1983)

p250 Gulch – Guy, p151

p250 harmless 'misogyny' – Guy, p154

p250 benefit comic – Ismo Santala, 'Alan Moore', *Ready Steady Book* (2008). *Strip Aids* was published in June 1987

p250 snowballed – *Headpress*

p250 a couple of weekends – *Idler*

p250 particular reverie – Sardinian

p251 best things I've ever done – *Works*, p161

p251 personal cycle – *Cerebus*

CHAPTER VIII

p253 communiques – *Feature* Vol 3, #2 (Summer 1997) [*Feature*]

p253 I am a wizard and I know the future – *NME* (2010)

p253 Radiant Powers – D.M. Mitchell, 'Moon and Serpent', *Rapid Eye* #3 (1995) [*Rapid*]

p254 up your sleeve – Jay Babcock, 'A Conversation with Alan Moore about the Arts and the Occult', *Arthur* #4 (May 2003) [*Arthur*]

p254 Tree of Life – *Cerebus*

p254 *Underland* – Robert Morales, 'Moore the Knife', *Reflex* #21 (December 1991) [*Reflex*]; *Fatea* #17 (1992), additional details from Moore, PC

p254 smouldering wrecks – *Wizard* #27

p254 selling tons – CC

p255 *Taboo* – #8 was published in 1995, with no content by AM

p255 macaroni and cheese – TCJ185

p255 private jet – *Supergods*, p242

p255 four or five million – ohdannyboy.blogspot.com.au/2012/09/when-i-am-working-for-marvel-i-am-loyal.html

p255 *Arkham Asylum* – Burton's Batman was so highly anticipated that the marketing firm collecting data for the UK cinema industry had revise its methodology after the old system calculated that more than 100 per cent of Britons intended to see it

p255 original graphic novel – as distinct from graphic novels like *Watchmen* and *From Hell* which collect previously published material

p256 freshness and charm – *Rebels*, p170

p257 takes good care – TCJ185, p82

p257 pimp – 'En Route, 1993', reprinted in TCJ185, pp82–3

p258 tread on that – suite101.com/article/neil-gaiman-on-hollywood-interview-a93886

p259 sustain interest – *Spawn* was still the biggest selling comic in August 1997, when #65 sold 165,000 copies. By #191 (May 2009), it was selling around 19,000 copies, 1 per cent of the sales of the first issue

p259 $100,000 – *Supergods*, p248: 'It was some of the easiest work I've ever done and the most lucrative . . . McFarlane paid ten times more than anyone else at the time.' Sim donated his fee – over $100,000 – to the Comic Book Legal Defense Fund. Hank Wagner, Christopher Golden and Stephen R. Bissette, *Prince of Stories: The Many Worlds of Neil Gaiman* (St Martins, 2008), reports: 'Spawn No 9 was a huge success, selling more than a million copies. McFarlane paid Gaiman

$100,000 for his work on it.' (Gaiman and McFarlane would soon enter a lengthy legal dispute, one aspect of which involved characters created for his issue of *Spawn*.)

p260 landed Alan – Alex Dueben, 'Steve Bissette, Part 1: To 1963 And Beyond', ComicBookResources.com (2 July 2010) [Dueben]

p261 computer games – The Image Info page in *Spawn* #43 (February 1996) announced that AM was writing a Spawn videogame. This would have to be *Spawn: The Eternal* (1997), but Moore receives no credit in the final product and has said he was never paid for anything. (*Works*, p237)

p263 real interests lie – Joseph P Aybandt, 'Moore Is Always Better', *Overstreet's Fan* #16, 1996

p263 purely for the money – Dueben

p263 superhero's muscles – *Rebels*, p171

p263 seems valid – *Feature*

p263 general directives – *Works*

p263 shaken it up – *Rebels*, p170

p263 sounded pretty good – *Works*, p171

p263 finish *Big Numbers* – *Reflex*

p263 Wilderness – CC92, p41

p264 misunderstanding – *Supergods*, pp248–50. Morrison had been surprised to read in *Comics International* that he was writing an issue of *Spawn*. He contacted McFarlane, who told him the magazine had made a mistake, but invited him to write one anyway. Morrison would end up writing #16–18 (December 1993–February 1994)

p264 farmhouse – Daniel Robert Epstein, 'Alan Moore – The Mirror of Love', *SuicideGirls* (28 July 2004) – 'it's a farm we bought as a ruin about ten years ago. We've been fixing it up ever since. It's about two to three acres of land surrounded by woods with loads of animals and birds that are there naturally. It's right on top of a hill in the middle of two Welsh valleys about two hours from the coast'

p264 'Heroes Reborn' – bleedingcool.com/2010/09/22/blast-from-the-past-how-the-purchase-of-wildstorm-was-reported

p264 bubblegum band – *Rebels*, p172

p265 The Emperors of Ice Cream – Curtis E. Johnson, email reply to lanceparkin.wordpress.com/2011/08/05/jukebox-with-a-j/, edited and reproduced with permission. The *Storyteller* CD includes the Satanic Nurses track 'Fires I Wish I'd Seen' and the Emperors performing 'Another Suburban Romance' and 'The Murders on the Rue Morgue' (both originally written in the seventies, as was another song they recorded not on *Storyteller*, 'Positively Bridge Street'), 'Me and Dorothy Parker' and 'Mr A'. There was a spoken-word-and-ice-cream-van-noises track recorded called 'Intro to Ice Cream'. Other Emperors songs are: '14.2.99' (Johnson didn't think the Emperors recorded this, but Pádraig Ó Méalóid has a recording), 'Chiaroscuro', 'London', 'Rose Madder', 'Age of Bavaria' (the 'goons' song mentioned by Johnson), 'To', 'The Lino Sleeps Tonight' and 'Secret Honour', none of which apparently were recorded. *Storyteller* includes two other songs from the period: Moore and the Jazz Butcher's version of 'Trampling Tokyo', and 'Leopardman at C&A', credited to Moore/Perkins. There's a recording of the UFO gig, with a running order of 'Another Suburban Romance', 'Murders on the Rue Morgue', 'Positively Bridge Street', 'Me and Dorothy Parker', 'Mr A' and 'White Light'

p267 unfinished – *Wizard*. Ten *Halo Jones* books were planned but only three were completed, so it possibly qualifies as 'unfinished'

p267 dippy and stupid – TCJ138

p268 Hindley – *Feature*

p268 constantly unnerved – *Cerebus*

p269 find an angle – *Egomania*

p270 gateway; Douglas Adams; Dionysiac – *Feature*

p270 Eno – CI12, pp22–3

p271 crushing misery – *Monsters*

p271 over and over – *Arthur*

p271 linear; Tarot – *Egomania*

p271 met his creation Constantine – *Wizard* #27

p272 magical act – *Spells*, p11

p272 our own meaning – *Egomania*

p272 landmarks – Elizabeth Ho, 'Postimperial Landscapes: Psychogeography and Englishness in Alan Moore's Graphic Novel From Hell', *Cultural Critique* #63 (Spring 2006)

p273 fast friends – *From Hell*, Appendix 1, p11

p273 patterns and divine – *Feature*

p273 ley lines – ballardian.com/iain-sinclair-when-in-doubt-quote-ballard

p274 wallpapering – *Caul*

p274 Watkins – *Feature*, p16

p274 introduced to Glycon – Steve Moore, 'The Fake, The Snake and the Sceptic', *Fortean Times* #276 (July 2011) [FT]

p275 potentially instructive; flowing locks; inevitable ridicule; imaginary playmate – *Egomania*

p276 the first experience – *Arthur*

p276 of course private – FT

p276 silver-white – philhine.org.uk/writings/rit_selenepw.html

p276 more mushrooms – *Arthur*. The interview was conducted in two parts, June 2000 and November 2001, so 'last year' could be 1999 or 2000

p277 feathers – *Works*

p277 diabolist – *Cerebus*

p277 'other magicians' – *Cerebus*. AM also mentions a third ritual exploring the sixth sphere with 'a musician'

p277 Bolland – *Works*, p107

p277 lucidly – *Cerebus*

p277 Focus, you – *Rapid*

p277 Asmodeus – *Arthur*

p278 *after* encountering – *Cerebus*. 'Days later, after the experience, I did some research to see what I could find relating to the demon Asmoday or Asmodeus as he is more often known.'

p278 Within a week – *Egomania*

p278 tumbled – AM, *Fossil Angels*

p280 spinning; Lovecraft – *Rapid*

p280 ISBN – *Hexentexts: A Creation Books Sampler* (1995)

p281 gauge reaction – *Rapid*

p283 build it myself; *Promethea* #12 – *Egomania*. 'I'd have to say that were someone to put a gun to my head and demand to know what was my single cleverest piece of work, I'd have to say *Promethea* #12'

p284 strangled – Wolk, p247

p285 magnified dreams – Quoted in episode 2 of *The Power of Myth*

p286 *sea change* – *Feature*

p286 shave off his hair – Grant Morrison, who had a very similar mystical experience in 1994, did end up shaving his head, travelling the world and embracing hedonism and materialism

p286 iambic – Wolk, p235

p286 Any cunt could do it – *Snakes and Ladders*

p287 beautiful chains – *Arthur*

p287 linear time – *Cerebus*

p288 literal landscape – *Writing*, p32

p288 persisted until 1985 – *Rapid*

p288 winking so hard – Wolk, p249

p288 cerebral cortex – *Egomania*

p289 Britney Spears – *Feature*

p290 Socrates – blogs.ocweekly.com/navelgazing/ill-lyteracy/rob-liefeld-shoots-on-alan-moo/
p290 thorazine – *Rapid*
p291 glorified New Age – *Mania*07
p291 amateur in lunacy – Dominic Wells, 'The Moore the Merrier', *The Times* (6 November 2002)
p291 weren't unified – *Rapid*
p291 Hydra – *Cerebus*
p291 Blake – *Arthur*
p291 grandiose . . . Jack Kirby – AM, 'Buster Brown at the Barricades', *Occupy Comics* #1 (2013) [Buster]. In *Mutants and Mystics* (University of Chicago, 2011) Jeffrey J. Kripal makes a lengthy case (pp131–50) for Kirby being part of a mystic tradition encompassing comic books (including Moore's), nineteenth-century popular fiction, twentieth-century occultists, Cold War science fiction paperbacks, Fortean accounts, West Coast UFOlogy and New Age mysticism. *Buster* is the closest AM has come to the suggestion
p291 Dick – *Arthur*
p292 tulpa – Alvin Schwartz, *An Unlikely Prophet* (Destiny, 2006)
p292 hydrogen – *Cerebus*
p292 shrine – Moore, PC
p293 new set of eyes – *Cerebus*
p293 exceeds – *Arthur*
p293 have a lot of fun – *Works*, pp172–4
p296 ironic – CBA25, p19
p296 no ABC without *Supreme* – millarworld.biz/index.php?showtopic=8739&st=1060
p296 *Glory* notes – Reprinted in *Alan Moore's Awesome Universe*
p297 physical damage – *Works*, p176
p297 stalker girlfriend – Susannah Clarke, 'Alan Moore: the wonderful wizard of . . . Northampton', *Daily Telegraph* (7 October 2007)
p297 be gone – nytimes.com/2006/03/12/movies/12itzk.html?pagewanted=2&_r=4pagewanted=all
p297 three things – bleedingcool.com/2010/09/21/how-dc-comics-killed-wildstorm/
p297 suddenly out of work – *Works*, p178
p298 extra $20 – Don Murphy, email correspondence for this book May 2013 [Murphy]
p298 puzzling – Moore, PC
p298 Rich Veitch – Veitch discusses this at comicon.com/ubb/ubbthreads.php?ubb=showflat&Number=447439&page=4, #447288 – 02/26/00 09:45 AM Re: Question about this week's CBG Cover Topic
p299 smugly proud – CBA25, p54
p299 Gorillaz – *Strange Attractor* #4 (March 2011)
p300 Glyconism – *Egomania*
p300 musical partner – *Arthur*

CHAPTER IX

p301 four adaptations – *Constantine* (2005) featured a character co-created by AM, but was not adapted from comics written by him
p302 make us rich – Lloyd
p303 intrigued and interested – movieweb.com/news/producer-joel-silver-and-director-james-mcteigue-talk-v-for-vendetta
p303 Samurai – *Interview*65, pp64–5
p303 Schwarzenegger – *Interview*65
p304 but killed it – Bob McCabe, *Dark Knights & Holy Fools: The Art and Films of Terry Gilliam* (Universe, 1999), p144 [McCabe]
p304 Therein lies – *Portrait* (Introduction)
p304 two fools – Holy, p144
p305 Paul Revere; *Rupert Bear* – Peter Murphy, 'Eroto-graphic Mania', *The New Review* (August 2007) [*New*07]
p306 Uslan – Scene7, pp55–6
p306 Battleship *Potemkin* – *Storyteller*

p307 Tundra – Murphy
p307 synopsis – *Companion* p167
p307 laundry lists – New07
p307 the first issue – CBA25
p307 idea sheet – Murphy
p307 lucrative for Moore – bleedingcool.com/forums/dc-comics/61526-did-alan-moore-turn-down-two-million-bless-watchmen-prequels-8.htmlpost403677
p307 under the illusion – Tim Franks, *HARDtalk*, BBC News 24, April 2012
p308 Barry Norman – news.bbc.co.uk/2/hi/entertainment/1295972.stm
p308 Robert Stam, 'Literature and Film: A Guide to the Theory and Practice of Film Adaptation (Blackwell, 2005), p3. Stam goes on to tease out seven common beliefs that lead people to think that novels are superior to movies: older arts are better arts; there's a rivalry between genres; the visual arts are inferior to the written; literature is seen as more thoughtful and less spectacular; movies are easier to watch than books are to read so spoonfeed their audience; class prejudice; movies are seen as parasitical. Interestingly, it's possible that none of these apply to comics as compared with movies, but when comics adaptations are discussed, the discourse is very similar
p309 convince a studio – *From Hell*, DVD 2-disc edition, 'Graphic Novel' extra
p309 parlour game – classic.tcj.com/interviews/the-eddie-campbell-interview-part-one-of-four
p309 American world empire – Iain Sinclair, 'Jack the Rip-off', *Guardian* (28 January 2002) [Sinclair]
p310 certainly improved – Deppey
p310 little substance – threemoviebuffs.com
p310 comics any day – Jennifer Vineyard, *The Last Angry Man*, MTV (2005)
p310 slasher film – classic.tcj.com/interviews/the-eddie-campbell-interview-part-one-of-four/
p311 reports from Prague – *Uncut*. Hawthorne was cast as Gull (after the original choice, Sean Connery dropped out to make *The Avengers* instead), but was diagnosed with cancer very shortly afterwards. He died in December 2001.
p311 sainthood – uncredited, 'Mad Man', *Newsweek* (17 October 2001) [*Newsweek*]
p311 on video – Steve Rose, 'Moore's Murderer', *Guardian* (1 February 2002) [*Guardian*02]
p311 had fun – Murphy
p311 unfilmable – *Exit*, p12
p312 quite the opposite – Scott Thill, 'Alan Moore: Comics Won't Save You, but Dodgem Logic Might', *Wired* (31 December 2009) [*Wired*]
p312 useless – villagevoice.com/2003-07-15/film/die-another-day/1
p313 literate pedigree – Charles Taylor, 'Review: The League of Extraordinary Gentlemen', *Salon*, 11 July 2003
p313 whim of an actor – MTV
p313 lawsuit – donmurphy.net/codgers.html
p314 *Lost Girls* – *Panel*08
p314 Still haven't – Murphy
p315 briefed to write it – andydiggle.com/alanmooreinterview.htm
p315 conspiring with the head of the studio – Murphy
p315 exonerate himself – NYT Notice of settlement retrieved from legalmetric.com/cases/copyright/cacd/cacd_203cv06906.html , 12-29-200315 Notice of settlement selection procedure by defendants Fox Entertainment Group and 20th Century Fox Film Corporation (mg) [Entry date 12/30/03]
p315 swearing off; they had nothing – Murphy
p315 funny side – *Exit*, p14
p316 within three days – *Chain*5. This is possible: the three days would fall in late

September or early October 2003.
p317 perplexed, 'Moore Leaves the Watchmen 15 Anniversary Plans', Newsarama (August 2000)
p318 not been reciprocated – *Exit*
p318 secretly wanted – comicbookresources.com/?page=article&id=1493720=article
p319 pure bliss – bigpicturebigsound.com/article_700.shtml Joe Lozito 17/03/06
p319 faithful to the book – *Exit*, p17
p320 au fait – comicbookresources.com/?page=article&old=1&id=6685
p320 retraction – *Exit*, pp19–25
p320 FedCo – *Lying*, 23 May 2005. It's not too difficult to deduce that AM's friend was Steve Moore, who had been hired to write the novelisation, not least because his book works in a few sly comments. When the colloqualisms of one character's dialogue are laid on a little thick, someone notes they 'half expected her to break into Cockney rhyming slang and refer to going up the apple-an-pears or talkin' on the ol' dog-an'-bone' (p47)
p321 core of it – Lloyd
p321 ever been understood – *Exit*, p51
p322 cowboy's guns – Spencer Lamm and Sharon Bray (eds), *V for Vendetta: From Script to Film*, (Universe, 2006), p176 [*Script*]
p322 serious advances – MTV
p322 James R. Keller, *V for Vendetta as Cultural Pastiche: A Critical Study of the Graphic Novel and Film* (McFarland, 2008) [Keller], p194. Keller's argument often seems to depend on the story having its genesis in 1988, the year DC started to publish it – for example his citing of Terry Gilliam's movie *Brazil* (1985) as a possible source (Chapter 5 passim)
p322 viral avenger – Keller, p15
p322 AIDS avenger – Keller, p199
p323 deemed homosexual – *Script*, p240
p324 liberal fantasy – MTV
p324 rudderless – *Mindscape*
p324 Yes it is upsetting – *Exit*, p47
p325 timid – MTV
p325 fascism and anarchy – *Exit*
p325 superhero – *Script*, p209
p325 regard to rulers – Buster
p326 fireworks – efilmcritic.com/review.php?movie=13855&reviewer=416
p326 People should not be – 'When the people fear their government, there is tyranny; when the government fears the people, there is liberty', attributed to John Jason Barnhill at monticello.org/site/jefferson/when-governments-fear-people-there-libertyquotation. Barnhill was a London-based poet, essayist, anarchist, socialist and Nietzschean who used his magazine *The Eagle and the Serpent* (written 1898–1902 under the pseudonym John Erwin McCall) to express the belief that certain individuals were supermen shortly to usher in an enlightened age, but they weren't to be found among the aristocracy. He declared approvingly, 'a race of free men is necessarily a race of egoists'. Barnhill was, then, an anarchist self-publisher obsessed with the concept of the superman. History does not record if he ever visited Northampton
p327 *Extraordinary Animals* – Sam Ashurst, 'Why Alan Moore Hates Comic Book Movies', *Total Film* (2 February 2009)
p328 validates it – *Storyteller*
p328 combination of both – *Wired*
p329 Prague – CBA25, p73
p329 spitting venom – Geoff Boucher, 'Hero Complex', *Los Angeles Times* (18 September 2008) [LA]
p329 devout – James Parker, 'The Sorcery of Alan Moore', *The Atlantic* (1 May 2009)
p329 hard R – LA
p330 computer graphic – FA100

p331 copious slo-mo – totalfilm.com/reviews/cinema/watchmen
p331 overlong – washingtontimes.com/news/2009/mar/05/movies-watchmen-leap-into-action/ixzz2FcUvuBYl
p331 hhhhhhhhhhmmmmm – comicbookmovie.com/comics/news/?a=9516cggwIFEjJvThG3tA.99
p331 check back – *Wired*
p332 full-blown ten – comicbookresources.com/?page=article&id=36726
p332 emotionally distant – newsarama.com/comics/jms-before-watchmen-details.htmlI
p332 fairly unremarkable – David Hughes, *The Greatest Sci-fi Movies Never Made* (Titan, 2001), pp146–8
p332 'multiple platforms' – *Wired*
p333 Altman or Coppola – *Writing*, pp4–5
p333 fragmenting – AV09
p333 box office – According to boxofficemojo.com, *From Hell* had a budget of $35m, an $11m opening weekend, total domestic box office of $31.6m and international take (excluding the US) of $42.9m. *LXG*'s figures were $78m, $23m, $66m/$112m, *V for Vendetta* $54m, $25.6m, $70m/$62m, and *Watchmen* was $130m, $55m, $107m/$78m
p334 yoghurt – Martin Cannon, *Critics' Choice Volume 1*, p12
p334 first murder – 4colorheroes.com/fromhell7.html lists the print runs for most of the issues, as follows: 1: 15,000; 3: 3405; 4: 4230; 5: 4355; 6: 4125; 7: 4090; 8: 4170
p334 total had doubled – eddiecampbell.blogspot.com/2008/12/c-hris-mclaren-has-posted-seven-photos.html
p334 oeuvre – One striking example is that on the back cover of *The League of Extraordinary Gentlemen Omnibus*, DC describe AM as the writer of 'From Hell and Watchmen', rather than naming another of his books they publish
p335 million copies – NYT
p335 Egyptian – youtube.com/watch?v=UNggw8xDaE0
p335 tide of idiocy – Bram E. Gieben, 'Alan Moore: Unearthed and Uncut', *Weaponiser*, 2010 – an uncut version of interview at skinny.co.uk/books/features/100258-choose_your_reality_alan_moore_unearthed) [*Weaponiser*]
p336 unfair – *Seraphemera*

Chapter X

p337 barely knew – Panel08
p337 works wonders – AV06
p337 between *Big Numbers* – CC
p337 great modern – Sneddon11
p338 anarchic visionary – Channel Four News, 11 January 2012 (see youtube.com/watch?v=FumNSfY7SfI)
p338 rural – Strictly, Dorothy and Wendy are not from different generations – Dorothy first appeared in *The Wonderful Wizard of Oz* (1900) and Wendy in the stage play of *Peter Pan* (1904)
p338 bowler hat – journal.neilgaiman.com/2007/05/interrogatory.html
p339 obsessed with rape – rollingstone.com/music/news/grant-morrison-on-the-death-of-comics-20110822ixzz2AQNXmauq. In fact Morrison's *The Filth* includes a number of rapes and examples of women coerced into having sex. One major subplot of his *The Invisibles* involves a videotape of Princess Diana being raped by an extradimensional monster
p339 child together – A common misreading is that the Comedian rapes Silk Spectre and Laurie is conceived as a result. The Comedian attempts to rape Silk Spectre in 1940, but is prevented from doing so by Hooded Justice. Laurie is not born until 1949

p340 windmills – TCJ118, p64

p340 rapture – Jess Nevins, 'A Blazing World' (*Monkeybrain*, 2004) [Blazing]. Reprinted in *Conversations*

p340 sexual act – *Mindscape*

p341 Sunday funnies – *Dodgem Logic*

p341 eight pages – Noel Murray, 'Lost Girls', *Onion* AV Club (20 September 2006)

p341 fiercest – AM, 'Bog Venus versus Nazi Cock Ring', *Arthur* #25 (2006). Reprinted as '25,000 Years of Erotic Freedom' (2009) [Venus]

p341 banjo – reason.com/archives/2004/12/01/disneys-war-against-the-counte

p341 Jupiter – Graham Lord, *John Mortimer: The Secret Lives of Rumpole's Creator* (Thomas Dunne, 2006), p152

p342 cure – *Reflex*, pp20–1

p343 sangfroid – *Works*, p158

p343 Chanel; fidelity – Panel08

p343 $350,000 – comicbookresources.com/?page=article&old=1&id=8374

p344 incredibly proud – AV06

p344 not obscene – comicbookresources.com/?page=article&old=1&id=8374

p344 Neil Gaiman, Signature Review: *Lost Girls*, *Publishers Weekly* (19 June 2006)

p345 Dworkin – Venus

p345 Denmark – AV06

p346 Dark Ages – Venus

p347 Freud – AV06

p347 warheads – AM, 'No More Sex', *Escape* #15 (1988)

p347 sixteen years – AV06

p348 *Patriot-News* – Chris Mautner, 'We Wanted to do Something Which Solved a Lot of the Abiding Problems that Pornography Has', *Patriot-News* (25 August 2006) [Mautner]. Reprinted in *Conversations*.

p348 In spite – Paul Gravett, 'Three Go Mad in . . .', *Independent on Sunday* (1 October 2006)

p348 higher demand – comicbookresources.com/?page=article&old=1&id=8374

p348 backordered – icv2.com/articles/news/9602.html

p348 artistic benefit – Sardinian

p349 happy new year – Today, BBC Radio 4, 31 December 2011

p349 Rosetta Stone – Todd A. Comer, Joseph Michael Sommers (eds), *Sexual Ideology in the Works of Alan Moore* (McFarland, 2012)

p350 slender thread – *Exit*, p9

p350 early 2007 – ratmmjess.livejournal.com/132469.html

p350 Jeez – CBA25

p351 John Nee – Murphy

p351 boot – comicbookresources.com/?page=article&id=14937%20=article

p352 fulsome – *Exit*, p36

p352 *The Walking Dead* – robot6.comicbookresources.com/2012/11/mint-copy-of-the-walking-dead-1-fetches-10000-on-ebay

p353 ruthless concept – rollingstone.com/music/news/grant-morrison-on-the-death-of-comics-20110822ixzz2HQdr0JHw

p353 insurance fire – PanelMagic

p353 top-flight – Tantimedh

p354 carrot – NYT

p354 unpretentious – Steve Rose, 'Unearthing the truth about Watchmen Genius Alan Moore', *Guardian*, 24 July 2010

p354 paranoid – Skinn

p355 imprisoned – web.archive.org/web/20011118115828/www.eddiecampbellcomics.com/fromhell/history.htmle schedule

p355 Click. That was it – AV09

p355 slightly longer – Moore, PC

p356 abandon us – TCJ185, p69

p356 trash – Moore, PC

p356 hates doing business – AV09

p356 canon – bleedingcool.com/2012/07/27/

dave-gibbons-dismisses-before-watchmen-as-really-not-canon/

p357 pay tribute – comicbookresources.com/?page=article&id=36724

p357 terminally ill – *Storyteller* David Uzumeri, 'Alan Moore Goes Beyond Paranoid in His Latest Crazy Old Man Rant', Comics Alliance (9 September 2010)

p358 creepy – Tantimedh

p358 talented as hell – Murphy

p358 politically savvy – Skinn

p358 charts – bleedingcool.com/2013/03/08/idw-gains-marketshare-from-marvel-and-dc-as-justice-league-of-america-1-tops-the-february-2013-charts/

p358 perennial – Respectively 29th, 32nd and 44th in 2011, 14th, 24th and 38th in 2012. www.newsarama.com/comics/diamond-2012-year-end-comic-book-sales-report.html; diamondcomics.com/Home/1/1/3/597?articleID=117102

p359 Meltzer – comichron.com/monthlycomicssales/2006/2006-08.html

p360 couple of years earlier – Morrison has objected to the idea he followed AM into the comics industry (e.g. at comicsbeat.com/the-strange-case-of-grant-morrison-and-alan-moore-as-told-by-grant-morrison), correctly noting that his first professional sales came before Moore's. There isn't the generation gap critics occasionally assert – they were both teenagers in the early seventies and broke into the comics industry a decade later. There are certainly a few years in the mid-eighties, though, where Morrison's career trails AM's. In 1986, the year *Watchmen* started, Morrison's most high-profile work was writing a back-up strip based on the Zoids toys for Marvel UK's *Spider-Man and Zoids*

p360 unfathomable – *Storyteller*

p360 couple of million – *Leftlion*

p361 sounds stupid – Moore, PC

p361 Ginger – *Observer*12

p361 empowerment – *Leftlion*

p361 bills – *Wired*

p362 thriving, vital – Joel Meadows, 'Alphabet Soupcon', *Tripwire* Spring Special (April 2000)

p362 occult school – *Arthur*

p362 *Borderland* – AM, *The House on the Borderland*, Introduction

p363 Stenographers – AM, 'Prism and Pentecost: David Lindsay and the British Apocalypse' (Introduction to *A Voyage to Arcturus*, Savoy, 2002) [*Arcturus*]

p363 significantly shared – Di Liddo, p172

p364 purer – *Rapid*, p172

p365 vaginal monsters – *Weaponiser*

p365 isn't a Too Far – *Writing*

p365 gone too far – *Weaponiser*

p365 back rooms – *Storyteller*

p366 phrasebook – Arthur

p366 2017 – *Nigh*

p366 orgasm – *Snakes and Ladders*

p366 great change – Moore, PC

p367 chasm – Occupied Times

p367 form of blog – *Dodgem Logic* #1

p368 anecdotes – Mindscape

p368 less cosmopolitan – Nicole Le Marie, 'Renowned writer Alan Moore pens huge book based in historic area of Northampton', *Northampton Chronicle* (13 March 2012)

p368 *nostalgie* – *Arkensword*13/14

p370 mythical – *Leftlion*

p370 pointy – bbc.co.uk/news/magazine-15359735

p370 glow – 'Alan Moore Still Knows the Score', *Entertainment Weekly* (16 July 2008)

p370 digging up – Sneddon11

p370 United Arab Emirates – thenational.ae/news/uae-news/guy-fawkes-masks-banned-from-uae-national-day-celebrations

p371 downtrodden – *Observer*12

p371 temper – Maxwell

p373 pamphlet – uncredited, distributed in 2011, and linking to aforanarchy.com. Reproduced at slackbastard.anarchobase.com/?p=170

p373 vested – AM, 'Preoccupying', *Occupied Times* (22 October 2012)

p373 illuminate – *Mindscape*

p374 minor works – Pádraig Ó Méalóid, 'Lunar Man', Forbidden Planet International website (11 November 2011)

p374 *Serpent* project – QuietusSM

p374 sublimated – *Wired*

p376 budgets of these films – *Observer*12

p376 2005 – 'eighteen months' before AV06.

p376 index fingers – *Observer*12

p376 three parts – Moore, PC

p378 unfair advantage; really proud – Moore, PC

p379 Arts Lab thinking – Moore, PC

p380 different stamps – *Works*, p193

INTRODUCTION

'A Letter from America', in *Heartbreak Hotel* #1, 1988, Script and Art: Alan Moore, courtesy of Alan Moore

The Ballad of Halo Jones, 1984, Script: Alan Moore, Art by Ian Gibson. Halo Jones™ REBELLION A/S, © REBELLION A/S, ALL RIGHTS RESERVED

CHAPTER ONE

First Comic-Con Convention Booklet, 1968 © Phil Clarke

'Dark They Were and Golden Eyed', advert published in *Cyclops*, 1970, Art: Alan Moore, courtesy of Alan Moore

Photo reproduced by kind permission of the *Northampton Chronicle & Echo*

CHAPTER TWO

'Lounge Lizards', cover for #3 of the Northampton Arts Group magazine, 1973, Art: Alan Moore, courtesy of Alan Moore

Anon E. Mouse #2 from *ANoN #2*, 1974, Script and Art: Alan Moore, courtesy of Alan Moore

'Stalin', in *Arcade #4*, Winter 1975, Script and Art: Spain Rodriguez

Cover of *2000AD*® #11, May 1977, Art: Brian Bolland. 2000AD®2000AD IS A REGISTERED TRADEMARK. © REBELLION A/S

'Yoomin' in *Back-Street Bugle*, 1978, Art: Alan Moore, courtesy of Alan Moore

'Malcolm McLaren', in *NME*, November 1978, Art: Alan Moore, courtesy of Alan Moore

Roscoe Moscow in *Sounds*, 1980, Art: Alan Moore, courtesy of Alan Moore

Maxwell the Magic Cat in the *Northants Post*, 1986, Script and Art: Alan Moore, courtesy of Alan Moore

CHAPTER THREE

Falconbridge, 1981, Script and Art: David Lloyd, © 2013 David Lloyd

V for Vendetta, 1982, Script: Alan Moore, Art: David Lloyd, DC Comics

'Our Factory Fortnight', *The Bojeffries Saga*, 1991, Script: Alan Moore, Art: Steve Parkhouse, © Alan Moore and Steve Parkhouse

Photograph, courtesy of Alan Moore

CHAPTER FOUR

'Script Robot Alan Moore' in *2000AD #322*, June 1983, Droid art by Robin Smith © REBELLION A/S, ALL RIGHTS RESERVED

Art and script of page 1, panel 1 of *The Killing Joke*, published 1988, Script: Alan Moore, Art: Brian Bolland, DC Comics. Batman and all related characters are trademarks of DC Comics. Batman created by Bob Kane

CHAPTER FIVE

Reinventing Comics, 2000, Script and Art: Scott McCloud, ©Scott McCloud

Swamp Thing #29, 1984, Script: Alan Moore, Art: Steve Bissette and John Totleben, DC Comics

Promotional artwork for *Comics Cavalcade,* 1986, Art: Dave Gibbons, DC Comics

Pacific Comics Order Form, 1984

CHAPTER SIX

Maxwell the Magic Cat in the *Northants Post*, 1986, Script and Art: Alan Moore, courtesy of Alan Moore

'Grit' in *The Daredevils* #8, 1983, Script: Alan Moore, Art: Pencils by Mike Collins, inks by Mark Farmer

CHAPTER SEVEN

Titan Books advertisement, 1988

'A Letter from America', in *Heartbreak Hotel* #1, 1988, Script and Art: Alan Moore, courtesy of Alan Moore

CHAPTER EIGHT

Big Numbers #1, 1990, Script: Alan Moore, Art: Bill Sienkiewicz, courtesy of Alan Moore

Violator v Badrock, 1995, Script: Alan Moore, Art: Brian Denham and Jon Sibal, Image Comics

'Risen', 1993, Art: Alan Moore, courtesy of Alan Moore

From Hell, 1991, Script: Alan Moore, Art: Eddie Campbell, © Alan Moore and Eddie Campbell

Glycon, 1993, Art: Alan Moore, courtesy of Alan Moore

Ectoplasm, 1994, courtesy of Alan Moore

CHAPTER NINE

Provisional artwork from *The League of Extraordinary Gentlemen*, 2000 © Alan Moore and Kevin O'Neill

CHAPTER TEN

Big Numbers #1, 1990, Script: Alan Moore, Art: Bill Sienkiewicz, courtesy of Alan Moore

Anarchy, c.2011

ENDPAPERS

Artwork for the cover of *Dodgem Logic* #3, © Alan Moore

THANKS

Tony Bennett at Knockabout, Stephen Bissette, Joe Brown, Mike Collins, Scott Dunbier, Dave Gibbons, Igor Goldkind, Oliver Harris, Bernie Jaye, Anthony Johnson, Curtis E. Johnson, Barbara Kesel, David Lloyd, Steve Moore, Don Murphy, Jeremy Seabrook, Dez Skinn, Ben Smith at Rebellion, all at Top Shelf.

Richard Bensam, Ross Byrne, Gary Gray, Maggie Gray (no relation), Gareth Kavanagh, Hannah Means-Shannon, Gary Spencer Millidge, Gábor Németh, Phil Sandifer, Smoky Man, Laura Sneddon, Dave Thompson

Captain Blue Hen (and his team-mates Joe Murray, Kita Roberts, Paul Stitik, Dave Williams), Halina Adams, Mark Clapham, Petra Clark, Jonn Elledge, Jim Figard, Ginny Garnett, Mark Jones, Chris La Casse, Jasmine Lellock, Kyle Meikel, Lars Pearson, Henry Potts, Eddie Robson, Jim Smith. The staff at the Morris Library at the University of Delaware.

My editor Sam Harrison at Aurum, along with Jessica Axe, Fran Higgins, Melissa Smith, Lucy Warburton, Steve Gove.

My agent Jessica Papin.

Alan Moore

Pádraig Ó Méalóid

Brie Parkin

INDEX

423

425

UEFUL NIGHTS
ABEROTHIS?